Swing Changes

Swing Changes

Big-Band Jazz in New Deal America

DAVID W. STOWE

Harvard University Press

Cambridge, Massachusetts, and London, England

Third printing, 1998

We gratefully acknowledge permission to use the following:
"Harvard Blues" (Count Basie, Tab Smith, George Frazier) © 1942 WB Music Corp.
(renewed). All rights reserved; used by permission.
"It's the Same Old South" (Jay Gorney, Edward Eliscu) © 1940 Mills Music Inc.
Copyright renewed and assigned to Piedmont Music Company; used by permission; all
rights reserved.
"Jitterbug" (Cab Calloway, Irving Mills, Ed Swayze) Copyright © 1934 (renewed 1962)
Mills Music c/o EMI Music Publishing; World print rights administered by CPP/Belwin,
Inc., Miami, Fla.; all rights reserved.
"Now They Call It Swing" (Norman Cloutier, Lou Handman, Walter Hirsch, Vaughn
De-Leath) © 1938 Chappell & Co. (renewed). All rights reserved; used by permission.

This book is printed on acid-free paper, and its binding materials have been chosen for
strength and durability.

Library of Congress Cataloging-in-Publication Data
Stowe, David W. (David Ware)
    Swing changes : big-band jazz in New Deal America / David W. Stowe.
        p.   cm.
    Includes index.
    ISBN 0-674-85825-5 (cloth)
    ISBN 0-674-85826-3 (pbk.)
    1. Big band music—History and criticism.   2. Music and society.
ML3518.S8   1994
784.4'8165'0973—dc20   93-47000
                            CIP
                            MN

For Linda and my parents

Preface

During the early stages of this project it struck me that writing a book on swing was a very pale substitute for experiencing the vitality of the music and the people who made it possible. Looking back now I can better appreciate the pleasures of writing about the past: not the exhilaration of a breakfast dance at the Trianon, quite, but the considerable rewards of intellectual camaraderie.

A number of people have given freely of their time, expertise, and experience to help make this book possible. John Szwed offered an inexhaustible supply of leads, sources, and anecdotes. Jim Fisher enthusiastically exhorted me that this project was worth doing, and suggested ways to make it better. In addition to early encouragement, Ann Fabian gave the manuscript a very careful reading and offered an incisive critique. The Music in History Project—Benjamin Filene, Margaret McFadden, Carlo Rotella, and Suzy Smith—provided a congenial forum for thinking about the issues with which this work is concerned. Dan Belgrad, Glenn Wallach, Chris Shannon, Steve Rachman, Krin Gabbard, John M. Blum, and several anonymous readers have made searching comments on various chapters. At Harvard University Press, Aida Donald and Ann Hawthorne skillfully guided the manuscript through its last stages and into book form.

Michael Denning deserves a special word of thanks. He has been involved in this project from the beginning, asking tough questions throughout and continuing to challenge me after I was ready to call it a day. On several occasions his casual remarks got me thinking in ways that profoundly influenced my approach to the subject. He subtly but persistently challenged me to theorize, warned me away from misinterpretations, and suggested several structural and conceptual changes that have greatly improved the book.

This study has drawn on the good offices of several librarians and archivists. At Yale University, I'm especially indebted to the staff of the Music Library. Ken Crilly with unfailing good cheer made dozens of trips to the basement to retrieve old magazines and scrapbooks and helped immensely with acquiring illustrations. I also owe thanks to Karl Schrom of the Record Library and Richard Warren of the Historical Sound Recordings Collection, and to the Film Studies Center.

Outside New Haven, I have made repeated use of the rich holdings of the Institute for Jazz Studies in Newark, where I benefited particularly from the assistance of Dan Morgenstern. I'm indebted also to the staffs of the Library of the Performing Arts, New York Public Library at Lincoln Center; and to the Schomburg Center for Research in Black Culture. Radio stations that provided the original basis for my knowledge of the music include New York's WRVR, Newark's WBGO, Washington's WUDC, Philadelphia's WRTI, and, most recently, Bridgeport's WPKN, where Victor Pachera's program provided a steady diet of historical and musical information during the time this project was under way. Of the many musicians from whom I have learned in performance and conversation over the years, I am especially grateful to my original partner in rhythm, Kurt Blickenderfer.

The most profound debts are personal: to Linda, for her support and patience through the sometimes exhilarating, often trying times during which this work was accomplished; to Henry, who has grown up alongside *Swing Changes* and provided the occasions for the long walks on which some of the most important and pleasurable progress was made; to Caroline, who has been a major presence since the manuscript entered the publishing process; and to my parents—musicians and music lovers, great inspirations in many ways, who started me down the road to music and history long ago without ever imagining it would come to this.

Contents

Introduction: Understanding Swing   1

1. The Tempo of the Time   17
   Song of the Jitterbug   30
   New Venues, New Audiences   40

2. Between Conjure and *Kapital*   50
   The Big Bringdown   54
   As American as Baseball and Hotdogs   64
   We Are All Americans   73
   Just Rich Men's Sons   80

3. The Incorporation of Swing   94
   Anyone Can Lead a Dance Band   100
   Broadcasting Swing   107
   The Jukes Take Over   112
   Are Colored Bands Doomed?   121
   Passing in Hollywood   130

4. The Conscription of Swing   141
   Soldiers of Music   145
   The Theater of Race   156
   The Gender Front   167

5. Swing and Its Discontents   180
    Tension Music and Concertitis   184
    Smothering the Market   191
    Crewcut, Jarb, Swixibop   199
    Swing *Redux*   202

6. Cracks in the Coalition   221
    That Modern Malice   223
    Jazz Is America's Own   230
    Epilogue: Shall We Dance?   239

Notes   247

Index   289

Illustrations

Following page 44:

Jitterbugs in New York City in 1938
    (Courtesy of the Frank Driggs Collection)
Dancers execute a breakaway at the Savoy in the 1940s
    (Courtesy of the Frank Driggs Collection)
A crowd outside Harlem's Savoy ballroom in the 1940s
    (Courtesy of the Frank Driggs Collection)
Dancing to the Erskine Hawkins Orchestra at the Savoy in 1941
    (Courtesy of the Frank Driggs collection)
Cab Calloway and orchestra at New York's Cotton Club in 1933
    (Courtesy of the Yale Music Library)
Benny Goodman at the bandstand in 1938
    (Courtesy of the Yale Music Library)
Couples at the Savoy in the 1930s
    (Courtesy of the Frank Driggs collection)

Following page 140:

Sarah Martin and Her Jass Fools in the 1920s
  (Courtesy of the Yale Music Library)
An early Benny Carter ensemble at the Savoy
  (Courtesy of the Yale Music Library)
Duke Ellington and orchestra in 1939
  (Courtesy of the Yale Music Library)
Fletcher Henderson, Ben Webster, and others at a fancy dress party in 1934
  (Courtesy of the Yale Music Library)
The Benny Goodman Orchestra at the Ambassador Hotel's Coconut Grove
  ballroom in Los Angeles in 1940
  (Courtesy of the Frank Driggs Collection)
Duke Ellington and orchestra on the RKO studio lot in the early 1930s
  (Courtesy of the Yale Music Library)
Advertisement by the Martin Band Instrument Company in *Down Beat*,
  May 1, 1945
  (Courtesy of the Yale Music Library)

Following page 204:

Earl Hines and His Orchestra, featuring the Bluebonnets, in 1943
  (Courtesy of the Yale Music Library)
A segregated wartime audience at a Duke Ellington concert at Fort Dix,
  New Jersey
  (Courtesy of the Yale Music Library)
Lionel Hampton with his 1950–1951 orchestra
  (Courtesy of the Yale Music Library)
Media speculation on the reasons for the sudden postwar decline of swing
  (Copyright © 1947 by the New York Times Company; reprinted by permission)
Dizzy Gillespie and fans in March 1948
  (Courtesy of UPI/Bettmann)
Benny Goodman with Mrs. Betty Henderson in January 1949
  (Courtesy of the Yale Music Library)

Introduction:
Understanding Swing

Ralph Ellison once described American culture as "jazz-shaped." He meant that African-Americans have provided the essence of the nation's cultural style: "the sudden turns, the shocks, the swift changes of pace (all jazz-shaped) that serve to remind us that the world is ever unexplored, and that while a complete mastery of life is mere illusion, the real secret of the game is to make life swing."[1]

What would it mean to describe American culture in the decade that ended in 1945 as "swing-shaped"? To begin with, swing's jazz-oriented dance music was the leading (though certainly not the only) form of popular music during those years. Large numbers of teenagers and young adults listened and danced to it. Swing was part catalyst, part product of the electronic mass culture industry coalescing during those years. At the same time, many others speculated about swing, seeking to explain its popularity and social significance. Swing was widely thought to express, for better or worse, a certain spirit of the age. The ways in which people thought about swing revealed new patterns of thinking about history, about racial and cultural difference, and about the nature of American society. The ideology that accrued to swing was closely related to the ideology of Americanism that appeared in many contexts during the Depression and war years. Its decline paralleled the end of a distinctive moment of self-definition for many Americans.

A few of swing's contemporaries recognized its cultural centrality, or at least ubiquity. "It has been reflected in the nation's literature, and has inspired novels, biographies, mystery stories, scholarly dissertations, countless magazine articles and newspaper features," wrote a reporter in 1938.

> It has served as a theme for Hollywood. It has been introduced in high school and college curricula. It is almost exclusively the subject-matter of a raft of trade journals published on both sides of the Atlantic. It is the gospel inviolate of a nation-wide organization of evangelists, the Hot Clubs of America. It has achieved immortality in recordings made especially for the Library of Congress by "Jellyroll" Morton. It has poked its way into the august chambers of newspaper editorial writers, where it shared consideration with such matters as the rearmament race, the Drang nach Osten, the C.I.O.-Moscow conspiracy and Charlie McCarthy. It has lent its name to toys, notions, games, women's clothing, jewelry and coiffure. It has tremendously stimulated an important phase of the nation's music business, as well as its entire night entertainment industry. It has been accepted in the lives of a sufficient portion of the population to have affected its mores and language.[2]

That a cultural product could be perceived in 1938 as pervading so many disparate realms of public consciousness, affecting everything from language and mores to scholarship to toys and notions, suggests that swing fed into the new concept of culture that was gaining currency in the 1930s. While swing was a cultural form, a product, it operated within a meaning of culture derived from anthropology: culture as a way of life. But this sort of cultural phenomenon could occur only amid the new technologies and industrial organizations that had emerged in the early decades of the century, particularly the 1920s.

Swing's trajectory, its rise and fall as a phenomenon of mass culture, tells us much about the society that produced it. Consider swing writ large—not just the big bands, but their audiences, the writers who critiqued and promoted them, the media conglomerate that supported them—as a microcosm of American society. The contradictions and tensions within swing—over race, politics, its own cultural status, the role of women—were the same as those played out in the larger culture. Swing's extreme self-consciousness and coupling of populist nationalism with a critical stance toward American society was distinctive to the 1930s. In its simultaneous challenge and acceptance of dominant racial, sexual, and cultural hierarchies and of large-scale industrial consolidation, swing acted out larger cultural impulses at the same time that it modified them. Swing was widely perceived, and understood itself, as both Other and Self—at once marginal and similar to an "ideal picture of America" the defining of which was a central cultural achievement of the years in which swing flourished.[3]

What exactly was swing? The question was of interest beyond the United States. In 1938 the Académie Française was debating whether to add the word to its dictionary, and, if so, how to define it. Then, as now, the word carried a variety of grammatical functions: verb *(to swing)* and adjective *(a swing band)*. But in the late 1930s the word generally appeared on its own, as a noun. Part of the fascination of swing as fad was undoubtedly its imperviousness to being pinned down and defined. The music itself may have been ubiquitous—in the airwaves, movies, books, and newspapers—but no one, it appears, was able to define it satisfactorily, or to resist attempting a definition. Swing seemingly had appeared so quickly and mysteriously that it was unclear whom to turn to for an explanation, or even what sort of definition would be appropriate.

Those most directly involved in the music, professional musicians, were of little help. Reporters writing articles with titles like "Swing: What Is It?" discovered that the definitions offered by "professional swingsters" (or their press agents) were hopelessly impressionistic. Benny Goodman was quoted as saying that swing "is as difficult to explain as the Mona Lisa's smile or the nutty hats women wear—but just as stimulating. It remains something you take 5,000 words to explain then leaves you wondering what it is." Chick Webb compared swing to "lovin' a gal, and havin' a fight, and then seein' her again," while Fats Waller offered the formula "two-thirds rhythm and one-third soul." For Louis Armstrong it was simply "my idea of how a tune should go." The difficulty of arriving at a consensus definition, various critics pointed out, was that swing referred not to a type of music, but to the way in which music was performed. "There is no such thing as a swing tune; when Duke Ellington plays 'In the Shade of the Old Apple Tree,' it swings. When Wayne King plays 'Riverboat Shuffle' it does not swing." To ask a musician to define swing is like describing the color red to a child who has never seen it, opined Goodman; it cannot be defined, only recognized.[4]

Others were willing to discuss the issue in musical terms. But many of these definitions linked musical properties of rhythm and improvisation to political concepts like "freedom" and "individualism." Perhaps the most widely publicized definition, one to which Goodman acceded, was advanced by critics John Hammond and Marshall Stearns: "A band swings when its collective improvisation is rhythmically integrated." For drummer Gene Krupa, swing was "complete and inspired freedom of rhythmic interpretation." Vibraphonist bandleader Red Norvo defined swing as "a pulsation of rhythm by individual interpretation of original or written phrases." A drum manufacturer defined swing as "simply a refined and cultured rhythm with clever emphasis on dynamics." Other definitions stressed the subjective responses it generated among listeners. Glenn Miller, for example, described swing as "a solidity and compactness of attack by which the rhythm instruments combine with the others to create within the listeners the desire to dance." Or acceleration: Wingy Mannone likened swing to "feeling an increase in tempo though you're still playing at the same tempo."[5]

In the most ambitious technical attempt to describe swing, the American composer and musicologist Virgil Thomson defined it as "a form of the two-step in which the rhythm is expressed quantitatively by instruments of no fixed intonation, the melodic, harmonic and purely percussive elements being freed thereby to improvise in free polyphonic style." At the core of the definition was a distinction between "beat music," whose rhythm was dominated by accents, and "quantitative music," in which rhythmic intervals were defined by rolls or trills— filled time—rather than by stresses. The former, according to Thomson, created a muscular music conducive to jerky dances and marches; the latter, which he associated with swing, produced a hypnotic response. "Notice the high degree of intellectual and nervous excitement present in any swing-audience," he wrote. "The listeners do not close their eyes and sink into emotional or subjective states. They sit up straight, their eyes flash, they applaud the licks. They occasionally jerk on the absent down-beat, but on the whole they seem to be enjoying one of those states of nervous and muscular equilibrium that render possible rapid intellection."[6]

In all these cases, defining swing required recourse to the social setting in which the music was performed or consumed, or to the political
ideas it seemed to express. Swing may have been primarily entertainment, but it struck its contemporaries as a form of entertainment that
might help them better understand their times.

A definition that was not given at the onset of the swing craze is the
one that has come to be accepted among historians: a stage in the development of jazz characterized by written arrangements and performed
by big bands—or small ensembles culled from those bands—during the
1930s and 1940s. One reason this definition was not available is that
jazz itself was a term with very little precision during the years during
which swing emerged. The "classic jazz" of 1920s New Orleans and
Chicago had seemingly evaporated with the collapse of the recording
industry in the years following the Crash. But even in its 1920s bloom,
"jazz" had no settled meaning. For most Americans who thought about
such things, jazz meant the "symphonic" product of Paul Whiteman
or the blackface vaudeville performances of Al Jolson, the success of
whose film *The Jazz Singer* (1927) created the most widely held public
image of jazz. The more widely read periodicals of the 1920s likewise
used "jazz" as a synonym for any kind of syncopated dance music, or
for "symphonic" jazz, as did the two best-known American books on
the subject, Osgood's *So This Is Jazz?* and Whiteman's *Jazz*. When
swing "burst" onto the scene in 1935, then, it understandably appeared
to most Americans to come out of nowhere, its historical links to 1920s
jazz having been elided.

Musicians, to be sure, were aware of those links and careful to
acknowledge them. Responding to the controversies provoked by
swing, and decrying the faddism that had come to surround the music
by 1939, Ellington reminded readers of *Down Beat* that swing had
already been performed for over a decade. His "Don't Mean a Thing
If It Ain't Got That Swing" had been recorded in 1932, and the term
had appeared in jazz recordings since the 1920s. "To speak of swing as
a fad is to define it as something similar to mah-jong or crossword
puzzles," said Goodman the same year. It had been "sinking its roots
in American music" for 100 years, he said. "Swing certainly wasn't
originated by myself or other current bandleaders. We simply helped
develop something that has been growing for decades." Whiteman,

who claimed that "swing" was first used in the musical sense by critic Olin Downes in a review of a 1924 Whiteman concert, went further. "There's no such thing as swing," he stated flatly. "Swing music doesn't exist, but swing musicians do. It is a verb, not a noun." Some musicians disparaged the swing of the late 1930s, charging that "in spite of all the ballyhoo," the public "gets less genuine swinging than it did ten years ago when most of the swinging was privately done in musicians' hideouts."[7]

The idea of this jazz tradition even appeared in the lyrics to a swing tune recorded by Billie Holiday the week before Benny Goodman's famous Carnegie Hall concert of January 1938. Ragtime had once "had its fling"; "this modern thing" featured "the same old syncopation," but "now they call it swing." The music they had played "jazz-time, to a buck and wing . . . again sweeps the nation." Singers who had once sung the phrase "hot-cha" now scatted a longer, more fluid melodic line: "Dee dee dee dee, Da da da da, *Ree* dee dee, *Da* da da." "Rhythm has its seasons, summer, fall, and spring," the lyrics conclude; "but for seven silly reasons someone pulled the string, and they started dancing; now they call it swing." By 1939 the notion that swing was essentially a new name for jazz was becoming commonplace among nonmusicians as well. "To call present-day jazz swing would be a lot like calling present-day football pass, just because there is more passing now than there was fifteen years ago," wrote John O'Hara, who considered swing a "disgusting fraud." But as late as 1944 the trade press was still soliciting musicians' opinions on the difference between swing and jazz, with most agreeing there was none, other than that the latter had a slightly archaic ring.[8]

Unquestionably, some of the distinguishing musical elements of swing had appeared in the work of bands as early as the mid-1920s. Certainly by 1932, three years before the swing phenomenon, orchestras led by Ellington, Fletcher Henderson, Bennie Moten, Don Redman, Glen Gray, and others were playing music clearly recognizable as swing. The music was also incubating among smaller groups in the jazz clubs of Manhattan's 52nd Street. But the beginning of swing as a popular phenomenon, one that reached a large national audience, is generally dated to the summer of 1935. The conventional account portrays the swing era as erupting unexpectedly in July 1935, when the Goodman orchestra wrapped up a disappointing cross-country tour with a sensational engagement at the Palomar Ballroom in Los Angeles. Late-night radio broadcasts from the "Let's Dance" show originating in New York had prepared the West Coast audience for the innovative Goodman sound. This tremendous response to the Goodman band followed it back across the country to Chicago and New York. The term *swing* began appearing in the popular press that fall in connection with Goodman.[9]

The notion that the "King of Swing" precipitated a musical movement squares with later conceptions of popular music centered on particular personalities or ensembles. But a more accurate if less mythic account of the swing era's beginning points to a specific piece of music: "The Music Goes 'Round and Around," ostensibly written (although its exact origins remained dubious) by two veteran white musicians, Mike Riley and Eddie Farley, who led a dance band known for clowning and novelty numbers at 52nd Street's Onyx Club. Recorded in September 1935, shortly after Goodman's West Coast triumph, the song became the Decca label's first big hit, selling more than 100,000 copies. According to *Time*, the sheet music was selling "a-copy-a-minute over sheet music counters": a necktie, a sofa, and a cigarette holder had been named after it; it was the most requested tune in hotels across the country; the three major record companies were distributing it under some dozen labels, while NBC and CBS announced it as the most popular song on the air; one station played it 28 times in one night in response to 428 requests, while another station prepared to broadcast it in Yiddish, Italian, Spanish, Hungarian, German, Polish, Ukrainian, Greek, "Negro dialect, Irish brogue and pig-Latin." The song was sung at parties throughout the winter. "It was like an echo that followed you around through the night and into the quiet and deserted streets of New Year's Day, 1936," recalled a writer. As late as 1939, when a movie based on the song was released, audiences joined in to sing the title tune. *Time* likened it to earlier "nut songs" but judged it "fundamentally a 'swing' tune," a view strongly disputed by others.[10]

Other signs, too, pointed to the emergence of a more broadly appealing musical hybrid. An article in early 1935 identified something new, not "the jazz of war days and of pre-Repeal," but a "jazz de luxe—romance with a golden glitter and the zip of a motorcar age." This new sound was not "hot," but "sweet," stressing melody over rhythm, "something that not only tickles the feet but also touches the heart," and designed less for dancing than for home consumption via the radio, while reading a newspaper. The big-name orchestras that played the new sound—led by Fred Waring, Wayne King, Guy Lombardo, Ben Bernie, Rudy Vallee, and Meyer Davis—resembled corporations managed by large-scale booking agencies with "West Point precision." This preswing "jazz de luxe" created a popular response associated with later swing: fans jamming into huge convention halls, cracking floors under their combined weight, attracting front-page headlines. Most important, it was accessible. "We don't try to educate or elevate or in any way change" the audience, according to Fred Waring, whose band grossed a record million dollars in 1934. "The new jazz and its gods know no class, no age, no boundary lines," the article averred. "The music of the new and very businesslike Jazzland is alike the music of Park Avenue and of Main Street." Though prescient, the article was off the mark on one key point: the "hot" qualities thought to be disappearing in the new jazz were the very ones that would define the new genre that had yet to be named swing.[11]

Swing acquired its name and gathered popular momentum during 1936 and 1937. It attracted its youthful audience through a complex media network of radio broadcasts, recordings, movies, and cross-country tours. Each year new band leaders—Benny Goodman, Artie Shaw, Tommy Dorsey, Glenn Miller—rose to prominence, competing for the loyalties of an expanding audience. A minority of dedicated listeners turned their attention to the African-American bands, discovering in ensembles led by Ellington, Jimmie Lunceford, Count Basie, and others what they considered a more vital and authentic music. By 1938 the swing phenomenon had acquired sufficient mass to become a national fad, the subject of articles and editorials in the country's most widely read periodicals and newspapers.

Although media interest waned as swing's novelty faded, the music's mass popularity continued through the Second World War. The heroes of swing were eagerly pressed into the war effort, lending their celebrity to war bond sales and transforming their music into a semiofficial morale-raising medium for military personnel around the world and war industry workers at home. The conscription of musicians, combined with an insatiable demand for entertainment, ensured that the war years were a financial bonanza for those big bands able to maintain their personnel. But musicians in the service returned to a much-changed swing industry. Squeezed by artificially inflated salaries, high overhead, and declining demand, many bands folded. Swing's audience also began fracturing after the war, with one segment following the popular vocalists who had risen to prominence in the big bands, others turning to a stripped-down riff-based "jump" style, while a small cadre of aficionados embraced the challenging swing offshoot known as bebop. By 1950 most of the big bands had dissolved, and swing would never recapture its popularity of the previous decade.

Studying culture through music depends on the fundamental assumption that some kind of meaningful overlap or continuity exists between the cultural form, music, and the broader entity of society or culture. Certainly, reducing swing to its aural dimension, by focusing on surviving recordings or various bands' arrangements and styles, would commit the same violence to the lived experience of its consumption as would reducing an actual performance to its song lyrics. The problem with using a musical form like swing as a historical source lies not so much in the abstractness of music, but in the arbitrary reduction of the scope of what is meant by "music." The solution lies not in musicological positivism, which privileges the written score above the experience of "sound-in-time" and elements of musical reference, but in broadening our conception of "the music" to include social elements: audience, performance context, ideology, and mass media. Historians must regard the score or recording as merely the sign of a large field of social forces that provide the ground for those texts. In other words, the arbitrary distinction between a musical performance and its origin or source can be abolished. Swing would then be understood not as a collection of written arrangements or recordings but as the field that makes such texts possible. In short, we should view the music not simply as text but as social practice.[12]

As musicologists increasingly acknowledge, music's meaning is constructed; thus the contradictions and ironies present in swing reflect the work of different social groups in constructing their own assorted understandings of it. This is not to strip musical texts of their particularity, to claim that musical performances or texts are homogeneous. Indeed, the point is that the qualities of music that produce meaning in the audience are culturally and historically specific. Different audiences actually hear the same music differently, and take different meanings away. The social meanings "read into" the music by contemporary listeners depended on how their ears and bodies were conditioned to respond, which in turn reflected the influence of family members, neighbors, ministers, magazine feature writers, and the like. In this sense swing was a cultural Rorschach test for its contemporaries.

Looking at music as a broad social field takes us closer to the idea of a swing-shaped culture that is developed in the following chapters. Changes in the ways the music was arranged, produced, distributed, and enjoyed reflected larger social patterns. Compared to the polyphonic, collectively improvised music of New Orleans and Chicago, swing was tightly structured through written arrangements that allowed relatively little room for spontaneous improvisation (even solos tended to be worked out in advance and performed with little variation). The twelve-bar blues and other, more complex forms that had provided the framework for much early jazz were largely supplanted in swing by popular songs written in the standard thirty-two-bar, AABA structure of Tin Pan Alley. As functional dance music, swing replaced the choppy two-beat "bounce" characteristic of early jazz with a more flowing, streamlined four-beat rhythm, partly a result of the substitution of the more rhythmically flowing stringed bass for the tuba in the rhythm section. Swing bands were larger than the typical early jazz ensembles, and they shifted the counterpoint from individual lines played by trumpet, clarinet, and trombone to two sections or "choirs," reeds (saxophones and clarinet) and brass (trumpets and trombones).

The turn away from the loose, open-ended, and nonhierarchical playing of 1920s jazz toward the more regimented modes of swing registered the move toward larger, more bureaucratic, and more rationalized units of organization characteristic of American society during the 1930s. It was analogous to the arrangements worked out among business, unions, and the government under the New Deal, for example. Swing's much-noted quality of enabling the individual voice to contribute to the collective whole also accords well with the notion of a cooperative commonwealth central to Franklin Roosevelt's vision of America.

Swing's jazz-tradition successor, bebop, drastically reduced ensemble size, typically to five pieces, and reinstated extended improvisation, sequential rather than collective. Bebop "arrangements" were not compositions in the sense in which swing arrangements had been; instead, they were open frameworks used to highlight the spontaneous creativity of the soloist. Bebop dramatically expanded the harmonic vocabulary and rhythmic idioms available for improvisation (and arrangements). Although most bebop compositions were derived from the repertoire of popular song on which swing drew, the familiar melodies were discarded in favor of the underlying harmonic structures.[13] The sharp contraction of the ensemble in bebop, together with the emphasis on individual virtuosity and dissonant (to swing-attuned ears) sonorities, suggests the heroic alienation of the postwar individual cut loose from Depression-era modes of commitment, or the racial militancy taking root among African-Americans in the late 1940s.

Swing's trajectory can be linked to those of several other aspects of American culture in the same years. For example, both the regionalist paintings of Thomas Hart Benton and swing expressed the ideals of progressive reform and a populist producerist ideology through symbols that embodied the uniquely American values of energy and democracy. Both swing and regionalism depicted a utopian vision of an "American way of life" that at once drew on and lent itself to Hollywood and advertising. Both clashed with the mores of the regional cultures in which they operated. And after the war both rapidly lost ground to styles that appeared abruptly discontinuous but were related through their defining artists; the abstract expressionist Jackson Pollock had studied with Benton, just as the jazz modernists had come up through the big bands. In its studied apoliticism, its emphasis on freedom, alienation, and the individual, its turn from society to self, from Marx to Freud, abstract expressionism was an apt reflection of the prevailing ideology of Cold War America.[14] Bebop likewise was taken to express this cultural mood of alienation; it too was abstract in the sense that its solos were based not on melodies but on chord changes (a practice that in fact predated bebop).

Baseball during those years affords still another parallel to swing. Baseball games, ranging from pickup scrimmages played by bands whose buses happened to cross paths on a highway on the Great Plains, to regulation games played in team uniforms, were a constant feature of big-band life. Harry James in particular took the sport with deadly seriousness and compiled an impressive record. "We made baseball fields out of cow pastures all over the eastern part of the country," according to a sideman. "We would practice all day, barely making it to that night's job." The two vocations had much in common, as Gene Krupa pointed out: "the living out of suitcases, the constant time pressures to get to another place so that you can perform on schedule, the working with the same people every day, being watched all the time by the public, trying to live up to a reputation, and, of course, all the mental and emotional intangibles that must affect ballplayers just the way they affect musicians."[15]

Moreover, both inspired a similar devotion among fans. "Hundreds of thousands of youngsters (and adults too, for it is a provocative diversion) know the personnels of the leading swing bands as a baseball enthusiast knows the roster of every major-league club," wrote an observer. To reach these audiences, both big band jazz and baseball required the new technology of the twentieth century—namely automobiles and radio—to assume what was to be their central role in the new culture of leisure apparent by the 1920s. Both galvanized their respective audiences through the force of personality: Ruth and Goodman, Robinson and Armstrong.[16] And both embodied the new sense of a transnational mass culture that was displacing a more localized, homegrown variety of cultural participation.

The parallel extends to the formal, ideological, and economic planes. In its choreographed symmetry, its balance of routine anonymous play alternating with moments of individual self-expression, baseball has much in common with swing. Both were performances within performances, in which spectators paid to watch professionals play. Both involved contestation, more subtle in swing, as different "choirs" (brass or reeds) played off one another, or a soloist played against the ensemble as a batter would face a defensive alignment. Both required teamwork at a high level of precision, and a balancing of the individual and the collective. Swing, like baseball, is regarded as quintessentially ✓ American. Both collected a bewildering range of political meanings, were championed at different times by both the Communist Party and the U.S. government. Baseball's "great experiment" of integration in the late 1940s has been cited as a watershed event in American race relations; swing performed a similar function a decade earlier. As jazz critic George Simon observed in 1947, when Jackie Robinson was struggling for acceptance with the Brooklyn Dodgers, the athlete's talents lay "in an unfortunate field"; as a jazz musician, he would have been immediately accepted. In both cases the legacy of integration was mixed. "Since Robinson's debut, blacks have done the same thing in Major League Baseball that they have done in popular music: entertain, make large salaries, and generate money for businesses that funnel precious little of it back into the black community," observes Nelson George.[17] The same argument was made about integrated big bands in the early 1940s.

The central cultural link, however, is the New Deal, understood not as a collection of legislative initiatives and alphabet agencies but as a broad-based cultural movement. Swing did more than symbolize this movement; it participated in it in direct, material ways. Swing was the preeminent musical expression of the New Deal: a cultural form of "the people," accessible, inclusive, distinctively democratic, and thus distinctively American. Like the politics of Franklin Roosevelt, swing provided the ideological terrain for ethnic and regional inclusiveness on a scale unprecedented in American history. It emerged in a culture defined by shocks and dislocations, divided by competing impulses toward political radicalism and social conservatism. Swing reflected those shocks and, as it evolved through the late 1940s, helped assuage them, producing a different kind of American culture in the process. To its proponents, swing was both proof and cause of an American society growing ever more egalitarian and progressive.[18]

Among its performers and their audiences, swing attracted a previously unrecognized constituency similar in many ways to Roosevelt's new Democratic coalition of organized labor, urban white ethnics, African-Americans, intellectuals, and farmers. Linking people across racial, ethnic, class, and regional lines, swing seemed to embody the American melting pot. Not since the heyday of blackface minstrelsy in the decades before the Civil War had America been forced to confront so directly its indebtedness to African-American culture, to acknowledge that its culture was unmistakably formed by a racial group systematically excluded from its society.[19] And in its alliance with the politics of the Popular Front after 1935, a highly visible sector of the swing community took part in a broad-based leftist coalition that sought to root itself in the American past and thereby define Americanism in its own terms.

Like the New Deal, swing also represented different and sometimes incompatible things to participants and observers. It struck proponents as the domain of healthy fun, critics as the source of hedonism and mindless exhibitionism eerily akin to the social effects of fascism. To some observers swing expressed escapism, a fantasy relief from economic hardship. To others it suggested the down-to-earth embrace of a reality obscured by much of the popular music that preceded swing. Like the New Deal, swing served to bridge polarities of race, of ideology, and of high and low culture. And like the New Deal, swing sometimes failed to fulfill its apparent promise in terms of actual social practice.

It was no coincidence that the big bands struggled and ultimately failed in the same postwar years that witnessed the ultimate fragmentation of the New Deal coalition. These centrifugal forces were reflected in various sectors: in the crisis faced by labor as it struggled with the challenges of congressional hostility, Red-baiting, and the renewed determination of business leaders; and in the travail of the Democratic Party, torn between the southern Dixiecrats and the Wallace progressives. These cleavages reflected comparable forces of race, ethnicity, geography, economics, demography, and technology. That they occurred at the same time and for similar reasons points to swing's cultural centrality. Its jazz-tradition successor, bebop, absorbed some of these ideological currents, producing an oppositional subculture whose politics of style were also rooted in swing.

this is a great to choice to end the course

Several metaphors already vie for the attention of those studying the Depression and war years. The figure of Roosevelt continues to loom over the period, and the New Deal, once almost synonymous with "the Thirties," still serves as a focal point. Broadening the field of inquiry to recover the experiences of larger numbers of people, historians have looked to expressive culture, especially movies and radio, for clues. Mickey Mouse, suggests Warren Susman, has superseded FDR as the central figure of the age. For others, the aesthetic of the documentary, expressed in journalism, photography, social science writing, fiction, and other popular culture genres, has been the defining cultural impulse.[20] A by-product of this cultural history is the tendency to ascribe psychological qualities to the decade. Susman and Lawrence Levine, for example, have identified strong currents of fear, shame, and guilt in 1930s culture as a consequence of unprecedented economic calamity. The postwar years have been linked to a mood of anxiety or doubt stemming from the technological forces unleashed by the war and by the new role of the United States in the world.[21] In these accounts, historical periods are identified above all as states of mind, collective and individual.

To propose the notion of swing-shaped culture is not to discard these or other suggestive attempts to characterize the culture of the 1930s and 1940s. Swing is only one of an unlimited number of maps that can be drawn from the culture of the period, none of which is reducible to any other. But because it operated in so many domains, swing offers a particularly suggestive map. A broad-based, unified but heterogeneous social practice with its own trajectory of rise and decline, swing captures the dynamic of change and movement in the period. Like other forms of expressive culture, it encompassed a variety of ideologies and touched the lives of people from a range of ethnic, class, and regional backgrounds. But it was also a national phenomenon, materially anchored in the complex mass culture industry. A unified but heterogenous area of social practice, swing complicates our understanding of a period that has frequently lent itself to reduction and oversimplification.

Finally, swing offers a useful way of periodizing the years that can only awkwardly be labeled "the 1930s and 1940s." It stresses the continuities between these two decades rather than the abrupt rupture caused by the beginning of the Second World War. The war in fact marked the culmination of the swing aesthetic just as it represented the climax of other cultural movements of the 1930s. By highlighting the ideals that swing was supposed to embody, the war revealed the contradictions implicit in swing as ideology and as social practice. If 1948 was "the last year of the Thirties," as Michael Harrington has written, "the very last moment when the philosophical preoccupations of the Great Depression were still primary," it is fitting that swing enjoyed a final surge of popular enthusiasm that year, in the appropriately deceptive guise of bebop.[22]

1

The Tempo of the Time

On a Sunday evening, January 16, 1938, an improbable audience assembled in New York's Carnegie Hall for what was to be one of the most celebrated concerts ever staged there. The featured performers, Benny Goodman and his orchestra, struck many observers as being as unsuited to the venue as the audience they attracted. There was a clear sense, among those who attended the event and those who wrote about it, that something historic was taking place: an invasion of one of the sanctums of High Culture by the roiling forces of a musical fad called swing.

That morning's *New York Times Magazine* used the occasion for a ponderous, pensive survey of the new music: its historical roots, Benny Goodman's by-then-familiar success story, the polarizing debates it was generating between cultural "Spenglerites" who dismissed swing as "unregenerate racket," and the "cultists" and "emotional boys who exalt swing to supreme artistic heights." The Carnegie Hall concert, according to the *Times*, would be a critical test for the music, the first major cultural opportunity since the failure of Paul Whiteman's "symphonic jazz" in the late 1920s. It would enable swing to exchange "the combustible atmosphere of the semi-darkened hotel grill room with its convivial and intimate tables" for "the cold and formal air of the concert hall, its sedate, red-plushed rows, its gilt, gingerbread boxes." How would the new music sound in "this strange milieu of righteousness and uplift," the author wondered; he felt confident that the concert would be "decisive in the history of swing." Perhaps more important, how would American society be affected by the cultural legitimation of this music?[1]

Not surprisingly, in view of such charged publicity, every available seat and area of standing room was filled. The estimated attendance of 3,900 was larger than that usually attracted by the New York Philharmonic. The audience filed in slowly out of the bitter cold, where picketers protested Goodman's having played a benefit for "Spanish Communists." The box seats were "full of important squatters," and the hall had set up a special jurybox onstage to accommodate some 100 additional spectators. "The audience," according to one observer, "was undoubtedly the strangest assortment ever gathered within the sturdy walls of Carnegie, from adolescent schoolboys attired like misprints in Esquire, who applauded everything, including the klinkers, to baggy-eyed pseudo-sophisticates who applauded nothing—including several enjoyable spots." In the first camp belonged the large number of "ickies," or exuberant swing faddists. The latter faction included famous classical musicians, society women wearing long white gloves and carrying lorgnettes, and bemused music critics from the major New York papers.

Although Goodman was the featured star and received a "real Toscanini send-off" that lasted for three minutes when he appeared onstage, the concert itself was an intriguing assortment of guest appearances and diverse acts. The event's organizers recognized an opportunity to define the music, to construct a history for it, and to stamp certain of its performers with legitimacy; it was also a chance to take racial liberties not previously witnessed in such cultural precincts. The big band opened the concert, nervously and stiffly, until incited by a "tremendous break" by drummer Gene Krupa. ("The crowd cheered, yelled, howled. Gene's hair fell into his eyes. The band fell into a groove.") But the Goodman big band itself was far from being the central focus of attention that evening. A smaller group performed a twenty-minute historical retrospective on jazz featuring satire-tinged tributes to the Original Dixieland Jazz Band ("Sensation Rag"), Bix Beiderbecke ("I'm Coming, Virginia"), and Louis Armstrong ("Shine"). Goodman hosted a small group of stars from the Ellington orchestra to play "Blue Reverie." A twenty-minute "jam session," judged the weakest part of the evening, allowed Goodman and his trumpeter Harry James to perform with luminaries from the Count Basie band, including Lester Young, Buck Clayton, Walter Page,

Freddie Green, and Basie himself. The concert's high point, according to the critics present, consisted of the segments by Goodman's trio and quartet, groups celebrated not only for their music but also for defying the color line by allowing pianist Teddy Wilson and vibraphonist Lionel Hampton to appear onstage with Goodman and Krupa.

If the musicians gave evidence of being intimidated by the Carnegie setting, the crowd itself apparently showed few inhibitions. "There was quivering excitement in the air, an almost electrical effect, and much laughter," wrote one critic. "The audience broke out before the music stopped in crashing applause . . . the great gathering was almost off its head with joy. The 'hotter' the pace, the louder the blasts, the better it went. Sometimes shouts threatened to vanquish the orchestra." Ickies clapped out of tempo, drawing indulgent grins from Goodman and Krupa, and shouted, "Come on, drummer, go to town!" and other encouragements. Krupa replied in kind, exhorting his colleagues to "take one more, Jack," at one point knocking a cymbal off its stand in his enthusiasm. Goodman, at least, found the crowd's enthusiasm excessive. He later castigated Carnegie's "hoodlum jitterbugs," a "noisy minority" who "blasted out the horns, yelled and stomped a dozen smooth passages of the trio into oblivion, wrecked a few numbers with trick ends completely." The mob applauded Martha Tilton's rendition of "Loch Lomond" for five minutes, prompting Goodman to inform them that the band was not prepared for encores (although the band played two at the end of the show).[2]

Normally this kind of event would monopolize the attention of the jazz community on a given weekend; it would certainly dominate a Sunday evening; and in fact this one continued to be discussed and dissected in the press for months afterward. But on this particular Sunday night, the Goodman performance at Carnegie Hall was succeeded by an event of comparable musical interest (although it didn't attract nearly the same publicity). Directly after their encore, Goodman and most of the musicians who had appeared with him left the stage to travel some eighty blocks uptown to a Harlem establishment known as the "Home of Happy Feet." The Savoy ballroom, largest of its kind in New York, was hosting a long-anticipated "battle" between the Chick Webb and Count Basie orchestras.

The Savoy, with its dual bandstands and enormous dance floor, hosted a succession of noteworthy band battles during the swing era. "There is something in the air here, a demand to be given something on the part of the people," wrote an observer, "that shapes matters, so that when a group needs to get really together and tightened up, this is where it books in." The previous May the Savoy had hosted a celebrated contest between bands led by Goodman and Chick Webb in which 4,000 dancers packed the hall, another 5,000 were turned away, and mounted police, the fire department, and a riot squad were called in to preserve order. But the Basie-Webb battle took on a particularly epic cast. It was a contest between West and East, pitting a Kansas City band with a revolutionary rhythmic concept against the local favorites, a house band that had vanquished all comers at the Savoy. The contest, according to one observer, was between "solid swing" and "sensational swing." Basie's band stuck to the blues, while Webb's played intricately arranged charts. The Kansas City group "devoted its attack to the body, to the heart, with a steady hammering of truly sending rhythm figures behind the truly sensational solos" of Lester Young, Buck Clayton, and Herschel Evans. "Webb's sensational, whirl-wind barrage," on the other hand, "was aimed chiefly at the ears and head with resounding arrangements played at breakneck tempos, and including all sorts of screeching and even novelty effects." Basie's men "settled into one unbeatable groove after another," while Webb's opted instead for "electrifying rhythm attacks, attacks which suffered by comparison through their lack of stability."[3]

Visitors to the Savoy walked up two flights of stairs, coming into a large low-ceilinged room; the dance floor was 100 yards wide and 30 yards long, framed by a long bar selling beer and wine, a row of booths, a section of tables, and the bandstand. "The place is packed solid," observed a journalist, "and the whole room seems to be one vast drum that some huge ebony jinni is beating . . . suddenly you are conscious that the floor itself is perceptibly swaying, perhaps as much as three inches." The narrow bandstand on which the bands performed, side by side, stretched some sixty feet down the far side of the ballroom. "It is the center of most of the light, but still dim enough," wrote a critic. "The wall behind it is painted into an extravagant blue background, and by means of trick spotlights, thin clouds seem to be drawn across it perpetually, giving the effect of motion and smoke, and the bands play under that, dominating the hall and bearing down on it, inexorable, all steam and iron, like freight trains."[4] On this stage the orchestras battled.

At about one o'clock the master of ceremonies asked the dancers for their verdict. The crowd cheered slightly longer for Basie than for Webb, and *Metronome* was glad to report that Basie appeared to be the winner of this plebiscite. "Had the battle been on a theatre stage before the usual un-hep, public audience, Webb would undoubtedly have won by a wide margin," but the knowing Savoy "swingsters"—an audience that included Duke Ellington, Benny Goodman, Gene Krupa, Lionel Hampton, and Red Norvo—knew better than to be beguiled by "break-neck tempos offered as true swing." But the result was not as clear-cut as the writer wanted to believe. A ballot conducted by the Savoy revealed a more than two-to-one margin in favor of the house band. Webb partisans pointed out that although the dancers were seen to bob up and down in front of the Basie bandstand, they were more enthralled by Webb's "terrific tempos" and "thrilling" rhythms. A separate ballot gave Webb's vocalist, Ella Fitzgerald, a three-to-one plurality over Basie's Billie Holiday.[5]

These two performances, though conjoined by a coincidence of time and place, help by their apparent difference to define the cultural field within which the phenomenon of swing operated. The incongruities within and frictions between these two performances of January 16 serve to illuminate the contradictions within the culture—and subcultures—of America in 1938, at the peak of the swing fad. The Carnegie Hall concert and the Savoy dance might be described as a series of polar oppositions: the first event centering on white artists and their audience, the second involving mainly African-Americans; the first paying tribute to the Anglo-American conventions of high culture, the second to an indigenous folk music tradition; the first a highly visible public event, the second submerged relative to the dominant American culture; Carnegie Hall stressing pluralism, inclusiveness, and consensus, the Savoy emphasizing contestation and difference; the first defining musical appreciation in terms of an ideal of spectatorship, as pleasure, the second as mere gratification, stressing physical participation; the first striving to impose its meaning on its audience, the second dissolving the barriers between performers and audience, by making the "spectators" cocreators of cultural meaning through their dancing, cheers, and partisanship.

To exaggerate or reify these distinctions, however, would be to miss the way in which the two performances, and swing itself, disrupted and frustrated these very cultural categories. To hear the audience participation in the Carnegie concert, the spontaneous applause after solos, and the shouts of approbation from the ickies, is to recognize a performance dynamic very different from that required by high-culture codes and ensconced in American concert halls since the turn of the century.[6] This audience was far from an assemblage of passive, disembodied spectators. Conversely, we know that dancing was only one way in which audiences expressed themselves at ballrooms like the Savoy; every performance generated a large cluster of spectators around the stage or bandstand, enjoying the performance as a musical experience, not an impetus for dancing. Swing was blurring the distinction between aesthetic enjoyment and pleasure of a less rarefied nature.

The artists themselves offer equally compelling evidence of the blurring of oppositions. They themselves overlapped the two performances; several of the guest performers at Carnegie were members of the Basie band, who occupied the spotlight later at the Savoy; many of the downtown concert's stars joined the uptown audience afterward. This type of fraternizing would have been unthinkable a few years earlier because of both racial and cultural distinctions that swing had already begun to challenge. African-American artists and popular music had been presented at Carnegie before the Goodman concert, to be sure, but with different symbolic resonances. For example, the Paul Whiteman orchestra's 1924 concert at New York's Aeolian Hall, an event considered a precursor to the Carnegie show by writers in 1938, presented itself as an elevation of jazz to "symphonic" status through the vehicle of George Gershwin's *Rhapsody in Blue*. Such goals were not part of the Carnegie program. And the racial integration that took place on the stage at Carnegie Hall and on the dance floor at the Savoy, proscribed as it was by carefully defined codes, would have been out of the question at the Cotton Club in 1930, let alone Aeolian Hall in 1924.

The repertoire provides further evidence for the syncretic impulse of swing. Several of Goodman's hits performed at Carnegie were originally written and performed by the Webb orchestra, including, ironically, "Stompin' at the Savoy," Webb's theme song. (For its encore, the Goodman band played "Big John's Special," reportedly named after the Savoy's doorman). Repertoire also linked Goodman to Basie; Goodman's versions of Basie tunes like "One O'Clock Jump" became hits, thereby aiding Basie's long-deferred commercial success in New York, which occurred that summer on 52nd Street, then the downtown center of jazz in Manhattan.

Beyond the parameters of Carnegie, swing served as a cultural bridge in the larger society as well. The controversy over the moral repercussions of swing paralleled the previous decade's debate over jazz, but it differed in important ways. Moralists had earlier stressed the threat that jazz, as they understood it, posed to civilized values and respectable culture. Through its physical manifestation, dance, jazz threatened to unleash forces that would undermine established gender, racial, and class hierarchies. The moral panic over jazz was rehearsed again in the early 1930s, focusing this time on "crooners" like Bing Crosby. Cardinal O'Connell of Boston, for example, expressed his "revolting disgust at a man whining a degenerate song, which is unworthy of any American man." Crooning was "immoral and imbecile slush . . . degenerate, low-down . . . a sensuous, effeminate luxurious sort of paganism." This line of attack was picked up by newspapers and even some radio program directors.[7]

Swing's threat was subtly different. The archbishop of Dubuque was capable of summoning the old rhetoric while addressing a meeting of the National Council of Catholic Women in Biloxi, Mississippi. "We permit, if not freely endorse by our criminal indifference, 'jam sessions,' 'jitter-bugs,' and cannibalistic rhythmic orgies to occupy a place in our social scheme of things," he thundered, "wooing our youth along the primrose path to hell." Such a culture robbed art of its "beautiful essence and meaning," leaving it "to die along the highroad of communistic endeavor." But among those opposed to swing, the considerations of personal morality and cultural decline that had so shaped the moral panic of the 1920s were overshadowed by concern over the rising totalitarian politics of the late 1930s. Some interpreted swing as a symptom of the loss of social and spiritual values brought about by a society of specialists and spectators; music could fill such an emotional vacuum, and the wrong music could yield disastrous results. "Swing is musical Hitlerism," declared a University of Chicago professor. "There is a mass sense of letting one's self go." Goodman was described as a "musical Billy Sunday"; more ominously, his fans were observed calling for him at a musical event "with the abandon of a crowd of Storm Troopers demanding their Fuehrer or a Roman parade greeting its Duce."[8]

Few went so far as to make a direct comparison between swing and fascism. But almost all observers seeking to make sense of swing agreed that, for better or worse, it was an apt expression of the times. "Swing is the voice of youth striving to be heard in this fast-moving world of ours," wrote one. "Swing is the tempo of our time." Another swing defender, bandleader Larry Clinton, called it "a reflection of a restless tense world. One can't expect this brittle age to produce anything but a brittle dance." Editorializing on the Goodman Carnegie concert, the *Times* concurred that swing is "strictly a spinal column affair," "in harmony with the major movements that are sweeping the world today." But, the piece continued, swing differed from these other trends "in having nothing repressive about it." It was not so much a "doctrine set to music as . . . a revolt against doctrine." The article concluded, "Dictators should be suspicious of swing."[9]

Others sought to correlate swing not to political movements but to domestic economics. The overcharged atmosphere of the Great War and its aftermath produced the first bloom of hot jazz; the "hangover" years of the early 1930s ushered in a more mellow, sweet sound; the mid-1930s, as the United States seemed to be recovering somewhat from the dislocations of the Depression, were producing something new.[10] "Our young people," declared the president of the Dancing Teachers Business Association in July 1938, "disturbed by uncertainties of their economic situation and wondering whether they will be on WPA or in a CCC camp tomorrow, have found in swing neurotic and erotic expressions of physical activity." Some linked swing to economic recovery. *Metronome* pointed out that "swing began to take hold in a national way about the time this country gave evidence of pulling itself out of the ruck. The economists call it recovery. But the effect on the mass mind is one of loosening up." In this view, swing as a cultural phenomenon resulted from the celebratory mood generated by the economic recovery under way by 1936, an interpretation that downplayed the role of the music itself in creating its own vogue. Asked whether the popularity of swing music accounted for the increased attendance figures of 1936 compared to those of 1935, a New York ballroom manager replied, "Not at all—you can give much more credit to the present administration in Washington and to the morale of the nation in general."[11]

Swing could also be explained less as a response to improving economic conditions than as a form of healthy compensation and escape from a disturbing world. "Fantasy is going to town," declared *Down Beat* in an editorial that linked swing to the release of *Snow White and the Seven Dwarfs*, and publication of the children's story *Ferdinand the Bull*. "A fantasy in motion pictures is a 'lift' to gloom-beridden folk. So is a fantastic story with equally absurd illustrations. And so is Swing music . . . By adapting himself to this trend, every orchestra leader and every potential orchestra leader stands a good chance to capitalize on the craving for fantasy which lurks in every Recession-minded listener." A letter to the *New York Times* urged bandleaders to shun the blues and instead, like movies or theater, help listeners escape "the tedium of life and events abroad. Light and frolicsome numbers, where the words don't mean very much but the gibberish lyrics are happily infectious, are best."[12]

For others, swing was a welcome development for precisely opposite reasons: its down-to-earth lack of the sentimentality that characterized most popular music of the first half of the decade. Swing "blows no bubbles in the air, offers no escapist Tin Pan Alley dream-castles, indulges in no tawdry heart-throbs," wrote one sympathetic observer. "This was the stock-in-trade of the crooner, whose extermination by swing deserves the gratitude of all parents, music lovers or no; his replacement by the killer-diller can be regarded only as a salutary step in social morality." To this line of thinking, swing was a form of good clean organized fun, not unlike organized athletics. "After playing for thousands of youngsters," wrote a bandleader, "I am convinced that swing is no more to them than a game—a good strenuous game after eight hours in an office or good solid study in a classroom ... It may seem wild, but it isn't." Swing received support from no less than tennis superstar Don Budge, who protested a finding by a college psychologist that swing adversely affected athletic performance by asserting that he regularly listened to Ellington recordings before playing matches.[13]

That swing could encompass such an array of conflicting interpretations is a sign of the vacillations in national mood during the years in which swing emerged and achieved mass popularity. The economic recovery under way in 1935–36 was followed by the "Roosevelt depression" in the succeeding two years, when the swing fad peaked and concern over domestic economics was joined by anxiety over events in Europe and the Far East. But the mixed response to swing also reveals a sense of historical relativism that had not been evident during the previous decade's moral uproar over jazz. Swing, one writer argued, was simply the twentieth-century counterpart of the eighteenth-century minuet and the nineteenth-century waltz. Those who condemned swing as "a fitting danse macabre for a society tobogganing to its grave" might take heart from the previous decade's panic over jazz; "recall that the dire prophecies of moralists and chiropodists now directed at the jitterbugs' dances were once resounding against that shameless exhibition of depravity, the Turkey Trot," one pointed out.[14]

American culture survived the Jazz Age: it might survive swing as well. After observing a dance to commemorate the local civic auditorium, newspaper editor William Allen White, the "Sage of Emporia," was prompted to nostalgic remembrances of the farm dances of his youth. Fond as his memories were, he recognized that the "slow and formal threnody of the waltz" no longer fitted the "new world picture." Each generation must construct "its own rowdy modern music." "So let Duke Ellington and his black boys blare and bleat and bawl with their saxophones and bull fiddles and muted trumpets syncopating the call of the wild," he concluded. "And it is all right. But it's the same old inner urge, the more we change the less we change."[15]

Although it had the effect of bestowing cultural legitimacy on swing, this historicizing line of thought threatened to strip swing of the formal qualities that supposedly made it unique and vaguely suspect. "While the jitter-bugs, killer-dillers, alligators and bobcats may 'truck' in the aisles with the belief that improvisation is the brainchild of the 'swing masters,' " wrote a conductor, "it dates back to the time of Handel in the eighteenth century." When controversy erupted over the practice of "jazzing" classical themes, the *Times'* chief music critic, Olin Downes, wrote a lengthy piece pointing out that the practice of appropriating and modifying musical compositions dated back to the thirteenth century and had been continued by Bach, Beethoven, Handel, Brahms, Rossini, and Schönberg. Moreover, he asserted, the "original" creators of the folk music from which Dvořák lifted the *New World* Symphony theme, or Rimsky-Korsakoff *Scheherazade*, would have been no more pleased with the appropriation than purists concerned about the defilement of Western art music by swing. The "real swingers," he concluded, "don't like attacking masters. They think that swinging a composition which is perfect in its own kind and after its own tradition is a compromise and a confession of weakness on the part of the performer. They say: swing for the swingers."[16]

As the boundaries between shorthair and longhair music, between lowbrow and highbrow culture, were demonstrated to be historically constructed and permeable, swing artists and their critics sought to position themselves on the median. Count Basie's goal, for example, was described as "the blues gone classic," a music aspiring to be "the language of all Negroes, high and low, upright and ornery, alley and avenue." Critics compared swing to the literature of the American Renaissance. "Some day . . . Americans will look back to Benny Goodman and Duke Ellington, to the Dorseys and Count Basie, Benny Carter and Coleman Hawkins . . . as the heroes of a Golden Age," gushed *Metronome.* "This is an era as important to American music as the time of Emerson and Thoreau and Whitman and Hawthorne and Melville was to American literature."[17]

Clarinet and bandleading rivals Goodman and Shaw prided themselves on their ability to play both hot and classical. After debuting at Carnegie in the swing genre, Goodman returned to perform as soloist with the New York Philharmonic; he performed Bartok with Hungarian violinist Josef Szigeti and Mozart with the Budapest String

Quartet. A kind of climax was reached when Goodman performed *Rhapsody in Blue* with the NBC Symphony, at the request of its conductor, Arturo Toscanini. The concert was a ready-made media event, pitting the "King of the Classics" against the "King of Swing." "Toscanini, usually a precisionist, allowed every sort of liberty in the famous rhapsody," according to a critic, even letting Goodman "blow the black stick hot." To Goodman, classical composers and swing arrangers "go about things pretty much the same way." The major difference, he thought, is that in performing classical music the musician attempts to capture the composer's intent, while swing provides the opportunity for a more individualized self-expression.[18]

Even the apparent incommensurability between the classical and swing audiences was less significant than it appeared, having more to do with age than any other essential difference. "It's unfair . . . to draw our symphony hall versus Savoy Ballroom generalization by comparing adults with their grandchildren," Goodman said. "The growing child naturally exhibits an immature reaction." Both concert music and jazz provoked a physical reaction. While the "tempo fiends" of swing cavorted and tapped their feet, the "sensitive concertgoer" got goose pimples. With time, "civilization and convention" would eliminate whatever differences remained. "The foot-tapper hasn't attended enough concerts or received enough dirty looks to stop his unashamed rhythmic movements," Goodman opined. "When he does, he'll sublimate them into goose pimples." He even held out hope that swing could elevate its audience to an appreciation of concert music by training its fans to really listen to music. "After all, a youngster reared on the rhythmic patterns of a Joe Jones, a Lionel Hampton, a Dave Tough or a Gene Krupa would hardly find Stravinsky's *Sacre du Printemps* perplexing; and the contrapuntal interweavings of a first-rate jam session have more relationship to a Bach fugue than even the musicians would consider possible." Goodman's hopes were not unfounded; the *New York Times* reported that 70 percent of swing record buyers also purchased classical recordings.[19]

If swing was in essence no different from, or at least equivalent to, European art music, some educators reasoned, why not incorporate the study of jazz into the school curriculum? New York City's Board of

Education led the way in May 1937, enlisting such swing luminaries as Goodman, Ellington, Gershwin, Rudy Vallee, and Wayne King to give weekly lectures in city high schools in order to improve jazz appreciation. A music teacher who directed a similar program in suburban Philadelphia admitted the need for courses in classical music appreciation. "But it strikes me that nowadays the kids are interested in dance music, and so long as they spend so much time listening to it, we might as well try to teach them what's good." Students were introduced to key musical concepts—instrumentation, arranging, structure, improvisation—before proceeding to practical analysis of actual recordings. The final exam included such questions as "List in your own words some effects which are responsible for Hal Kemp's style. Where were those effects shown in the recording of 'So Lovely'?" The students, according to a reporter, seemed to know more about dance music than even "more mature jitterbugs and even some musicians." A lecture-recital on jazz and swing sponsored in 1938 by New York's decorous Town Hall as part of its Short Course Division exposed a dignified audience of subscribers to the Goodman orchestra. The audience, many of whom were encountering swing for the first time, responded to the musical illustrations in a fashion "altogether encouraging to friends of swing," the *Times* reported. "Although occupants of orchestra seats maintained a concert-going reserve those in the balcony were not ashamed to sway their shoulders and paid no heed to restless feet."[20]

Predictably, these experiments in swing pedagogy generated skepticism. "American schools are certainly going the limit to break down education resistance," offering "the growing boy and girl everything they can get at the neighboring theater, except bank night," observed a syndicated columnist. As one concerned partisan asserted: "To wage a successful war against the anti-jazz prejudices of most planners of school music courses, it will be necessary for brave, far-sighted prophets ... to establish beyond question the premise that this medium of musical expression is so fundamental, so completely ingrained in our national character and national feeling, that it can no longer be ignored." In fact, despite scattered alarms and misgivings, swing enjoyed a far less hostile reception from cultural arbiters than had the jazz of a decade earlier. Differences in the music itself and in the image projected by its creators undoubtedly accounted for some of this. But American culture itself had changed. It had moved further from the genteel codes challenged in the 1920s, but it had also embraced a sense of historical and cultural relativism.[21] Ironically, it was within swing itself that some of the most heated resistance to the swing phenomenon appeared.

Song of the Jitterbug

Recalling his first exposure to a jitterbug, Benny Goodman wondered if there was "something rotten in the arrangements," whether his music had become "morbid" or a "Mad Ophelia note had crept in." "The bugs, literally glued to the music, would shake like St. Vitus with the itch," he recalled with distaste. "Their eyes popped, their heads pecked, their feet tapped out the time, arms jerked to the rhythm. They joined in background choruses, ran temperatures up and down in unison with the heat and coolness of the music." If swing enjoyed a certain amount of cultural acceptance, its uninhibited cultists, known as jitterbugs or ickies, inspired alarm and derision among moralists and musicians alike. Few observers of jitterbugs refrained from a tone of ridicule in describing them. A jitterbug was a dervish, a kangaroo, a jack-in-the-box, a person vaccinated with a riveting machine. If swing was a "mass contagion," as some believed, jitterbugs were the carriers of the virus, who needed to be quarantined from impressionable youngsters for the good of society.[22]

Jitterbugs offended swing partisans and opponents alike, for different reasons. For moralists, jitterbugs combined two unsavory tendencies in American culture: the hedonism and uninhibited exhibitionism of African-American culture coupled with the mindless "mass-man" behavior symptomatic of and conducive to totalitarian societies. "Bugs" thereby conflated a racial and a political threat. There was something sinister in their appearance of mass hysteria. A psychiatrist speculated that "a combination of circumstances has made them one-minded and their inhibitory checks have broken down. Some individuals are more suggestible than others, and those individuals start them piling into the aisles. They do sound like goats, don't they?" Swing festivals staged outdoors at Randalls Island in New York City, or indoors at arenas like Madison Square Garden or Boston Garden, frequently threatened to degenerate into riots. A jamboree at Chicago's Soldier Field in August 1938 attracted an "overwrought mob" of 100,000 that caused it to be ended early; the field later required reseeding. A riot reportedly provoked by saboteurs hired by a rival promoter engulfed a "Jimmie Lunceford swingaroo" at Los Angeles' Shrine Auditorium in March 1940. "Their angers flamed by free liquor, 6,000 assorted white, Negro, Mexican, and Filipino jitterbugs . . . suddenly went wild, smashing windows, flashing razors, and swinging fists." Twenty-five officers were called in to quell the riot, and seven people were injured. Free broadcast-dance dates by the Goodman band at New York's Manhattan Center were moved back to the more restrained precincts of Radio City after "more than 6,000 wild jitterbugs and rowdies" jammed the hall and broke up the show. "Spiels advertising the cigaret were booed and hissed by youthful exhibitionists," a most ominous affront to the broadcast's sponsor, Old Gold.[23]

By late 1939, some localities in the Midwest actually were cracking down on jitterbugs, ostensibly for taking up too much space on the dance floor. In Milwaukee, a dance hall ran an advertisement warning: "Positively No Jitterbug Dancing Allowed." And an Indianapolis ballroom, after an altercation between jitterbugs and more conservative dancers, took the draconian step of banning "stomping, heel clicking, back kicks, worm wiggling, acrobatics, breaking contact beyond arm's length, floor hugging, and, the dancers were told they must stay with the line of direction."[24]

Concern over the rise of authoritarian movements, from fascism in Europe to domestic leaders such as Huey Long (by then deceased), Father Charles Coughlin, Gerald L. K. Smith, and even Franklin Roosevelt, fueled concern over the psychological impact of swing music, particularly the loss of rational individuality it seemed to produce. An apparent cottage industry of psychological experiments sprang up during the late 1930s as academics put the impact of swing to empirical test in the laboratory. An Oberlin professor conducted a study of syncopation by having ten musicians tap out rhythms of "normal" and syncopated measures with their fingers and feet, which were attached to recording devices; the results were published in the *Journal of General Psychology*. Several universities tested the effects of swing on apes: a team at Temple found that monkeys "enjoyed" recordings of the Tommy Dorsey orchestra, while gorillas did not. Psychologists at Wayne State tested Benny Goodman records on monkeys.[25] Some of the experiments may have been public relations hoaxes or examples of the racist humor that circulated in certain circles of the swing community.

Probably the most widely known experiments were conducted by Arthur Cremin, a music educator from New York City. He placed a young man and woman alone in a room and played a series of recordings. During the classical and waltz selections, according to Cremin, the two remained friendly but formal, but when jazz was played they became noticeably "bolder"—acting "familiar" and "personal" toward each other. Cremin reportedly attributed a wave of sex crimes to the popularity of jazz. Another psychologist attributed the concupiscent effect of swing to its being "cunningly designed to a tempo faster . . . than the normal pulse." Such an effect could be expected "to break down conventions and lead to moral weakness" among impressionable young people.[26]

The Cremin experiment, at least, was taken seriously enough to provoke Duke Ellington, who was falsely reported to have studied psychology at Howard University, to attack the experiment—on methodological grounds. The test lacked a " 'proper constant'—a prerequisite of an accurate experiment of this nature," Ellington charged, adding that no two people would be affected the same way in such circumstances. "Music invigorates emotions to certain degrees," he acknowledged, "but on the other hand, so do baseball and football games. If music can be proved a neurotic influence, then I'm certain you will find Stravinsky's 'Le Sacre du Printemps' a great deal more exciting, emotionally, than a slow 'ride' arrangement of 'Body and Soul' or even a fast rendition of 'Tiger Rag.' "[27]

Not all of these experiments yielded results unfavorable to swing. A University of Kansas professor argued that the complex variations evident in the best swing recordings were comparable to the musical sophistication of the best of European art music. "The difference between Beethoven's Fifth Symphony and Benny Goodman's 'Opus ½' is one of degree, and not one of kind," he argued. Moreover, the lyrics

of many swing tunes, he wrote, were sophisticated from a psychoana-
lytic point of view, and psychologically beneficial. Swing was successfully deployed in a variety of settings where a therapeutic result was
sought. After playing a concert for patients at the Philadelphia State
Hospital, bandleader Vincent Lopez was favorably impressed by the
efficacy of "swing therapy," believing that the music's "physical invig-
oration" had a therapeutic effect on patients. Inmates were encouraged
to form swing bands and broadcast their performances as part of pris-
oner rehabilitation in Huntsville prison in Texas. But a University of
Pennsylvania experiment on the value of music as an "aid to work" in
a manufacturing plant yielded mixed results. The workers tested reportedly liked music in the workplace; it raised their spirits and made the
time go faster. But the experiment also found that the workers "spoiled
more work and also made more protests against the kind of music when
swing was on."[28]

But testing the effects of swing on subjects in an "experiment" was
not the same as observing those effects among jitterbugs in their natural
environment. To those with a firsthand knowledge of swing subculture,
it was clear that jitterbugs were a more variegated group than they
appeared to appalled outsiders. Jitterbugs got their label from a dance
of the same name, sometimes known as the Lindy Hop, a step that had
appeared in New York dance halls in the late 1920s. The Lindy originated among secret gangs in Harlem, a neighborhood in transition in
the late 1920s and 1930s as African-Americans moved in to replace
departing white ethnics. Although its exact date and place of origin are
not known, the dance was refined by dancers at the Savoy ballroom
during the early to mid-1930s, when preswing dance-centered subculture was taking shape. The jitterbug, according to its historian, was
essentially "choreographed swing music." In contrast to the bouncy
vertical steps of earlier jazz dance, the jitterbug flowed horizontally,
with more rhythmic continuity. The fundamental innovation of the
dance was called the "breakaway"—a moment, often during an instrumental solo, when dancers would spin away from each other and improvise a break. By 1937, the best jitterbugs were incorporating acrobatic
"air steps," judolike variations in which partners would roll and flip
each other over the back.[29]

Musicians and swing insiders tended to favor these skilled dancing jitterbugs. "In ballrooms, where there's dancing like I was raised on, when everybody is giving to the beat, and just moving, and the house is bouncing—that inspires you to play," said Lunceford drummer Jimmy Crawford. Musicians played more relaxed, less self-consciously. "I've always felt," wrote Dicky Wells, a Basie sideman, "that if they could screen the bandstand with glass or something at a place like the Savoy and record while the band could see those dancers, they'd get a wonderful effect." Goodman admitted being "crazy about the chandelier-kicking type of jitterbug dancing. It's rhythmic mathematics, sometimes as gifted as the music that inspires it." "The white jitterbug is oftener than not uncouth to look at," reported the *New York Times*, "but his Negro original is quite another matter. His movements are never so exaggerated that they lack control, and there is an unmistakable dignity about his most violent figures." The reporter judged jitterbugs "unquestionably the finest" of any ballroom dancers he had seen. These jitterbugs usually followed a strict set of codes governing dress, access to restricted portions of the dance floor, and prohibitions against copying too closely someone else's dance innovation.[30]

In contrast to these respected jitterbugs, skilled dancers who were generally black and attended urban ballrooms, were the more widely publicized and despised variety: the white youth of high school and college age who alarmed moralists and generated disdain among more sophisticated enthusiasts. The ever-volatile Artie Shaw's diatribe against jitterbug "morons" in late 1939 during one of his periodic retirements from the business was the most widely publicized. Although jitterbugs crowded the bandstand, interfering with musicians and occasionally pilfering "souvenirs," it was their musical ignorance—their habit of applauding the wrong moments while missing the passages of musical excellence—a lapse so conspicuous at Goodman's Carnegie concert—that most irritated bandleaders and "serious" listeners; "The ordinary jitterbug expresses no rhythmic interpretation or artistic creation," reported *Metronome*, "and his disgusting habit of shouting to his swing idols is most annoying to the musicians and ruins the music." These jitterbugs were often labeled "ickies" and did not dance, at least according to any recognized canon. Rather, a jitterbug

> places himself in a conspicuous place and annoys the leader by constantly shouting out his requests such as "Dinah" and "Tiger Rag,"

etc. He claps his hands (usually dragging or rushing the tempo), dances a sort of mad dervish dance on one foot, or trucks, while his head is held to one side, eyes are rolled up in the corners, eyebrows raised so that the forehead is furrowed with premature wrinkles. This attitude alternates with a joyously, painful expression induced by pushing the brows down formidably over the eyes, resulting in a squint. The teeth are bared in a violent smile, chin down, while the head is moving in a rhythmically, negative shake. This is accompanied by a springs-under-the-heel bounce, hands are held loosely at the sides, palms up, fingers close together moving vertically in a hinge effect. These are his best "sent" expressions.

The critic and producer John Hammond, who took offense at the suggestion that he was a jitterbug, was emblematic of a third type of fan enthusiast, sometimes known as an "okay" in distinction to "icky." Such fans wore crewcuts and "Esquirish" clothes, read "fanzines" and gossip columns on swing stars, and were willing to drive hundreds of miles to see their favorite bands, to which they were tremendously loyal. An okay would stand transfixed in front of the bandstand, listening intently for deviations from the recorded versions he knew so well. "He wears a wide smile, an alert expression and is genuinely thrilled if he can meet the musicians."[31]

As they set about recruiting and educating their audience, most bandleaders sought to position themselves on a middle ground, resisting the apparent excesses of their youthful followers while rejecting the moralists' and cultural elitists' criticisms of swing. "To me the swing icky is as dismal as the high-brow music icky," Goodman asserted. "Swing isn't as important as the icky thinks it, and certainly not as unimportant as the long-haired classicist thinks it." Most bandleaders went out of their way to please their public, to cater to their preferred tastes, and saw nothing improper about it. "Our appeal is not limited," boasted Jimmy Dorsey. "We have the swingiest of jitterbug kids to the most conservative of middle-aged dinner dancers, and we have arranged our repertoire to such a degree that we can please all persons." Although his unexpected 1935 Palomar triumph had been based on his willingness to risk performing the band's new, "hotter" Henderson arrangements, Goodman agreed that bands should play for audiences, not for fellow musicians. "We don't try to force the audience around to our way of thinking." Krupa, leading his own band in 1941, lashed out at "sideline jivesters" who urged him to play less commercial swing. He took his orders from hotel managers, who had to meet expenses before giving consideration to aesthetic ends. "I get paid for dance music, the art's thrown in extra," he was quoted as saying. After observing college audiences, another bandleader concluded that "the present status of unadulterated swing is overrated"; a noisy minority of jitterbugs frequently gave the impression that the audience preferred their music, when in fact most preferred a sweeter sound.[32]

Not all bandleaders positioned themselves as forces of cultural moderation and consensus, striving to produce music accessible to a wide range of audiences while distancing themselves from their more extreme followers, the jitterbugs. Cab Calloway, the inveterate popularizer of swing culture, strongly identified himself with the swing "counterculture." His "Song of the Jitterbug" (1935), which was made into a film short, offered this recipe for attaining the desired status:

> Now if you'd like to be jitterbug
> The first thing you do is get yourself a jug
> Put whiskey, wine and gin within
> Shake it up and then begin.

According to one account, the original jitterbug was a bibulous trombone player with Calloway, whose propensity for curing his shakes with "jitter sauce" became well known around 1932 through broadcasts from the Cotton Club. Among the listeners was a group of Yale students, who quickly organized a Jitterbug Society complete with membership cards and the secret password "Palsaddictinsomnidipsomaniac." During the preswing and early swing periods, Calloway and other prominent bandleaders, including Armstrong, Don Redman, and Fats Waller, capitalized on the mystique of urban drug culture. In tunes like "Minnie the Moocher" and "Reefer Man," Calloway alluded openly to narcotics and marijuana, a theme that figured in Armstrong's "Song of the Vipers," Don Redman's "Chant of the Weed," and even Goodman's "Texas Tea Party." It was later said that whereas Dixieland musicians were drawn to alcohol, and bebop players to narcotics, swing musicians adopted marijuana as their substance of choice. Calloway was also able to commercialize the special argot of swing musicians and followers in his *Hepster's Dictionary*, first published in 1936 and republished several times afterward.[33]

But by the late 1930s musicians themselves began a backlash against these excesses of language and behavior. That Ivy League collegians would form a Jitterbug Society suggested that there were limits to the social deviance of this swing subculture. Calloway's foreword to the 1944 edition of his dictionary suggests how much its subcultural élan had been neutralized. Swing's "colorful language . . . should be called to the attention of as many people as possible," he wrote. "That the general public agreed with me is amply evidenced by the fact that the present issue is the sixth edition since 1938 and is the official jive language reference book of the New York Public Library." "Jive talk," he went on, was now an accepted part of the language, one that Calloway thought would be spread internationally to Australia, the South Pacific, North Africa, China, Europe, "and wherever our Armed Forces will serve." Calloway was assisted in his efforts by Dan Burley, whose weekly column for the *New York Amsterdam News* made him perhaps the nation's leading authority on "jive"; and by Gene Krupa, who delivered a twenty-five-page lecture on "The Lexicon of Swing" to an audience of nearly 700 gathered in the Egyptian Wing of New York's Metropolitan Museum of Art.[34]

While Calloway tamed his own jive talk through commercialization, other bandleaders relegated it to ickies. "Swing fanatics who discuss the swing musicians with an absurd terminology and farfetched slang . . . give me the well-known pang," Goodman wrote. A veteran of the music industry in Chicago backed him up. "You should hear Benny Goodman and his men put on the flutter tongue when Benny reads a term like 'killer diller' from the typewriter of a radio script genius." " 'Out of this world' is a columnist's dream and 'hep cat' is used for a laugh on Bing Crosby's programs." Such presumably hep terms as *jive, skinbeater, gate, gob stick,* and *swingeroo* were similarly relegated. "Leave the 'jive' lingo to the 'ickies,' for that's where it belongs," the insider concluded. Otis Ferguson complained that hep talk was partly responsible for "all these little nursery hotshots from Princeton, with their heads clipped and clothes not matching and ten-pound feet in golf socks, clomping all over stands and crashing into instruments and yelling 'Give with the git-box, gate' and getting into everybody's hair." The situation was bad for swing, he added: "a lot of quiet citizens who might like the music when it's good still can't be made to touch it with a coast-to-coast network because of the way it is surrounded, in print or in public, with all this false enthusiasm, wordy vacuity, and false shoptalk."[35]

The sensationalized attention to drugs prominent early in the decade likewise generated a moral backlash on the part of the music industry itself. The notoriously vice-free John Hammond celebrated the impact of swing on musicians' lifestyles, rescuing them from "drink and weed." In an article titled "Musicians Desert Gin and Weed to Swing Again," he wrote: "Since the public's acceptance—almost amounting to insistence—of rhythmic improvisation it is not an unusual sight to see once hopeless drunkards emerge as sober and world-beating trumpeters, percussionists and guitarists." The following year *Down Beat* published a series of articles on marijuana for the guidance of musicians; the question of whether the drug was harmful, helpful, or neither remained current through the 1940s, with federal researchers conducting experiments in prison hospitals on the impact of marijuana on musical performance.[36]

A steady stream of incidents involving marijuana, which was criminalized in 1937, notably the highly publicized bust of Gene Krupa, put musicians on the defensive. A "boiling" Lionel Hampton wrote an angry screed defending fellow musicians against "the popular conception that all we do is get high off our tea, and use grog for chasers." The intense competition for jobs in top bands and the pace of touring discouraged musicians from such distractions, Hampton stressed. But after marijuana was discovered at the site of an accident in which members of the Charlie Barnet band were involved, the swing press found itself responding in an editorial to negative publicity surrounding drug use among musicians. While claiming that marijuana smokers were a tiny minority, and castigating the press for creating a public image of musicians as dope fiends, *Down Beat* and *Metronome* strongly condemned marijuana use and urged the musicians' union to discipline its members. "Tea and Trumpets Are Bad Mixture," scolded one editorial, while another reminded readers, "They Are Innocent until Proven

Guilty!" Publicized crackdowns on marijuana use recurred during the war years, especially on New York's 52nd Street and in Hollywood, where racial mixing apparently provoked intense police scrutiny.[37]

As was often the case during these years, Hollywood's representation of swing offers valuable clues to its cultural meaning. Busby Berkeley's *Strike Up the Band* (1940) celebrates a wholesome, lily-white version of swing as an exemplar of the traditional virtues of duty, loyalty, and hard work. Bridling at the traditional music of his high school band, drummer Jimmy Connors, played by Mickey Rooney, convinces the principal to let him form a "modern dance orchestra." "I want to make American music just as important as any other country's music," he pleads. "Look at Gershwin. His music's as good as Beethoven or Bach—better, maybe. Best of all, it's American." He must also win over his widowed mother, who has dreamed of his becoming a doctor and exacts a promise that Jimmy will conduct himself in his chosen vocation with honor.

Jimmy meets his idol Paul Whiteman at a high school party thrown by a wealthy new girl. Learning of his aspirations, the bandleader reminds the youth that music has become a "mighty important" profession, its bandleaders celebrities comparable to movie stars and baseball heroes: "But with this popularity comes a great responsibility. Rhythm can either excite the worst in us or bring out the best. Take that little fellow on the street, Jimmy. Teach him to blow a horn and he'll never blow a safe. Sometimes I think rhythm almost runs the world." Jimmy decides to enter his band in a nationwide talent contest hosted by Whiteman. After struggling to raise travel fare, he turns the funds over to pay for an emergency operation for a classmate. Out of loyalty to his high school, he even turns down an offer from Whiteman to join a professional band in New York. But with the help of the wealthy girl's father, who charters a special train, the Riverwood band enters the contest, which is decided, of course, by the response of a radio audience. In the end, as the American flag rises, loyalty and sacrifice are rewarded. Jimmy fulfills his duty to his mother, his sick friend, his community—and still wins the contest. Despite appearances— Jimmy's manic baton work suggests Cab Calloway, while his frenetic drumming mimics Krupa—Jimmy is as red-bloodedly American as

Tom Sawyer. And swing has been redeemed from whatever moral taint had shadowed it since the 1920s.

New Venues, New Audiences

At the same time that many in the swing industry distanced themselves from the subculture they helped spawn, bandleaders acknowledged that the jitterbugs, with all their excesses, had crucially changed the consumption of jazz. Swing enthusiasts helped transform swing from functional music for dancing to an art music performed for attentive spectators. This change in the performance practices surrounding jazz is generally thought to have occurred later, with the rise of bebop during the mid-1940s, but even the early days of swing gave evidence that the cultural status of jazz was beginning to change, at least among its adherents, from dance music in the direction of "art" music. As early as 1937, Ellington observed a change in the audience response to music, detecting a shift to "relative quietude" from the rowdy audiences characteristic of the 1920s. "Audiences, today, invariably crowd around the bandstand, eager to grasp every solo note and orchestral trick and certain to 'shush' down any rowdiness that may hamper the enjoyment of the music," he wrote. "The new jazz movement has served to enlarge the public's knowledge of music, mainly in the world of modern American jazz, which is being accepted, at present, as a recognized form of music." The willingness of jitterbugs to stand and listen rather than dance, Goodman agreed, freed arrangers to create more musically inventive arrangements and musicians to engage in more creative expressive improvisation. "In other words, jitterbugs helped us drag jazz out of the old saloon mechanical piano and give it new life and dignity . . . the jitterbug godfathered swing." Perhaps the jitterbug had something to offer, after all. "Don't Spit on the Jitterbug—Educate Him," *Down Beat* urged in an editorial. Have patience: the obnoxious excesses are only a passing phase.[38]

This new mode of audience participation seems to have emerged with the explosive popularity of the Goodman band. "Society and Musicians Sit Spellbound by Brilliance of Goodman Band," ran a *Down Beat* headline on a three-and-one-half-hour performance in the Urban

Room in Chicago in late 1935, an event organized by the Rhythm Club, an organization of swing fanciers dedicated to bringing swing before properly appreciative audiences. A single attempt at dancing "was instantly booed," according to the report. The pattern continued. The *Boston Herald* reported that "any sociologist frivolous enough to be interested in the changing modes and manners of Boston society would have found something to ponder at the Ritz Roof the other evening when Benny Goodman and his quartet gave a midnight concert . . . The gathering was distinctly on the social side [Franklin Roosevelt, Jr., was present] and it was a little strange to see people who up to a year ago hardly deemed swing music worthy of their notice listening as raptly as at a Stokowski concert. No one danced—in fact the feeling seemed to be that this would be desecration!—and after every piece there was applause and howling for more, thunderous enough to bring down the roof had there been one overhead." A mood of quasireligious reverence seems to have been the dominant style of these audiences. "Usually a group of youthful music-lovers is gathered worshipfully before [the] bandstand, while others sit at their tables bobbing up and down and groaning in tribute to each hot passage. Those who dance pause frequently and just quiver to the rich blend of brass, reed, and percussion."[39]

In 1939 *Metronome* asserted that "the vast majority of dancers stop dancing when real swing bands begin their swing numbers . . . The tempos of these pieces prove to be either too fast or too slow for enjoyable dancing, and the real fans are beginning to realize that swing is appreciated more by those who listen and watch than the ones who attempt to dance to its music." The article cited even a Count Basie engagement at a "swank" Westchester club as being tailored to listening rather than dancing. In some clubs, such as the Onyx in New York, no room whatever was provided for dancing. On the other hand, at centers of innovation like the Savoy, dancers made a point of being able to keep up with even the fastest swing numbers. "The bands seemed to be swinging faster every night," according to one renowned Savoy dancer, "and all the best dancers could follow them, in new and different ways."[40]

The fact that a sizable number of the audience stood rapt around the bandstand during performances of the more musically stimulating big bands means neither that people weren't dancing to the majority of swing bands nor that jazz had lost its participatory quality; but the convolutions of jitterbugs represented a less directed, less regimented form of physical expression than most Americans were willing to recognize as dance. As Virgil Thomson had observed, swing's quantitative rhythms engendered very different sorts of physical responses from those customarily associated with dance. Moreover, a high proportion of swing performances took place not in ballrooms, where dancing was to be expected, but in theaters. To several contemporary industry observers, the presentation of big bands in theaters was the key innovation undergirding the swing boom of the late 1930s. Bands would generally play several daytime shows at theaters, which is where younger audiences were more likely to attend. "Early shows were the norm everywhere, because our music was the entertainment of youth," recalled Woody Herman. "Kids would skip school to hear us before the prices changed after noon." The moral panic stimulated by jitterbugs was based largely on observations made at Goodman's stand at the Paramount Theatre in New York, when the band played between screenings of Mae West movies. The audience, mainly high school students from the boroughs, began showing up before the sun came up and lit bonfires to stay warm; the theater opened its doors early on the advice of a police sergeant.[41]

The conventions of ballrooms and dance halls themselves changed in important ways during the swing years. With the repeal of Prohibition in 1933, nightclubs began to lose the covert, illicit quality that had characterized them during the 1920s and became acceptable and popular in regions and small cities that earlier would have resisted them. As a result of this cultural change, dancing venues became more inclusive, more open to a range of class backgrounds, and, perhaps most significant, more racially integrated, at least in certain large cities.[42]

The Savoy, for example, located on Harlem's "main stem," Lenox Avenue, had a policy of welcoming and encouraging white dancers and spectators. A report on the redecoration and modernization of the Savoy in the fall of 1936 reported that the ballroom "now resembles any other downtown palace except for the fact that about 20 percent of the crowd is colored. Ofays have muscled in something awful." During his sojourn in Harlem in the early 1940s, Malcolm X estimated that one-third of the sideline booths off the dance floor contained whites, mainly spectators, but some of whom danced, a few even with blacks. According to poet Langston Hughes:

> The lindy-hoppers at the Savoy even began to practise acrobatic routines, and to do absurd things for the entertainment of the whites, that probably never would have entered their heads to attempt merely for their own effortless amusement. Some of the lindy-hoppers had cards printed with their names on them and became dance professors teaching the tourists. Then Harlem nights became show nights for the Nordics.

Even in provincial Boston, where Malcolm X was introduced to swing subculture, he observed that "white girls always flocked to the Negro dances" at the Roseland Ballroom, although most of the dances there were white-only and featured white bands. Calloway played nearly exclusively at white theaters and was especially popular among Jewish audiences, according to a musician.[43]

Appreciation for particular swing performers caused racial boundaries to be crossed from both sides. White youth constituted the largest proportion of the audience for either black or white swing bands, but African-Americans were willing to cross the line for the right white bands. At Goodman's Paramount engagement in 1937, black patronage was reportedly increased from 3 percent to 15 percent of the total, hurting attendance at shows by the black Earl Hines orchestra at the Apollo Theatre. *Metronome* reported that the "biggest and pleasantest surprise around New York these days is the great reception accorded white bands in Harlem recently. The colored folks have been vociferous in their acclamation, as for example the near riot that broke out when Charlie Barnet shattered all precedent and opening day records as he brought the first white band into the Apollo Theatre." Harlem was "really white" on Christmas Eve, according to the same report, with Glenn Miller attracting more dancers than ever to the Savoy. "Meanwhile sepia artists have been going over well in downtown spots" such as the Arcadia ballroom. In Philadelphia, Bud Freeman recalled, a black theater regularly attracted sellout crowds for the white bands it booked. "Their black audiences really loved the white bands, and when I got out in front to do my solos, the black people would get up in the aisles and dance."[44]

Dance hall culture changed in other ways as well. The institution of check dancing, or "taxi-dancing," in which men would pay a slight fee, usually 10 cents, for a three-minute dance with one of the hostesses employed by the dance hall, gave way to non-exchange-based coupling. Customers were charged an entrance fee at the door and were free thereafter to dance with anyone. "The fact that they can dance whenever they want to without thinking of the money involved each time, encourages them," reported the manager of the Arcadia, a large Broadway ballroom. Indeed, with the advent of the big bands, at the Savoy, originally a taxi-dance hall, "you'd get slapped in the face or worse if you offered a dime to some beautiful lady for a sprint around the magnificent dance floor," according to one participant. Ballrooms made other changes as well, including providing more floor space for dancers and additional table space for those who chose to sit out dances and watch the bands. The rising popularity of nightclubs and other nondance establishments across the country, coupled with the availability of radio, led ballrooms to encourage bands to emphasize visual entertainment and specialty numbers rather than just providing background for dancing.[45]

Another feature of the democratization of dance hall culture was the promotion of "stunt nites" designed to attract a wide range of customers. At the Palomar in Los Angeles, Monday was a "candid camera" night; Tuesday featured free dance lessons; Wednesdays featured a Mardi Gras carnival atmosphere; Thursday featured the "Palomar Handicap" race of mechanical horses around the dance floor; Friday was devoted to college students from USC and UCLA; and Sunday featured a dinner-dance special. Every night included two raffle drawings. Harlem's Savoy also featured special attractions such as Thursday Kitchen Mechanics' Nights, bathing beauty contests, and Saturday night car giveaways. Every Sunday afternoon was called Opportunity Day, when amateur dancers would compete for cash prizes and admis-

Jitterbugs in New York City in 1938, the height of the swing craze.

Dancers execute a breakaway at the Savoy in the 1940s.

A crowd waiting for admission to Harlem's Savoy ballroom—"the Home of Happy Feet"—in the 1940s.

Dancing to the Erskine Hawkins Orchestra at the Savoy in 1941.

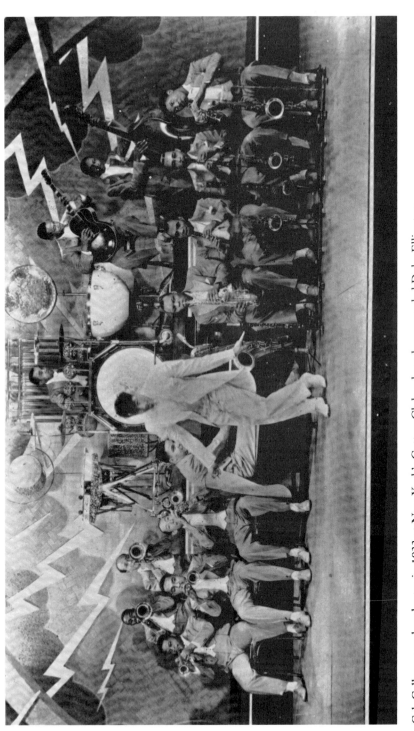

Cab Calloway and orchestra in 1933 at New York's Cotton Club, where he succeeded Duke Ellington.

Benny Goodman surrounded at the bandstand by youthful music lovers in 1938.

Couples at the Savoy in the 1930s.

sion tickets.[46] Dance contests were institutionalized at many dance halls, providing a forum for the development and dissemination of dance innovations.

Even the architecture and decor of swing establishments reflected a difference in the culture of swing, one that rendered it more inclusive, democratic, and culturally acceptable. Whereas the emphasis of the cabarets and nightclubs of the 1920s had been on intimacy and "atmosphere," the ballrooms of the swing era reflected size, grace, and elegance. The European-influenced theatrical architecture, characterized by vertical axes and art deco motifs, gave way to the horizontal strokes of the *art moderne* style, modeled after the streamlined power of airplanes and trains. The new clubs were dominated by parabolas and constructed to maximize unobstructed views. "By stripping away the facades and excesses of the architecture associated with failure, the moderne theater-restaurants conquered the moral chaos of the consumer society to offer a vision in miniature of a smoothly operating futuristic world," writes Lewis Erenberg. "American technology, embodied in the chrome, steel, glass, and curvilinear electrical motifs, now came to dominate nightclub design."[47]

Swing musicians themselves were inscribed with the look of *art moderne*. The big bands arrayed their musicians in resplendent uniforms. Top bands like Duke Ellington's, which had a reputation for sartorial splendor, would order new uniforms for different engagements. For band photographs, musicians lined up in order of ascending height to create an effect of perfect symmetry. The typical visual image of a 1920s "hot jazz" band, by contrast, was of musicians mugging and clowning, instruments thrown up at oblique angles, lounging over pianos. Music stands and stage backdrops for big bands were generally impeccably designed, usually marked with the initials of the bandleader.[48] The celebrity bandleaders with whom the American public associated swing in the late 1930s—Goodman, Dorsey, Shaw, Miller—embodied in their very persons the visual style of the musical fad. The men were impeccably groomed, not surprisingly, but their appearances also suggested moderation and sobriety. All three wore eyeglasses, and Goodman was once described as looking like a high school science teacher. Black bandleaders in particular were highly educated, and many looked it; Lunceford, Henderson, Benny Carter, Don Redman, and others all had college educations.

To be sure, swing artists and audiences were not homogeneous. According to bandleader Glen Gray, whose touring experience with Casa Loma Orchestra began in the early 1930s, class differences played a role in determining audience preferences:

> The kids who work hard somehow seem to be ballroom types. The cities and their white collar workers are night club types. They like their fun sophisticated, like in the movies. That means a cocktail lounge, a floor show and the trimmings. Bands usually play in big, unadorned barn-like amusement parks and the dancehalls. The mining and industrial towns, the farmers and steelworkers take their dancing straight.

Ensembles that played local circuits away from urban centers were known as territory bands, and necessarily became more familiar with local tastes.[49]

The new look and sound of big band jazz only partially concealed an ethos of harmonized conflict and contestation that had characterized jazz since its earliest days. Alongside the conspicuous attempts to make swing inclusive and temperate, accessible and morally responsible—the Benny Goodman concert at Carnegie—remained the contrary impulse: swing as *agon*. "There's conflict *inside* music," wrote a critic in 1940. "In classical music you call it counterpoint. In American music you call it swing. The soloist swinging against the rhythm section is battling it so as not to get sucked into an 'on beat' [square] solo." As the Basie-Webb and innumerable other "battles" at establishments like the Savoy indicate, big bands were at some level competing with one another, with the audience as a democratic referendum. This same ethos was at work among individual artists as well, in the form of after-hours jam sessions, at which artists would attempt to "cut" their instrumental rivals by outdoing them in terms of originality, volume, and musical brilliance. In addition to providing a form of release, these cutting contests served as informal laboratories for the development of improvisation. "There's got to be conflict, swing, counterpoint," wrote the critic. "That's what's good about a jam session, an old fashioned 'carving' session. Everyone fight[s] everyone to give out or to give up—then you produce your best music."[50]

This same ethos of harmonized competition can be glimpsed amid the multitude of polls and honorific titles bestowed on the stars of the swing era. Jazz had always included a kind of titled nobility among its most renowned artists: King Oliver, Duke Ellington, Count Basie, Earl Hines, and so on. But during the swing era these labels became formalized, commercial properties determined by readers' polls and bestowed by music magazines. Goodman had emerged as the "King of Swing" in 1935, and the popular press eagerly reported on the progress of various "pretenders" to the Goodman throne. In February 1939, for example, Artie Shaw and Goodman waged an "ordeal by battle" in two neighboring theaters in Newark, New Jersey. "At week's end," *Time* reported, "Benny Goodman could claim technical victory." Box-office receipts were equal, but admission cost less at Goodman's theater, meaning he attracted more customers; and Shaw fans were "disappointed by their idol's cold stage personality." *Time* mentioned a number of other challengers, including Bob Crosby and Bobby Hackett, but by that fall was reporting that a dark horse challenger, Glenn Miller, was "now undisputed King of Swing." Fans picked up this spirit of partisanship; one could be either a Goodman or a Shaw fan, but not both.[51]

That swing was a music of "the people," subject to the plebiscite of its audience, was perhaps expressed most clearly in the popularity of magazine-sponsored polls. *Down Beat* introduced its "all-time swing band" poll in 1936, and it became an annual feature; *Metronome* quickly followed suit. Various controversies haunted these polls, ranging from scandals over ballot stuffing (ballots were simply printed in magazines, and it was not unheard of for a press agent to request hundreds of copies of the issue that contained the ballot in order to promote his client) to alleged discrimination against African-American musicians. The point of such polls was the process as much as the end result, with magazines reporting the tallies issue after issue as if announcing a close horse race. The *Chicago Defender*, for example, conducted its poll over the course of four months, reporting the standings each week. "Never before in history has any contest captured the fancy and imagination as this one did coast to coast," announced columnist Al Monroe in the final week (in which Ellington edged out Lunceford, Basie, Calloway, Ernie Fields, and Erskine Hawkins, who were in a virtual dead heat for second). The contest proved both that white musicians and readers were interested in black bands, and vice versa. "You will perhaps be interested, if not surprised to know that even though not entered in the contest many votes were cast for Glenn Miller, Benny Goodman, Dorseys, Tommy and Jimmy and Artie Shaw," averred Monroe. "That shows something, my fans, but definitely."[52]

Swing as ritualized combat staged for a plebescite of dancers receives perhaps its clearest representation in Harlem Renaissance writer Rudolph Fisher's short story "Common Meter." Set in a Lenox Avenue ballroom clearly modeled on the Savoy, the story concerns two rival bandleaders who duel for the affections of a young hostess. Like Basie and Webb, the men are a study in physical and musical contrasts. Bus Williams is round, dark, and ingenuous; Fess Baxter is angular, jive-talking, with a "Swiss-cheese-colored face." (Fess Williams was a real-life musician who led a house band at the Savoy in the late 1920s.) Williams' "philosophy of jazz" subjugates tone to rhythm, while Baxter considers rhythm "a mere rack upon which to hang his tonal tricks." When the two nearly come to blows over Miss Jean Ambrose, the Arcadia's manager delivers an ultimatum. "You birds fight it out with them jazz sticks, y'hear?" he orders. "Them's your weapons. Nex' Monday night's the jazz contest. You'll find out who's the best man next Monday night." The rules of this contest—the "jazz championship of the world"—are simple. Both bands are to play a one-step, a fox-trot, and a blues. The band that inspires the longest total applause, as measured by an official stopwatch, will be declared the winner. Baxter achieves an early lead by sabotaging his rival's all-important drum set, but Williams struggles back with an inspired rendition of the blues. In the end, Williams garners twenty seconds less total applause than Baxter, but the crowd, sensing foul play, refuses to accept the timekeeper's objective verdict. Miss Ambrose impulsively delivers the trophy loving cup to the trusty Williams, a clear victory for integrity, both musical and personal.[53]

By standing for different ideas and taking different ideological shapes, swing managed to bridge some of the oppositions and contradictions that characterized the culture of the 1930s. How it did so is another question. As is frequently the case, those closest to and most knowledgeable about the cultural form, the musicians themselves, had little interest in a politics of swing; the music was a livelihood, at most a means of personal expression. Its musical language was not readily translatable into a verbal language, political or otherwise. Swing's meanings were instead defined largely by the community of writers and critics who took it up as an avocation during the period: the same writers who prepared the public for Goodman at Carnegie Hall and deemed Basie the victor in the Savoy battle with Webb that night.

2

Between Conjure and Kapital

In May 1939 *Down Beat* published a retraction by Duke Ellington of an article that had appeared the previous month describing the relationship between swing critics and the musicians they reviewed as "laughable." While critics are necessary to any art, Ellington had acknowledged, criticism of jazz was missing the mark; a less confrontational approach, more sensitive to the differing aspirations of musicians and the pressures of the music industry, was needed. Ellington had singled out John Hammond for special censure. Hammond, he wrote, had simultaneously provoked the "greatest resentment" and "deepest gratitude" among musicians. "He appears to be an ardent propagandist and champion of the 'lost cause.' He apparently has consistently identified himself with the interests of the minorities, the Negro peoples, to a lesser degree, the Jew, and to the underdog, in the form of the Communist party. Perhaps due to the 'fever of battle,'" Ellington speculated, "Hammond's judgment may become slightly warped, and his enthusiasm and prejudices a little bit unwieldy to control."[1]

One month later Ellington found himself offering a correction in *Down Beat*. "It was my intention to merely infer that the political affiliations of Mr. Hammond bordered on the 'left wing,'" he wrote. "The impression conveyed that he is in any way associated with the Communist party was both accidental and erroneous."[2]

That impression, it seems, was not unique to Ellington; Hammond was widely considered a "fellow traveler." J. Edgar Hoover had Hammond under investigation for much of the 1940s, and the Federal

Bureau of Investigation gathered much information on Hammond's myriad left-wing political associations (and Ellington's, for good measure) during those years. But Ellington was no workaday redbaiter, and the *Down Beat* exchange of 1939 was only the latest incidence of a curious tension between swing's most prominent African-American bandleader and its most respected talent scout and producer. In 1935, in an article titled "The Tragedy of Duke Ellington, the 'Black Prince of Jazz': A Musician of Great Talent Forsakes Simplicity for Pretension," Hammond had castigated Ellington for distancing himself and his music from the troubles of his people. "It would probably take a Granville Hicks or a Langston Hug[h]es to describe the way he shuts his eyes to the abuses being heaped upon his race and his original class," Hammond charged, obscuring the fact that Ellington came from a middle-class Washington family. Because of his indifference to the plight of southern sharecroppers, northern working-class blacks, and such victims of southern justice as the Scottsboro boys, Hammond argued, Ellington's music had "become vapid and without the slightest semblance of guts." Ellington's tact and suave manner disguised a willingness to tolerate racial indignities for the sake of commercial success, according to Hammond, and stripped both the bandleader and his music of the moral authority he thought they should possess. Hammond's attack on Ellington was not the first published by *Down Beat.* As early as 1935, a front-page article by Marshall Stearns charged: "The 'Duke of Ellington' Steps Out—of the Picture? 'Jungle Style' and 'Wah-Wah' Effects Are in Class of 'Horse and Buggy.'" Ellington's music was then evolving in a way that several influential critics found disconcerting. But Hammond's critique was unusual for being based as much on political as musical grounds.[3]

Hammond's criticism is ironic, given that Ellington's music of the 1930s was explicitly and self-consciously concerned with African-American cultural expression. The unique sonorities of the Ellington band, whose tonal coloration owed much to the pioneering use of plunger mutes by trumpeter Bubber Miley and trombonist Tricky Sam Nanton, was sometimes labeled a "jungle" sound; it was developed in part to meet white audience expectations of exoticism at Harlem's Cotton Club. In compositions like "Creole Love Call," "Black and Tan

Fantasy," "Harlem Speaks," "Drop Me Off in Harlem," and "Harlem Air Shaft," to name only the most obvious examples, Ellington's orchestra sought to give aural representation to urban black experience.[4] But by 1938 Hammond had positioned himself as the arbiter of African-American musical authenticity, a domain in which Ellington was suspect. Hammond's patronage ran rather to Ellington's New York rival bandleader Fletcher Henderson; to Count Basie, whom Hammond "discovered" through a radio broadcast from a Kansas City nightclub, brought East, prodded and promoted, and eventually made into a national success; to vocalist Billie Holiday; to the "boogie-woogie" piano players; and of course to Benny Goodman, whose 1935 band Hammond helped select and promote, leading to its Palomar triumph. If these diverse artists had anything in common, it was certainly not a sense of racial consciousness or dedication to radical politics, those areas in which Hammond found Ellington lacking.

The Ellington-Hammond "feud" was unique but emblematic of a relationship that was crucial in shaping the music and cultural meaning of swing: the relationship between musicians and their critics. No other critic would have been as forward in calling into question both Ellington's racial loyalty and class consciousness; certainly no musician would have even considered making such a charge. But the impulse that Hammond expressed was widespread among the dozen or so writers most influential in shaping public perception of big-band jazz and, in consequence, in defining the music itself. Writing for specialized publications like *Down Beat*, *Metronome*, *Swing*, *Tempo*, and the Paris-based *Jazz Hot*, as well as periodicals aimed at a more general audience, a small coterie of young white men, typically from privileged social backgrounds, exercised enormous influence in shaping America's understanding of the swing phenomenon. They promoted and denigrated particular artists and styles of music through reviews of concerts and records; they bickered among themselves and with musicians over developing critical standards for evaluating the new music. And they told and retold the story of jazz and its most prominent artists to an eager audience with little understanding of how the cultural force of swing had emerged.

It was through these writers that jazz took on the remarkable ideological content that it acquired during the swing period and with which it has contended ever since. Since coming to public attention in the late 1910s, and throughout the 1920s, jazz—or what passed for that still largely undefined region of popular music—had served as both a symbol and a vehicle for cultural rebellion and, in a most indirect way, social protest. Although its musicians for the most part were unconscious of issuing such a challenge, the cultural establishment perceived their music as a direct threat to established cultural values. Racially, jazz was perceived as uncouth and primitive, a variety of music associated with African-Americans, and the arena for a dangerous social miscegenation. In class terms, it stood for an assault on middle-class propriety waged by both the lower-class criminal elements associated with Prohibition speakeasies and brothels, and the decadent upper-class socialites who "slummed" them; this reaction was not limited to whites, but was felt among the black middle class as well. In terms of gender relations, jazz and the dances it inspired were perceived as a direct threat to moral propriety, sexual decency, and American womanhood.[5]

But during the 1930s and 1940s, when jazz answered to the label "swing," the music took on a more explicit set of ideological meanings. Instead of simply eliciting negative responses from respectable journals, women's associations, civic organizations, and dance federations—as was the case during the 1920s—jazz evoked more complex responses. Many of the writers who criticized or reviewed jazz sought to define a political meaning for the music, one that correlated with the Popular Front ideology influential in intellectual circles during the latter half of the decade. Like the communism of Earl Browder, the U.S. party head, jazz seemed to express both all-American values and progressive leftist ideals. It challenged the ironclad rigidity of Depression-era racial segregation, crediting blacks with unique powers of spontaneous artistic creativity, among other things. Jazz represented a musical thumbing of the nose at fascism, whose Nazi theorists regarded swing as a debased creation of Jews and blacks. Jazz, to its proselytizers, was above all a democratic music, a product of "the people," accessible to all classes and cultural types, marked both by a spirit of collective cooperation and by spontaneous individuality. Like the Popular Front, the surface clarity of this ideology disguised darker dissonances and inconsistencies that would emerge during the war and after, but during the 1930s it stayed intact, largely as a result of swing's community of writers. The contradictions of jazz criticism were a symptom of the difficult task with which these writers saddled themselves: explaining to America that swing was in a fundamental sense an African-American music, that somehow, for the first time since antebellum minstrelsy, black culture had become for many of its young people the American culture of choice.

Not that the critical community was a place of consensus, political or aesthetic. The ethos of harmonized competition that characterized the swing-era big bands had its more unbridled counterpart in the community of writers who critiqued and promoted the music. The pages of journals like *Down Beat* and *Metronome* resounded with generally good-natured but occasionally biting ripostes and ad hominem attacks against bandleaders, recordings, and rival critics. Typical controversies—Did Ellington's post-1935 music represent a failure of misplaced highbrow pretensions? Was big-band swing a commercial adulteration of a golden age of Armstrong, Sidney Bechet, Beiderbecke, King Oliver, Bessie Smith? Were vocalists merely pretty ornaments who detracted from the important instrumental work of the bands? Did African-Americans play better jazz than whites?—would be debated in issue after issue, drawing heated responses from readers as well as commentary from specialists. These exchanges were symptomatic of deeper reservations about the qualifications of the critics and about the criteria (or lack thereof) that governed critical evaluations of the music. By the late 1930s, the realm of swing had become nearly ungovernable, with calls for a new basis for jazz criticism appearing alongside parodies of its best-known writers.

The Big Bringdown

No figure was central to more of these debates than John Hammond. Identified by his contemporaries as the most influential person in the swing industry, Hammond was in many ways *sui generis*; but his background, career, and politics were not unrepresentative of others in his generation of swing critics. Born in New York City in 1910 to a Yale-educated lawyer from Kentucky and a pious Christian Science convert who was a Vanderbilt and a cousin of minister Henry Sloane Coffin, Hammond grew up in a mansion on Manhattan's East 91st Street that included, among other things, two elevators and a private ballroom. After prepping at Hotchkiss, where he first become intrigued by African-American music, Hammond attended Yale for a year and a half, making regular trips to Harlem to attend theaters and cabarets until he dropped out, in 1930. With an annual trust income of about $9,000 Hammond could live comfortably while pursuing the myriad jazz-related ventures and social causes that caught his attention through the 1930s and 1940s. He developed as a writer through stints as the American correspondent for the British music journals *The Gramophone* and *Melody Maker,* and covered the Scottsboro trial in Alabama for *The Nation;* later he would contribute to *Down Beat,* the *New Masses,* the *Brooklyn Eagle,* the *Daily Worker, Tempo,* and the *Chicago News,* among others, and cofound *Music and Rhythm.* At the same time he worked at various publishing ventures, musical and otherwise, was employed by an advertising agency, and ran a downtown theater. A colleague explained Hammond's predilection for constantly shifting employment: "Every place he goes he presently spies the taint of commercialism in art or the sordid hand of capitalism clutching workers. He burns. He speaks out. And then he *is* out."[6]

Hammond's most important move, for himself and for swing, came in 1933, when as American recording director for the English division of Columbia records he lined up some recording dates for Benny Goodman, then a disenchanted New York studio musician. By prodding Goodman to replace band personnel with such key members as Krupa and Jess Stacy and to hire Fletcher Henderson as arranger, Hammond pushed him away from the mainstream, "sweet" commercial dance music toward the more adventurous jazz-inflected sound that would captivate audiences in the summer of 1935. At the same time Hammond urged Goodman to break with the segregated tradition that had governed public performances and recordings of jazz up to that time. The coronation of Goodman as "King of Swing" brought a corresponding increase in prestige for Hammond in the music industry.

Hammond's position as talent scout, recording consultant, and technical adviser for Columbia Recording Corporation, which issued records on the Columbia and Brunswick labels, coupled with his friend-ship with Willard Alexander of the powerful Music Corporation of America (MCA), provided him with access to key networks in the emerging swing industry. As a roving "talent scout" who drove 30,000 miles a year seeking out fresh talent, Hammond "discovered" a number of swing's leading stars. Four of the top bandleaders of 1939—Goodman, Basie, Teddy Wilson, and Harry James—were directly indebted to Hammond's patronage, not to mention scores of other instrumentalists and vocalists. "In fully fifty per cent of the best bands the soloists [swing fans] would mention approvingly are Hammond dis-coveries and Hammond enthusiasms," wrote one observer. He was equally influential in forming critical opinions, through both his own writings and the opinions of other journalists influenced by his enthu-siasms and tastes; each of the three book-length studies of jazz pub-lished in 1938–39 acknowledged Hammond's advice. "Hammond's opinions, expressed with the frankness of a man who has nothing to lose by any reaction his words may arouse, are conned eagerly by jazz 'critics' and college boys from coast to coast, thereafter to reappear almost verbatim in their own periodicals when they review records or discuss jazz performers to be heard on the air."[7]

Until 1938 all of Hammond's work had been done behind the scenes: backstage after shows, at musicians' bars, during intermissions at clubs, at late-night record-listening or -trading sessions. It was Hammond's performance as master of ceremonies at "From Spirituals to Swing," a concert sponsored by the Marxist weekly *New Masses* at Carnegie Hall in December 1938, that first fixed his image in the public eye; his con-tribution generated nearly as much interest as the musical performances themselves. During the next year profiles appeared in *Harper's, Collier's,* the *New Yorker,* and elsewhere. Thin, lanky, "rather sallow-faced," and sporting his trademark crewcut, Hammond struck some at the concert as looking even younger than his twenty-eight years. Appearing nervous and self-conscious, he delivered his annotations before each act in what one observer described as a "poised inarticulate way." Sitting on one side of the stage during the show, his head wagging and foot tapping drew the attention of several reporters present. "From a position in one of the red-plush wooden-armed chairs in the hall, where dowagers had nodded in acceptance of Toscanini's Beethoven, Hammond's performance was hardly less engrossing than any of the official ones," *Harper's* reported. "An ear-to-ear grin, a slap of the hand on the thigh, a bobbing from right to left showed the pleasure that lesser (more inhibited) folk merely expressed by a pounding of palms." The *New Yorker* reported that "Hammond in action is the embodiment of the popular conception of the jitterbug . . . When the music jumps, he begins to move his head, his feet, and sometimes his whole body. His eyebrows go up, his mouth opens wide and reveals a set of even, gleaming teeth, and a long-drawn-out 'Yeah' slides out of his throat." Hammond angrily disclaimed the jitterbug label. "A jitterbug is an exhibitionist," he told a reporter. "I'm not. I just like music, that's all, and all kinds." He drank little and never danced, incurring the wrath of hostesses at dance halls he visited in search of talent.[8] Instead he would take up station at a table, bobbing and beaming to the music, and perusing the periodicals (*New Masses, New Statesman, Variety*) he regularly carried under his arm.

Hammond's unselfconscious physical ebullience, which helped define the popular image of the youthful 1930s swing enthusiast, was only one manifestation of his legendary personal energy. "Not having to be in any one place, he is in all places; not having to do one thing a day, he does a hundred," wrote a colleague. "I've tailed him for just one day and I estimate that five days in a row would drop anyone's arches." That "typical" day began with a drive to Philadelphia to scout talent at the University of Pennsylvania; an interview with the head of the glee club; attending a penny arcade and two shows, including a Fats Waller performance, and meeting people backstage afterward; a return to New York for a working dinner and floor show; a session of listening to and trading old records; a midnight drive uptown for more record talk. "I had only been conditioned to bear up under a routine of doing ship's work from five to five and standing four hours' watch six nights out of eight," commented the writer, who dropped out exhausted along the way. Another colleague confirmed that "restless and driven with an energy few others possess, John on many a night has worn out as many as three others who tried to keep pace."[9]

His driving exploits were equally daunting. Crisscrossing the country in his Terraplane in constant quest of new talent, Hammond drove in obsessive Dean Moriarty fashion, taking his shoes off so that his cold feet would keep him awake for the long stretches between New York, Memphis, Chicago, Kansas City, and New Orleans. "He can go anywhere but east out of New York for hundreds of miles without looking at road signs," observed a colleague. "Chicago and Kansas City he takes off for in the same way you would propose going up to [Harlem's] Savoy because there is a good band in." Another writer recalled a trip to Kansas City: "With Hammond at the wheel we fought an Ohio River flood and a whole series of Indiana, Illinois, and Missouri cloudbursts. But Hammond steered his Terraplane along at a 55-mile-an-hour average the whole route, leaving the wheel only long enough to trade seats. Once away from the steering gear Hammond would throw back his head, fall asleep in 30 seconds, rest maybe 40 minutes or an hour, and then suddenly jump up and grab the wheel for another 5-hour stretch." Upon arrival he immediately set about locating pianists.[10]

Hammond's physical vigor was matched by an equally strenuous sense of musical and moral rectitude. Known by various nicknames— "the Critic," "the Little Father," "the Guardian Angel," "the Big Bringdown"—that reflected the patriarchal authority he projected, Hammond was positioned to promote or derail musical careers, a prerogative he undertook with evident relish. But he refused to temper his power with critical equivocations. A friend pointed to his "invincible certainty, whether in praise or blame—a rare attribute in a forum peopled largely by neophytes and blind enthusiasts." Others were less charitable. "As a working critic, John Hammond suffers mainly from a complete lack of temperance and caution," wrote Otis Ferguson, whose contributions to the *New Republic* were much admired by Hammond, among others. "He hasn't established for himself the intervening marks on the scale of achievement between 'it's terrific' and 'it stinks.' " Ferguson continued: "As Dean of the Swing Critics, accustomed to deference and not having his word disputed, he has developed a habit of knowing the answers and what's more giving them to you—it doesn't matter whether you asked." For a time he took to referring to himself in the third person.[11]

Hammond's strong and mercurial critical judgments, combined with his tendency, not uncommon among other leftist critics of the period, to judge art partly according to its ideological utility (as in the Ellington incident), combined to make Hammond less than universally popular among both musicians and critics. According to Ferguson, whose acerbic but respectful depiction of Hammond stands out among the more flattering press coverage, Hammond's enthusiasms generated anger and resentful jokes among musicians: "the phrase 'Uh-oh, the Bringdown's here' is as familiar in some quarters as 'Soup's on,' with different effect." Ellington charged Hammond with conflict of interest for "freely condemning and condoning" bands in which he had no financial stake, a "right" Ellington believed he had "forfeited" as a result of his activities as a producer and talent scout. "Such tactics would not be tolerated from the business man and they are doubly unappreciated when employed by one whose name and position allow him to remain immune from counter-attack."[12] Hammond's political fervor could be disconcerting. His constant state of high moral purpose, of principled indignation, could irritate even those in basic agreement with his principles, or the beneficiaries of his zeal. "He'll rush up to a well-meaning bird who never heard of the war against Fascism in his life and cut him clear to the floor because the bird went to see [Max] Schmeling fight," observed Ferguson. "He'll urge a demonstration for Loyalist Spain on trumpet men who think that is just another tango job."[13]

Fellow critics were also put off by Hammond's sense of zealous self-importance, and regularly took satirical swipes at him. *Down Beat* published a gently mocking poem, "The Hammond What Am!" in 1937. A *Metronome* parody of Hammond and other critics from that year took the form of a fictional review of a Mezz Mezzrow recording. Hammond had recently written a pseudonymous series of articles for *New Masses* documenting shady and discriminatory practices at Decca.

> The fact that labor conditions at the Victor factory are lamentable, dooms this weak attempt at a poor record, for which I have nothing but praise. When I see the president of Victor next time, he may have some explanation to offer. Further, this is simply another case of Comrade Mezzrow being exploited again by the colored race. Of course,

they in turn were exploited by the Victor people. We shall have to wait until the revolution to see people swing. By the way, the music on this record is quite good.

Hammond's "Harvard" accent, family connections, and trust income also generated some resentment. Appearing to be a man of simple tastes who gave of himself endlessly in support of the many artists and causes he took up, Hammond's consumer habits struck some as resembling "velvet over a box-spring mattress." "He lives very modestly on Sullivan Street below Washington Square but his telephone-answering service costs more than the majority of our population pays for rent," observed Ferguson, one of the few jazz critics not of patrician background. "He keeps a car and turns it in so fast you barely have time to put a cigarette burn on the upholstery." Most revealing of all to Ferguson, Hammond actually bought his own magazines instead of waiting to read someone else's copy. Hammond's relations with his family remained cordial despite their divergent politics; he hosted recitals in his mother's ballroom, and regularly had his laundry done at home. His father attended "From Spirituals to Swing," but avoided buying a box in favor of anonymous orchestra seats. "Typical of the caviar cocktail crowd" was how one FBI informant warily described him.[14]

Perhaps most controversial among Hammond's critical positions was his outspoken belief that blacks played superior swing. "The best of the white folk still cannot compare to the really good Negroes in relaxed, unpretentious dance music," he was quoted as saying, an opinion that struck many as "clearly intolerant," according to the *New Yorker*. Ferguson objected:

> He is all for the working class. Fine. He's dedicated to the cause of the Negro. Fine. But he is too apt to shut his ear to the music of someone who didn't pay off on a date or said nuts to the lettuce pickers, and call it criticism. And when he goes around saying "white musician" the way you'd use the term "greaseball," he not only confuses his readers and upsets his own standards but starts the Jim Crow car all over again, in reverse.

Hammond was not alone among jazz critics in his belief that race made a difference in the performance of jazz, and that blacks had an innate superiority. But no other critic weighed "extraneous" political factors as heavily in his critical evaluations. At the same time, Hammond opposed the campaign for black separatism in the swing industry led by a *Pittsburgh Courier* columnist who urged musicians to shun the newly integrated white bands, promoters, and unions as the "enemy." History has "proved" that strategy "wrong," Hammond asserted. "Only by unity between Negroes and whites will they be able to survive and flourish." Moreover, race was only one component of Hammond's canon of musical authenticity. In choosing the program for "from spirituals to Swing," he deliberately rejected well-known black entertainers like Ethel Waters, Marian Anderson, Paul Robeson, the Hall Johnson Singers, and what he described as "the highly publicized Negro jazz bands, some of whom have made serious concessions to white taste by adding spurious showmanship to their wares and imitating the habits and tricks of the more commercially successful white orchestras." Instead, Hammond recruited what he regarded as the genuine authentic performers of African-American music: Mitchell's Christian Singers; blues artists Bill Broonzy and Joe Turner; boogie-woogie pianists Meade "Lux" Lewis, Albert Ammons, and Pete Johnson; New Orleans artists Sidney Bechet and Tommy Ladnier; and, his great mission of the late 1930s, the Count Basie Orchestra. What linked these performers, imbued them with authenticity, was a negative quality: "These are artists who, for the most part, have had no formal musical training of any kind, cannot read musical notations, and have never played before white audiences or in any formal way before colored audiences," Hammond announced in the *New York Times*.[15] The exceptions to that statement were the Basie sidemen who had appeared at Carnegie Hall earlier that year under the auspices of the pathbreaking Goodman concert—an event at which Ellington sidemen (and compositions) appeared but Ellington himself did not, choosing instead to wait and appear in his own right.

While Hammond's notion of musical authenticity was clearly rooted in his attitudes toward race and commercial adulteration, his politics struck contemporaries as notably more equivocal. "He might be called a fellow-traveller today except that there is some doubt about where he is travelling to," concluded the *New Yorker* in 1939. "Hammond does not know himself." In fact, his politics, with their incongruities and lacunae, help illuminate the cultural work performed by swing in the Popular Front. Even in a decade marked by intense enthusiasm for commitment, political and other, Hammond stands out. In 1933 Hammond was listed as a member of the National Scottsboro Action Committee. The following year he became a member of the National Committee for Defense of Political Prisoners. In 1935 he joined the National Association for the Advancement of Colored People and traveled to the Soviet Union, where he was entertained by filmmaker Sergei Eisenstein. But it was Hammond's formation, along with Orson Welles and English professor F. O. Matthiessen, of the Citizens' Committee for Harry Bridges in April 1941 that set off the loudest alarms at the FBI. The committee, whose sixty-five sponsors included writers, clergymen, and artists, was formed to protest the effort by a federal judge to deport the West Coast labor leader as a Communist.[16]

Beginning in 1941, J. Edgar Hoover took a personal interest in Hammond's case; he was interviewed by FBI agents in that year and the next. By 1941 Hammond had also joined the National Committee for People's Rights; he was a sponsor of the American Council on Soviet Relations and of Russian War Relief, Inc.; he was guest of honor at the American Peace Mobilization Testimonial Dinner for Vito Marcantonio and at the Fourth American Writers' Congress and Congress of American Artists dinner. Hammond was later identified as a sponsor of the Artists' Front to Win the War and of the Musicians' Committee to Aid Spanish Democracy. He made repeated donations to the Federated Press and served as director and a principal stockholder of the Trade Union Service, Inc. During and after American involvement in the war, Hammond continued to add to his commitments, serving on the Musicians' Committee of the National Council of American-Soviet Friendship, the National Negro Congress, the Council on African Affairs, Progressive Citizens of America, and the Maryland Committee for Peace. He served on the executive board of the Theatre Union, on the board of directors of People's Songs, and as an owner of the People's Press.[17]

Despite this welter of affiliations, and skeptics like his *New Yorker* profiler, Hammond's ideology was remarkably clear and consistent. He was fundamentally a Progressive, a high-minded crusader whose social background, energy, and temperament in a previous generation might have attracted him to, and evoked comparisons with, Theodore Roosevelt. To charges that he enjoyed playing Pygmalion Hammond admitted that he could not "plead total innocence. After all, my mother passed on to me the urge to change the world I thought needed changing. Sometimes that even included jazz." Hammond proudly recounted his career as a series of encounters between his own hard convictions and entrenched wrongdoing; his celebrated triumphs— fighting segregation in the armed forces and taking on David Sarnoff's policy of whites-only orchestras at RCA—were won, as Hammond told it, by unrelenting moral suasion coupled with that old Progressive weapon: threat of public exposure, usually through the press.[18] An aura of noblesse oblige emerges from his writings, along with a clear sense of his own agency in making musical history; it was *Hammond* who was responsible for discovering and marketing fresh talent, making the personnel changes, arranging recording contracts, and the like, which advanced the careers of his clients; the musicians themselves, like the hapless Fletcher Henderson or Count Basie, who let himself be duped into signing to an inferior contract without Hammond's knowledge, seemed often to be helpless hindrances to their own success.

Hammond's success in his field was also due to a kind of professional expertise associated with Progressive reformers. "Had he been the lawyer his father . . . hoped he would be, John Henry, Jr., would no doubt have been a research man of prodigious qualities," wrote Irving Kolodin. Hammond's business was "omniscience," achieved through his "extraordinary memory" for details and "all-inclusive knowledge of his specialty . . . In a field where scholarship is unknown and documentation largely by word of mouth, Hammond's arsenal of facts and experiences is an impregnable resource."[19]

But if Hammond's methods were quintessentially Progressive, his ideals were not. He was almost exclusively committed to the goal of racial equality, an end he felt could be achieved by individual effort, especially by broadening cultural awareness. Hammond's "idea of a terrestrial heaven," according to the *New Yorker*, "would probably be a place with a low ceiling and doubtful ventilation where white and colored friends of his could play blues together in racial and musical harmony." His overarching commitment to civil rights had the effect of distancing him somewhat from the Communist Party. Hammond's experiences with what he considered the party's cynical exploitation of racial difference as an organizing strategy left him cool to the sort of comprehensive program that Marxists proposed. Although he could write that "once again, as in other forms of labor, a vicious system keeps the Negro and white in competition while the inevitable exploiters take advantage of their rivalry," Hammond rarely evinced an interest in revealing the systemic causes of racial inequality in the swing industry. Throughout his life Hammond steadfastly denied any Communist sympathies, apparently regarding the label as something of a slur. He voted Democratic in 1936 and for the American Labor Party in 1937, 1938, and 1940. His association with *New Masses* began when it allowed him editorial space to attack racist practices in the recording industry, and ended when he directed his attention to discrimination in what he considered leftist musicians' unions. He made clear, for example, that he allowed *New Masses* to sponsor "From Spirituals to Swing" only on condition that the journal agreed to keep the concert free from any sort of explicit political message; Hammond turned to the magazine only after being turned down by both the NAACP and the International Ladies Garment Workers Union.[20]

In short, the inclusive ideology of the Popular Front, in which a patriotic American could be a committed radical, was for Hammond the ideal political orientation. Even Hoover's FBI concluded in 1943 that although Hammond could be considered a "so called 'fellow traveler,'" there was no evidence showing him to be a member of the Communist Party, and that the case on custodial detention for Hammond should thereby be closed, "subject to further information being received."[21]

As American as Baseball and Hot Dogs

While Hammond's primary allegiance was to African-American culture and he was adamant in denying a personal affiliation with the Communist Party, many Communists during the same period were eagerly aligning themselves with swing and other forms of black music. This had not always been the case. Before the redirection of policy under the Popular Front, jazz and most other popular music had been regarded as ideologically suspect by the party both in the Soviet Union and in the United States; noncommercial rural folk music and protest songs were perceived as the "correct" radical music. This demonization of "decadent bourgeois music" was consistent from the early days of the Soviet Union, with brief thaws occurring in the mid-1920s and mid-1930s, during the Second World War, and early in the Khrushchev and Brezhnev eras.[22] Given the party's desire to recruit members of oppressed groups such as African-Americans, this dismissal of vernacular music resulted in a dissonance between the party leadership and its rank-and-file organizers. The more tolerant, inclusive atmosphere that prevailed in the party after 1935 led a number of younger Communists, including writers for the *Daily Worker*, to express enthusiasm for both "traditional" jazz and swing. The popular music of the big bands came to be seen as an important vehicle, along with black theater, literature, and professional sports, for promoting the idea that African-American culture was integrally American, quintessentially democratic and progressive. Harlem, already the headquarters of swing, came to be at the center of this ecumenical push.[23]

Beginning in 1937, the *Daily Worker* began publishing articles favorable to swing and regularly reviewed jazz records. During 1938 and 1939 three major programs of contemporary black music were sponsored by organizations with ties to the Popular Front: a Carnegie Hall benefit for the Spanish Children's Milk Fund; a program sponsored by the American Labor Party called "Negro Music, Past and Present"; and Hammond's "From Spirituals to Swing." Harlem's Communist Party founded an interracial "swing club" and promoted jitterbugging, while the Young Communist League sponsored a "Swing America" pageant at its 1939 convention. Echoing Earl Browder's description of communism as "one hundred percent Americanism," a *YCL Review* article in 1939 claimed that "Swing is as American as baseball and hot dogs. A good hot band can claim as many raucous rooters as the Dodgers. There is a good deal of audience participation in swing, a kind of give and take and mutual inspiration for the musician and the crowd, a rough democratic air invading the sacred halls of music." Another writer stated bluntly: "Jazz is the music of the American proletariat. If Negroes have been more prominent in its development, it is because more Negroes are proletarians." Poet Norman Macleod, writing of the inspiration provided by Louis Armstrong, recalled carrying a recording to Oklahoma City: "Louis Armstrong's music became familiar to the packing house strikers and on the Fourth of July at a farmers' picnic where the Russian October Revolution was being celebrated I took *Star Dust* and a portable out that the king of swing might be better known to the cohorts of communism and the veterans of the Green Corn Rebellion in Oklahoma." The record was lost when "Federal dicks" arrested the friends with whom he left it.[24]

Many musicians' most vivid contact with Communists came at dances, particularly those held at Camp Unity, a retreat north of New York City on the Hudson River. All were struck by the extent of interracial dating. "I think they were trying to prove how equalitarian they were by throwing together the white or the black counterparts of the opposite sex," recalled Dizzy Gillespie, who played Camp Unity in the late 1930s. According to a musician who spent most of the summer of 1943 there, "all 'racial equality' boiled down to there was that the black musicians had to be with the white women since there were no black women in the camp." Still, he "got hip to communism a week after I got there. The game seemed to be to make Blacks embrace their philosophy." Gillespie also recalled efforts to "convert" him at dances, and signed a membership card. "I never went to a meeting," he said, "but I was a card-carrying communist because it was directly associated with my work."[25]

Swing intersected the Popular Front most conspicuously at Café Society, a Greenwich Village nightclub founded in 1938 by a former shoe salesman from New Jersey named Barney Josephson. A white-owned establishment in a white neighborhood, Café Society was unique both in featuring integrated musical acts and in welcoming interracial audiences. With advice from Hammond, Josephson showcased vocalists Billie Holiday and Big Joe Turner; boogie-woogie pioneers Ammons, Lewis, and Johnson; pianists Hazel Scott, Teddy Wilson, Mary Lou Williams, and Art Tatum; and numerous others. He hired Village artists to paint wall murals lampooning the "society" set, eliminated chorus girls and cigarette salesgirls, and offered artists better working conditions than prevailed in typically mob-controlled nightclubs. "The wrong place for the right people" was the club's motto.

During the early 1940s both Café Society and its uptown counter-part, opened in 1940, attracted much favorable press publicity. Eleanor Roosevelt attended a performance of the Golden Gate Quartet there and later invited the group to the White House. But Café Society also attracted the attention of J. Edgar Hoover, who in July 1943 ordered a full-scale investigation of Josephson and his brother, Leon, an avowed Communist and lawyer with International Legal Defense, both of whom were suspected of Soviet espionage. Hoover described the estab-lishments as "known hangouts for Communist 'intellectuals' " and kept them and their proprietor under surveillance. "Not only were Reds assigned as entertainers, waiters and captains," alleged a 1947 FBI report, "but Josephson was advised to use Communist propaganda in shows for the cover-charge customers." *Daily Worker* staff reportedly were admitted free in exchange for favorable publicity in the Com-munist newspaper.[26]

Despite the syncretic energy of the Popular Front, tension persisted between the swing partisans and less permissive old-school Commu-nists. One such dispute was played out publicly in the pages of the *Daily Worker*. A music critic named Bruce McCall delivered a scathing review of the S. C. Handy Birthday Concert at Carnegie Hall. The show, a benefit for the Spanish Children's Milk Fund, featured a stellar lineup, including Cab Calloway, Jimmy Lunceford, Teddy Wilson, Roy Eld-ridge, Lionel Hampton, Fats Waller, and Maxine Sullivan, but McCall was not impressed. "During the entire evening, there was hardly a sug-gestion of genuine and sincere jazz," he wrote. "Evidently, it was assumed that the audience consisted of jitterbugs, and the hypothetical droolers were given their money's worth of noise and vaudeville." McCall, with a clear preference for "authentic" hot jazz over more "vulgar" commercialized swing, was particularly affronted by the more exhibitionist and comedic elements of the show: Calloway's musical comedy, Roy Eldridge's facile virtuosity, Waller's boisterous clowning.[27]

Response to McCall's review was rapid and incisive. The next issue carried a letter from John Hammond excoriating McCall's "arrogant and dyspeptic" review and defending the musicians who performed at the benefit (while acknowledging that "the concert was badly arranged and atrociously presented"). But Hammond's complaint expressed more than a difference in musical judgment. "I think it highly impolitic for the *Daily* to be a party to insulting treatment of great Negro artists, who, for the first time, are becoming interested in the cause of democracy in Spain and are contributing their services to help it," he wrote. On the same page the paper's editorial board offered a three-column apology for McCall's "errors," criticizing at length his vituperative language. The editors appeared especially embarrassed that his review played directly into the hands of those who would debase and disparage African-American culture. "The Negro people have made profound and original contributions to American culture, and particularly in the field of music," the board affirmed. "Comrade McCall, who has himself recognized and emphasized this contribution, failed to consider this in this review, saying the 'music itself was disgraceful' when he described the orchestra renditions of swing and jazz."[28]

Entrusted with a review of "From Spirituals to Swing" a month later, McCall delivered a much more favorable appraisal. The concert was "eminently successful," its "shortcomings" due not to the performers but to the concert's "thesis" and presentation. While the concert attempted to trace a continuous line of musical influence, the program failed to make these relationships clear, and suffered from an overall lack of balance. "The absence of white musicians in the latter [swing] half of the program hardly helped to explain a number of musical phenomena," McCall wrote. And McCall subtly questioned the extent of the audience's understanding and appreciation of the program, charging that "in view of the uncertain relationship between audience and musician, there never was a greater necessity for enlightening and charged criticism."[29]

As the party took pains to treat black music with respect, its efforts to mobilize mass support in the black community were dealt a debilitating blow by the announcement of the Nazi-Soviet pact in August 1939. The party's hasty retreat from the Popular Front strategy, the embrace of the New Deal and militant opposition to fascism that made it relatively palatable to the American public, left it deeply vulnerable to latent American anticommunism. But the cultural links forged with African-American artists, writers, and musicians weathered the fallout better than most. "Whatever the Communist Party embodied as a political and social phenomenon—as an agent of Soviet diplomacy, an advocate of working-class power, a vehicle for the Americanization of ethnic minorities—it had become, by the late '30s, a major force in American society promoting systematic cultural interchange between whites and blacks and encouraging whites to recognize the black contribution to the nation's cultural heritage," writes one historian. "So long as Communists remained the most visible advocates of cultural and racial democracy, some black artists and intellectuals clung to the Party milieu with a stubborn loyalty, even when Communist mass-organizing in Harlem almost sputtered to a halt."[30]

Swing musicians were not prominent among those artists, despite some appearances to the contrary. Ellington, who had labeled Hammond a Communist and been forced to retract it, himself attracted FBI attention for his political activities both before and after 1939, generating a list of left-wing associations that rivaled Hammond's. In May 1938 he was listed as an endorser of the first All-Harlem Youth Conference, and in July 1941 he appeared with part of his band at a barn-dance fundraiser for the Hollywood chapter of the Veterans of the Abraham Lincoln Brigade. That summer also saw Ellington involved with the musical revue "Jump for Joy," which premiered at the Mayan Theatre in Los Angeles. Written by a team of "scholarly Hollywood writers" and backed by "top-bracket film people," the show aimed, as Ellington recalled, to "take Uncle Tom out of the theatre . . . and say things that would make the audience think." The show was constantly in flux, according to Ellington, its writers "always on guard against the possibility of chauvinism creeping in, of saying the same things about other races we did not want said about Negroes." He remembered an unusually diverse audience ranging from "the most celebrated Hollywoodians, middle-class ofays, the sweet-and-low, scuffling-type Negroes, and dicty lawyers as well." Later that year Ellington was a sponsor of a dinner given by the American Committee to Save Refugees, the Exiled Writers' Committee, and the United American-Spanish Aid Committee, all regarded by the FBI as suspect organizations.[31]

Ellington's political activities picked up significantly during the war. Along with Hammond, he sponsored the Artists' Front to Win the War in its debut at Carnegie Hall in October 1942. The following summer he appeared at a "Tribute to Negro Servicemen," a program supported by the Negro Labor Victory Committee and the National Negro Congress, among others. He endorsed and appeared at a tribute to Benjamin J. Davis, Jr., the Communist Party candidate for New York's City Council, in October 1943. The following January Ellington mailed out some 1,500 fundraising letters on behalf of the National Committee to Abolish the Poll Tax. In April 1944 he appeared at a Carnegie Hall "Tribute to Fats Waller" sponsored by American Youth Democracy, which reportedly "turned into a tremendous, spontaneous demonstration of inter-racial unity." He volunteered his services for another Carnegie concert, sponsored by the Joint Anti-Fascist Refugee Committee. Ellington was on the executive boards of the Hollywood Democratic Committee and of the Independent Citizens' Committee of the Arts, Sciences, and Professions. Like many other swing musicians, Ellington campaigned for Roosevelt in 1944, lending his photograph to an advertisement paid for by the Independent Committee of Arts and Sciences for Roosevelt. And he sponsored a benefit concert at New York's Town Hall for the American Committee for Yugoslav Relief in January 1946.[32]

As in the case of Hammond, though, these disparate affiliations added up to less than a strong ideological commitment. "I've never been interested in politics in my whole life, and don't pretend to know anything about international affairs," Ellington wrote in 1950. "The only 'Communism' I know is that of Jesus Christ." He claimed that his political activities during the war (he confessed only to helping sell war bonds) had been undertaken with the sole intent of defeating the Axis powers, and that he would help in similar efforts in the future. Ellington's explanation, "No Red Songs for Me," appeared in the *New Leader* in the wake of a contretemps with the *Daily Worker*, which published several stories in May and August 1950 to the effect that Ellington had signed the antinuclear Stockholm Peace Petition while on a European tour. Ellington denied the report and threatened legal action against those he described as "trying to defame my name and reputation."[33] The bandleader's disapproval may have represented an act of political expediency mandated by the changed political climate of 1950. But there is no evidence that Ellington ever aligned himself with the Communist Party directly or embraced any part of its program apart from its general policy of racial equality and respect for and promotion of African-American culture.

Benny Goodman was also linked to Popular Front antifascism. Like Ellington a member of the Musicians' Committee to Aid Spanish Democracy, Goodman supported a May 1937 benefit concert for the Spanish Loyalists. His support for the cause was well known and provoked controversy, as evidenced by the picketers outside the 1938 Carnegie Hall concert. A *Down Beat* reader wrote to complain about the magazine's coverage of the Musicians' Committee: "Did you stop to think what form of government this so called Democracy represents? Well if you haven't it represents Spanish Reds, Communists." The reader enclosed on article on "our No. 1 Communist swing band leader 'Benny Goodman,'" and asked: "Why not expose these fellows?" When Goodman delivered a lecture on jazz at City College of New York in 1939, he was sent to an auditorium where an anti-Nazi protest meeting was just breaking up. "It is better to hail a band leader than *heil* a *bund* leader," the protest leader reportedly quipped by way of introduction. Goodman began his talk, which eventually turned into a "jitterbug jamboree," by telling the audience: "What just went on here is important too, and I'm sorry I wasn't here." At Hammond's urging, even the Basie band was inspired to record a politically charged piece, "It's the Same Old South." Taken from a revue, *Meet the People*, that opened in Hollywood and was performed across the country, the lyrics sharply satirized southern poverty and racial practice. The South was "a regular children's heaven, where they don't start to work 'til they're seven"; it made time for "old-fashioned get-togethers—'Colonel, pass me the tar and feathers!'"; "bloodhounds that once chased Liza" now "chase the poor CIO organizer." Sung by Jimmy Rushing, the song concluded: "Let the Northerners keep Niagara; We'll stick to our Southern pellagra." According to the lyricist, "no one wanted to record it and the only reason Basie [did] was due to John Hammond's enthusiasm." Released during a feud between the radio networks and the songwriters, the recording got no air time and failed.[34]

Despite these alignments, the fit between the Communist Party and big-band jazz was never a seamless one. The class contradictions embedded in the production and consumption of swing made it difficult for the music to maintain the symbolic force its proponents on the left wished it to have. "I confess that I am getting just a little tired of hearing jazz described as a proletarian art, when it is not only supported by middle-class enthusiasts, but also is played by musicians whose thinking (in almost all cases) and whose pocketbooks (in many cases) are predominantly middle-class," complained a *New Republic* reader. Rex Stewart, a trumpet player who read Marx and Spengler during the early 1930s "when most of the Harlems all over the country began being exposed to the stratagems of various shades of political thought," concluded: "our [American] way best represented a road to the dreams and aspirations of men living in our society." Stewart's reading led him to consciously resist "the blandishments of the far left which concluded that the American system was unworkable," as it indeed seemed "during those dark Depression days."[35]

Still, the relationship between swing and the left carried benefits for both sides. For Communists, swing coupled the obvious pleasure of music and dance, the glamour of popular culture, with a means of attracting new partisans and creating new coalitions. For swing musicians and critics, the Popular Front offered an unusual experience of cultural recognition, as well as a vehicle for commitments to racial equality, antifascism, and other attractive political causes. In this sense, those drawn to the fringes of the Communist Party after 1935, like Hammond, Ellington, and Goodman, were typical of most "fellow travelers" who embraced the Popular Front not out of deep partisan loyalty to the party, but because it provided the only plausible vehicle by which to pursue their own highly variegated political agendas.[36]

We Are All Americans

If swing melded only imperfectly with Marxist politics, it came to stand as the epitome of a broader, ambiguously left-leaning ideology of the 1930s—a version of American exceptionalism, which equated democracy with the United States and posited an "American way of life" as the medium in which political ideal and nation were blended. The United States was a domain of economic and social opportunity, of ethnic pluralism, of freedom of expression, of unharnessed creative energy. And while these ideals were at times imperfectly fulfilled in the broader society, they achieved their highest expression, according to its proponents, in the musical realm of swing.

Big-band swing appeared to be a music based on spontaneity and improvisation, which moved its audience to liberating self-expression; it seemed to be relatively free of hierarchal distinctions, produced in conditions of mutual respect and communal purpose. And swing was the point at which the racial and class boundaries of brutally segregated 1930s America were most permeable, for both musicians and their audiences. Against the expanding backdrop of fascism, the linkage of music, democracy, and America seemed especially potent. "Jazz, black and white, and democracy go hand in hand," as a *Down Beat* letter writer concerned about the threat of "Hitlerism" put it in 1941. "One cannot exist while the other is suppressed." These swing virtues were at times justified and were widely and proudly acknowledged by the music's supporters. "A man who improvises with a musical instrument is using the same freedom as that exercised by an editorial writer who spouts his own ideas, or an architect who throws over past ideas and builds a house of glass," said Benny Goodman.[37] But at times these beliefs bordered on a self-righteousness that made it possible to justify social practices that contradicted these stated ideals. Such inconsistencies provide an entry point through which to examine the broader political impulses of the 1930s.

This "swing ideology" needs to be sited within the larger discourse of "Americanism" of the 1930s and 1940s. Emerging in the early decades of the century as a result of Americanization campaigns during the first World War, scientific management practices, and the diffusion of

"American" cultural values through the mass media, Americanism provided a vocabulary for articulating a variety of often-contradictory political programs. The Americanist ideology combined a strong nationalistic current with a deep faith in democracy; indeed, democracy had seemingly reached its ultimate expression in the United States. Americanism revered national traditions while maintaining a belief in a better future achieved through progressive reform. It held that the interests of the individual were compatible with those of the community, that a harmony of interests made social cooperation both inevitable and desirable. Swing's ideology, as articulated by both its artists and enthusiasts, shared in these assumptions. The swing ideology expressed reverence for such cherished American ideas as liberty, democracy, tolerance, and equality, while holding firmly to the conviction that the experience of swing was both sign and engine of a fundamentally rational and ever-improving American society. Not coincidentally, the decline of this "working-class Americanism" as a salient political language among U.S. industrial workers after 1946 coincided with the inability of swing to maintain its mass audience in the late 1940s.[38]

Nowhere were the politics of swing better epitomized than in *Down Beat*, the journal that did the most to shape critical and popular opinion on jazz during the swing era. Other journals directed primarily at musicians also made swing the focus of their coverage, while the trade journals *Variety* and *Billboard* included extensive coverage of the swing industry. Some publications were directed less at musicians than at swing enthusiasts of various levels of sophistication: *Swing* for jitterbugs, *Tempo* and *Jazz Hot* for Hot Club members, and, by 1940, the *H.R.S.* [Hot Record Society] *Rag* and *Jazz Information* for serious listeners and collectors. In addition, some general-interest publications ran regular articles on jazz by well-known writers: the *New Republic*, *Colliers*, *Saturday Evening Post*, the *New Yorker*, *Mademoiselle*. But *Down Beat* combined the most in-depth coverage of swing developments with a quality of Chicago earnestness, yellow sensationalism, risqué girlie photos, and distinctively freewheeling editorial atmosphere that made the exchange of sharp polemics irresistible to both writers and their audience. "Hardboiled and sentimental, inaccurate and thorough, unpredictable and consistent, patriotic and rebellious, idealistic and cynical," charged one writer, "the paradoxical 'Beat' is the image of the screwball business it serves and the direct reflection of the God-damndest staff that ever handled a magazine." In this editorial climate, paeans to America as the land of racial opportunity coexisted with blackface-style depictions of jazz musicians dressed in African tribal garb and speaking in Joel Chandler–like dialect; musicians were occasionally referred to as "jigs." Celebrations of American democracy and toleration overlapped with editorials titled "Communists and Nazis Should Be Run out of the Country."[39]

At the time of its founding in 1934, no other American magazine gave regular attention to African-American music. *Down Beat* proudly noted its editorial policy of judging musicians "strictly on their ability and not on any basis of the complexion of their skin," and ventured that "most white musicians do not recognize color lines in music." This became the dominant trope of the magazine's editors. Hailing America as a land of racial equality and opportunity, the magazine reported the progress toward racial equality taking place within the music profession. In an editorial criticizing the decision by the Daughters of the American Revolution to prohibit Marian Anderson from singing in Constitution Hall, the editors again voiced a familiar refrain: "There are no color lines in music."[40]

Efforts at integrating jazz were generally noted with approval. "With the popularity of swing music (in which the Negro is at his finest) mixed orchestras have been quite common in recording studios, and in clubs where white musicians have sat in and jammed with colored musicians; and fine colored arrangers have sold many arrangements to top-notch white swing bands." Bemoaning "a world sick with carbuncles of hate, ravished with fevers of race discrimination, and nauseated by dictatorships," *Down Beat* noted with "a great deal of pleasure" Goodman's hiring of Teddy Wilson, whom it described as "a colored boy of great talent." Then followed the predictable creed: "We still like to believe that regardless of race, creed or color we are all Americans, and that as Americans we are all free and equal, and deserving of the respect and admiration of our fellow men according to the extent of our abilities and talents." Ironically, the editorial reserved its greatest praise for

Goodman's other pianist, Jess Stacy, who in a "noble gesture" of "rare sportsmanship" stood nightly "in the shadow of the colored man" to enjoy, "without the slightest trace of resentment," Wilson's genius. And the magazine hedged its bets on the controversy, balancing a front-page review by Hammond of the Goodman quartet's success in Dallas with a more skeptical article: "Can a Negro Play His Best in a White Band? Goodman Quartet Proves Artistry Can Overcome Prejudice—But Is Idea Good?"[41]

Down Beat also seemed to back away from the prospect of an integrated big band, as opposed to a combo playing between regular sets. Commenting on the third failure to sustain a mixed band in Harlem, it argued that such experiments aroused racial prejudice and focused attention on social instead of musical values. Although music was a "democracy of talent" with "no racial lines," the editors asserted, "real democracy is equality of opportunity, not the fact that a Negro can sit side by side with a white, BUT THAT HE CAN BUILD A BAND AS GOOD AS CASA LOMA OR BENNY GOODMAN." In a symposium titled "Should Negro Musicians Play in White Bands?" occasioned by Goodman's adding Charlie Christian and Fletcher Henderson to his regular big band, the journal solicited a variety of opinions from other bandleaders. The editors themselves claimed a position of neutrality on the issue, stating their intention to get musicians to *"think* about [the issue] instead of feeling about it," and noting critically that most musicians opposed to integration refused to give their names. "Free expression of opinion—WHATEVER IT IS! in free America! Criticism, whether it be good or bad—WITHOUT FEAR OF ARREST OR PUNISHMENT." "One thing sure, we want to see a square deal," the article concluded. "And any American, no matter what his race, his color, or his creed, is entitled to that."[42]

Music was depicted as the ultimate American melting pot, an occupation that traditionally welcomed people from a range of ethnic backgrounds. *Down Beat* stressed the advantages of cultural pluralism to both the assimilated and the assimilators. Efforts to organize an all-Jewish symphony in a midwestern city provoked an editorial extolling "the stimulation of creative impulses that comes from the exchange of ideas and the intermingling of different racial stocks." But such pluralism required "the modifying influences of American free thought" in order to turn those stocks into "real Americans." "We don't want large groups of unassimilated peoples here perpetuating un-American ideals, and breeding hates among themselves and disrespect for American institutions." This nativist strain sounded most stridently in a screed against Communists and Nazis, who, the editor warned, were stealthily scheming to take control of the American Federation of Musicians. *Down Beat* promised to expose "how these foreign rats bore from within to undermine our country, our ideals and our free institutions . . . they 'howl' for fair play and freedom with which to carry on their bastardly [*sic*] work unhindered, trying to destroy the very government which grants them those privileges of living as free and untrammeled men in a world surrounded by fear, treachery and tyranny!" Elsewhere the magazine argued the essential equivalence of communism and fascism, both being systems that "feed on hate" and "sacrifice the individual to a one-party dictatorship which regiments and purges every fragment of society to its will."[43]

At the same time that it printed Hammond's left-leaning pieces, *Down Beat* expressed a deep suspicion of the Popular Front. Perennially concerned about Communist infiltration of musicians' locals, one editorial warned readers how "professional propagandists and party workers . . . take money from your union treasury under the false impression that it is being donated to charitable and patriotic institutions but which in reality goes to support Communist Party propaganda, under the clever disguise of these 'Trojan Horse' institutions, that they control and run behind a camouflaged 'united front' of misled but decent American citizens." An unusual front-page editorial excoriated Hammond for supporting the Citizens' Committee for Harry Bridges, citing the need for Americans to pull together against Stalin and Hitler. The debate continued through several issues, with a letter of rebuttal by Hammond and a follow-up editorial.[44]

Any suggestion that the swing fraternity itself harbored racial bias was met defensively. In response to rumors that Paramount Picture executives had blocked the appearance of Teddy Wilson with the Goodman band in *The Big Broadcast of 1937*, substituting Jess Stacy in musical sequences actually performed by Wilson, *Down Beat* published an editorial berating the black press for "building resentment in the hearts of colored people over an imagined race discrimination that never took place." Citing Goodman's denial of the story, the editorial warned that waving the "editorial red flag" in front of "sincere people" could erode racial goodwill and understanding built up over years. "The plight of the Negro Musician is difficult enuf, without further endangering his position by feeding the fires of racial animosity," it warned. But the following year the magazine reported the same incident, this time as an example of racial progress; noting the commercial success of Goodman's mixed group in New York City, Paramount executives this time actually requested the quartet, which included both Wilson and Lionel Hampton. A similar issue arose in 1941 when the black press charged *Down Beat* with racism for not awarding Duke Ellington the top ranking in its annual poll. In response, the magazine published an article by Ellington himself criticizing those in the press who suggested the possibility that the poll was racially biased.[45]

The sharpest exchanges occurred not over integration or bias in the swing industry but over the issue that won Hammond notoriety: who played better jazz, whites or blacks, and why. Paul Eduard Miller concluded, like Hammond, that "Negroes are superior. As regards technique, emotional expression, originality of phrasing, and rhythmic impulse they are supreme, and any argument to the contrary is mere sophistry, the philosophy of a misled neophyte." Black superiority sprang from "tradition," according to Miller, an innate familiarity with unspecified "essential requirements of swing" that white musicians had to "laboriously" strive to acquire. As a result "the important landmarks in the process of evolution [of jazz] are curiously though definitely all very dark in colour." In a rebuttal the next month, Reed Dickerson charged Miller with drawing "a color line in jazz" that had never been there before. Citing Goodman, Beiderbecke, and Joe Venuti as counterexamples, he argued that "it is high time we stop wasting our energies classifying musicians according to skin pigment, nationality, or religion." Dickerson acknowledged two factors that would tend to support black superiority in jazz: "a certain vitality and abandon which most white men either lack or are reluctant to express," and the fact that black musicians had no other musical outlet than jazz. The real distinction was not between races, according to Dickerson, but between "classical" and "romantic" schools of jazz; if the former included more whites and the latter more blacks, musicians were perfectly capable of crossing categories. Clarinetist Buster Bailey "betrays hardly a negro trait," for example, while trombonist Jack Teagarden "is essentially negro in his conceptions."[46]

Essentially negro: Even while claiming to call into question the color line, Dickerson betrayed an assumption of racial essentialism that pervaded nearly all writing about jazz. One could argue whether black jazz was superior to white, but difference was taken for granted. The issue was not necessarily biological. "Any good scientist will tell you there's no difference between the blood of a Negro and the blood of a white man. But you can still tell the color of a jazz musician by listening to the music he plays," wrote Marvin Freedman. "White jazz is colder, cleaner, more gracious; black music is richer, looser, more relaxed." And black jazz was clearly in the ascendant, as it had been since the beginning of swing. "There's no white vitality anywhere in jazz," he charged. The successful white bands—Artie Shaw, Glenn Miller—represented diluted versions of the Basie band, while "Charlie Barnet's [white] band is as black a band as you'll ever hear." "In the last year or so you hear white musicians say that they've got to play like colored musicians, or their music doesn't swing. Even a great musician like Harry James forsakes the white cause, and carries out the ideas of colored musicians."[47]

Occasional articles did argue the superiority of "white" jazz. A 1938 piece claimed that while blacks excelled as soloists, white bands had the advantage as ensembles, and "only Ellington has an organization worthy of being called an orchestra." An angry rebuttal shot back that the writer was either a "musical moron" or prejudiced; the popular white swing bands merely copied blacks, and moreover, in jazz, ensemble work was secondary to individual improvising ability. But rarely did writers doubt either the superior originality or ability of African-American players (or that an essential difference existed between the musicianship of blacks and whites).[48]

One sign of the development of swing's critical community was a growing concern with origins (as in Goodman's Carnegie retrospective), with getting the historical record straight, which provided another ground for racial controversy. By the mid-1930s jazz critics had acquired an acute interest in the music's historical origins, and occasional disputes flared over the question of primacy in the invention of jazz. Marshall Stearn's serialized history of jazz, which began appearing in *Down Beat* during the summer of 1936, generated continuous controversy with its claims about origins and influences. Both *Down Beat* and *Metronome* published claims by Nick La Rocca, founder of the Original Dixieland Jazz Band, that his all-white band had "invented" jazz. La Rocca's band, organized in New Orleans in 1908 and brought to Chicago in 1914, is credited with popularizing both the word *jass* and creating a vogue for the music during a four-week stand at Reisenweber's in New York City and through recordings made in 1917. But few critics accepted his claim that New Orleans' blacks had merely imitated the ODJB. It is revealing of the critical climate that La Rocca felt compelled to write a letter to *Down Beat* afterward to allay any impression that his claim to be the originator of jazz was motivated by race. "Please allow me to state most emphatically that I am in no wise prejudiced against the negro race," he said. Similar historical debates among critics took place regarding the first instance of an integrated jazz band. Although Goodman was popularly associated with breaking the color line, various writers gave that distinction to Benny Carter, Mezz Mezzrow, and others.[49]

Just Rich Men's Sons

Who were these contentious interpreters and historians of swing? Jazz criticism was, during the swing era and afterward, a preserve of white males. While black newspapers such as the *Chicago Defender* and *New York Amsterdam News* regularly covered jazz events on their entertainment pages, the coverage was limited to straight reportage, often based on press releases, with virtually no critical commentary. *The Crisis* occasionally profiled jazz artists; its piece on Benny Goodman was written by Hammond, a director of the NAACP. But according to Hammond, NAACP leaders like Roy Wilkins and Walter White were "typical black bourgeoisie" who "couldn't stand" jazz, blues, gospel, and other forms of African-American popular music.[50] *Down Beat* did hire an African-American, Onah Spencer, as Harlem correspondent in 1938, but its action appears to have been unique. (The black press had its own critics, of course, like the *Amsterdam News*'s Dan Burley.) Women were similarly excluded from the critical discourse. With the exception of Helen Oakley, a Canadian-born writer who contributed to various publications, including *Jazz Hot* and *Down Beat*, jazz critics were men whose social backgrounds resembled Hammond's.

These white male swing enthusiasts were bound by a strong sense of group loyalty. While committed political activists congregated in cells, swing fanciers came together in organizations known as Hot Clubs. Founded by European jazz fans on the Continent around 1934, the United Hot Clubs of America (UHCA) was launched with a flourish in late 1935 (the same year as Goodman's Palomar triumph and "The Music Goes 'Round and Around." A declaration by the new secretary general of the International Federation of Hot Clubs, Marshall Stearns, appeared in the Paris-based *Jazz Hot:* "The time has come when a worldwide organization of Hot Clubs, exercising a tremendous influence for the betterment of swing music along many fronts, is no longer an idle dream," he wrote, his language capturing the republican flavor of the movement. "At last, the numerous organizations of the western hemisphere, composed of truly appreciative hot-fans, will have the opportunity to unite and make their convictions felt as one all-powerful man. Such an organization will have tremendous power, and justly so, for there is much that needs to be done." Stearns described the aims of the federation as "the universal progress of swing music," which would be accomplished by four primary activities: commissioning "special hot records" whose personnel were to be chosen by "international committee"; reissuing "rare old classics"; staging jazz concerts by "orchestras freely offered by the record companies"; and publicizing the accomplishments of swing musicians, "as well as generally propagating the swing-gospel, throughout the world." Hot Club chapters were founded that fall in New York, Chicago, Boston, Los Angeles, Cleveland, Birmingham, and New Haven, where the Yale Hot Club, under the direction of Stearns, was recognized as the American base of operations. French critic Hugues Panassie was named as president of the international federation, Hammond as president of UHCA; news of the various Hot Clubs appeared regularly in *Jazz Hot*.[51]

In a sense the Hot Clubs served as a union of jazz consumers. By organizing into similar clubs, Europeans had been able to exert pressure on recording companies to issue jazz disks, and their American counterparts hoped to mobilize a comparable collective action. A chief organizer in New York was Milton Gabler, owner of the Commodore Music Shop, the retail epicenter of swing recordings, who looked on the clubs as a way of promoting sales of classic jazz reissues. To this end, clubs sponsored a number of notable swing performances: the Goodman orchestra's pathbreaking stand at the Urban Room in Chicago, which held spectators rapt for more than three hours; and a March 1937 jam session in New York City that was cohosted, photographed, and reported by *Life* magazine. This collusion led to a falling out with Hammond, who charged that the "good old UHCA was used as a pawn by determined and competing interests," including Gabler, *Life*, Brunswick records, and Irving Mills, who managed Ellington. Were Hot Clubs really, as they claimed, charitable organizations trying to erase swing's stigma of "sensationalism and puerile ignorance," asked *Down Beat*, or an attempt by Gabler to sell "a bill of goods" to the swing public?[52]

These contretemps at the national level notwithstanding, most Hot Club activity at the local level was amicable. For the cost of a ten- or fifteen-dollar club charter plus a two-dollar individual membership fee, members got free copies of official UHCA recordings, a magazine subscription, lapel insignias, and discounts on musical equipment. They provided forums for members to trade and listen to records, exchange discographic intelligence, and occasionally meet musicians and sponsor concerts. For example, the Newark Hot Club, founded in 1939, met Monday nights in a Jewish community center—the Fuld Neighborhood House—located near the black neighborhood. A critic who joined as a teenager in 1940 recalled the club as a "family," a "tightly knit band despite wildly disparate origins." The members were not jazz *buffs*, the sort of people who called Louis Armstrong "Satchmo," but *fans*: "Cadre, hardcore. The kind who seized you by the arm and told you that the clarinet solo by Bill Creger on *She Wouldn't Do What I Asked Her To* by Naylor's Seven Aces (Gennett 5376) was the best damned unknown solo by a white musician . . . and so on." By contrast, the Boston Hot Club, which met in a rented clubhouse on Massachusetts

Avenue directly above the headquarters of the Socialist Labor Party, comprised mainly students and recent graduates of Harvard.[53]

Many such fans were to be found at elite universities. Marshall Stearns, a young professor of English literature at Yale during the 1930s, attracted several protégés, including George Avakian, who began contributing to *Down Beat* as an undergraduate before becoming a producer for Columbia records after the war. George Simon, who produced most of *Metronome's* swing coverage, assigning letter grades to performances, and George Frazier, known for the biliously patrician tone of his reviews, were both recent Harvard graduates. Frank Norris, who freelanced for various publications, including *Town and Country* and the *Saturday Evening Post,* was educated at Princeton. Universities had been centers of jazz enthusiasm during the 1920s, and during the early post-Crash years, when the music and recording industries were crippled by the Depression, the Ivy League sustained its demand for hot music. This was the period during which many of the most important critics were in college, presumably forming their musical tastes.

This entente between patrician writers and African-American musicians, of whom even those from middle-class backgrounds (Ellington, Lunceford, Henderson, and many others) existed in a distinct caste within American society, was not unprecedented. Elite universities had since the late nineteenth century produced young men eager for "authentic" experience of various kinds who gravitated to the bohemian quarters of cities like New York where ethnic boundaries were blurred.[54] But never before had an elite vanguard exerted such an influence on both the production and the consumption of a subcultural form, functioning at once as patrons of particular artists and as evangelists to the broader American public. This is not to claim that swing artists—black or white—were pawns who depended on the good graces and marketing talents of critics and impresarios. The role played by the critics was limited, and often overshadowed by the businessmen who operated the large booking agencies and more directly brought the artists to their public—and vice versa. These realms overlapped; Hammond and later Leonard Feather operated easily in both, and an early theory for the rise of swing proposed that "influential young admen, just arriving at positions of importance, created a wide market for jazz by loading commercial radio programs with the hot music they had learned to like a decade before at college."[55] In any event, these critics did force Americans to confront the fact that a conspicuous portion of their popular culture was undeniably indebted to African-Americans. By observing the rituals of swing subculture and reporting them to a broader public, these writers helped create and shape both the expectations of the swing public and, to a degree, the behavior and self-conception of the musicians themselves.

Occasionally the relationship between critics and artists was inscribed in the music itself. "Harvard Blues," a piece recorded by the Basie orchestra in 1941, provides such a recorded icon, its ventriloquism marking the intersection of swing's producers and mediators. George Frazier wrote the lyrics, which concern the ennui of a Harvard student, after seeing Basie perform at the Ritz in Boston. "I wear Brooks' clothes and white shoes all the time," Rushing sings: "Get two Cs, a D, and think check-from-home sublime." "I don't keep dogs or women in my room," goes the second verse, "But I love my Vincennes, baby, until the day of dawn." Arranged by altoist Tab Smith and sung by Jimmy Rushing, the great Oklahoma City–born tenor blues-shouter, the tune featured a much-praised two-chorus saxophone introduction by tenor Don Byas and a trombone obbligato behind Rushing's lyrics.[56]

This kind of inverted blackface, comparing the cryptic ennui of a jaded Harvard sophisticate to the sexual or socioeconomic sorrow usually depicted in blues lyrics, could be interpreted as an expression of existential solidarity. It may have been a way of paying tribute to an admired artist, or merely an inside joke. Swing bands often had little control over their repertoire, and if Frazier had lined up a recording date, performing his lyric would not have seemed an excessive favor to Basie. A parody of collegiate life may also have been intended. On the other hand, a recording of the Yale "Whiffenpoof" song was a national hit for Andy Kirk's big band. Swing artists were often invited to receive unofficial "honorary degrees"; Harvard students, for example, awarded Count Basie a doctorate in "swingology" in 1942. Enthusiasts at Yale and Harvard extended the schools' rivalry to swing. A disgruntled Harvard student complained in 1937 of student ignorance and even the lack of a Hot Club, while Yale's club, under Marshall Stearns, was the headquarters of UHCA. Harvard tightened the race in 1939, establishing a collection of swing records in Widener Library. When Goodman donated 100 of his rare disks, President James Conant announced a $250 annual budget to build a collection. For swing enthusiasts, this kind of playful link between jazz and the academy could take place only at an elite level; insiders looked with disdain on Kay Kyser, one of the most popular novelty-style bandleaders of the swing era, whose popularity was largely based on the radio show "Kay Kyser's College of Musical Knowledge." But successful bandleaders from Goodman to Calloway adapted the format for their own radio programs.[57]

A similar move, less ventriloquism than race/class inversion, occurs on the Lunceford band's recording of "Slumming on Park Avenue," a sendup of the white socialites who poured into Harlem's exotic nightclubs and speakeasies during Prohibition. After the ensemble states the theme, with short solo spots for trumpet, piano, and saxophone, a vocal chorus suggests an anthropological excursion to the exotic East Side. Safely disguised by pretentious eyeglasses, the slummers grimace and sniff at the Park Avenue natives, turning the tables on the privileged classes who regularly invade their precincts. Like "Harvard Blues," "Slumming" was written by a white, Irving Berlin, and performed by blacks.

While swing critics reveled in their associations with African-American musicians willing cheerfully to accept Ivy League honorary degrees, some enthusiasts were less amused by these incidents of cultural exchange. "I am getting a little weary . . . with having to accept as gospel the *ex cathedra* pronouncements of the scion of an old New York family, of a sometime Harvardian, of an English instructor at New Haven," complained a *New Republic* reader. "I would like to suggest furthermore that the words 'terrific,' 'solid,' 'simplicity,' 'sincerity,' and 'inviolate' have after all outlived their usefulness in critical writings." A young Boston heiress who had herself written a tune for the Basie band inquired in *Down Beat* "why they can't get colored critics, who really know what they are talking about, and can sense true jazz far better than us whites. After all, they ARE jazz, practically. I find that an ordinary colored tap dance teacher knows much more regarding jazz, swing, etc., than one of our most famous critics by just talking to him."

For that matter, wondered another reader, why did it take "a Javanese or a Frenchman or some other foreigner to become our noted critics on a naturally American form of music—jazz?" Even *Down Beat* conceded that "the best work, the most serious, painstaking research has been done on American jazz by foreigners: Swedes, Englishmen, Frenchmen, Lowlanders."[58]

The fact that the critical evaluation of big-band jazz was largely in the hands of recent Ivy League graduates and foreigners raised a question that resonated throughout the swing era: What gave someone the right to label himself (rarely herself) a critic? On what basis were critical standards established? As writers took sides in the endless and sharply polemical debates that ran through the pages of *Down Beat*, many wondered how such disputes could be resolved. The inherent subjectivity of criticism was of course nothing new, but the apparent speed with which jazz emerged and was taken seriously had left the institutions and conventions of a critical community—journals, academic departments, and the like—little time to establish their legitimacy or authority. These issues were raised repeatedly not only by fans and musicians, who were occasionally awarded space in music publications to voice their displeasure with the way in which their music was being reviewed, but by the critics themselves. The problem of jazz criticism was twofold: *who* was doing it, and *how*.[59]

Writing that could be construed as jazz criticism, assuming a loose definition of the words *jazz* and *criticism*, had been produced for more than a decade before the advent of swing in 1935. In the United States, criticism had been published as early as 1917 and throughout the 1920s in such publications as *Literary Digest, Harper's, Atlantic Monthly, The Dial*, and the *New York Times Magazine*. Carl Van Vechten's articles on African-American show business, published by *Vanity Fair* in 1925, Abbe Niles's music reviews for *The Bookman*, published in 1928 and 1929, and especially Robert Darrell's reviews of the late 1920s and early 1930s for *Phonograph Monthly Review* and *Disques* are regarded as the best of the early criticism.[60]

In Europe, jazz criticism had appeared as early as 1919, written by the Belgian Robert Goffin, who published *Aux frontières du jazz* in 1932. Magazines in Britain (*Melody Maker, Rhythm, The Gramophone*, and *Hot*

News), France (*Revue du jazz* and *Jazz Tango*), and Sweden (*Orkester Journalen*) included some coverage of jazz as early as the mid-1920s. The dominant European figure, Hugues Panassie, who exerted an influence comparable to Hammond's in the United States, began publishing regular reviews in *Jazz Tango*. His influential volume, *Le Jazz Hot*, was published in 1934, the English translation appearing in 1936, while the monthly *Jazz Hot*, which published articles by a number of the most prominent American writers on jazz, appeared in 1935. But with the exception of Hammond, who had traveled and written for European publications, little if any of this critical literature was known to swing-era critics, who had developed their appreciation for jazz during the early 1930s, when writings concerned with jazz, as well as the music itself, had largely dropped out of sight. The critics of the era, writing regularly for *Down Beat* and *Metronome*, were in a position of creating critical standards and criteria *ex nihilo*, based on personal preferences and their often-impressionistic listening habits. As George Frazier put it in an early survey of his colleagues, "Swing criticism, like swing music, should send you."[61] Never before, it seemed, had an art form arisen so quickly or been so in need of informed criticism.

That their criticism lacked conceptual or institutional foundations was not lost on these writers. While acknowledging their superiority to daily newspaper reporters, who often simply rewrote press releases, writers for the swing-oriented publications engaged in ruthless self-criticism. Under headlines like "Says Most Critics Are Not Qualified" and "They Don't Look at Both Sides of the Question," critics lambasted themselves as "dogmatic," "misguided," guilty of "deplorable lapses of taste." "When will people remember that a critic approaching jazz must have the same approach as a critic viewing any other art?" complained an erudite critic. "Yet what jazz critic has read Aristotle, Longinus, Horace, Du Bellay, Sidney, Boileau, Dryden, Pope, Wordsworth, Taine, St. Beuve, Arnold, Spingarn, Bergson, Croce, Kruth?" Musicians could hardly be blamed for regarding the average critic as "an ignorant sonovabitch that needs a poke up side the snoot."[62]

Occasionally musicians were enlisted to address the problem of defining critical standards. Benny Carter dismissed critics with a quip: "They sing not, neither do they play, hence forget them or forgive them

. . . for they do not what they know." But Ellington had no quarrel with the project of criticism, acknowledging "that any art worthy of the name requires its own critics, whose responsibility is to 'maintain and elevate standards,' the same principle applying to any respected profession." Nor was the problem that critics were not musicians, as some argued. "In fact," he asserted, "the critic is more likely to deliver impartially if he is not personally musically talented." The problem stemmed instead from the fact that musicians believed criticism should be based upon the artist's intent, not his or her sincerity, while critics appeared to feel a duty to "expose" commercial leanings or other deviations from the high-minded pursuit of artistic excellence. The normally politic-to-a-fault Ellington singled out, in addition to Hammond, Stearns for his "misinformation or inaccuracy," Oakley for her "hasty judgment" and "impressionability," Frazier for "flagrant overstatement," and Panassie for his "closed mind." Writing on behalf of all musicians, he called for "honest constructive criticism by persons familiar with both the fundamentals and business of music, and conscientious about their responsibility to musicians for maintaining professional standards."[63]

The sharpest criticism came from the writers themselves. *Down Beat*'s editor contributed an article titled, with typical subtlety, "What the Hell Good Is a Swing Music Critic?" which singled out Frazier, Hammond, and Simon for particular censure. "There are no intelligent critics," declared Carl Cons. "There are only press agents for their own artistic prejudices. And finding an impartial and intelligent piece of criticism is like finding a period in a haystack of adjectives." Like Benny Carter, critics seemed to be sensitive to the fact that many of them lacked musical knowledge. "Just about all the silly, snippy, smatterings of the reviewers' are just such because of one thing: THE LACK OF ACTUAL EXPERIENCE," *Metronome* concluded. "They don't know WHY WHAT HAPPENS WHEN. All their stuff is based upon a view from the outside in, and usually a very warped view at that."[64]

Most of *Metronome*'s swing coverage was handled by George Simon (often writing under pseudonyms), who prided himself on having acquired musical experience playing drums with a big band at college, while Hammond was an accomplished classical viola player. Other critics, like Otis Ferguson, acquired an insider's knowledge of jazz not by playing an instrument but by close association with musicians. But many "authorities" were thought to be virtually indistinguishable from their readers. "Very often they're just rich men's sons who buy batches of phonograph records with the money which their dads had sent them at college to pay laundry bills," *Metronome* asserted. "They listen to the records, not knowing what to listen for, and proceed to form all sorts of opinions. After a while they form more concrete opinions, and, talking big, convince an uninformed editor that they know all about swing. And their stuff gets into print."[65]

A few critics strove to develop a rationale for criticism. Panassie, for example, described the "chief aim of the critic" as being "to recognize the beauties and virtues of a musician or a music, and to write about them in order to bring them to the public's attention, to make the readers understand the reasons for his enthusiasm so that they can share them." Another writer, citing the number of "once great artists now languishing in insane asylums, jails, and hospitals, their minds shattered by lives of debauchery and overindulgence," dismissed musicians as being "in the moron class"; fellow critics had an obligation to develop intellect, good taste, and delicacy as prerequisites for their calling. "We cannot dispense with criticism," he argued. "Jazz musicians must be brought to realize that. Perhaps if they were able to read and understand [Oscar] Wilde's excellent treatise on 'the Critic as Artist' they would sooner be resigned to the truth." Acknowledging his colleagues' lapses, the writer maintained that their work "is the essential part of the creative spirit. It is the critic who throws the pure light of reason upon each work of art to determine its worth and value. In many cases the artist is dependent upon the critic to explain and translate his creations not only to his patrons but often to himself." Not surprisingly, this writer found being introduced to musicians as a critic comparable to announcing he had bubonic plague, and considered escaping "to a convenient rest-room to dissolve in tears."[66]

The issue of musical ignorance and a lack of critical criteria was not the only area of contention among the critics of swing. By the late 1930s a notable rift had opened between writers favorable to swing and those who dismissed most swing as nonjazz, a commercial travesty. Yale undergraduate George Avakian, who later supervised Columbia's first jazz reissue series, lashed out at the musical clichés of the "swing craze," which he distinguished from "the golden age of jazz." "Instead of a band like Duke's or Fletcher's, with first-class instrumentalists playing intelligent stuff, we have meaningless noise thrown at us by incompetent bands whose leaders are flashy second raters," he charged. He lambasted swing's simpleminded and repetitive arrangements, designed to appeal to the most undiscriminating listener; its trumpet blasts and legato clarinet runs, "hacksaw" saxophone work, and "tom-tom interludes." Avakian rejected the notion that swing was an evolved form of jazz, built on the great innovators of the 1920s. "Jazz is jazz; it can't be modernized or streamlined," he wrote. "King Oliver was playing as hot as anyone can play in 1922, and the records prove it." Deeming recordings "the sole preservation of music," Avakian by 1939 was ready to give up on live music and take refuge in records: "So it's back to the ivory tower and dust off the old turntable." Expressing a similar sentiment, a group of "hot music addicts" in Los Angeles signed a petition in 1940 protesting some of the bands Hammond was recording for Columbia, denouncing him as a "rat" for "selling out to commercials" and reportedly delaying reissues of Armstrong, Beiderbecke, and Bessie Smith recordings.[67]

These purists generated equally splenetic reactions from their critical and musical antagonists. One writer attacked record collectors as "jerks," insincere "bores" more concerned with the commercial utility of a rare record than with the quality of its musical performance. The article quoted Dixieland guitarist Eddie Condon, who compared collectors to "gnats": "Everywhere you go, and always in the way; always coming back; no way to get rid of 'em. They ask who played second kazoo on a 1927 Okeh disc I don't even remember making." Another writer offered this "formula" for becoming a jazz critic:

> Spend four years at least in an exclusive eastern college. Become acquainted with old Bix and Louis records and talk about these men in hushed whispers. Never listen to a record made after 1936 . . . it just can't be good, it's too new. Get to know a few old musicians and give them some publicity. It doesn't matter if they can only play in two keys and have no technique. Remember, if it's old, it's good. Sneer at all records made by Dorsey, Goodman, Miller, Barnet, [Jan] Savitt,

[Woody] Herman, Crosby. Make some musician your god (some old musician—don't forget) and refuse to talk about any other musician in the same breath. Above all, remain completely ignorant of the technical aspects of music. Don't know anything about chords, about tone, or keys. That's *commercial.* In short, become a romantic, a charlatan, a poseur, a pseudo-intellectual, an aesthetic snob, and you are well on the way to success.

This recipe suggested a new negative image of the jazz critic: musically ignorant yet socially privileged, elitist, obsessed with the past and with its commodified traces, rare recordings.[68]

Disenchantment with the existing periodicals' sensationalism and anti-intellectualism, coupled with the desire for a more serious critical study of jazz, gave rise in the late 1930s to a number of short-lived "little" jazz magazines. *H.R.S. Rag*, associated with the Hot Record Society in New York City and edited by Russell Sanjek and Heywood Hale Broun, son of the famous journalist, was formed in 1938 and lasted two years. Its competitor, associated with the rival Commodore Record Shop, was *Jazz Information*, formed in 1939 by a group of Columbia students, including Ralph Gleason and Gene Williams, which also lasted for two years. According to Sanjek, the pronounced difference in attitude between these two groups resulted in a "kind of Montague-Capulet situation." The former clique took a relatively lighthearted approach to their avocation, while the latter was serious and scholarly; neither could abide the other.[69]

In 1940 Hammond and two *Down Beat* colleagues founded *Music and Rhythm*, a combined trade journal and fan magazine in which Hammond editorialized against discrimination in the recording companies, radio networks, and musicians' union. "We believe 100% in modern democratic unionism, and will . . . challenge exploitation of artists, racial discrimination, unfair practices, insufficient wage-scale, undue commercial pressure wherever we find it," wrote Carl Cons, who sold his share in *Down Beat* to join the new venture. One issue included a well-publicized attack by Hammond on his old comrade Benny Goodman for "bowing" to "popular tastes," "following the path laid down by his own imitators." Worse, wrote Hammond, Goodman "no longer defies convention by breaking down racial barriers, and thinks primarily of the commercial appeal of his music."[70] These fault lines within the swing community foreshadowed the more corrosive schisms that developed after 1945 between traditional jazz enthusiasts and proponents of the variant of swing that came to be known as bebop. Several of the main combatants in this postwar controversy had participated in the earlier swing wars, while others were formed in the already-polarized critical climate of the late 1930s and 1940s.

The divisions and rivalries within the community of swing-era jazz writers reflected a number of things: the age of the participants, nearly all of whom were under thirty, as were the musicians they wrote about and the audiences for whom those musicians played; a jazz ethos that celebrated the virtues of controlled competitive rivalry and individual accomplishment harmonized by group spirit; the related tendency of jazz writers to serve as advocates as much as critical commentators, with the sort of allegiance to a particular orchestra one would expect in a fan rooting for a baseball franchise. Moreover, the line between critic and publicist was often hard to define because some writers had direct commercial interests in particular musicians or ensembles.

These tendencies were not unique to swing, of course. The interest in historical origins and genealogies, the preoccupation with a strict canon of authenticity, the disagreement over critical standards, the disdain for the market—all these impulses, formed in a contentious climate of intolerance and sectarianism, were typical of other twentieth-century artistic and literary movements. And they expressed a pervasive cultural pattern of the 1930s: the valorization of commitment, whether to a political cause, a literary movement, or a community.[71]

But a large part of the aura of combativeness that surrounded swing had to do with its own distinctive qualities, both formal and sociological. Big-band jazz was a cultural form whose meanings were overdetermined, "up for grabs," open to a variety of interpretations by an audience that brought strikingly different assumptions and expectations to the music. Swing music could be held up as a proletarian protest music, a cultural expression of oppressed Americans that carried an implicit political message. It could just as easily be hailed as a product of the American way of life, the flowering of those qualities of individual liberty, social equality, and illustrious ethnic pluralism thought to be unique to the United States. Thirties jazz could be hailed as an authentic folk music, the end product of a lineage that began with work songs and spirituals. But it could also be reviled as trite commercialism: music debased by the need to win the widest possible segment of a new audience constituted by the new media of recordings, radio, and movies.

Swing's range of meanings was determined partly by variations in the music itself, differences in the expectations of its consumers and critics, and something more: the intrinsic difficulty raised for the dominant culture by a cultural form produced or associated with a marginalized group, in this case African-Americans. It also reflected the ambiguities implicit in the language of Americanism that held such currency in New Deal America and lent its vocabulary to a wide range of ideological causes. Swing participated in this larger discourse, and shared its tensions and contradictions.

Each of these interpretations was voiced by different members of the small and relatively homogeneous group who wrote about swing. But divided as they were on many critical issues, these writers by definition shared an opinion that distinguished them both from most Americans and from many musicians: they conceived of big band jazz primarily as art music. It was to be appreciated for its own sake, apart from any utilitarian appeal as dance music. As Eric Hobsbawm has argued, American critics exerted less sway over popular taste than did their European counterparts, who controlled the flow of American recordings. American audiences were more likely to experience the music unmediated, live or through radio. As a result, the distinction between "authentic" jazz and commercial swing was less clear, and the power of commercial media greater.[72] Much as the critics were implicated in it, the music industry—the nexus of corporations, managers, and agencies that made swing available to consumers—was for the critics a corrupting influence, a necessary evil. Few were fully aware how deeply swing was indebted to the "culture industry" for its emergence and popularity, and to what extent the music was shaped by the intervention of the corporate apparatus that distributed it.

3

The Incorporation of Swing

In October 1938 the *New York Times* carried a front-page story on the Bach Society of New Jersey's campaign to halt radio broadcasts of "jazzed" versions of European concert music. The organization's president, Alfred Dennis, wrote of the "genuine distress to lovers of fine music" caused by the current "rage of playing classical and traditional songs over the radio in swing tempo." "Recently, on two occasions, we heard a jazz orchestra giving a rendition of Bach's 'Toccata in D Minor,' " Dennis complained. "All the beautiful fugue effects were destroyed by the savage slurring of the saxophone and the jungled discords of the clarinet. By no stretch of the imagination could such performances be tolerated except by people of no discrimination. As a group interested in bringing the best of Bach's music to the people in our State, we must protest against the jazzing of Bach's music. If this is permitted to go unchallenged, swing renditions of the Mass in E Minor will follow, offending listeners on both religious and aesthetic grounds." Suspend an offending station's license for a first offense, then revoke it, suggested the society, reported to comprise some of New Jersey's "most prominent persons." Swing would survive, Dennis reassured its less determined foes, because the supply of modern compositions was "endless."[1]

The practice of "swinging the classics" was a distinctive feature of swing through its peak years of the late 1930s and early 1940s. The list of composers "desecrated" by swing was a virtual *Who's Who* of European concert music. The Tommy Dorsey band had been among the earliest to participate, playing jazzed versions of Rimsky-Korsakoff's "Song of India" and Strauss's "Blue Danube." Earlier that year Dor-

94

sey's rendition of the Scottish folk song "Loch Lomond," sung by Maxine Sullivan, was cut off in midbroadcast by a Detroit station manager who had supplied a list of songs not to be jazzed, an order that was quickly rescinded. Goodman's "Let's Dance" was based on Carol Maria von Weber's "Invitation to the Dance." Raymond Scott drew on a Mozart theme for "In an Eighteenth-Century Drawing Room," while Larry Clinton transformed Debussy's "Reverie" into the hit "My Reverie." Flotow's "Martha" was "covered" by both Connie Boswell and Larry Clinton. Ravel's "Pavane" became "The Lamp Is Low"; fragments of Tchaikovsky's symphonies were transformed into "Moon Love" and "No Star Is Lost"; "Romeo and Juliet" yielded "Our Love." Alec Templeton recorded such tributes as "Mozart Matriculates," "Bach Goes to Town," and "Mendelssohn, I'll Mow You Down." Wagner and Liszt were similarly appropriated, particularly the latter's Hungarian Rhapsody No. 2. Folk songs also became swing numbers: "Comin' through the Rye" became "Swingin' through the Rye," while "Bei Mir Bist du Schön" was a big hit for the Goodman band (performed at Carnegie Hall). Even the songs of Stephen Foster ("I Dream of Jeanie with the Light Brown Hair") were performed endlessly.[2]

Widely reported in the media, the controversy over swinging the classics produced strong opinions among partisans on either side of the debate. For most, the salient issue was censorship, not aesthetics. One self-described "lover of good music" charged that penalizing jazzed versions of classics "would be just a bit against our much cherished freedom of speech." Another "private citizen" expressed a willingness to "defend to the death the right of any broadcasting station to put a broken-down jazz band on the air with a swing version of the Mass in B Minor." On the basis of mail it received, the *Times* concluded that regardless of their personal preference for jazzed classics, most listeners stood "shoulder to shoulder defending the greater issue" of freedom of expression. Pointing out that the Communications Act of 1934 specifically declined to give the Federal Communications Commission (FCC) power to censor or interfere with free speech, the *Times* averred that "science has made ... listener[s] the only censor[s] of radio in America" by allowing them to turn off programs or selections they deemed offensive.[3]

Others turned to the same historicist arguments used to defend swing from its moralist critics. Attempts to curtail the swinging of classics would fail, according to one listener, "because swing is a new form of an old eroticism, an eroticism as old as sex itself. And to the jitterbugs of swing nothing is sacred, let alone the classical music of dead men. To dipsy-doodle to Bach is the real McCoy for emotionalists, kinder-gartners in the evolution of the savage dance of ancient days." Those with proper erudition turned to the history of art music itself to rebut charges of desecration. Critic Olin Downes showed "that processes of rhythmical and harmonic and melodic variation had been present since music was consciously composed, and probably before that"; even such sacrosanct figures as Beethoven, Handel, Haydn, Rossini, and Debussy had engaged in it. "Copyright laws exist for the world of business and practical affairs," Downes asserted. "In the realm of art they are not wholly enforceable." An assistant program director for CBS pointed out that in the particular case of Bach, authenticity was a moot point; pianos had not existed when he composed, the organ was today virtually a different instrument, the full symphony was unknown to him, and Bach himself had constantly arranged the work of other composers for his own purposes. "It is a question whether Bach would have been more annoyed with modern symphony conductors or modern dance band conductors," he asserted.[4]

"Let us not forget that Johann Sebastian was once dismissed from a job as church organist because he improvised so much the hymn singers couldn't follow him," pointed out Paul Whiteman, arguing that there is "nothing inherently irreligious about swing, or four-four rhythm . . . a bad classical orchestra can mutilate Bach just as well as a poor swing band." Whiteman also echoed the argument made by Goodman, that popular treatments of the classics "invariably" increased the public's interest in the originals themselves, therefore providing a sense of cultural uplift.[5]

To be sure, taking the position that the FCC should avoid even the appearance of censoring radio was not to endorse the practice of swinging classics, and many expressed a sense that the whole controversy was regrettable, a matter of poor taste. Magazines solicited the views of various opinion makers. In a survey of Hollywood figures' position on the controversy, *Metronome* found that Cecil De Mille, John

Barrymore, Claudette Colbert, and W. C. Fields were opposed to the practice; Dorothy Lamour, George Raft, Shirley Ross, Fred Mac-Murray, Ginger Rogers, and Douglas Fairbanks saw no harm. Maxine Sullivan, whose "Loch Lomond" was the most celebrated of the remakes, wrote to Eleanor Roosevelt asking her advice on the issue. "My dear Miss Sullivan," the first lady responded, "I can't imagine what the songs you mention would be like in swing tempo, but there is nothing wrong in doing it. If people like it and you succeed, you will be doing other things. You cannot please everyone all the time." Presumably those "other things" would be more uplifting than jazzed classics, although Roosevelt was too diplomatic to make the point so baldly.[6]

Even members of the jazz community were critical. "They're desecrating American's beautiful old melodies and favorite music," charged Count Basie. "Mine is an out and out swing band, but I'll not go on the air if I have to resort to those beautiful compositions for my swing material." A *Down Beat* writer urged that "something should be done about the loose application of the word 'swing,' " which "now embraces not only the music which it was originally intended to describe, but likewise almost every conceivable form of jazz composition, arrangement, and technique." "There is a vast difference between a swing arrangement of a popular tune or a semi-classic and the truly rich and wholesome jungle jazz of Duke Ellington or Nat Leslie," he continued, and "swing fans of real discernment" should be able to "extricate the good from the bad."[7]

The proximate cause on which the controversy hinged—the Bach Society's petition—was quickly resolved, with the FCC suggesting only that broadcasters use "a high degree of discrimination" in selecting their programs. It is tempting to dismiss the whole episode as what would come to be known as a pseudo-event, its significance wildly exaggerated by news media, which generally adopted a tongue-in-cheek tone in their reporting of it. At most it would seem a reflection of the aspirations of popular swing musicians to elevate their music by associating it with the established canon of European art music, thereby gaining a certain type of cultural legitimacy. Or perhaps, to shade the point slightly differently, the musicians were attempting to undermine or subvert those very cultural hierarchies, by tweaking the notion of an autonomous tradition of art music that existed apart from and above the commercial market of popular taste.

While there is something to these interpretations, the craze of jazzed classics also points to the broader domain of the entire culture industry in and through which swing emerged in the 1930s. The reassurance offered to swing lovers by the Bach Society, that the supply of jazzable tunes was essentially unlimited, was not true. In fact the years during which swing peaked as a popular phenomenon was a period when the big-band repertoire had been constricted by a complex struggle between the guild of songwriters and publishers, American Society of Composers, Authors, and Publishers (ASCAP), which controlled rights to roughly 90 percent of those compositions, and the radio networks, without which commercial success for big bands was impossible. During the late 1930s ASCAP decided that the royalty fees paid by radio for the broadcast of music was inadequate. The ensuing campaign to pressure the networks to comply culminated in the ASCAP strike of 1941. Bandleaders, then, were inspired to "swing the classics" partly because those classics were in the public domain and could be per-formed without paying royalties; arrangements of such tunes could even bring royalty payments to the arranger.[8]

This struggle, which pitted two powerful industries against each other while leaving musicians in the crossfire, was only one eruption in the complex, large-scale, and stressful process of reconfiguration under-gone by the music industry concurrently with the reign of swing as American popular music. The period witnessed the participation of var-ious cultural institutions in a series of shifting feuds and alliances, con-solidating and increasing their own power as they attempted to van-quish rivals. Music publishers feuded with radio networks; the recording companies challenged radio's right to broadcast their prod-ucts; the American Federation of Musicians fought both radio and recording companies over compensation for its musicians; the union disciplined musicians who evaded union regulations in the illicit jam sessions so important to the development of the music; bandleaders regularly fell out with the booking agencies, which had established an oligopoly during the 1930s; these booking agencies in turn waged a long campaign against radio networks.

But if the swing industry resembled a Hobbesian state of nature, fraught with the tensions and stresses that signaled the growing pains of what has been labeled mass culture, it was also marked by an equally complex series of alliances and partnerships, the symbiotic marketing relationships that would increasingly characterize the industry of popular culture during the remainder of the century. Consolidation was the order of the decade. The dozens of record labels of the 1920s were reduced to three, later four, major labels during swing's peak years. A similar multiplicity of independent radio stations came under the domination of two national networks, NBC and CBS.[9] Touring swing bands, whether more or less jazz oriented, numbered in the hundreds by the crest of the swing craze, but most willingly surrendered some of their autonomy by signing up with the national booking offices: Music Corporation of America, General Amusement Corporation, William Morris, and others. Hollywood increasingly exploited the popularity of top bands, and musicians were attracted to Los Angeles in hopes of gaining valuable cinematic publicity for themselves and their ensembles. Links between big bands and commercial sponsors such as tobacco companies became increasingly common and lucrative. These various configurations released synergies. Association with a major booking agency, for example, provided entree into the more desirable hotels with radio wires from which remote broadcasts originated; publicity from these programs boosted record sales, increased attendance at one-night stands (the major source of income for most bands), and sometimes led to lucrative corporate sponsorships, which in turn generated publicity, in a recurring cycle.

Swing as a national phenomenon, in short, was made possible by a nexus of cultural forces and institutions, many of which emerged concurrently with swing. The particular forms the music took, its evolution from its pre-1935 "underground" origins to its peak in the late 1930s and early 1940s, the size of the bands, the songs that were chosen and the way they were arranged, even the way solos were improvised, all bear the signs of the culture industry that supported swing. It was inevitable that those who deemed themselves arbiters of musical authenticity, as well as many musicians themselves, would regard these market-driven, corporate-supervised changes as signs of commercial adulteration and decline.

At the same time, however, swing exerted its own influence on the evolution and development of this culture industry. The utopian impulses that big-band jazz seemed to embody and express—freedom, individualism, ethnic inclusiveness, democratic participation—were ones that inevitably put the music and its practitioners into conflict with the tendency of the swing industry toward consolidation, vertical integration, and homogenization. If swing was the popular music of most of the 1930s and 1940s, and therefore the first music to be acted upon by a new kind of culture industry, it was a particular *kind* of popular music, one that marked the media through which it gained its mass appeal. More easily assimilated to large-scale corporate sponsorship than to the politics of the Communist Party, swing nonetheless was not digested without incident.

Anyone Can Lead a Dance Band

A front-page story in the December 1936 *Down Beat* carried the headline "More Bands Go Co-Operative; Will They Eliminate Name Leaders?" Sometimes referred to as "commonwealth" bands, these cooperative ensembles posed an alternative to the more autocratic management styles that characterized many dance bands. In a commonwealth band, all earnings after expenses were pooled and distributed equally; band decisions were made by democratic vote. Chiefly associated with "territory" bands located at a distance from urban centers, and especially with those based in the southwestern United States, the cooperative system was adopted by at least one major national band, the Casa Loma Orchestra, which produced a strong national following and exerted an important stylistic influence during the early swing period. Casa Lomans were paid quarterly dividends in addition to their salaries and were required to sell their stock in the band to the corporation upon leaving. Fines against drinking and lateness were strictly enforced by fellow band members. Still, according to leader Glen Gray, "the band is harder to get into than a college frat or an exclusive club."[10]

Proponents of the system pointed to a number of advantages. By improving musicians' morale, commonwealth bands provided a defense against raids by other bands seeking to recruit musicians and increased the group's bargaining power in negotiating with employers. "The men no longer felt they were working for whoever happened to be paying their salaries at the moment," said Gray. "They were working for themselves, and that makes a lot of difference." Musically, according to its supporters, the system encouraged better musical teamwork: crisper attacks, more precise ensemble passages, and so on. And it seemed appropriate to the democratic ethos associated with jazz and swing. But some commonwealth bands, like the ill-starred Blue Devils of Oklahoma City, some of whose members eventually gravitated to the early Basie orchestra, found that the system was prone to the well-observed difficulties of democratic decision making; because of lack of leadership, the group passed up potentially lucrative opportunities and eventually disbanded. Still, the advantages of cooperation were palpable enough to inspire predictions that "name leaders" would eventually be eliminated in favor of collectives.[11]

Within a few years it was clear that these prophecies were dead wrong. The industry was dominated by celebrity bandleaders whose drawing power gave them near-total control over their sidemen. Many of the most commercially successful bands were led by domineering personalities known for the intimidation through which they controlled their musicians: Goodman's "Death Ray" glare, Tommy Dorsey's chronic pugilism, Glenn Miller's ruthless calculation. Yet even successful bandleaders found themselves powerless, overwhelmed by the market pressures unleashed by the success of swing. If leaders gained power relative to the musicians they employed, they surrendered much of it to the impersonal institutions and corporations that increasingly controlled the business. No longer could bandleaders function as entrepreneurs, making business decisions. The musical and business functions were bifurcated, with business decisions left to managers who were either attached to particular bands or affiliated with the national booking agencies.[12]

Some bandleaders surrendered these responsibilities willingly, while others resented the commercialization of the business. Artie Shaw, who stormed out of the business in 1939 after netting $250,000 and collapsing from exhaustion, lashed out at the booking offices and music publishers who he felt controlled the destiny of swing. Shaw testified from personal experience to the reduced power of bandleaders. "Anyone can lead a dance band," he charged. "The average band leader is only a front, a window dressing"; with $50,000, fourteen good musicians, and a press agent, Shaw promised to "make Joe Doakes, who doesn't know a C scale from a snare drum, one of the most popular band leaders in America." With effective management and backing from a national booking office and music publisher, virtually any band could achieve success, provided it was willing to relinquish a significant percentage of its profits to its benefactors and to perform commercially successful "musical monstrosities." But potential bandleaders must be prepared to "fight politics, corruption and a system of patronage" to succeed in a field that was "10 per cent art and 90 per cent business."[13]

Shaw clearly exaggerated the extent to which bands could be foisted on the public from above, and overstated the contrast between the craven late 1930s and what he called "the golden era of [jazz's] birth when every member of a band was a musician at heart." Other observers noted that swing had actually increased the level of musicianship among bandleaders. And the management style to which Shaw objected had, ironically, been pioneered in the late 1920s by Irving Mills on behalf of a bandleader for whom Shaw had the utmost respect: Ellington. Soon after hearing the band at New York's Kentucky Club in 1926, Mills, whose background was in music publishing, had become Ellington's manager and had turned the cooperative ensemble into a corporation in which Mills owned 45 percent. Through astute deals and public relations, Mills by late 1927 had won Ellington a job at Harlem's preeminent cabaret, the Cotton Club, a regular broadcast carried by CBS, and a recording contract with RCA Victor, which had never before handled African-American artists. Mills also secured the band's entry into movie theaters, an important innovation; won him a movie contract; arranged interstate tours of the South and of Europe; and engineered Ellington's entrance into ASCAP. By exploiting the synergism of these media, Mills and Ellington were able to triumph over their chief New York rival of the 1920s, Fletcher Henderson, "the Mahatma Gandhi of the jazz age," who remained true to the bandleader-entrepreneur model and was unwilling to hire a manager. During the early 1930s Mills accomplished the same feat with Cab Calloway, building his band into one of the most successful in the country.[14]

The Ellington-Mills partnership and its methods were unique in big-band jazz of the late 1920s and enabled the Ellington band to prosper in the difficult years of the early 1930s, when most big bands were hard hit by the Depression. "We worked clean through the Depression without even knowing that there was one," recalled Barney Bigard. But with the ascendancy of swing, the Mills method had become the rule instead of the exception; if Shaw exaggerated in saying that the new method was *sufficient* for any band to achieve success, certainly by 1936 it was *necessary* for survival. Personal managers like Mills and Joe Glaser, and later the national booking offices, served as gatekeepers of the venues and media that enabled swing to become a national phenomenon of popular culture.[15]

Although these agencies achieved their most dramatic success during the swing period, their origins lay in the 1920s and earlier; William Morris was founded in 1898 to manage theatrical and vaudeville acts. An early alternative to the Mills management style was developed by the Boston-based Schribman brothers, who owned and operated a network of ballrooms in New England. The Schribmans sought out unknown bands, financed them through engagements on their circuit and college dates, and secured radio exposure for them. If the band became successful—and Woody Herman, Tommy Dorsey, Artie Shaw, and Glenn Miller were among those whose bands started in the Schribman network—they repaid the loans. Profits from the self-sustaining Schribman bands were channeled to less successful newcomers.[16] Similar networks of dance halls owned by individuals who enjoyed more or less exclusive arrangements with bands existed throughout the country.

Moe Gale, owner of the Savoy, likewise functioned as a kind of patron to up-and-coming bands. Known as "the Great White Father of Harlem," Gale was credited with discovering and developing Calloway, Chick Webb (the first drummer to lead a big band), Ella Fitzgerald, and the Ink Spots. He also managed and booked the Benny Carter, Erskine Hawkins, Lucky Millinder, and Coleman Hawkins orchestras, among others. A 1941 profile credited Gale's "uncanny flair for discovering unknown sepia swingsters and developing them into stars" with making him "the most important single factor in Negro jazz." Unlike the high-profile Hammond, Gale was a shy, unassuming family man from the lower East Side who had originally aspired to be an accountant. A patient patron, in some cases Gale would sustain a loss of tens of thousands of dollars over several years on an act before it became profitable. "I guess I got the gift for knowing what the masses of people will like," he told a reporter. "I just tell it by my reaction . . . wait and see if something happens to me." His successful patronage enabled him to build an entertainment empire worth an estimated $10 million.[17]

Despite the significant role played by these individual entrepreneurs, the bulk of swing was controlled by a very different type of operation: large corporate booking offices headquartered in New York near Radio City. The dominant agency, Music Corporation of America, was founded in 1924 by two musician-doctors in Chicago. Barely surviving the early Depression, it began its rise in 1930 by proposing to the American Tobacco Company the idea of regular sustaining broadcasts by major dance bands originating in a different city each week. MCA reportedly consolidated its domination of the booking business in 1934 by cornering a large supply of liquor just as Prohibition was repealed and offering it to hotels in return for booking MCA clients. In 1936 MCA gained control of CBS bands for $1 million and scored early triumphs in signing Goodman and Basie. In 1937 the "Star-Spangled Octopus" handled approximately $18 million, nearly one-third of the $60 million reportedly grossed by 1,400 licensed bookers for their big-band clients; MCA's nearest competitor, Rockwell-O'Keefe, handled $4 million. In 1938 MCA controlled seventy-five top orchestras, including such commercial favorites as Tommy Dorsey, Guy Lombardo, Wayne King, Horace Heidt, Sammy Kaye, and Xavier Cugat. In 1941 it managed two-thirds of the country's most prominent white swing bands, according to an industry expert.[18]

"Working out of plush, handsomely furnished, distressingly formal offices, MCA's approach was strictly business," wrote a historian of swing: "cold, dry, hard but tremendously effective business." The agency preferred to work anonymously, behind the scenes, telling reporters that "it neither seeks nor desires publicity for itself." With salesmen, a contract department, lawyers, talent scouts, and various other experts, MCA was a highly efficient, vertically integrated operation. "Its files contain the pedigree and up-to-date performance record of every important radio and dance band in America, as well as others reported by its scouts as worth watching. No dreamy, impractical musicians man its polished desks but alert business men who know the market." For swing musicians, the presence of MCA loomed large enough to have inspired a blues lyric sung by Jack Teagarden: "I started up to see Bud Freeman but I lost my way, / and I thought for a minute I was on the road for MCA."[19]

The second-largest booking office, originally called Rockwell-O'Keefe and later General Artists Corporation, was regarded as more sensitive to its clients' musical goals, and controlled Glenn Miller, Artie Shaw, Woody Herman, Jimmy Dorsey, and Casa Loma (in its postcooperative incarnation). William Morris became an important force in the swing industry in 1939, when it acquired Willard Alexander, the Hammond confidant who originally signed both Goodman and Basie for MCA; the new agency quickly lured Basie and recruited Ellington, Whiteman, and others. Joe Glaser, who for a time handled "colored-band" interests for Rockwell-O'Keefe, managed Armstrong, Lionel Hampton, Andy Kirk, Les Brown, Jan Savitt, and others. Along with Consolidated Radio Artists and other smaller agencies, these offices controlled some 98 percent of the dance-band business by 1938.[20]

The relationship between swing and the booking agencies was one of mutual dependency. Swing as a national fad of the late 1930s would have been impossible without the agencies, which served as liaisons between radio networks, commercial advertisers, and the big bands. These arrangements netted top bands as much as $250,000 a year in addition to providing the broadcast publicity that boosted record sales and theater and ballroom receipts. The logistical difficulties of putting together itineraries of one-night engagements across the country, as successful bands did, would have been insurmountable without the kind of centralized management that the offices provided. Moreover, by securing exclusive rights to choice hotels, dance halls, and theaters, booking offices made it a requirement of the business that bands have some corporate affiliation.

Booking offices also took charge of the range of public relations activities used to promote bands. Agencies sent promotional brochures, which included photographs, window cards, newspaper mats, and press manuals, to local promoters, ballrooms, hotels, and other locations. Agents sent press releases to newspapers or magazines, placed favorable stories in trade magazines, and arranged for their clients' mention in syndicated columns like Walter Winchell's. They arranged for band-leaders to be photographed with Hollywood stars and other celebrities, judge beauty contests, and enter other media events. They cultivated disc jockeys in order to set up interviews or get air time for their clients' recordings. They won endorsement contracts with musical instrument manufacturers. Sometimes agents would precede a band on the tour, "crashing" the editorial departments of the local papers, buying drinks, and so on. Then the agent would arrange so-called tie-ins, "the terrific ballyhoo stunts that knock the town dead": arranging to have the mayor present the bandleader with a key to the city, setting up a mid-afternoon talk to the YWCA, appearing in a department store to buy a new suit and announce a sale, signing sheet music and records in the local music store before playing the band's theme song on a piano. Fans were also targeted. Calloway fans would get copies of the *Hepster's Dictionary*, Kay Kyser partisans a diploma from the "College of Musical Knowledge."[21]

The agencies provided less tangible benefits as well; affiliation with a top agency such as MCA conferred prestige on the client band. "To ballroom operators and dancers alike the three magic letters on a dance poster soon became a guarantee of quality comparable to the Good Housekeeping Seal of Approval on a product for the home," wrote one former band promoter.[22]

The reasons for big bands' reliance on booking agencies are perhaps more apparent than the obverse; but the booking offices could not have made themselves indispensable in the absence of those very complexities that were unique to swing: the high overhead involved in main-taining large ensembles of musicians and their equipment, the com-plexities involved in negotiating the various media and institutions involved, the fact that the swing audience dictated that bands play fre-quently before live audiences and therefore move often. As the swing industry expanded, so did the opportunities for profit making by the agencies, which charged a fee of 10 percent of gross receipts before expenses. A sizable proportion of big-band revenues accrued to the agencies, as much as $15 million in 1937, when total swing industry earnings were roughly $80 million, according to a *Variety* survey on the industry.[23] Only with the emergence of swing as big business could an industry based on a percentage of gross receipts develop the kind of scale the large booking offices did.

Broadcasting Swing

Radio more than any other medium was at the heart of the synergy that drove the swing industry, and radio highlighted the gatekeeping role of the booking offices. A big band could no more hope for sustained national success without radio than it could without the support of MCA or William Morris. Numerous anecdotes testify to the fact that radio was an invaluable conduit of information on swing for consumers, critics, and musicians. Most famously, radio is widely thought to have kicked off "the swing era" when late-night transmissions of NBC's "Let's Dance" reached the West Coast during "prime time" and attracted audiences prepared for the innovative arrangements that non-radio-prepared listeners had rejected in New York City and across the country. It was via Kansas City's W9XBY that John Hammond first heard the Basie orchestra as he sat in a cold car with Goodman outside the Chicago club where Goodman's orchestra was currently appearing. Broadcasts from Harlem's Cotton Club were instrumental in securing the national success of Ellington and Calloway. Kay Kyser, probably the most commercially successful of all swing-era big bands, built his early success on the college prom circuit almost entirely through Monday night broadcasts over Chicago's WGN, "the only radio station folks down south listen to." And radio transmissions introduced musicians to one another when recordings did not exist or were unavailable.[24]

These anecdotes illustrate the structural centrality of radio to the swing industry. Radio broadcasts, either the "sustaining programs" that originated late at night in hotels and clubs, or the regular commercially sponsored programs that were awarded the country's most popular bands, were the primary means by which a band and its agency found and prepared its audience. A widely observed irony of the time was that the most desirable swing engagements were often locations where bands expected to lose several hundred dollars weekly. These hotels and ballrooms attracted top-name bands despite the low wages they paid only because they had radio wires. The broadcasts generated the publicity that was transformed into tours of one-night stands in the large ballrooms or theaters that accounted for the bulk of a band's earnings. In other words, these locations served as the loss leaders of swing. The Bob Crosby band, for example, grossed only 16 percent of its 1939 earnings from locations such as hotels and ballrooms, while earning 29 percent and 31 percent in one-night engagements and theaters, respectively. (Radio commercials, recordings, and royalties made up the rest).[25] The value of radio publicity was such that by 1939 bands were paying for their own wires, risking union penalties to pay for the radio hookups that had traditionally been paid for by the location. By controlling access to key locations, such as New York's Pennsylvania Hotel, which served to launch Goodman, Tommy Dorsey, Shaw, and Miller, booking agencies essentially controlled a band's commercial horizon.

At times the swing industry actively sought out and created new locations from which sustaining broadcasts could originate. Some were created specifically for radio. A large dance hall was built in Cedar Grove, New Jersey, twenty-five miles from midtown Manhattan, in order to duplicate the conditions of a New York hotel. With a permanent glassed-in radio control room, the Meadowbrook Club broadcast twelve network shows a week, including a one-hour Saturday afternoon program for CBS. With its low overhead, the Meadowbrook could offer more attractive terms than a New York City hotel, and it soon booked Miller, the Dorseys, Woody Herman, and other top bandleaders. "Of course the band does not win such prestige as at the Pennsylvania, but the radio listener in Omaha who hears this chromium-trimmed barn described as 'the beautiful Meadowbrook Country Club' can imagine it as he pleases." Similarly, 52nd Street's Famous Door was one of many cellar clubs on New York's downtown jazz strip until MCA designated it the originating point for live broadcasts over CBS, which finally won national recognition for Count Basie in 1939. This tendency reached its logical culmination in programs like Martin Block's "Make Believe Ballroom," which dispensed with live music altogether in favor of recordings.[26]

Reserved for the most successful big bands and entertainers was the swing industry's greatest prize, a commercially sponsored program. The concept, a watershed in commercial radio, was pioneered in the 1920s in such shows as Rudy Vallee's "Fleischmann Hour" for NBC. In 1933 the Whiteman, Waring, and Casa Loma orchestras were sponsored by Kraft Cheese and Old Gold and Camel cigarettes, respectively. Lucky Strike had pioneered its movable "Your Hit Parade" broadcasts from different cities in 1930, and tobacco companies backed virtually all the top swing acts. Goodman replaced Casa Loma on "Camel Caravan" in 1936; Lucky Strike sponsored Kyser in 1937; Raleigh and Old Gold sponsored Tommy Dorsey and Shaw, respectively, in 1938; and Chesterfield signed Miller in 1939. The big bands of Bob Crosby, Hal Kemp, Harry James, Horace Heidt, Larry Clinton, and Woody Herman were among others awarded sponsored radio shows. The financial benefits could be substantial: Miller's contract for three fifteen-minute broadcasts a week yielded $250,000 in the first year. The success of these programs eventually made nonsponsored "sustaining" broadcasts obsolete. CBS's "Saturday Night Swing Club," first aired on June 13, 1936, was the first radio program devoted solely to swing; it was on that show that Maxine Sullivan's swinging version of "Loch Lomond" was cut off by the Detroit station manager. The show was abruptly canceled at the height of its popularity in 1939, reportedly to be replaced by "a new type jazz" program expected to reach a larger audience. According to *Down Beat*, even CBS acknowledged that the show was its most valuable unsponsored program and that the network had moved it to a larger location in order to accommodate the increasing number of people requesting tickets.[27]

Another sustaining program popular with jazz listeners, "Mildred Bailey and Company," was cancelled by CBS after eight weeks, reportedly because it refused to drop the racially mixed bands that appeared on it. Such actions produced an attitude of barely disguised contempt among many in the swing community, although only a few could risk expressing their views openly. *Metronome*'s George Simon spoke for many when he wrote: "When it comes to putting across new ideas in music and actually discovering top talent in the rough, you can put in last place . . . the artist bureaus of the networks and the radio departments of just about all the advertising agencies in the business."[28]

As radio acquired its mature form by exploiting previously unrecognized commercial partnerships, which benefited the most successful swing outfits, broadcasters collided with songwriters and publishers. Tension over the payment of royalties for ASCAP material performed over the radio had simmered throughout the 1930s, with a number of compromises arranged and abandoned. In 1936, when the Warner conglomerate resigned from ASCAP for six months, songs written by Gershwin, Cole Porter, Richard Rodgers and Lorenz Hart, Jerome Kern, and others were withdrawn for that period. Despite the fact that some 20 to 40 percent of the total ASCAP repertoire was not available to radio, the networks received few complaints. But swing further affected an already precarious playing field. The percentage of ASCAP income paid by radio broadcasters rose from $750,000 in 1932 to $5.9 million in 1937 (it dropped somewhat in the two succeeding years, probably as a result of the "Roosevelt recession").[29]

By late 1940 a more serious crisis loomed: ASCAP was demanding a 1941 contract with broadcasters of between $7.5 and $9 million, roughly double the fees paid in 1939. That amount, according to Broadcast Music, Inc., was 65 percent of ASCAP's *total revenue*, nearly twice as much as fees paid by movies, dance halls, and other commercial consumers of music. Moreover, the networks would be required to pay a fee of 7.5 percent of their undistributed revenues. Refusing to meet this demand, the three networks decided to ban ASCAP-controlled music, including many swing theme songs written by big-band leaders. Setting up [BMI] as an alternative source of broadcast music, the networks quickly had "a large staff of musicians" working to arrange public domain songs, contracted for 200 new pieces written by non-ASCAP writers, and claimed to have available 250,000 copyright works in the event of an ASCAP strike.[30]

Musicians, particularly bandleaders, found themselves caught in the middle as networks tightened the screws on ASCAP by requiring bands to play a certain percentage of BMI tunes when broadcasting. Jimmy Lunceford lost radio air time for refusing to balance his performance of ASCAP tunes with an equal number of BMI numbers. By October the proportion of ASCAP tunes broadcast fell from 80 percent on sustaining broadcasts and 76 percent on commercially sponsored programs to 25 percent and 31 percent, respectively. Musicians remained neutral in the clash, urging both sides to submit to arbitration. *Metronome* ascribed the impending clash to "too much 'dictatorship' . . . an overdose of demand and an underdose of suggestion." Claiming that "the American way is the compromise way," the journal observed: "One look at modern Europe should be enough to discourage the philosophy of force, for commands and demands have desolated an entire continent." Calling musicians "goats" in the clash, *Down Beat* urged the American Federation of Musicians to mobilize "the combined strength of 150,000 musicians" in order to force a compromise.[31] By December the U.S. Justice Department became involved, with Assistant Attorney General Thurmond Arnold announcing criminal charges against all parties, ASCAP, BMI, CBS, and NBC, thus widening an earlier antitrust suit filed by the department in 1934.

All efforts to force an agreement failed. For most of 1941, from January through November, the songs of Gershwin, Irving Berlin, Harold Arlen, Johny Mercer, and other popular writers were banned, including most big-band theme songs. To prevent any strains of ASCAP-controlled music from inadvertently slipping into broadcasts, the networks instituted a ban on ad-libbing, requiring that all solos be transcribed and submitted ahead of time for clearance; station managers hovered anxiously, prepared to cut off soloists who interjected forbidden strains. Swinging the classics suddenly became less preference than necessity, with such public domain tunes as "I Dream of Jeanie with the Light Brown Hair," "London Bridge Is Falling Down," "My Old Kentucky Home," "Comin' through the Rye," and others achieving a second life. The third network, Mutual Broadcast System, had settled with ASCAP in May in order to beat its two rivals to the air with the ASCAP repertoire. By November all three had settled on terms that were generally regarded as a "substantial financial victory" for the broadcasters.[32] ASCAP, it appeared, needed radio more than radio needed ASCAP.

BMI, set up by the broadcasters as a temporary source for music, was established as a permanent rival to ASCAP.

The Jukes Take Over

Radio, it has been argued, was a medium uniquely suited to the social stresses of the 1930s, offering Americans "ritualistic solidarity" that elsewhere took the less benign form of fascism. Radio provided its Depression-era listeners "the solace of solidarity and of predictable, structured time." Lawrence Levine has demonstrated the sense of community produced by radio in the 1930s through its serials and political speeches by politicians such as Roosevelt, Huey Long, and Father Coughlin. Phonograph recordings, in contrast, typically produce a diametrically opposed set of audience responses; in place of solidarity, "solitude; the occlusion of the musician; the use of music as an object and a commodity; the collapse of a public architecture of time and the creation of a private interior design of time." For jazz musicians, however, things have been different; recordings have served a crucial role in creating community, providing the medium through which techniques, styles, and performances could be studied, imitated, and disseminated. Records, according to this critic, have functioned as "the conservatory of jazz: its school, its treasure-house and thesaurus, its way of husbanding resources."[33]

At no time was this privileged relationship between jazz and recordings more evident than during the swing period. While radio sat at the hub of the swing industry, driving the cycle through which bands gathered their audience, toured, and recorded, swing passed these benefits along to the recording industry. The trajectories of big-band popularity and record sales between 1930 and 1940 show a striking alignment. Like the 1920s dance bands, recording companies were devastated by the Crash, although record sales had been falling since 1925, partly because of competition from radio. After bottoming out in 1932, when some 10 million records were sold, the industry showed a moderate steady increase in record sales through 1938, when 40 million records were sold. Then began four years of rapid acceleration, with 80 million sold in 1940. In 1932 the industry grossed $2.5 million, by 1939 $36 million. In the best year since 1921, 1941 produced sales of some 130 million records.[34] This recovery was accompanied by the sort of consolidation that characterized the swing industry as a whole. The Depression had served to purge the industry; in contrast to the swarm of recording companies that had operated before 1929, only two major companies survived by 1932: Victor, which had merged with Radio Corporation of America in 1929; and Columbia, acquired by CBS in 1938.

Of course, records were perceived as a significant component of success for big bands. "Waxing a half-dozen sides a month is not unprofitable for any leader, or his side men, and yet the scale paid musicians actually is the least important aspect of a recording date," *Down Beat* reported. "The leader knows that once his records are released by any one of the major companies, his band will be exploited via a dozen methods, and over hundreds of radio stations in the hinterlands—all of which adds up to publicity which, in many cases, the leader himself couldn't buy in a lifetime on his own."[35] Most potent of all was a hit record's potential to somewhat inexplicably crystallize a band's sound and create a national market virtually overnight: Tommy Dorsey's "Marie," Artie Shaw's "Begin the Beguine," Andy Kirk's "Until the Real Thing Comes Along," Larry Clinton's "My Reverie," Count Basie's "One O'Clock Jump," Bunny Berigan's "I Can't Get Started," Miller's "Little Brown Jug."

The correlation between the recovery of the record industry and the success of big-band jazz was no coincidence; by 1939, swing fanciers were thought to account for one-quarter of all record sales. To be sure, other factors than the popularity of swing were involved, causes that had contributed to the rise of swing itself. The gradually recovering economy of mid-decade played its part, as did the entry of Decca into the recording field in 1934, particularly its introduction of a 35-cent popular record when the standard price had previously been at least 75 cents. For the remainder of the decade the three major recording companies engaged in periodic price wars, usually paced by Decca. By 1940 even the classical market was affected; Columbia cut prices from two dollars on its premium recordings to one dollar or even 75 cents.[36]

But perhaps the single most important factor in the recovery of recordings lay in a technological development, the jukebox, a device that deprivatized the experience of consuming records. After the repeal of Prohibition, the five-cent jukeboxes placed in bars, cafés, diners, and roadside dance establishments rivaled movies as a source of public entertainment for those with lower incomes. By 1940 the jukebox industry was grossing some $150 million, with 350,000 machines scattered across the country; incredibly, these machines consumed nearly *one-half* of all records produced at that time. Much of Decca's success during the swing period resulted from its policy of dominating the jukebox market by underselling its competitors, controlling 90 percent of jukebox sales in 1939.[37]

Writing in the *American Mercury*, a young jazz enthusiast expressed alarm at the musical "monster, part intellectual and part idiot, fattened by the men who run the industry of the Jukes." Linking jukeboxes to other commercial forces that seemed to be threatening the "tumultuous creative spirit" of genuine jazz, the writer was "certain . . . that greater mechanization is in store for our music: gears and sprockets will displace musicians and originality will make way for the standardized output necessary to feed the market created by the proliferating Jukes. For good or ill," Barry Ulanov concluded, "the Jukes have taken over Swing and will twist it to their own profit."[38]

This voracious appetite for recordings helps explain the otherwise puzzling campaign against "canned music" waged by the American Federation of Musicians. The threat to musicians' employment posed by radio, phonograph recordings, and Vitaphone had long concerned the union. Especially disturbing was the way these technologies reinforced one another to the detriment of live musicians; not only did recordings appear to make them obsolete, but records could be broadcast, thereby depriving musicians of additional employment and whatever royalties would have accrued from record sales. Of course, many artists, particularly African-Americans, were simply paid a flat fee for their work, receiving neither publishing rights or record royalties. Jukeboxes, which proffered music in venues that had traditionally employed many live musicians, presented still another problem. Proprietors both were freed from the expense of hiring bands and profited directly from the machines; many of their patrons even came to prefer the polished, familiar music of the jukebox recording to the vagaries of live performances.

While the AFM had protested the broadcast of commercial records over the air as early as 1930, and forced recording companies to place labels on records forbidding them to be played on the radio, it was union president James Petrillo who brought matters between the musicians and the media to a head. Although he did not become national president until 1940, Petrillo led a strike of the Chicago local he headed against "canned music" in 1936–37. He led another effort at the 1937 AFM convention, resulting in a contract with radio networks ratified the next year that guaranteed use of a minimum number of staff musicians during broadcasts.[39]

Meanwhile a series of court decisions in the nebulous area of commercial property rights set in motion a showdown with recording companies. In July 1939 the federal appeals court in New York ruled against radio station WNEW (home of Martin Block's "Make Believe Ballroom") in a suit filed by Paul Whiteman, awarding the bandleader licensing rights for his own recorded music, but only in conjunction with his manufacturer, RCA Victor. Recording companies quickly exploited this opportunity by sharply increasing their fees to broadcasters, a move that seemed intended to drive commercial recordings off the air. But in December 1940 the U.S. Supreme Court issued a more momentous ruling in a case brought by bandleader Fred Waring against station WDAS. By refusing to take up a federal appeals court reversal of a decision by the Pennsylvania Supreme Court in Waring's favor, the court ruled in effect that property rights ended with the sale of a recording; broadcasters were therefore free to use commercial recordings on the air. Labels specifying "Only for noncommercial use on phonographs in homes" were suddenly irrelevant. Partly because of this decision, the contract between the AFM and the networks was not renewed when it expired at the end of 1940. The musicians' union found itself lacking any leverage over the networks.[40]

Petrillo turned instead to the recording companies to force radio and jukeboxes to compensate musicians for their services. Although he had initially hoped to involve representatives from all sectors of the music industry in negotiating a compromise, Petrillo decided to announce the strike after the National Association of Broadcasters commenced a hard-hitting public relations campaign against him, in hope of generating public opinion and congressional action. By waiting until June 1942 to announce that no recordings would be allowed beginning that August, Petrillo made it difficult for the recording companies to stockpile music as they had on previous occasions. A national ban on recordings went into effect on August 1. Petrillo was attacked personally, often with ethnic insinuations, by periodicals ranging from the *New Republic* to *Forbes*, the *New York Post* to the *Herald Tribune*. The trade press criticized Petrillo with varying degrees of ferocity. John Hammond expressed sympathy for his goals but recommended that the union get a "good press agent." *Metronome*, on the other hand, labeled him "brazen," prone to "complete delusions of grandeur," and editorialized against "the vain, the clumsy, the unethical, the tyrannical attempt . . . to fight technological progress." *Down Beat* likewise pleaded with the union leader to end his "octopus-armed battle" with all forms of mechanical reproduction.[41]

As in the ASCAP-radio dispute, big-band musicians found themselves in an awkward position. Swing-band leaders "almost to a man disagreed violently" with the strike, according to George Simon, who covered swing for *Metronome*. According to *Down Beat*, swing musicians were underrepresented at the AFM convention at which the recording ban was decided. The union was divided between its older, less mobile constituents, often members of brass bands and strongly affiliated with particular locals, and its younger, more mobile constituency, which comprised most swing musicians. The recording ban reflected the interests of the former group. A journalist complained that because African-American musicians lacked access to network broadcasts and depended heavily on record sales for their earnings, they would be hurt disproportionately by the ban. Although union members reportedly lost $4 million in the first year of the strike, and despite the campaign by the National Association of Broadcasters, hostile hearings by a Senate committee, and an adverse decision by the War Labor Board capped by a personal appeal from President Roosevelt, the union ultimately prevailed. Decca and the new independent labels like Capitol acceded to the AFM demands in September 1943, while the two biggest labels,

Columbia and RCA, held out until November 1944. The key provision won by the union was a performance trust fund for unemployed musicians to be funded by a fixed fee on all recordings sold.[42]

But the technological depredations of canned music were not the only threat posed to the AFM by swing-driven changes in the music industry. The constant mobility characteristic of the swing bands made it difficult for the union to maintain jurisdiction over their activities. "Only with great difficulty did the union organize the dance field," according to a historian of the AFM. "Years of militant pressure, picketing, and policing were necessary." One union response was a levy on traveling bands. Any band that included members not affiliated with the jurisdiction in which an engagement occurred was required to file a contract showing 10 percent above local scale; the band, in other words, paid the local a fee of 10 percent. Black-staffed bands sometimes had to deposit their contract with the white local when playing a white hall or club. Because of rules governing the workplace, high-profile leaders like Tommy Dorsey and Charlie Barnet periodically incurred union wrath by sitting in at after-hours jam sessions. The union hired "walking" delegates to monitor these sessions, for which musicians could be fined as much as $500. "On our level we never saw [the AFM] as being of any real benefit," recalled Dizzy Gillespie, "and sometimes it kept us from gaining experience . . . the union has always been just a dues collector." One-night engagements also posed enforcement problems for the AFM and were brought "under the union scale slowly, and only after many leaders were expelled and many agents and bookers had their licenses revoked."[43]

As well as being the first to feel the technological and legal shocks that affected the music industry during the 1930s and 1940s, big-band musicians contended with other unique circumstances. The same forces that produced a consolidation and incorporation of swing through the booking agencies, radio networks, and recording companies also shaped the local "corporate culture" in which swing musicians operated. In contrast to the stereotype of the hard-drinking dissolute jazz musician, many artists of the 1920s were formally trained, sober, and conscientious. The stereotype was more likely to fit star soloists, who unlike section players could not be as easily replaced and thus were under less pressure to comport themselves. With the growth in popularity of swing, this tendency toward professionalization continued. The complex, highly arranged music required excellent technical ability and reading skills, and a level of motor control not generally compatible with debauchery. Moreover, the consolidation of the swing industry at the national level, chiefly in New York, increased competition for employment and persistence in the top bands. More than ever musicians were expected to conform to standards of musical and personal decorum.[44]

The demands made on bandleaders and musicians alike by national success were daunting. The swing industry required simultaneous activity in broadcasting, recording, and touring, entailing enormous amounts of time. At one point, for example, the Miller band was rehearsing for and broadcasting three "Chesterfield Shows" a week (with repeats for the West Coast audience), four to five hours an evening at their location at the Pennsylvania Hotel, also wired for radio, the same number of shows during the day at the Paramount Theatre, and recording sessions at two in the morning. Occasional days off were generally booked for one-nighters. In its initial flush of success, the Goodman band was filmed for "The Big Broadcast of 1937" while playing an engagement at the Palomar. After playing an exhausting evening that ran until at least one in the morning, musicians were required to rise at five in order to reach the studio by seven. "We continued to double for three weeks, every man dead on his feet," according to a musician. In addition, working conditions were designed to maximize musical output. Bandleaders like Tommy Dorsey were known for packing music into the four hours of a location job, playing the first hour and a half without a break and forbidding musicians to wear watches. Bandleaders designed a system of penalties and fines to ensure promptness, neatness, and comportment.[45]

Despite the pressures on bandleaders, the financial and other rewards of leading a top ensemble served as a potent centrifugal force on established bands during the peak years of swing. Better-known sidemen were constantly quitting the bands in which they had made their reputations in hopes of duplicating such success on their own. In 1939 *Metronome* editorialized against the glut of new bands, which made it difficult for bandleaders to keep groups together, depressed prices for all bands, and frequently failed. "What Are the Chances for All the Sidemen Now Starting Bands?" asked a *Down Beat* headline for an article that detailed the proliferation of bands and the tough odds against success.[46] The problem was exacerbated further when the war siphoned off a large percentage of big-band musicians. Whatever its other benefits, bandleading did not provide relief from the work discipline imposed by the market. Many bandleaders, including Miller, Goodman, and Shaw, collapsed and required hospitalization during the height of their careers.

Glenn Miller perhaps more than any other bandleader exemplifies the way in which the components of the swing industry interacted to promote success. Miller's wartime exploits, capped by his disappearance over the English channel in 1944 and immortalized by James Stewart in *The Glenn Miller Story* (1954), have made Miller a national icon, an exemplar of the successful mating of popular culture and patriotism. A recent historian has charged Miller with effecting "a subtle taming of the musical and utopian vision of swing" during wartime by fusing "the spontaneity of popular culture and a new social purpose."[47] But Miller is an equally apt choice as an icon of success in the swing industry. Despite national exposure in dance bands led by Ray Noble, the Dorsey brothers, and the Ben Pollack band, which during the early 1930s also included Goodman and Krupa, Miller ascended slowly during the early years of swing. His first band was formed and failed in 1937; after reorganizing during February 1938, Miller barely kept the ensemble together for the remainder of the year, paring his band roster and accepting one-night engagements for as little as $400.

Then a series of rapid developments enabled Miller to assume *Time*'s mantle of "undisputed King of Swing" by the fall of 1939. That February he was booked to play New Jersey's Meadowbrook Club starting in March. A few days before that engagement began, Miller received an even bigger break, a summer booking at New York's Glen Island Casino, a prime Westchester County location graced with "a whole slew of coast-to-coast radio wires" that had aided the rise of such diverse big bands as Casa Loma, Tommy Dorsey, Charlie Barnet and Ozzie Nelson.[48] At the Meadowbrook, a sustaining broadcast carried by CBS six to ten times a week provided a national audience and allowed Miller to polish his new style. In April his band recorded twelve sides for RCA Victor, including future hits "Sunrise Serenade," "Little Brown Jug," and the band's theme song, "Moonlight Serenade." During the remainder of 1939 Miller achieved dominion over the country's 300,000 jukeboxes, contributing as many as one in four recordings to some machines. In October he received a $250,000 annual contract from Chesterfield to replace Paul Whiteman on its CBS program, beginning December 27, playing three quarter-hour broadcasts per week at 7:15 p.m. The band broke one-night attendance records from Harlem's Savoy to the Kansas City Convention Hall. In 1940, its first full year of success, the band grossed $630,000, with 52 weeks of Chesterfield programs, 25 weeks of hotel engagements, 16 weeks of one-nighters around the country, 10 weeks of theater shows, and two record dates a month for RCA Victor, cutting four to six sides in each session. The next year Miller transported his fame to Hollywood, filming *Sun Valley Serenade*.[49]

Miller's rapid ascent was not due solely to business acumen. The band's success had much to do with its distinctive reed and brass sound, particularly the use of a clarinet, often paired, playing lead over the saxophones, in unison but an octave up. While the Miller band also perfected a smooth, readily accessible four-beat rhythm designed to appeal to the least practiced dancers, the band's forte, according to its leader, was not rhythm but harmony. "The years of serious study I've had with legitimate teachers finally is paying off in enabling me to write arrangements employing unusual, rich harmonies, many never before used in dance bands," Miller told *Down Beat* early in 1940. He made no pretense of musical "authenticity," which he implicitly associated with rhythm. "I haven't a great jazz band, and I don't want one," he said. "Some of the critics among us . . . point their fingers at us and charge us with forsaking the real jazz. Maybe so. Maybe not. It's all in what you define as 'real jazz.' It happens that to our ears harmony comes first. A dozen colored bands have a better beat than mine."[50]

But whatever Miller's musical innovations, at least as much credit should go to his sophisticated knack for using the various media of the swing industry to his advantage. According to those who knew and worked with him, Miller was above all a businessman, interested in bandleading primarily as a moneymaking venture. "It's an inspiring sight to look down from the balcony on the heads of 7,000 people swaying on a dance floor—especially when you are getting $600 for every thousand of them," he was quoted as saying. He was particularly astute in the use of radio. In effect, the deeply leveraged Miller of early 1939 bet everything on the ability of radio to create an audience. "Miller's theory," according to a sideman, was "go on the air as much as we can." He paid for radio wires, when necessary, in order to reach the broadest possible audience. In addition, Miller employed the technique of saturation broadcasting. To build name recognition, the band would perform a relatively small number of tunes repeatedly. "We'd shove the music down their throats," recalled the sideman. "Then when the band toured and came to your home town, you'd say: 'That's the band we've been listening to every night.' And you'd want to see what the hell you had been listening to." Miller then used the audiences to help him decide which tunes to record. At live engagements, members of the audience would request tunes that the band had broadcast but never recorded; Miller would keep track of such requests and record the most popular numbers. He even paid to have his radio checks recorded, some of which are still being released and earning revenues.[51]

Are Colored Bands Doomed?

"Colored attractions are now definitely in demand throughout the entire country," wrote Helen Oakley in 1938, "and they have become unmistakable box-office draws with which to be reckoned." She cited the competition among the three top booking agencies as evidence for her claim that the "colored market," once considered "limited" and relegated to individual bookers like Mills and Glaser, was now becoming profitable. MCA was rumored to be considering a separate department for black bands, while William Morris, Consolidated Radio Artists, and Rockwell-O'Keefe were all reported to be augmenting their capacity to handle black artists. Calloway, Ellington, Waller, Lunceford, and Henderson had consistently proved their box-office drawing power. Armstrong, under the management of Glaser, had been the first

African-American awarded a commercially sponsored radio program in 1937 and received three "outstanding" Hollywood film contracts.[52]

Within two years this bubble had apparently burst. *Down Beat* ran a two-part article detailing the plight of the black bands. "Are Colored Bands Doomed as Big Money Makers?" ran one headline: " 'Negro Leaders Could Make More Money Running a Rib Joint.' " The controversy was joined by the *Amsterdam News* in articles with headlines like "Does Blackout Loom for Negro Bands?" and "Negro Bands Are Not Doomed Says Millinder."[53]

The conditions and prospects faced by African-American and white big bands had never been equivalent, and as swing became profitable business the disparity between the two groups increased. That swing's mass popularity worked to the detriment of black bands by inspiring white imitations of the music that proved more acceptable to a mass audience has been well documented by historians. In the early 1930s, when the popular white dance bands led by Whiteman, Lombardo, Leo Reisman, and others played a "sweet" music, the protoswing orchestras led by Ellington, Benny Moten, Don Redman, and Calloway enjoyed a monopoly of the more jazz-inflected music popular at colleges and theaters. After 1935 white swing bands were playing a music that struck many listeners as indistinguishable from that of their black counterparts; indeed, white bands sometimes drew stronger audience responses than black ones, even from African-Americans. No longer perceived as having anything unique to offer, black bands could hardly be expected to overcome the structural obstacles to parity built into American society. At a time when the swing industry was glutted with more bands than it could profitably sustain, blacks were the first to be pushed out.[54]

By 1940 the crisis affecting the black bands had been widely publicized, although disagreement existed over the reasons for it. Some pointed to black bands' lack of showmanship, a factor of increasing significance given changes in the swing audience. The "swarms of jitterbugs of the 1937–39 period" who "knew no color lines" had dissipated by 1940, leaving more affluent patrons who preferred the "corn and schmaltz crews."[55] But the more fundamental structural problems faced by black bands were well recognized. Denied access to the urban hotels from which sustaining broadcasts originated, the black bands were unable to benefit from the all-important publicity afforded by radio. Moreover, they were passed over by commercial sponsors for sponsored programs. As a result, of the five major sources of big-band receipts—record sales, one-night engagements, theater shows, hotel location jobs, and commercially sponsored programs—black bands were essentially restricted to the first three. This situation posed particular hardships because commercial broadcasts, in addition to involving substantial fees from the advertiser, generated much of the publicity that drove record sales and boosted ticket sales at dance halls and theaters. Location jobs, though frequently costing rather than earning money, also provided a much-needed respite from the rigors of touring, given the long jumps often demanded from one night's engagement to the next. Without them, bands faced the prospect of endless strings of one-nighters, with daily trips of 200 to 500 miles being common, compounded by the chronic lack of accommodations. The challenge of keeping a band intact under such conditions was formidable.[56]

The appropriation by white bands of a particular style invented and popularized by African-Americans may have been central to the crisis faced by the black bands. But the issue of artistic exchanges between whites and blacks has had a long, contentious history, and arguments that the history of jazz represents a one-sided appropriation by whites overlook the personal testimony of numerous African-American musicians. As Gerald Early has observed, "the relationship between black American artists and white audiences and white patrons is surely more complex than most people think . . . it is always difficult to tell who is copying whom."[57] White orchestras such as the Jean Goldkette Orchestra, Coon-Sanders Nighthawks, and even Paul Whiteman were much admired by early black big-band leaders, at least for their sophisticated arrangements and precise ensemble execution; instrumentalists such as Frank Trumbauer, Bix Beiderbecke, and Miff Mole influenced a wide range of black stylists. This admiration often extended to sweet bands not generally respected by swing critics. Armstrong's enthusiasm for Guy Lombardo was well known, and Thad Jones listened regularly to Lombardo, Kyser, and Kaye, both for their musicianship and for their arrangements.[58]

To be sure, some of this black admiration for white artists was related to a desire to duplicate their commercial success by appealing to white audiences (who in many cases sought out the black bands precisely because they offered an *alternative* to white music). In the preswing and early swing period many African-American bands passed as white, a phenomenon aided by the nonvisual media of radio and recordings. The Andy Kirk band, for example, reached an audience in the Southwest through sustaining broadcasts from a white nightclub in Oklahoma City. "Since they came to know us only by radio," according to Kirk, "they didn't know whether we were white or black." Appearing opposite a band led by trombonist Jack Teagarden, Kirk recalled that his ensembles "played more white than Jack's band." Earl Hines experienced a similar reaction to his broadcasts from Chicago's Grand Terrace, receiving letters inquiring about his race because the band's repertoire included waltzes, ballads, and other forms not associated with "race" outfits.[59]

On the other hand, much of the appeal of black bands was precisely their "otherness": Ellington's early fame was based largely on his exotic "jungle" effects, while the canon of authenticity promoted by Hammond and others valued precisely those musical qualities that set African-Americans apart from their white imitators. And some musicians professed their ability to recognize racial differences in swing. After much radio listening, Roy Porter discovered a "world of difference in feeling and soul" between black and white bands and instrumentalists. "White bands were note for note, so precise and tight," he recalled. "The black bands were loose and swinging." Still, Porter admired the ensemble execution and arrangements of certain white bands.[60]

For a time the recording industry discouraged musical "passing." What was permissible in live performances and, by extension, on remote broadcasts was discouraged in the recording studio, ostensibly because executives believed that the audience for race records— African-Americans, they assumed—would not accept it. The Henderson orchestra, for example, whose shows at whites-only Roseland featured a number of waltzes and other non-"race" pieces, was prevented from recording much of its repertoire by the "unwritten custom among record people that no negro orchestra should be allowed to record anything that wasn't blues or hot stuff."[61] Hoping to enlarge his "breakthrough" audience by recording a ballad, Andy Kirk was discouraged by Decca founder Jack Kapp, who told the bandleader, "You've got something good going for you. Why do you want to do what the white boys are doing?" Finally recorded with new lyrics and released in the summer of 1936, "Until the Real Thing Comes Along" became a huge hit for Kirk, the theme song that signaled the band's escape from the proscribed race-record market.[62]

"There was a whole lot of black music that wasn't played on white jukeboxes, radio stations, theaters and Hollywood movies," agreed Danny Barker, who played guitar for Calloway and Millinder. "Of the millions of jukeboxes around the country, many did not spin black artists." At the same time, "many black jukeboxes only played two or three white artists," preferring to carry instead Ellington, Calloway, Lunceford, and the Mills Brothers. Moreover, recording artists "had to confront these black entrepreneurs, who were subtle rip-off artists," like Mayo "Ink" Williams, who as head of the "race" department for Decca routinely bilked his musicians out of royalties. Decca executive Dave Kapp's treatment of Basie was the most infamous instance of an unfair recording contract. "Without realizing what I was doing, I had agreed to record twelve records a year for $750 a year outright, no royalties," recalled Basie. "I didn't know anything about royalties. John [Hammond] couldn't believe it. He couldn't get us out of the contract, but he was able to get Decca to raise the musicians' pay up to minimum scale."[63] It was these practices that goaded Hammond to write his pseudonymous exposé of Decca for *New Masses*.

Despite the ideology of pluralism and racial equality promulgated by the swing critics, then, racial prejudice pervaded the swing industry. At the broadest level, of course, African-American musicians had to cope with racism from the audiences they played for, both North and South. Because of their inability to get most hotel location jobs or lucrative commercial contracts, black bands were forced to travel more extensively than their white counterparts, frequently in regions where they encountered inconvenience if not outright hostility. Because there were only about a half-dozen hotels for African-Americans in the southern states, musicians were often forced to canvass black neighborhoods for places to sleep, after arriving late at night. Because of the dearth of toilet facilities, black touring musicians generally had to relieve themselves beside the highway; singer Blanche Calloway was arrested and fined in Mississippi for using an unauthorized restroom at a Shell station. Attempts by these northern urbanites unfamiliar with local customs to be served at roadside diners could precipitate murderous rages. Bandleaders that could afford it, like Ellington and Calloway, hired private Pullman cars; others bought or chartered buses. Even so, local conditions occasionally required musicians to move preemptively to the back of *their own* vehicles so as not to attract attention.[64]

Even when performing, black bands faced physical threats, as in a recently oil-rich region of Texas where inebriated patrons fell over one another to attack black musicians playing dances, taking advantage of a law that allowed a white to assault a black for a $300 fine. Fraternizing with whites on or off the bandstand, even when initiated by whites, was especially taboo; members of the Calloway band playing in Fort Lauderdale required a police escort to leave the stand for water during intermission. The same band played the Dallas World's Fair in 1936; forced to leave the fairgrounds to find a bar where they could listen to the first Louis-Schmeling fight and devastated by Joe Louis' loss, Calloway's musicians were then compelled to pay to get back into the fair where they were working. Another musician recalled that when Calloway announced the fight's outcome, whites in the audience stood and applauded. Andy Kirk, who had a relatively benign view of race relations, attributed the band's success in avoiding threatening situations to their early experience playing white ballrooms in Oklahoma, where they imbibed the ethos: "Keep your place. You're here as servants. Please the customers, and everything will be fine."[65]

Racially motivated incidents were not limited to the South. A New York hotel at which Billie Holiday was performing forced her to enter through the back door. In Detroit, a white trumpet player was beaten unconscious and kicked in the mouth for having a drink with Holiday, while the theater's manager forced a troupe of white dancing girls to perform in blackface and wear Mammy costumes to lessen the shock of appearing onstage with the Basie band. Deciding that Holiday herself appeared to be dangerously Caucasian under certain lighting conditions, the management provided the singer with grease paint to darken her complexion. And in Minneapolis, police raided the Harlem Breakfast Club, an after-hours establishment, known for hosting interracial jam sessions between local musicians and members of traveling bands. More than fifty musicians were arrested and jailed overnight, apparently because the club was thought to attract young girls and marijuana users.[66]

In addition to manipulation by record companies and exclusion from many hotel locations and commercially sponsored radio programs, African-American artists faced discrimination from within their own union. Of the 673 AFM locals organized in 1943, 631 were exclusively white and 32 African-American; 8 admitted blacks to "subsidiary" groupings, and only 2—New York's Local 802 and Detroit's Local 5— were fully integrated. Lack of union affiliation meant exclusion from the preferred locations. But sometimes union membership was not enough to ensure fair treatment. Black union musicians in New York and Chicago charged recording companies with hiring only nonunion blacks to make race records, thus ignoring union-mandated standby provisions and enabling the companies to acquire all rights for a small sum to avoid paying royalties. In a rare show of support for the black locals, the AFM pressured RCA Victor and Decca to eliminate these practices. But as *Music and Rhythm* pointed out repeatedly, the AFM was often implicated in the practices of discrimination faced by its African-American members.[67]

White bandleaders and musicians could demonstrate courage in defense of their African-American colleagues. Although the earliest prominent proponent of swing integration, Benny Goodman, hired Wilson and Hampton only after prodding from John Hammond, other bandleaders took up the effort more militantly.[68] Artie Shaw, who stood resolutely by Holiday during various racial incidents when she sang for his band, later cancelled thirty-two one-night engagements in the South in order to avoid trouble over black trumpeter Oran "Lips" Page. Gene Krupa, who in April 1941 became one of the first bandleaders to hire an African-American as a regular band member as opposed to a special attraction, was jailed after punching out a restaurant owner in York,

Pennsylvania, who refused admission to his trumpet star, Roy Eldridge. "This much I can say for Krupa: he's for Negro musicians," attested Eldridge, whose experiences as a featured soloist in white bands were especially traumatic.[69]

Still, an undercurrent of racial hostility existed among musicians themselves. Violinist and bandleader Joe Venuti, for example, reportedly stormed out of a party hosted by white singer Mildred Bailey because Teddy Wilson and his wife were there. One musician announced he would be unwilling to play "beside a jig for even a thousand dollars a week." Asked for their opinion of integrated bands in 1939, at a time when Goodman had added Charlie Christian and Fletcher Henderson (who had long worked behind the scenes as an arranger) to his band, a number of musicians attacked the prospect. "The north has spoiled the Negro and success has made him insolent and overbearing," said a southern musician; another claimed that "the musical ideas of the Negro and White are too far apart for the best results." A third charged that "White people do not want to mix socially with Negroes . . . There have been many instances of Negro musicians making overtures to white women in the cafés they were playing."[70]

Not all racial animosity was aimed at blacks. Glenn Miller considered Italians and Jews "troublemakers" and tried to avoid hiring them, although he conceded that the former made great lead trumpeters (even if they couldn't play "good jazz") and that "You can't have a good band without at least one Jew in it." And Dave Tough, whose career suffered after he married an African-American woman, was supposedly the victim of "reverse discrimination" by blacks in Harlem who were willing to let him sit in but would not drink with him. A few African-American musicians were distressed to discover discrimination by lighter-skinned blacks against those with darker skin. "I was deeply pained to find that colored people in show business were as racist as those crackers that I left in my home state of Alabama," recalled vocalist Viola Jefferson. Conversely, trumpeter Bill Coleman remembered a light-skinned trombone player named Billy Burns turning down a plum job with Paul Whiteman because he didn't want to be taken for a white.[71]

By 1941 the barriers that had previously stood against integrated bands had fallen, with Goodman's hiring of Christian and Henderson and Krupa's hiring of Eldridge. Ironically, this apparently progressive step added still another hardship to the financial prospects of the top black bands. Everything else being equal, white bandleaders and musicians were paid more than their African-American counterparts. The end of the taboo against integrated ensembles made black bands vulnerable to raids by higher-paying white bandleaders. As Goodman sought to rebuild his orchestra in 1940, rumors flew that such stars as Ellington's Cootie Williams and Ben Webster, Basie's Lester Young (and Basie himself), and Lunceford's Trummy Young were soon to join Goodman. Williams did in fact leave Ellington, supposedly for a salary increase of twenty-five dollars a week, a defection that caused even *Metronome* to editorialize against the raiding of established black bands and inspired Raymond Scott to write "When Cootie Left the Duke."[72]

The speculation inspired an impassioned article by Dan Burley in the *Amsterdam News* charging Goodman with "wrecking the topnotch colored bands that he might have the nation's No. 1 all-star mixed combination":

> To dangle such tempting bait as fat salary checks, plus a chance to play in swing music's big leagues, is to the colored musician what a chance to pitch for the Brooklyn Dodgers in the major baseball circuit would be to a member of the N.Y. Black Yankees. In such an instance, the athlete would drop his colored league connections in such a hurry, it wouldn't even be funny. The Negro musician figures to do the same thing. Few would blame them since the money isn't as abundant as the press agents aver in the all-colored field. And the future isn't as bright as we'd like to see it for the average musician buried in a Negro band.

One's first inclination, Burley acknowledged, was to "loudly applaud [Goodman's] courage, his spirit of fair play, his sense of justice in giving Negro musicians the chance they so richly deserve in playing the music they originated." Swing had made it possible for black and white musicians "to know each other on grounds of intimacy never dreamed of in the stilted days of ragtime and jazz": sharing instruments, rooms, cigarettes, money, "while the leaders smile benignly on such intermingling." And white bandleaders had hired blacks as vocalists and featured performers. But because it undercut the precarious existence of the black bands, according to Burley, recruiting star soloists was different, another instance in a long tradition of white appropriation of African-American musical innovations. To claim that the color line did not exist in music was therefore specious: "The Negro has a definite place in swing music—to originate, not to profit . . . the other fellow will tolerate him only so long as he can learn something new." Others observed that the work of artists like Williams and arranger Sy Oliver suffered perceptibly when they deserted their longtime musical bases for lucrative white bands.[73]

To claim that white musicians like Benny Goodman became "hegemonic by colonizing a black art form," to use Cornel West's phrase, is thus to echo an accurate charge that dates back to the high-water mark of swing.[74] A band leader like Basie made the same point, if more obliquely. "He's got some damned good colored boys writing for him," he said of Goodman, "and the white boys have to play because the music is there for them." But it is important to distinguish the "colonizing" impulses of swing as an industry from the intentions of individual artists, many of whom were significant innovators in their own right or went out of their way to credit their African-American mentors. That Goodman's recording of "One O'Clock Jump" sold substantially better than Basie's original reflected the structural bias built into the music industry, not insidious intent on the part of Goodman, who went out of his way to credit Basie during broadcasts of the "Camel Caravan" show.[75]

Passing in Hollywood

In 1942 New Orleans–born clarinetist Barney Bigard quit Ellington's band, moved to Los Angeles, and declared he was not a Negro. A member of Ellington's orchestra since 1927, and earlier associated with King Oliver, Bigard wanted to join the all-white Local 47, knowing that as a black his employment opportunities would be limited. The issue had never come up before, Bigard claimed, because New York's Local 802 was integrated. The union rejected Bigard's petition. The same year, while making *Jammin' the Blues*, one of the more respected swing-era jazz films, guitarist Barney Kessel was persuaded to stain his hands with "berry juice" so as to appear African-American. Warner Brothers was worried about distributing a film, even a short, that appeared to show racial mixing. According to Kessel, the treatment was so successful that in photographs he appeared much darker than the light-skinned Lester Young, prompting jokes that perhaps Young should have been removed from the group.[76]

Incidents of racial passing, whether of black for white or the less common white for black, were not uncommon in the world of jazz or jazz-oriented swing. Bands led by Andy Kirk and Earl Hines could be taken for white by radio listeners, while the Chicago-born Jewish protohipster Mezz Mezzrow's dedication to the jazz subculture of the late 1920s and 1930s inspired legends that his skin grew darker and his nose wider.[77] The conversation depicted in Dorothy Baker's *Young Man With a Horn*, the novel inspired by Bix Beiderbecke but published at the peak of the swing craze, was not farfetched:

> Jack seemed mixed up. He was beginning to feel the gin. "You mean to tell me a white man would play in a coon band? Art Hazard really plays for Jeff Williams?"
> "Hazard isn't white," Rick said.
> "You mean Art Hazard isn't a white man?" Jack said, his jaw way down.
> "Heck no," Rick said, and Tracy, the drummer, backed him up. "He's black as your hat. Haven't you ever seen a picture of him? He's a nigger, all right."

In fact, after leaving Goodman to form his own band, Lionel Hampton was booked by a number of managers who, not having seen photographs of the famous Goodman quartet, assumed Hampton was white. The apparent fascination provoked by the displacement of racial boundaries was not limited to popular music. In his study of the radio-show-turned-television-comedy "Amos'n'Andy," Melvin Ely describes the fascination produced by the racial transgressions of the two white men who performed the show, particularly a 1929 live performance in which the duo appeared in blackface and gradually stripped it off while continuing in dialect.[78] This fascination with the color line seems to have been a well-established feature of American culture since the beginning of the century, as it had been before the Civil War. By rendering the performing subject invisible, the new aural media of recordings and particularly radio facilitated the crossing of racial boundaries.

That Bigard's and Kessel's less successful episodes of racial passing should have occurred in or near Hollywood (Bigard moved to Los Angeles in part to take advantage of employment opportunities in the movie industry) is fitting. First, the racial climate of southern California was extremely inhospitable. Lionel Hampton was one of many African-American musicians who likened conditions in Los Angeles to those in the deep South. "You had to sit in the back of the bus, go into the white nightclubs by the back door," he recalled. "Taxis wouldn't stop for you." And blacks were paid about one-fifth what white musicians made.[79]

More important, the relationship between swing and movies lacked the creative synergy that existed in other sectors of the swing industry. Not that film and music did not enjoy a mutually beneficial arrangement. Most of the swing era's most popular songs came from movies. Because many studios were in partnerships with New York music publishers, they profited from royalties from air play and sheet music sales at the same time the latter helped promote the movies from which they were drawn. But profitable as Hollywood's representation of swing may have been both to studios and to certain bandleaders and entertainers, the fit between the two forms was not without friction, judging from the accounts of those musicians who made movies, the contemporary reaction of the swing press, and the films themselves. Central to the problem of the film version of swing was the problem of race; by rendering visible what the aural media had elided, film created difficulties for a musical form that had always included a latent sense of racial experimentation.[80]

The relationship between film and jazz or, more broadly, the music industry had been problematic well before swing. Al Jolson's *The Jazz Singer* (1927) had little to do with the "jazz" of that era, even with Whiteman's "symphonic" material; but the film's popular success inevitably gave the musical form visual and aural definition for millions of

Americans who had not otherwise encountered it. By converting the racial ambiguities of "authentic" jazz into a clash between first-generation urban Jews and their assimilated offspring—between Old World religious tradition and New World secular culture—the film figured the cultural journey enacted by the Warners and other transplanted easterners who built Hollywood during the 1920s. As Michael Rogin argues, the film obscures the African-American origins of jazz by replacing the "exotic other" with "the split self, the white in blackface," albeit a Jewish white.[81]

But the film's internal ironies are compounded by an external, materialist twist: Vitaphone, in destroying the job market for the live musicians who accompanied silent films, released some of the musical personnel who would staff the swing-era big bands. In 1926, the year before Vitaphone, some 22,000 musicians, about one-fifth of the AFM's membership, were employed in movie-theater pits. By 1929 that number had dropped to 19,000, and after 1930 the number fell drastically, to roughly 5,000. String players were especially hard-hit, as dance bands generally eschewed violins, and musicians had to retool their skills.[82]

Hollywood was quick to sense the commercial possibilities of dance bands, casting Rudy Vallee in *The Vagabond Lover* (1929) and Paul Whiteman in *The King of Jazz* (1930). Ellington's cinematic potential was recognized early, his band featured in a short, *Black and Tan*, as early as 1929. The next year Ellington's orchestra appeared in a ballroom sequence in the Amos'n'Andy film *Check and Double Check* (1930); the radio team was then at the peak of its popularity, far better known than Ellington, whose career received an important boost from the publicity. The Ellington band made two films for Paramount in 1934, *Belle of the Nineties*, starring Mae West, and *Murder at the Vanities*. In January 1936 in Manhattan, Twentieth Century–Fox sponsored what it described as "The First Swing Musicale Presented in America," featuring Fats Waller. "Sandwiched in between examples of piano playing Waller had just recorded for a Twentieth Century–Fox picture (are you beginning to get the idea?) was Waller's version in four-four time of some waltz music to a children's poem by Robert Louis Stevenson," wrote a disdainful critic for the *New Republic*. But "the zenith in wretched pretense," according to the writer, was a parody of Shake-

speare's "The Lover and His Lass." "The upshot of this sort of promotion, of course, is going to be that the public will be sold a great
deal of spurious music masquerading under the label of jazz," a familiar
lament.[83]

With the onset of swing as a popular craze, Hollywood rushed to
enlist its most prominent artists. By the late 1930s the old relationship
between music and film, in which (silent) movie theaters provided jobs
for musicians, had been reversed. Swing bands, in a final irony, attracted
large audiences to theaters where even mediocre movies were playing,
leading Hollywood to consider integrating big bands directly into the
films themselves.[84] The issue then became: In what capacity should the
bands be used? Should they be functionally emplotted, or simply spliced
in to provide musical variety, much as live bands in theaters did? Most
moviemakers chose the latter strategy, with the result that scores of
films during the late 1930s and 1940s featured swing bands and personalities.

In *Swing It, Professor* (1937), Kay Kyser plays a pedantic academic
whose professed dedication to the eternal, autonomous realm of European art music makes him recoil from the "barbaric" tom-tom
rhythms of swing, identified in the film as a musical fad that fits the
rapid tempo of contemporary life. Quitting his job because he can't
abide the swing craze sweeping the campus, the professor becomes a
happy Depression hobo, falling in with an ethnically diverse hobo camp
and avoiding arrest at one point by serenading an Irish cop with a Celtic
folksong. He eventually straggles into a nightclub, where he is mistaken
for a fearsome gangster, and manages to bumble along in his new identity. Attracting a hoodlum's moll, who teaches him to enjoy swing
despite himself by dancing with him, the professor ultimately falls in
love, while the erstwhile gangster falls for a farm girl and becomes an
agrarian.

This type of plot resurfaces in *Ball of Fire* (1941) and its virtual
remake, *A Song Is Born* (1947). In both films, a laughably unworldly
professor falls for a nightclub singer/moll in the course of research that
takes him outside the monastic Manhattan foundation in which he is
cloistered with a team of émigré scholars. In the first, he is an English
professor (Gary Cooper) preparing an encyclopedia article on slang; in

the latter, he is a musicologist (Danny Kaye) conducting field work on popular music for an ambitious world *History of Music*. Gene Krupa's orchestra makes a cameo appearance in *Ball of Fire*, while *A Song Is Born* makes more extensive use of a star cast comprising Benny Goodman (who plays one of the émigré scholars), Louis Armstrong, Lionel Hampton, Charlie Barnet, Tommy Dorsey, Mel Powell, Louis Bellson, and others.

Whereas these films invoked swing's challenge to cultural hierarchies by satirizing academia, *The Duke Is Tops* (1938) (later renamed *Bronze Venus*) focused on the novelties of the new transnational culture represented by swing. When a talent scout for a New York booking office sees Ethel (Lena Horne) sing in the South, her boyfriend-producer Duke (played by Ralph Cooper of Apollo Theatre fame) "sells" her off, hoping to free her to fulfill her talent without being inhibited by her loyalty to him. She eventually bombs on Broadway, and his next show fails badly. Duke then teams up with an old-fashioned medicine show promoting "Doctor Durando's Elixir," in the course of which a variety of African-American acts perform. His producing talents make the show a huge success, saving Doctor Durando from bankruptcy. Hearing news of Ethel's failure over the radio, Duke leaves the quack to rescue her in New York. They finally find success starring together in a stage spectacular in Philadelphia; the New York agents who initially "stole" her away attend the show and express their approval of the collaboration.

In nearly all these films, swing appears only for atmosphere, its performers making brief and improbable cameo appearances, a fact that consistently riled supporters of the music. (Miller's *Sun Valley Serenade* [1941] and *Orchestra Wives* [1942] are exceptions.) *Down Beat* had complained as early as 1938 that the movies, along with Tin Pan Alley, were lowering public taste and causing a loss of respect for musicians. "Go to any musical picture and tell me that anything but trash is coming into your ears," the article challenged. "Not only doesn't it swing—not only is it not jazz—it's even stinking as sweet music." Rather than promote the careers of real musicians, movies have "publicized [Irving] Berlin as the spirit of American jazz." By 1941, when such stars as Charlie Barnet, the Dorseys, Woody Herman, Harry James, Sammy

Kaye, Gene Krupa, Jimmie Lunceford, Freddy Martin, Glenn Miller, and Jack Teagarden converged on Hollywood, lingering because of the AFM recording ban and wartime gasoline rationing, the swing press had launched a biting critique of the practices of Hollywood.[85]

In an editorial titled "Hollywood Is Jazz' Deadliest Enemy," *Down Beat* attacked the flat stereotypes projected by the movies, especially the notions that all classical music was stuffy and that jazz was merely a fad. A fan wrote to complain of Hollywood's tendency to represent African-American musicians solely as comedic showmen, while a serviceman from Louisiana wrote, "Hollywood's present attitude to our jazz greats stinks. I'm eagerly looking forward to the day they get out of their Mickey Mouse suits and give us jazz as it should be played." A later editorial, "Will Hollywood Ever Get Hep?" decried the use of big-name swing stars for promoting films in which they appeared only briefly. "Hollywood is suffering from a frustration complex," concluded a *Down Beat* writer. "It is excruciatingly aware of the box-office value of dance orchestras, but it hasn't the faintest idea of just what to do about it . . . No one has, as yet, come up with a sure-fire formula for the use of dance bands in pictures—a formula, which by Hollywood tradition, must eliminate the necessity for imagination and inspiration." Barry Ulanov of *Metronome* agreed, calling the situation "very sad, worth weeping over, in fact."[86]

The same article explained how swing had been reduced to such a predictable and, to its closest admirers, disappointing role. The AFM local with jurisdiction over Hollywood required bands not affiliated with that local to play a "featured role" in films in which they appeared, thereby requiring screenwriters to invent often fantastic stretches of plot to integrate them. Moreover, because of the high scale for local musicians, it frequently cost less to make movies using nationally known "name bands." Scale ran from $30 to $60 an hour for musicians actually playing in the films, but only $16.50 for musicians who only *appeared* to be playing. Musicians would record the soundtrack first, then play-act to their music, often excessively. This system created its own implausibilities, which further galled those dedicated to the music; Tommy Dorsey's *Las Vegas Nights* (1941), for example, showed a conventional big band on the bandstand, while the soundtrack gushed the sound of a full string section.[87]

Disdain for Hollywood's representation of swing was part of a larger wave of resentment against the industry's depiction of African-Americans. Citing a long tradition of racist films, the black press and others called for more realistic and respectful portrayal of blacks. Confessed writer Dalton Trumbo:

> In Hollywood the most gigantic milestones of our appeal to public patronage have been the anti-Negro pictures, "The Birth of a Nation" and "Gone With the Wind." And between the two, from 1915 to 1940, we have produced turgid floods of sickening and libelous treacle. We have made tarts of the Negro's daughters, crap shooters of his sons, obsequious Uncle Toms of his fathers, superstitious and grotesque crones of his mothers, strutting peacocks of his successful men, psalm-singing mountebanks of his priests and Barnum and Bailey sideshows of his religion.

A poll conducted by the *Negro Digest* found that an overwhelming majority of both blacks and whites believed that the portrayal of blacks in films was "degrading." A study by the curator of the Schomburg Collection found that of approximately 100 films that included black themes or characters, three-quarters were "anti-Negro." Efforts to harmonize race relations on behalf of the war mobilization brought pressure from the Office of War Information and a well-publicized meeting between the NAACP's Walter White and Wendell Willkie and movie executives Darryl Zanuck and Walter Wanger. Meanwhile, southern censors reportedly excised sequences from films featuring Cab Calloway, Lena Horne, and others, often at the expense of plot continuity.[88]

By some measures, these efforts to upgrade the depiction of blacks yielded some improvements. Consider *Ball of Fire*, which cut Eldridge from the few scenes showing the Krupa band; the version released six years later (*A Song Is Born*) showed interracial jam sessions and gave prominent roles to Armstrong and Hampton. But to a large degree Hollywood's conservative attitudes outlived the war. In July 1946 *Down Beat* reported that Monogram pictures, in deference to southern sensibilities, had substituted white actors for black musicians in a movie featuring Charlie Barnet's integrated band. The editors charged that "no American industry has failed so completely to meet its aesthetic, civic and moral obligations." [89]

138 — Swing Changes

Two films epitomize the way in which the expectations of swing enthusiasts were raised and dashed by Hollywood. Organized around the flashbacks of a retiring dance star (Bill Robinson), the talent-packed *Stormy Weather* (1943) provides yet another version of the history of African-American music: a post-Armistice cakewalk performed by returning black servicemen; minstrels on a cotton-packing riverboat; Fats Waller's bravura performance of "Ain't Misbehavin'" in a Beale Street club where a female blues singer also performs; a blackface vaudeville routine in a Harlem club; Cab Calloway's jiving hipsterism set in the film's present. The plot, just enough to provide continuity between the various acts, depicts Bill's romantic pursuit of Selina (Lena Horne), which is frustrated when Selina resists motherhood to pursue her career; eventually she relents. *Down Beat*'s review was sharply critical of both the film itself and the system that produced it. The magazine reported that its black "musical supervisor" had quit when his bosses at Twentieth Century–Fox insisted on the "hot, sexy, primitive" dance scene that ended the film. "'Stormy Weather' is just another filmusical," the review stated, "except that its cast is composed of Negroes—sincere, hard-working, highly talented Negroes who are conscious to varying degrees of the fact that their white bosses insist that Negroes be depicted not as what they are but as what the white bosses think the American white public wants them to be."[90]

Another talent-rich production, *New Orleans* (1947), suffered a similar fate at the hand of its studio. Joe Glaser recruited an all-star crew for a film purporting to be about New Orleans jazz. According to producer Jules Levey: "Hollywood films dealing with jazz in the past have shown Negro musicians who created this rich art as children playing with primitive rhythms, as savages bringing the jungle into the dance halls, or as melody drunk clowns. We intend to break with all these 'traditions.' I believe that the men who gave America the gift of this exciting music ought to be treated with the respect due all creative artists." In addition to Armstrong, who led the band, Glaser lined up New Orleans luminaries Kid Ory, Barney Bigard, Zutty Singleton, and Bud Scott, as well as the Woody Herman orchestra. Billie Holiday, then near the apex of her career, was also hired. She had assumed she would be playing an entertainer; learning that her role was a maid,

Holiday was restrained from backing out only by Glaser's threat that she would never work in Hollywood. The studio sent in a dramatic coach to help Holiday "get the right kind of Tom feeling" in her lines, which as she recalled were limited: " 'Yez, Miss Marylee. No, Miss Marylee,' in twenty-three different kinds of ways." She also feuded with the film's female lead. According to Bigard, who generally enjoyed the filming, Holiday showed up twelve days late for shooting and was " 'ornery' at the time, and kind of nasty." By the time the film was released, nearly all the musical footage had been excised, and the film was generally conceded to be a failure.[91]

New Orleans was the pallid product of an ambitious project initiated in 1941 by Orson Welles. The director had cultivated a number of jazz artists as they passed through California, including Billie Holiday, who introduced him to the African-American nightlife of Los Angeles' Central Avenue. The morning after seeing Ellington's band perform "Jump for Joy" at the Mayan Theatre in the summer of 1941, Welles summoned the bandleader to his office at RKO and proceeded to offer a detailed critique of the performance—"both a review and a mass of suggestions," according to Ellington, who recalled it as "the most impressive display of mental power I've ever experienced." Welles then offered the bandleader $1,000 a week to cowrite and codirect a film on the history of jazz, which was to have been included in the epic four-part production, *It's All True*. Ellington accepted the offer readily. A large team of researchers and writers was hired for Ellington, but Welles had a falling out with RKO and the project was dropped, Ellington having written twenty-eight bars of music. But the writer whom Welles engaged for *The Story of Jazz*, Elliott Paul, turned up years later in the credits to *New Orleans*. And in 1944 the New Orleans band that Welles hired for his CBS radio show included many of the musicians who would appear in *New Orleans*: Kid Ory, Zutty Singleton, Jimmie Noone, and eventually Barney Bigard, who described Welles as a "real swell fellow" and very knowledgeable about jazz.[92]

The romance of swing and Hollywood was riddled with ironies and frustrated expectations. The movie industry first made jobs for musicians, eliminated those positions after 1927, then created a different category of employment, putting musicians in the films themselves.

The theater musicians who provided the sound for silent movies were rehired, albeit in much smaller numbers, because only top national bands were considered. In effect, swing became an appendage of Hollywood's publicity engine, an advertising image for a poster or a marquee. The prevailing impulse of the 1930s culture industry, toward national consolidation, was further confirmed.

Illusion and simulacra were integral to other sectors of the swing industry, of course. Such techniques were crucial to the success of radio in creating its audience-communities. The Meadowbrook, a barn in New Jersey, was capable of conjuring images of glittering Manhattan for listeners around the country. "Make Believe Ballroom" created its effects by dispensing with live bands altogether. Records likewise created effects in listeners not fully accounted for by the technological process alone. The irony of Hollywood is that the nation's shrine to simulacra defeated one of the illusions that had worked to broaden the possibilities of African-Americans in music. By reinscribing the visible signs of race that had been elided by the aural media of radio and recordings, Hollywood was forced to make a choice: either to confront directly the fetish of race around which all swing artists negotiated, or to accept and indulge that fetish by evading it. It was the latter course, with its berry-juice blackface, stereotyped casting, and requisite sexy and primitive jungle dance scenes, that the movie industry chose. In this sense, Hollywood's racial contradictions served as a fitting microcosm of the larger mass culture industry, which both exploited and advanced the music with which it was so closely bound during the 1930s and 1940s.

Sarah Martin and Her Jass Fools in a "hot jazz" pose typical of the 1920s.

An early Benny Carter ensemble on the bandstand at the Savoy, arranged in the dignified symmetry favored by swing bands.

Duke Ellington and orchestra in 1939.

Fletcher Henderson, Ben Webster, and other distinguished musicians at a fancy dress party in 1934.

Bands in Hollywood to shoot movies usually secured engagements at local ballrooms. The Benny Goodman Orchestra at the Ambassador Hotel's Coconut Grove ballroom in Los Angeles, 1940.

Duke Ellington and orchestra on location on the RKO studio lot in the early 1930s.

WHERE A SAXOPHONE
HAD TO BE GOOD!

One letter in our mail the other day drew special attention. It was from a war prison camp in Germany. The writer was a member of the Royal Canadian Air Forces.*

He was unlucky enough to be captured by the Germans. But he was lucky, too, in the prison camp—but let him tell it:

"I am using a Martin Alto Sax (serial number 145206) issued by the American Red Cross. *Here in the prison camp we have no repair facilities and a sax must be really good.* My Martin has given exceptionally good results."

By now it's a familiar story—the way Martins have stood up under the severest conditions of military service. Not a single Martin instrument supplied to the armed forces has been rejected or returned because of any defect. And mu-

sicians in the service have written us from all parts of the world to praise the performance of the Martins they play.

The reason is clear. In addition to their superb musical qualities, Martins have always been durably built for dependable and lasting service. Naturally the splendid new Martins which will be available after war restrictions are lifted will be distinguished for this quality.

Incidentally, our RCAF correspondent asked us to send his Martin Post-War Purchase bond to his folks in Canada. Remember, this Martin bond is worth $25 cash on a new Martin instrument—and *it's free to any musician in the service now playing a Martin*—his own, or government issue. Send name, address, and serial number of the instrument and we'll mail the bond.   * Name supplied on request.

THE *MARTIN* BAND INSTRUMENT-COMPANY
ELKHART, INDIANA

"Here in the prison camp we have no repair facilities and a sax must be really good." From an advertisement by the Martin Band Instrument Company, *Down Beat*, May 1, 1945.

4

The Conscription of Swing

"Jazz is the wail of America's weeping soul." So begins a vignette about the chance meeting of two enlisted musicians in a southwestern railroad yard in 1944. An eastbound train of marines pulls in from the California desert alongside a westbound army train. After a stifling half-hour, sitting motionless in the nighttime drizzle, a soldier named Franklin pulls out a trumpet and begins playing. ("The throbbing melody resolved into a distinguishable melody—the St. Louis Blues played slow and hot. The liquid tone spread in agonizing ripples of sound; the last note echoed far over the still desert night.") A marine private, Schwartzman, moves down the train to a window facing Franklin, pulls out his horn, and challenges Franklin to a cutting contest. (Franklin: "Ah ain't touched this horn in six months. Ah'm beat, man! My lip—no good!" Schwartzman: "Hell with it! I ain't played this one in two years! Let's go!")

The men play ("with each other, at each other, around each other, and apart from each other") for over an hour, eyes closed, shoulders hunched, sweating profusely, egged on by a "crying, stamping, rocking audience." "Melancholy Baby." "Honeysuckle Rose." "Blue Skies." "One O'clock Jump." "Chinatown." "Somebody Stole My Gal." "Darktown Strutter's Ball." ("The two men played each to a fare-thee-well. They played after their lips were so sore they were without feeling, after the ache of their breathless chests, and legs cramped at the open windows, had grown sickening.") Their audience sits rapt. Unable to restrain themselves, six white-jacketed porters get off the train and begin "to jitter on the ties with graceful, slithery movements and burlesque high knee action."

Finally one train begins to pull away; the trumpeters break simultaneously ("as if at the behest of an invisible baton") into "Auld Lang Syne"; soldiers and marines cheer, break into song, and wave goodby.

> On the soldier train, headed westward into the California desert—westward to where a ship lay at anchor waiting for them—the men prepared for sleep that night, oddly refreshed. A catalyst, the music called jazz had drawn out their souls. It had said, plainly and confidingly to each of them, some of the personal things about life back home, about their sweethearts, about the strange lands they were traveling toward, which these guys had wanted to say but for which they hadn't been able to find the proper words. Further, they had lost some of that loneliness which is paradoxically each soldier's lot in an army of ten million. For jazz had bared other souls to them that night, souls of utter strangers, which had yet proved wonderfully and warmly kin to their own. Jazz by its magic had done all this in one, brief, incidental hour while rain fell and railroad smoke clogged the air.[1]

To its partisans jazz was indeed the ideal music with which to roll into what was widely considered a Manichaean struggle against fascism. As the railroad yard tableau suggests, jazz was a music that spanned East and West, capable of uniting a disparate military around the trumpet performances of two musicians who might be taken as figures of the rural black South and the urban ethnic North. Although some people in and out of the military yearned for the shared marching music and martial songs of the Great War, American culture and its music had been irrevocably changed by the ascendancy of swing in the half-decade before 1941. The scandalous music just entering public awareness during the previous conflict had metamorphosed into swing, a music that by 1940 many Americans and foreigners recognized as America's most distinctive contribution to the world's musical culture. Not surprisingly, swing found itself transformed into a galvanizing symbol of national purpose.

Swing was not the only cultural form to receive a special commission in the war effort, of course. Its deployment was a small part of a vast cultural mobilization that enlisted conductors and composers, poets and writers, comedians and filmmakers. "As never before do we realize that art and culture are a stronghold against the aggressor and his devastating, demoralizing forces . . . this is a war of the people as much as of the armies, of the artists as much as of the soldiers," asserted Boston Symphony conductor Serge Koussevitzky. The war inspired an unprecedented output of cultural and intellectual work aimed at linking the democratic ideology with a sense of American identity, and at demonstrating the existence of a unique American character through its cultural and political traditions. Music was a crucial component of this American identity. Koussevitzky urged musicians to compose "hymns of freedom and victory" and "marches to vanquish the foe" on behalf of the "ageless ideals of independence and democracy." In the U.S. war effort, jazz was part of a much larger cultural impulse whose urgency blurred the schisms that had divided the swing community into rival camps: hot jazz versus swing, swing versus sweet.[2]

But the distinctive ideology that had accrued to swing during the 1930s—a belief in American exceptionalism, in ethnic pluralism and democratic equality—was ideally suited to the collective needs of a nation battling fascism. They were the very ideals thought to inspire the heroism needed in Europe and the Pacific, and the sense of sacrifice needed domestically. A few months before Pearl Harbor, President Roosevelt addressed the National Federation of Music Clubs in language bearing clear traces of this swing ideology. Music, a "universal tongue," has the power to make people aware of their "common humanity," to "strengthen democracy against those forces which would subjugate and enthrall mankind," the president wrote. More specifically, music "can help promote tolerance of minority groups in our midst by showing their cultural contributions to our American life," and even "promote hemispheric friendship and understanding by popularizing the music of our Latin-American neighbors." Fittingly, it was Benny Goodman whom Roosevelt later named musical coordinator for the Pan-American Committee; the bandleader also served as honorary chairman of the Popular Music Division of Russian War Relief.[3]

The Second World War was a watershed moment in the formation of American society, creating new forms and linkages in industry and government, new notions of gender and racial identity, and a host of other fundamental changes in the culture. In particular, the unprecedented demands that the war placed on the nation's labor force transformed traditional attitudes toward the economic participation of blacks and women. As President Roosevelt warned in 1942: "In some communities employers dislike to hire women. In others they are reluctant to hire Negroes. We can no longer afford to indulge such prejudice."[4]

Beginning in the mid-1930s, the swing industry had anticipated the changing racial attitudes that became national ideals during the war. Whatever forms of racial discrimination it still harbored, the swing industry was clearly in the forefront of the new ideology of pluralism and racial tolerance, demonstrating the virtues of integration in a highly conspicuous way. It set a standard that other sectors of American society—the military and professional baseball, for example—took years to match. By adapting and underscoring the ideological content that swing had already assumed, the war conferred patriotic legitimacy on the music. And by enlisting it in the military deployment, it also dispersed the music throughout the globe, preparing the way for the quasi-evangelical function that jazz would provide in the postwar era.

Yet by highlighting the national ideals that swing was supposed to embody, the war called into question the symbolic content of swing. The war heightened its contradictory cultural impulses, and bridging these cultural and social oppositions became doubly difficult in the stress of wartime. Above all, a music that had drawn much of its power for its audience from its hostility to racial barriers was confronted both with a Jim Crow military and a populace unexpectedly intransigent in adhering to the racism that swing took credit for helping dissolve.

The war also revealed a significant blind spot in the swing ideology. Although the shortage of civilian musicians created some opportunities, women did not benefit from the militant spirit of inclusion that had characterized the swing community on the race issue. War revealed, on the contrary, that this community was far better labeled a fraternity. A handful of women were accepted in predominantly male bands, and all-female bands enjoyed popular audience support; but these facts triggered no fundamental rethinking of women's place in the musical world. Neither the swing ideology nor the larger discourse of Americanism that comprised it had much need for women, a fact revealed by the strikingly homoerotic ritualism of the military train vignette.

Women appeared to lie outside the realm of the thinkable among the more influential members of this otherwise open-minded subculture.[5]

Soldiers of Music

Within weeks of Pearl Harbor, the swing industry faced a variety of challenges to its economic viability. Blackouts were decreed in urban areas where clubs and halls were located; the manufacture of jukeboxes was banned, and production of musical instruments was drastically curtailed; rationing of gasoline and rubber combined with restrictions on civilian use of railroads and buses to limit sharply the national tours that had delivered the bulk of big-band revenues (incidentally making location jobs more lucrative); shortages of shellac dictated that recording (already curtailed by the AFM recording ban) proceed only under zero-sum conditions in which old records were traded in and their shellac recycled; wool conservation efforts even forced musicians to wear tuxedos instead of band uniforms. New policy decrees continued to handicap swing until almost the war's end. In the spring of 1944 a 30 percent cabaret tax was levied; the following winter a national midnight curfew was decreed. Some felt that the war was being used as an excuse to persecute and ruin the popular music; others blamed the fractious nature of the industry itself. "Unless the music industry and the American Federation of Musicians take immediate steps to effect a united front among all those interested in providing music," predicted *Music and Rhythm*, "there will be a dimout of creative activity in the music business and a shutdown in jobs."[6]

Compounding these formidable material obstacles was an additional challenge: to prove that a musical form associated by much of the American public with mild rebellion and frivolous antics had relevance to winning a deadly serious war against fascism. The ability of popular music to lift morale was well known and widely touted among military experts. Citing the preternatural capacity of "Alexander's Ragtime Band" to "regenerate" a column of "sweaty, weary infantrymen," a soldier described the sundry activities sponsored by the army to guarantee the presence of music in the war zone; "the longest march actually becomes fun with the aid of a good snappy march tune," he said.

Familiar music seemed to have unique powers to raise morale and promote solidarity in stressful conditions. A group of Americans caught in Shanghai after the outbreak of hostilities had assembled a torrid dance band in their internment camp. As a group of internees left the camp, the band broke into "God Bless America." "Tears were rolling down the cheeks of dusky Jimmy Brown, crack trumpet player but he played as never before," an eyewitness reported. "Others, too, were misty eyed. A mighty cheer went up from the prisoners and the alarmed guards came running from all directions, bayonets fixed." One of the band members assured the guards that "it was only music and not an uprising," but the order was given not to play that number again. Even advertisements for musical instruments exploited this theme. One instrument manufacturer published an advertisement under a drawing of prisoners of war jamming in a prison camp while a German soldier patrolled outside the barbed wire. "Here in the prison camp we have no repair facilities and a sax must be really good," wrote a soldier, adding that his own had held up.[7]

Maintaining civilian morale was equally important. According to a former postmaster general, "Entertainment and sports are the greatest antidote against hysteria, and we need them to win the war!" *Down Beat* observed: "Working people newly burdened with war production pressure at home, and with casualty reports from abroad, are seeking the gayer atmosphere of clubs for entertainment and relief." But with abundant jobs and income, "normal moral repressions may vanish" amid "a fatalistic spending spree," the writer cautioned. "IT WILL BE OUR JOB TO KEEP EMOTIONS NORMAL AND HEALTHY." With demand for entertainment rising dramatically, and American workers adjusting to twenty-four-hour factory production schedules, musicians endowed the term *swing shift* with a double meaning by adding extra dances for workers just completing early morning stints.[8]

But acceptance of swing faced more difficulties than an Irving Berlin tune or "snappy march." Though not generating as much moral opprobrium as 1920s jazz had, swing provoked ambivalent reactions among the arbiters of mainstream American cultural life, and the elements of resistance were heightened by the crisis atmosphere of war. The perception of rising juvenile delinquency apparently caused by working mothers and absent fathers, coupled with race riots in Harlem, Detroit, and Los Angeles, led to calls to close "jook joints" and ban jukeboxes. A U.S. senator opined in 1943 that "if the ban on recordings wipes out jitterbug music, jive and boogie-woogie, it might be a good thing all around." New York Philharmonic conductor Artur Rodzinski created a furor the following year by calling "boogie-woogie music . . . one of the greatest causers of delinquency among American youth today," singling out teenage devotees of Frank Sinatra as "pitiful cases."[9]

As during previous moral panics, swing proponents were quick to develop an aggressive defense of the music. "Can't Blame Jazz for Flaming Youth Delinquent Acts," proclaimed a *Down Beat* editorial. A panel assembled to rebut Rodzinski's charges resurrected many of the relativist arguments that had been deployed to defend jitterbugs against moralists. Swing was a symptom of the times, no more dangerous than earlier dance forms like the waltz or Turkey Trot, which had also been condemned in their time. "The world doesn't lilt today," an educator pointed out. "It rocks, it staggers, it reels, it writhes, shudders and quivers—well, that's swing." Even the "extreme behavior" associated with Sinatra groupies "has its normal and healthy aspects, because it is a means of helping to solve *erotic* drives and of sublimating them," insisted a psychologist. Although juvenile delinquency was a palpable problem, the educator acknowledged, it was attributable not to swing or boogie-woogie but to social dislocations created by the war mobilization: "both parents at work, the home demagnetized, adolescents with plenty of spending money, the feeble influence of religion and failure of education."[10]

Some went further, claiming that swing was a positive good. A doctor with American Flying Services commended Benny Goodman for his music's salutary impact on the reflexes and conditioning of young fliers. "Results of our mental and physical tests prove conclusively that young men who are dance fans—specifically jitterbugs—have a better sense of rhythm, timing, and muscular coordination than those who have no musical knowledge or appreciation," he said. "Indirectly, you and your fellow orchestra leaders have done much towards sharpening and bringing out the faculties so essential to flying and the activities incurred during flights."[11]

There were more traditional ways for swing artists to demonstrate their support for the war effort, of course. Many volunteered for military service. A "Band Leaders' Honor Roll" from March 1943 showed thirty-nine former band leaders enlisted in the army, seventeen in the navy, three in the merchant marines, and two in the coast guard. Glenn Miller, after proposing that musicians' late hours made them natural air-raid wardens, enlisted in the army with the express purpose of volunteering his musical services. Drummer Buddy Rich, on the other hand, joined the marines in order, he said, "to beat a tattoo on the heads of a lot of Japs with lead." Artie Shaw won widespread plaudits, including *Metronome*'s "Musician of the Year" award, for assembling and leading a crack navy band that toured the South Pacific, playing shows at Pearl Harbor, New Caledonia, the Solomon Islands, New Hebrides, Guadalcanal (where the band came under air attack), New Zealand, and Australia. Shaw recalled the reaction when the band would show up "on some God-forsaken island unexpectedly. Some of them throw gifts at the band. Others cry. Most of them just listen, devouring everything we kick off."[12]

Other musicians lent their support as civilians. Within a month of Pearl Harbor, 200 name musicians volunteered for United Service Organization (USO) tours of military bases. On Christmas Day 1942, Coca-Cola hired forty top bands, including Ellington's, James's, and Goodman's, to play from noon until midnight over 142 radio stations across the United States. Saxophonist Frank Trumbauer, whose 1920s recordings with Paul Whiteman and Bix Beiderbecke influenced Lester Young among many others, quit the music business to become an aeronautics inspector; the war found him testing new bombers in Kansas City for North American Aviation. Swing's most prominent artists, including Fats Waller, lent their services to selling war bonds.[13]

As in other sectors of American society, this spirit of patriotic sacrifice competed with impulses toward private self-interest. For every swing musician accepted by the military there were others who received deferments, sometimes against their will but often because they sought a 4-F classification. Woody Herman, for example, had a doctor induce a hernia to help him avoid service, later claiming to have believed that he would be contributing more to the war effort as a bandleader than as a gun carrier. Fletcher Henderson turned down an army commission for similar reasons, preferring to boost civilian morale by touring with his band. Musicians leery of military service exchanged tips on how to evade conscription. Basie trumpeter Buck Clayton attempted to emulate musician friends who had escaped induction by eating soap and drinking Benzedrine; he nearly killed himself but was accepted for service anyway. Dizzy Gillespie succeeded in being deferred by behaving eccentrically and implying that he might shoot American whites rather than Germans in a combat situation. "Well, look . . . here in the United States whose foot has been up my ass?" he claims to have said by way of explanation.[14] The constant mobility of the big bands made it relatively easy for unwilling musicians to avoid conscription, but nearly all were eventually tracked down by draft boards, sometimes receiving draft notices at dance halls.

As draft boards proved themselves relentless enforcers of the "work or fight" edict against even the best-known bandleaders, the trade press elaborated its rationale for sparing musicians. "Should Name Band Heads Be Deferred to Build Morale?" a *Down Beat* editorial rhetorically asked, referring specifically to Kay Kyser, who was deferred but remained extremely active with the USO. "Bandsmen today are not just musicians," insisted another editorial. "They are soldiers of music." Servicemen preferred that top ensembles be kept together so that their quality would be maintained:

> Is a despondent man with a gun more effective in wiping out the enemy, just because he has a gun, than a man with a horn? Not at all . . . The soldier in Africa inspired by Muggsy [Spanier] . . . thinking back to the night he listened to him in New York, is very likely thinking ahead to the time he can get back and take up that listening where he left off. *And it's hardly stretching it to say he's a better fighter, a safer fighter, for knowing Muggsy's still in there blowing his head off, rather than getting it blown off in battle somewhere.*

In this war, morale was best protected not by creating the kind of national pride associated with patriotic songs, but by appealing to an exclusive and privatized notion of aesthetic experience.[15]

Apparently not all the rank and file accepted such a rationale. Servicemen in the South Pacific wrote angrily to protest effusive coverage of Artie Shaw's heroic tour that ignored the deprivation experienced by GIs in the trenches. Although most enlisted personnel appeared to accept the fact that many musicians had genuine deferments and frequently doubled at defense factories, they reportedly taunted some with the epithet "slacker." In some areas musicians risked being assaulted by resentful servicemen. *Metronome* periodically scolded musicians, particularly name bandleaders, for shirking their patriotic responsibilities. The "little guys, the tiny bands, all over the country have responded handsomely to the USO call, while you big fellows have been, with very few exceptions, quick to refuse, fast to find excuses, shamefully absent from soldiers' camps and sailors' bases." Despite the efforts of Goodman, Kyser, Herman, Norvo, Sammy Kaye, and Guy Lombardo, some musicians were "griping," "not showing up for Army record sessions and broadcasts, working grudgingly, grumblingly, not really cooperating at all." These musicians apparently "can stay up all night to have a ball, but not to make records for the Army." The press made the most of exceptions to this pattern, like a band composed of Seabees who played jazz in addition to their full work details. "The Seabee swing band is becoming known as the band that won't quit—come air raids, or high water, plagues of insects, windstorms or torrential rains," reported *Down Beat.*[16]

Invidious comparisons were inevitably made with the music and musicians of previous conflicts, when a more general sense of commitment presumably governed. Some decried the war's "comparative songlessness," looking back nostalgically to the Great War, when both enlisted men and civilians shared a repertoire of popular songs: "Over There," "Tipperary," "K-K-K-Katy," and "Keep the Home Fires Burning." "So far this war has produced no war songs which have spread through the armed services and the entire nation," observed the USO's music coordinator. He attributed this absence to "the specialization of modern war—with motorized infantry, paratroops, ski troops, commandos and others—the men want a song of their own."[17] Major Glenn Miller offered two theories on why the war was not producing the great songs previous wars had. One was that Americans were too angry to sing. But he also speculated that a more profound change had taken place: radio had dulled Americans' fervor for public participation, turning the United States into a "listening nation." Admitted an army major: "The Army is not singing as a whole. When we went into this thing none of us was singing. But we're getting a song in our heart . . . We are breaking some barriers in the Army itself and it is rapidly becoming a singing army."[18]

Some blamed the military itself for undervaluing and mishandling music. "The military authorities have apparently not yet recognized the great spiritual power of serous music in a time of war," charged Lawrence Tibbett, a famous baritone angered by the decision to force a "well-known American composer" (and army private) to turn down an invitation to compose a symphonic musical greeting to the Russian people. "The OWI [Office of War Information] has sent out helpful hints to pulp magazine fiction writers and has tried to inspire Tin Pan Alley experts to turn out ditties about saving scrap. But it would appear that serious musicians are not considered of potential value to their country in this crisis." "Why Isn't Music Being Permitted to Do Its Part in Winning This War?" asked a *Down Beat* editorial stressing the importance of music for parades and in military camps and factories. "Now, is the time for America to harness music's full powers in its drive to STAMP OUT OUR ENEMIES AND SWEEP ON TO FULL VICTORY!"[19]

To others, Tin Pan Alley rather than the military was "out of step," producing inferior patriotic songs. "What happened to the industry that yesterday made America ask, 'Brother, Can You Spare a Dime?' and today fails to make America sing for the defeat of fascism?" wrote a coast guard musician frustrated with songs like "When Yuba Plays the Thumba on the Tuba" and "Dance with a Dolly" for War Manpower Commission broadcasts and blood donor campaigns. "Why isn't there a rousing 'Give-your-protector-blood-plasma' song? Where is the throbbing song to inspire the boys still in training here at home? Why do we never hear them rally, at home, to 'Get the dirty fascists!' and by what rule of saving our lives do the song publishers actually prohibit the name of Hitler in the title of a war song?" Music publishers accused bandleaders of refusing to play their patriotic fare, while leaders charged publishers with trying to foist defective merchandise on them. The head of OWI's Radio Section expressed hope that exposing Americans to "worthy war songs on radio" would "drive away" the "drivel" that dominated the airwaves. "What [Americans] need are songs that will help sustain them through the losses and sacrifices," intoned ASCAP's general manager. "They need songs that glorify the fight the United States are waging, songs that say *what* we are fighting for." Presumably in response to this crisis of music, the U.S. government began suggesting themes for songwriters to follow. "New Batch of Patriotic Music Set to Flow Soon," *Down Beat* reported, as ASCAP and BMI snapped into action with new songs.[20]

Possibly because of concern over a perceived decline in group singing, the army also undertook programs to encourage soldiers to make their own music. One initiative purported to teach soldiers to play toy or miniature instruments like harmonicas and ukeleles in ten minutes. In the last year of the war alone, the army issued nearly a million instruments; half were harmonicas, along with flutes, ocarinas, and ukeleles.[21]

But new technology was radically transforming the function of music in the armed services, reducing the need for traditional marching music and simultaneously making possible new applications for popular music. Both radio and recording, barely developed commercially during the First World War, were pressed into widespread service. Radio in particular lent itself to morale-building and propaganda. Through the American Expeditionary Service, which established portable broadcast systems overseas wherever American troops were stationed, more than 100 programs were shipped abroad each week via transcription disks. *Spotlight Bands* organized live, prime-time network broadcasts of name bands from military installations several nights a week during much of the war. Some radio programs originated overseas and were broadcast back to the States or to enemy troops. Broadcasts by the Glenn Miller band, with announcements in German, were beamed at enemy troops every Wednesday during the German *Wehrmacht* hour. Sometimes the emotive power of swing was turned against Americans. Every night at nine, Tokyo broadcast a shortwave program featuring American music at Allied troops in order to "create discontent and loneliness"; while on Guadalcanal, Shaw heard his own "Begin the Beguine" between snatches of enemy propaganda.[22]

Above all it was the army's "V Disc" program that lent itself to the militarization of swing. The program was established in September 1943 by the Special Services Division, with a team of experienced recording producers and engineers recruited from Columbia and RCA Victor. Soon the operation was shipping waterproof and pressure-resistant cartons of 20 twelve-inch disks to 8,000 foreign installations and 1,200 domestic bases each month, amounting to approximately 250,000 individual recordings a month. Produced in commercial studios in New York City, the recordings were exempted from the AFM recording ban and came from a variety of sources: dubs from commercial records and films, air checks, and live recordings. V Discs included recordings by many of the most critically and commercially successful swing artists. Benny Goodman reassembled his trio; Mildred Bailey recorded with Teddy Wilson; Paul Whiteman offered "Rhapsody in Blue." The disks included some of Fats Waller's last recordings, a jam session featuring *Esquire*'s All-American Band at the Metropolitan Opera House, Lena Horne's vocals from *Stormy Weather*, and recordings by Norvo, Hampton, Miller, and Crosby. Servicemen in Italy "who had had just enough of the music of the local outfits in Naples and Palermo, and vicinity" responded gratefully; " 'O Sole Mio' will never replace 'Stardust,' " said one. In the Pacific, 20,000 popular recordings and 275 portable phonographs were ordered for artillerymen, who rigged amplifiers throughout jungle outposts. In all, more than 124,000 phonographs were distributed.[23] Through the broadcasting capability of the American Expeditionary Service, V Discs also reached a substantial radio audience in Europe.

Musical tastes were formed or altered by this unprecedented mobilization of technology. Because of the presence of radio and phonographs in barracks and service centers, some soldiers who had not previously heard it were becoming fanciers of swing and jazz. After completing a tour of Europe, bandleader Shep Fields observed that as a result of wartime experiences "some of the jitterbugs" had "grown up." But the war had also increased the interest in jazz. "A lot of fellows who never cared much about music are real hounds now," he observed. "The jam sessions within their units, often their only diversion for long periods of time, have made a lot of men jazz conscious." A serviceman confirmed this: "Swing's the kind of stuff we go for. It's great morale music. On our trip to the Pacific, some of my shipmates had musical instruments. Every day they used to get together in a jam session. That's all they played, and that's all they wanted to hear. And when my brother got back after 26 missions over Japan, do you know what he wanted to hear? Drum boogie." The same soldier claimed that his company would refuse to accept shipments of V Discs that weren't swing, and that the army had converted him to jitterbugging. A *Down Beat* reporter marveled at the variety and originality of dance steps among his fellow GIs, theorizing that their uniforms somehow allowed them to shed a self-conscious dignity.[24]

Despite the emergence of enthusiastic swing converts, a majority of service personnel were attracted to less "hot and rugged" music. Sentimental ballads—"White Christmas," "Johnny Doughboy Found a Rose in Ireland," "As Time Goes By"—and novelty numbers like "Praise the Lord and Pass the Ammunition" and "Pistol Packin' Mama" were among the popular favorites of the war. But tastes shifted as U.S. fortunes changed. Ray McKinley, who played with Miller in England, observed that during the "grim" early years both servicemen and civilians were drawn to the "extreme sentimentality" of commercial dance music; although "warworkers liked to dance for relaxation, neither minds nor bodies could relax to any but sweet music." But by mid-1943, as "the country sensed victory . . . swing began to crop up a little more often." Possibly the associations conjured up by ballads became "too painful." Finding that its audience "responded loudest and longest to the swing numbers," the Miller band adopted a swing-to-sweet ratio of seven to three, according to McKinley. War columnist Michael Levin was similarly impressed by the way such music affected other soldiers who reacted cynically to sentimental movies. "That's why old songs and sentimental ballads as such have seen more interest than was ever thought possible in as desperately bitter a war as this; why war songs, and patriotic marches by and large have fallen flat," Levin hypothesized. "The GI may feel he has to scoff at his own hopes when he bumps into them on the printed page or on the screen, but give it to him via reeds and brass, and it makes a tremendous impression."[25]

After *Metronome* published an article by a serviceman criticizing the

Glenn Miller army band as bland and unadventurous, another soldier wrote an emotional defense of the bandleader. "No, it doesn't sound like Nick's or the Onyx or even the Apollo midnight show," he wrote. "Perhaps they're not bringing us things that are far ahead musically." But "the average G.I." had less interest in "weird harmonies" or "the very latest Lucky Strike Hit Parade songs" than in familiar music that would provide an "avenue of escape," "cheer and joy and light moments." Servicemen wanted "music that is musical . . . things that remind them of home, that bring back something of those days when we were all happy and free and when we used to be able to put on a Miller record or listen to a Miller broadcast or even hear the band play 'In the Mood' in person."[26]

But it was becoming virtually impossible to determine what the "average G.I." or American wanted to hear. Swing was only one of several genres of popular music competing for listeners during the war. Hillbilly or country and western attracted many whites, while African-Americans were drawn to jump, a blues-oriented music usually played by small bands.[27] Meanwhile, vocalists like Bing Crosby, Dick Haymes, Perry Como, and especially Frank Sinatra enjoyed a spectacular boom during the war. Debates raged within the swing community over the merits of this "swoon craze," which was sometimes linked to juvenile delinquency; purists held up Crosby ("the Groaner") rather than Sinatra ("the Voice") as the true jazz vocalist. A friendly rivalry between the two persisted during the war. The press reported that while Crosby was supporting Dewey for president in 1944, Sinatra was a Roosevelt man. "We didn't talk about politics, but the President kidded me about the art of making girls swoon," Sinatra reported.[28]

With the entire world locked in what seemed a life-or-death conflict, the stakes had never seemed higher for developing an appropriate national music. But with cultural pluralism the new ideal, the challenge of creating inspiring music for troops and civilians was made more complex; the music industry now had to accommodate increasingly segmented audience preferences. Furthermore, it wasn't always clear whether the purpose of this music was to exhort, to energize, to unify, to comfort, or to relax. The harder the music industry worked, the more perplexing these problems appeared. Fortunately, the technology of mass culture that had developed since the Great War made possible the distribution of audience-tailored music on an unprecedented scale.

The Theater of Race

That African-Americans were rejecting the by-then-mainstream popular music of swing in favor of a new vernacular variant was in some ways predictable, in other ways unexpected. Given the ideological congruity between a war perceived by many Americans as a campaign against totalitarian racism and a music that had come to symbolize the uniquely American virtues of freedom and pluralism, the Second World War should have represented a kind of moral apotheosis for big-band jazz. To some, swing did fulfill its utopian promise in the armed services. "Many times I have been told that the bands were more morale building and good will promoting between races than any other factor," said a member of a seventeen-piece swing band stationed at Barber's Point Naval Air Station. "Swing knew no barriers. A musician was idolized for his performance from the lowest rank enlisted men to the highest gold braid." Bud Freeman recalled how jam sessions and concerts defused racial tension among personnel stationed in the Aleutian Islands, where the saxophone player led an army band during the war.[29]

But for many others, swing's utopian promise was betrayed by the war experience, as were the aspirations of those who felt that a victory over fascism would exorcise the racial demons that prowled American society. Few aspects of the Second World War have lived as vividly in the memory of its participants as the gap between American ideals of racial toleration and the experiences of African-Americans both in the military and as civilians.[30] Nowhere were these contradictions posed more starkly or played out more vividly than within swing. Racism remained the dominant experience of the many black musicians inducted into the service. Even more offensive to the swing community was the way in which racial hostility infected the domestic culture of war mobilization. The persistence of institutionalized racism in a war ostensibly against racism was painful enough; that this occurred within a subculture marked by a tradition of racial tolerance and equality was doubly disturbing.

Not infrequently this contradiction appeared in a symbolically charged form. Early in 1945 bandleader Earl Hines was invited to address the University of Louisville on "American Jazz, the Expression of Democracy and the Enemy of Fascism." Jazz, he told the interracial audience, "expresses the hope of a free people" who "hunger for a better life. It is based upon individuality which is contrary to the very fundamentals of Nazism." But Hines's lecture was nearly canceled; originally scheduled for an all-white audience at the segregated university, it proceeded only because it was moved to the music school, where interracial assemblies were permitted.[31]

The indignities of Jim Crow weighed especially on African-Americans inducted into the military, many of whom were northerners unused to its most virulent forms. For musicians acclimated to an artistic subculture in which racial mixing was tolerated, even encouraged, the shock could be substantial. The experience of average enlisted personnel, and of the entertainers brought to them through the USO, was defined by the need for maintaining strict segregation. Despite Roosevelt's June 1941 Executive Order 8802 banning racial discrimination in defense industries and establishing the Fair Employment Practices Commission, the entertainment sector of the war industry remained deeply segregated. Black entertainers who toured with USO Camp Shows, Inc., reported that no provisions were made for them to eat or sleep after performances. African-American soldiers were sometimes not informed of performances or were prohibited from attending. Bandleader Horace Henderson and Lena Horne cut short a 1945 tour to Camp Robinson in Arkansas because black soldiers were not allowed to attend their show, while Nazi prisoners of war were "welcomed." Blacks also charged that the few "Negro" shows booked were outdated musical comedies and vaudeville. Several top black bands—including those of Ellington, Calloway, Hampton, and Waller—were not asked to go abroad to entertain troops. Resistance came from other sources as well: Philadelphia's AFM Local 77 banned the USO show *Dixiana* because it employed black musicians.[32]

Furthermore, because black musicians had a harder time being admitted to service bands than their white counterparts, they were more likely to join combat units and have their musical careers seriously disrupted. Saxophonist Lester Young, for example, was one of several Basie sidemen who ignored draft notices but eventually ended up doing stints in the army. Despite admitting regular use of marijuana and a medical exam revealing syphilis, Young was inducted in September 1944, completed basic training, and was sent to Fort McClellan in Alabama in December. Injured while running an obstacle course, Young spent a number of days in the base hospital, where he was diagnosed as being in a "constitutional psychopathic state manifested by drug addiction (marijuana, barbiturates), chronic alcoholism, and nomadism." His behavior after leaving the hospital led to a search; after marijuana and barbiturates were found, Young was court-martialed, dishonorably discharged, and sentenced to a year in disciplinary barracks. While serving his sentence at Fort Gordon, Georgia, he played regularly at dances on base in groups that included pianist and arranger Gil Evans and guitarist Fred Lacy.[33]

A small number of African-Americans did get chances to play in segregated military bands, some of which were excellent by any standards.[34] The vicissitudes of military life could make an enormous difference in the plight of musicians. Young's Basie colleague Buck Clayton, for example, had the good fortune to run into an old musical friend immediately after induction. Despite some hazing for his celebrity status and presumed disdain for military discipline, Clayton was protected by musician friends in the clerical department from being shipped away for basic training. Eventually they allowed him to join a military band in New Jersey that included Mercer Ellington and arranger Sy Oliver. The main duty involved playing at New York piers for war-bound soldiers, beginning as early as five in the morning and continuing all day. Clayton recalled the army as providing an excellent opportunity to rest and gain weight after the harrowing pace of Basie tours; by arranging charts for name big bands, he was soon earning more than he had as a civilian.

After a year Clayton was requisitioned by another New Jersey camp which struck him as being more a recreation center: "soldiers wouldn't salute officers unless they felt like it and the officers didn't seem to give a damn." The band included swing musicians from several top black bands including Lunceford, Jay McShann, Redman, and the Ink Spots.

In addition to playing for pier embarkations, Clayton continued to compose, arrange, record, and play weekend concerts in New York, where he kept a room at the Theresa Hotel, "the place to be during the war if you could be so lucky as to keep a hotel room and be in the army at the same time." Because he was one of the last to be inducted, Clayton remained at Kilmer after nearly all the other musicians had been discharged. "It was kinda bad," he recalled of being the sole trumpeter in military parades; "in fact it was very bad." But on V-E Day Clayton was in the Theresa Hotel, "blowing [his trumpet] out of the window onto Seventh Avenue, down to the people on the streets who were dancing and carrying on." Soon Clayton was discharged and married a woman he met while in the army.[35]

Working in characteristically zealous fashion to combat the conditions he observed after being drafted, John Hammond experienced an army tenure nearly as traumatic as Young's. "I could never quite remember that I was Private Hammond in a military hierarchy whose patterns of behavior had nothing to do with my principles," he wrote later. For nearly three years, at a succession of bases in Virginia, Louisiana, Oklahoma, Alabama, and Georgia, Hammond tangled with southern superiors enraged by his stubborn fraternizing with blacks and persistent efforts to end segregation and improve living conditions at "separate but equal" facilities. After being marched to the point of collapse by an Alabama drill sergeant, Hammond was transferred and began the work that was to occupy most of his energy in the army: arranging entertainment for troops for the Information and Education Section. He managed to book Count Basie, Ella Fitzgerald, the Ink Spots, Cootie Williams, Louis Jordan, Jan Garber, and the bebop-incubating Billy Eckstine band. Using his family connections and "leaking" reports to newspapers and NAACP colleague Walter White, Hammond was able, in his view, to dent the army's system of segregation. "No one at Fort Benning even dreamed that a mere private had caused the wheels to turn in Washington," he recalled proudly. "It was my last contribution to World War II."[36]

Even outside the orbit of the armed forces, service bands, and USO tours, the systemic hardships imposed on black bands by the music industry were exacerbated by wartime conditions.[37] One-night engagements, which accounted for a disproportionate amount of income for black bands barred from other opportunities, were made more difficult by the rationing of gasoline and rubber, while an Office of Defense Transportation edict in June 1942 prohibited the use of buses by big bands. Realizing the certain consequences, Cab Calloway and Walter White of the NAACP organized a lobbying campaign for better bus service in the South, where Jim Crow made rail travel onerous. Many musicians who had partially shielded themselves from Jim Crow by hiring private buses were shocked when their bands were forced to travel by train. When Calloway's efforts appeared fruitless, the trade press speculated on the likelihood that black bands would be eliminated; *Down Beat* lambasted the hypocrisy of asking blacks to fight for liberty they did not enjoy at home. Eventually lobbying efforts by booking agent Moe Gale and others secured the allocation of five buses for southern tours by African-American bands. But by 1943 bus service had been ended for all ensembles.[38]

Transportation was only one of the difficulties faced by African-American musicians. As long as they adhered to a code of behavior considered proper for entertainers, swing artists had generally enjoyed grudging toleration and sometimes respect among white audiences, North and South. Trouble arose when the invisible line between performers and their audience, or between whites and African-Americans in the audience, was crossed. This pattern became disturbingly familiar during the war as news reports filed in from various regions of the country.

By displacing people in ways that resulted in cultural dissonance, the war was indirectly responsible for these incidents; but the war also changed the moral calculus of racism. For perhaps the first time in American history, overt racism was unpatriotic. Symbols of national unity like "The Star-Spangled Banner" could be invoked as musical talismans to quell racial violence. In 1943, for example, Erskine Hawkins helped avert a race riot at a jitterbug contest in the Little Rock city auditorium that had attracted 3,000 blacks and 1,800 white spectators by striking up the national anthem. The following year, in Boston, a race riot nearly erupted when white navy shore patrols attempted to arrest a black sailor dancing by himself at the Tic Toc

Club. As reinforcements poured in on both sides, "Earl Hines, sensing what was taking place, raised his arm and stopped his men from playing and ordered them to play 'The Star-Spangled Banner.' Immediately everyone stood at attention. Raised clubs and clinched fists were brought down and arms raised to salute." As the shore patrol quietly escorted the sailor away, patrons and management applauded Hines for "saving the day" by his "timely gesture."[39]

Although comparable incidents occurred in cities across the country, Los Angeles in particular was associated with war-generated racial tensions that reflected the increasing importance of Hollywood to the swing industry. The war created a massive influx of labor and capital into the region: civilians to work in booming defense industries like shipyards and aircraft manufacturing, and to support the large military population. Likewise, the popularity of films featuring big bands, coupled with the AFM recording ban and government limitations on touring, made southern California a magnet for many in the music industry. Hollywood attracted an increasing proportion of the commercial radio broadcasts that accounted for perhaps three-fourths of the income of the top white orchestras. With bands flocking to the West Coast in search of film contracts and radio commercials, *Metronome* anointed Hollywood "the newly crowned capital of the song business . . . well on its way toward equality with New York in the business of making and breaking bands, if not superiority over Gotham."[40] These demographic and industrial changes created both the need for entertainment on a massive scale and the potential for racial conflict provoked by friction among different cultural mores and competition for housing and other amenities.

Among Los Angeles' several large ballrooms, the Hollywood Canteen best conveyed both the scale of swing in wartime Los Angeles and the racial tension surrounding it. Described as the "largest nightclub" in the United States (Hollywood's Palladium was already the largest ballroom), the Hollywood Canteen hosted some 25,000 servicemen each week. The establishment was organized by over forty unions and guilds, including both white and African-American musicians' unions, and staffed by 7,000 volunteers, including some of Hollywood's leading stars. Volunteer entertainment worth millions of dollars was booked by

Local 47, including swing's top attractions: Ellington, Basie, Carter, the Dorseys, Horace Heidt, Cugat, Crosby, Vallee, and others. Kay Kyser's orchestra had a standing engagement on Saturday nights, and the Harry James orchestra on Wednesdays. Symphonic, radio, and movie orchestras also performed there.[41]

Trouble at the canteen was precipitated by volunteer dance hostesses who struck some as too willing to cross racial lines to entertain servicemen. Local women who raised objections to mixed dancing were decisively overruled by celebrity hostesses Bette Davis, Lana Turner, and Betty Grable. But numerous racial incidents continued to plague the canteen and the broader community, climaxing in riots in the summer of 1943, when gangs of U.S. sailors attacked Mexican *pachucos* attired in zoot suits. Nightclub policies of excluding African-Americans and friends of black musicians attracted national press attention. Further publicity followed reports that the owner of a string of Los Angeles dance halls had banned black orchestras, that bandleader Horace Heidt's Trianon ballroom practiced Jim Crow, and that a white researcher at Caltech had been fired for bringing black friends to the Pasadena Community Dance. The last year of the war was marked by a Los Angeles Chamber of Commerce campaign to suspend the licenses of fifteen nightclubs, allegedly because of racial fraternizing, and by lawsuits to block black musicians, including Benny Carter, from occupying their homes in predominantly white neighborhoods.[42]

Contemporary observers attributed the heightened tension in this traditionally conservative city to the migration of large numbers of southerners to Los Angeles. "The South has won Los Angeles," concluded Chester B. Himes in *The Crisis*. "Army, navy, and marine corps staffs seemed to have chosen Los Angeles as the ideal place in which to give white southerners leave . . . we find huge numbers of uniformed southerners in the city." But the Los Angeles incidents were part of a larger migrational trend that brought southerners to the North and vice versa. For northern liberals, southern whites served as convenient scapegoats for these incidents, as they had before the war. "In the swing world we take it for granted that colored and white persons get along well," a booking agent told *Down Beat*. "But with the influx of persons from Jim Crow sections of the country a new problem presents itself":

the specter of the race riot, "that dynamite dreaded by all." Citing a spate of racial incidents of varying seriousness in Los Angeles, Little Rock, Philadelphia, Detroit, and Harlem, *Down Beat* pointed out the irony that a war against racial supremacy was the catalyst for so many incidents of domestic racism. "One of the prime purposes of this war is . . . to actually eliminate the false cry of racial supremacy which the Hitlers and the Hirohitos utilized as the clarion call to rally the fanatic hordes that brought world conquest by these 'Master Races' too close for comfort," the editors asserted. "How can we hope for one world in peace, when we fail to check the spread of the same insidious poison within our own vaunted civilization?" Curiously, the editors took pains to blame not the club and ballroom operators for instituting Jim Crow policies, but the public for making the policies necessary.[43]

Because New York City was the spiritual home of swing (and of many musicians) and had long symbolized the cultural and economic opportunities available to African-Americans, the occurrence of similar racial incidents there was particularly troubling for swing partisans. The black community was outraged when the Savoy was closed down by the city in the spring of 1943, ostensibly because a number of servicemen had contracted venereal disease from women to whom they were directed while dancing there. After pressure from religious organizations and liberal lobby groups, the ballroom was reopened in October. More persistent was racial tension surrounding 52nd Street's clubs, associated with jazz since the 1920s and the most important incubator of swing innovation outside Harlem. The street's establishments were by no means racial utopias themselves; policies regarding racially mixed bands and audiences varied from establishment to establishment, and changed under different managers. But wartime conditions highlighted the anomalous liberties apparently encouraged there, and triggered moral panics and police crackdowns.[44]

The most publicized of these crackdowns occurred in July 1944 and inspired a three-part article in the *New York Amsterdam News* documenting an environment of unprecedented (for midtown Manhattan) racial mixing. While the majority of those attracted to 52nd Street were "worshippers at the shrine of jazz," according to the article, a small but conspicuous minority of "riffraff" were drawn by the "promiscuous mingling of the races" promised there. "Customers literally check their racial identity along with their hats and coats as they enter one of the places," it reported. "A sociologist or student of race relations might say that a new social order has invaded New York City." The White Rose Inn, a bar that catered to musicians, provided this "typical midnight scene":

> a puzzled faced group of white sailors or soldiers standing with their mouths aghast on the edge of the curb (and the edge of contempt) as the mob inside beef and drink. A little mahogany colored girl draped over the bar sneaking laughs in a glass of beer as a white boy with a pronounced Carnarsie accent whispers in her ear; a pajama-clad 53rd Street resident allowing her sniffing poodle dog to pull her up to a strange man as she says: 'Don't Fifi, I don't know that man!' (As if it made any difference); 'Hep-o-crats,' with neatly trimmed Van Dykes, demonstrating the latest music rift [sic]; a stiff business man with head hung low trying hard to make himself feel at home in a mixed party; a box back blond, standing 5 feet 10 inches, guffawing and nudging a refugee jitterbug from the Lenox Avenue home of happy feet; a quiet Chinese boy; zoot suiters; playgirls; playboys; scalliwags and scoundrels—altogether just a scene signifying nothing—except a slice of colored and white relationships which to some folks is THE EXCEPTION!

After weeks of pressure on the White Rose's manager to exclude blacks, the bar was charged with solicitation involving a white prostitute and black pimp. The manager was also warned that negative press coverage was forthcoming. On July 11 Ed Sullivan's *Daily News* column warned that a "race riot" was brewing at the location; Walter Winchell followed with the observation that 52nd Street was "looking more like Beale Street in Memphis every night." With scores of uniformed police patrolling the block, the manager consented to close at midnight and to allow a policeman to be posted inside during business hours.[45]

While one manager attributed the police crackdown to professional jealousy at the drawing power of black musicians on 52nd Street, and others attributed it to prostitution and drug peddling, observers blamed the recurring problems there on discomfort with racial mixing. The *New York Amsterdam News* charged that the police campaign against the White Rose was "the climax of a well organized plan to rid 52nd Street not only of its undesirable characters, but ALL Negroes—including even the Negro musicians!" As in Los Angeles, tension was exacerbated by the presence of white servicemen unfamiliar with the permissive social conventions of swing. "The Street was the jumping off point for all the crackers from down South going overseas to different places," recalled Dizzy Gillespie. "They'd come down to Fifty-second Street to start some shit." In one brawl triggered by a conversation with a woman who appeared to be white, Gillespie used a carpet knife and his trumpet to fight off a crowd of white sailors before hiding on a subway catwalk.[46]

For some African-Americans the conspicuous public mixing of races jeopardized precious opportunities to demonstrate the ability of blacks to maintain decorum in public settings. The booking of the Basie orchestra at the Lincoln Hotel's Blue Room on Broadway and 45th Street, for example, was considered a major milestone for a black band and attracted "all the world of showlife, cafe society, and the glitter and glamour crowd." *New York Amsterdam News* columnist Dan Burley observed three slightly inebriated black servicemen enter the room and sprawl at a table near the dance floor to order drinks. When one of the sailors attempted to cut in on a white couple, many guests "looked askance"; even the musicians "nearly had apoplexy" before cutting the set short to defuse the "ominous air pervading the room." Burley credited Basie with averting a "cause celebre for front page news plus extra work for racial experts." The serviceman "who tried to cut in on the white sailor [was] merely following a ballroom custom among jitterbugs who change partners frequently . . . But downtown it simply isn't done . . . persons out night-clubbing downtown should stick with their own party and dance with the girls they bring with them." "It usually happens in this way," Burley observed. "We scuffle for years to break down doors and places where we've never been before and then something happens or someone does something and the door is forever closed." Fellow columnist Abe Hill was more concerned by nightclub seating policies that relegated African-Americans to the least desirable locations.[47]

Despite periodic discomfiture, swing partisans continued to maintain that music could defuse racial tensions inexplicably inflamed by a war against racism. After *Down Beat* editorialized that "music is the most logical field of endeavor in which we may hope to tear down the age old hatreds between races and creeds," a reader asserted:

> Liberty and freedom like art and culture are indivisible. If they are suppressed in one part of the world and nothing is done about it, sooner or later they are bound to be suppressed in other parts of the world. Musicians therefore should use their art to fight such suppression and prove that the cause for which we fought abroad and for which we are now fighting at home is a just one.

African-Americans' war-boosted aspirations were dramatized on a massive scale in the Negro Freedom Rally, held in Madison Square Garden on June 26, 1944. Sponsored by the Negro Labor Victory Committee, the rally featured such prominent speakers as Mayor Fiorello LaGuardia, Vito Marcantonio, Adam Clayton Powell, Jr., Benjamin Davis, Jr., and Wilhelmina Adams. The rally's centerpiece, "New World A-Comin'," enlisted some 200 performers, dancers, and singers, including Langston Hughes, Pearl Primus, Josh White, and Canada Lee. (Duke Ellington was also advertised but apparently did not perform.) The *Amsterdam News* likened the pageant to "a million dollar movie, as powerful in its implications as anything ever assembled for the screen, only more so, for here were living people, voicing indignation against bias and discrimination." One critic compared it to a Greek political satire infused with technical innovations introduced by the Federal Theater's "Living Newspaper." Speaking afterward, LaGuardia expressed regret that the program could not be staged around the country for the purpose of challenging race prejudice.[48]

These powerful demonstrations were accompanied by angry denunciations of the racial status quo. Michael Levin, John Hammond, and others inveighed angrily against the continuing presence of Jim Crow in the musicians' union despite six years of international struggle against such restrictions. "We are fighting Hitler and Hitlerism, and yet we are practicing Hitler's own racial theories," wrote Hammond, who advocated a strategy of "trade union militance" for the AFM. "This is a war in which we are relying to a large extent on colored allies—

Chinese, Indians, Brazilians, and millions of others—but every day that we countenance racial discrimination we are affronting our own partners ... Segregated unions are a national disgrace, and all musicians whatever their race or color should demand real unity." Wrote Levin: "If we come back, and allow the kind of thing we have going on in the AFM to continue, we all either ought to give up or go back as permanent KPs." An impassioned editorial asking why black musicians continued to be excluded from hotels, network orchestras, and sponsored radio programs generated an outpouring of support from around the country. In tandem with the campaign to improve Hollywood movies, bandleaders detected a new spirit of militancy among their musicians, making them less willing to accept either Jim Crow or band rules. Entertainers and journalists sought strategies to combat discriminatory nightclub policies. Sinatra barnstormed in a high-profile national campaign for racial tolerance.[49]

As the war wound down, it remained unclear whether the status of African-Americans had undergone lasting change. Swing, it seemed, had exploited the social and cultural flux that accompanied the war to encourage a broader social intimacy between the races than had previously been possible. But it was a profoundly precarious intimacy, requiring an urban environment easily disrupted by hostile forces, and one that was received warily by whites and, to a lesser extent, blacks. Swing proved more acceptable as an ideology, an abstract symbol, than as flesh-and-blood musicians or dancers, if they happened to be black. More far-reaching and permanent than any statutory or institutional changes in racial practices were the changes that swing figured in the race consciousness of African-Americans. The contrast between swing's utopian potential and the stubborn intractability of attitudes and institutions made necessary a new politics of swing.[50]

The Gender Front

Whatever bias African-Americans experienced from the armed services, the entertainment industry, and the American public, their status was secure among the cognoscenti, critics, and fellow musicians who constituted the swing community. For female swing musicians the situation was just the reverse: the sharpest hostility to them emanated from the swing subculture—or, more accurately, fraternity—itself. As a result, wartime conditions promised to transform their status more drastically than it did the attitudes and institutions of racism.

Shortly after the United States entered the war, Connie Berry, a pianist appearing at Manhattan's Café Society, speculated about the impact of the war on the prospects of female musicians. "So many of our best young musicians will be taken by Uncle Sam that there will be nobody left soon to play real jazz except the older men or the women," she said. The draft did in fact drastically reduce the number of musicians available to the swing bands, and broke up many bands whose leaders weren't themselves in the service. With demand for dance music at an all-time high, draft-exempt musicians found themselves in an extreme seller's market, able to command high wages while rival bandleaders engaged in bidding contests. Leaders also faced competition from radio house bands, which offered musicians both a less strenuous existence than cross-country touring and, when combined with freelancing on commercial programs, a higher income.[51]

But Berry wondered whether even market forces would be enough to drive a wedge into what had been an almost exclusively male preserve. Despite the apparent opportunities, "there aren't enough girls who want to lead bands or even play in them," she mused. "Too many women are scared to take up an instrument like the saxophone or trumpet, though they'd find much less competition and more work that way than by following a conventional occupation. I wish I'd been brought up to be a trombone player myself—maybe by now I'd be a female Higginbotham or Tommy Dorsey!"

Historians have documented a substantial "secret history" of women's participation in jazz dating back to the music's origins. But despite the recovery of this tradition, those women appear as exceptions that prove the rule. That a music identified with democratic participation and ethnic inclusiveness resisted the participation of women as coequals is less incongruous by contrast with the general exclusion of women from nearly all contemporaneous public life. The heated polemics of the period about the musical capability of women demonstrate that gender relations in jazz were affected even more deeply by the dominant culture than were race relations. But as in the case of race, war heightened the contradictions represented by the exclusion of women from this most egalitarian of cultural forms. "Girls work right along beside men in the factories, in the offices, in nearly every trade," as one woman drummer put it. "So why not in the dance bands?"[52]

Women entering the jazz world confronted long-standing and apparently transcultural taboos, including "the notion that certain musical forms or instruments [were] 'unfeminine.' "[53] With its tradition of aggressive self-assertion, embodied in quasi-combative rituals like cutting contests and band battles, jazz further emphasized the traditionally masculine qualities associated with instrumental performance. Jazzmen prided themselves on their masculinity, distinguishing themselves from more effeminate "long-haired" (classical) musicians. The swing subculture as represented by its trade press was rife with images and terminology of masculine sexual fantasy and domination, including photographs of scantily clad women and "Heartthrob of the Month" layouts. Occasionally readers wrote to protest the cheesecake coverage. "I've waited and waited for you people to get wise and stop plastering pictures of 'femmes' all over your magazine," wrote a Connecticut reader. "Yours is a music magazine, not a beauty contest. Whether you know it or not you have plenty of girl readers," she wrote, urging *Metronome* to grant equal exposure to such "good-looking boys in the music world" as Sinatra, Ray Eberle, Dick Haymes, and Mel Powell. Some readers demanded that magazines provide regular coverage of women musicians.[54]

Just as most big bands remained racially segregated after the line began to be broached in the late 1930s, a rigid gender division characterized the swing bands. All-female outfits led by Ina Ray Hutton and Rita Rio achieved substantial popular followings during the late 1930s, while Phil Spitalny's "All-Girl Orchestra" had a record-breaking run at New York's Paramount Theatre and won praise from Toscanini. The female bands enjoyed certain commercial advantages. "First of all, the novelty can always be counted on to drag in paying customers," explained *Swing*. "And if that won't work, the girls may be relied upon to attract gaping males to the box office." A female trumpet player agreed that women musicians were "a good drawing card for any band, even though they may not play as well as the men." The fact that such bands comprised only women didn't preclude exploitation. Spitalny's orchestra was incorporated, requiring band members to buy stock that they forfeited in the event they left the band—or married. "Girls will be girls—even when they're playing in a band," mused Spitalny, who prided himself on managing the band through "the power of suggestion." If a band member was concerned about her weight, for example, "I take her to task by weighing myself after lunch every day in her presence. Then I observe out loud that I am losing weight rapidly and that I'm glad of it. After some days of this," Spitalny boasted, the musician "suddenly takes a deep personal interest in her own weight reducing."[55]

Much less frequently were women hired by male orchestras. Mary Lou Williams, a mainstay of Kansas City's fertile Pendergast-era jazz community and later the star pianist and arranger for Andy Kirk and other top orchestras, was *sui generis*. Sometimes women were recruited to play stringed instruments, as by Earl Hines, whose orchestra hired eight women; both strings and piano were widely considered to be relatively "sympathetic" to women's "temperament." Trumpeter Billie Rogers, who played during the war with Woody Herman, was the only regular member of an otherwise male name band to play a nonstringed instrument. Her style was likened to Roy Eldridge's, although she admired the tone of Bunny Berigan and Bobby Hackett. "I prefer a big, deep rich tone and good ideas . . . rather than a long range, which is weak in quality," she said, criticizing Eldridge's tendency to play "high screeching tones." Adorned in a "man-tailored shirt and jacket" that made no attempt to "glamorize" or "capitalize on her femininity," Rogers was reportedly considered "one of the guys" by her section mates.[56]

Whether members of all-female or of mixed bands, women often encountered hostility from the jazz community. Attacks on women's musicianship followed two lines: that women were congenitally incapable of that ineffable quality that made jazz "swing," or that their exclusion from the environment that produced jazz left them irremediably handicapped. "It would seem that even though women are the weaker sex they would still be able to bring more out of a poor, defenseless horn than something that sounds like a cry for help," averred the author of a *Down Beat* article juxtaposed with a photograph of a woman saxophonist pressing clothes under the caption, "Should Stick to Their Ironing." "You can forgive them for lacking guts in their playing but even women should be able to play with feeling and expression and *they never do.*" Women's manifest inferiority as musicians had little to do with a lack of "masculine strength." Rather, "women are as a whole emotionally unstable which prevents their being consistent performers on musical instruments"; "gals are conscious of the facial contortions so necessary in 'blowing it out' and limit their power for fear of appearing silly in the eyes of men"; women's economic dependence deprived them of the "time, ambition, or the patience" for the "woodshedding" so necessary for mastering an instrument; "tradition" and "heredity" also militated against female competence in a historically male preserve. Nearly all female bands remained locked in vaudeville or novelty acts whose scanty musical requirements further restrained the development of musical skills. "If more girl drummers had cradle rocking experience before their musical endeavors," the article concluded, "they might come closer to getting on the beat."[57]

Women responded to this prevailing attitude in various ways. Rogers agreed, ironically, that women lacked the "physical stamina" to play horns in name bands. "Men have more fortitude and so it's easier for them to stand the strain of continuous playing," she said. "Too, women aren't as serious about their playing as men, because they look forward to settling down to a home and family ... I certainly don't intend making this my life's work, and most of the other girls I know feel that way too." Viola Smith, drummer and leader of the Coquettes Orchestra, disagreed. "There are many girl trumpet players, girl saxophonists and girl drummers who can stand the grind of long tours and exacting one-night stands," she wrote in *Down Beat*. "The girls of today are not the helpless creatures of an earlier generation." Moreover, Smith claimed to know "at least a dozen girl musicians" qualified on musical grounds to win regular jobs with top national bands.[58]

Even those like Rita Rio who believed women possessed the necessary attributes to succeed in male bands accepted the essentialist notion that women were biologically different in ways that affected their musicianship. First, the women in her band possessed endurance for rehearsing, travel, and performance that was thought to exceed what men would put up with. Second, women's "aesthetic nature" was reflected in their "warm vibrant tone" and phrasing, which contrasted favorably with the "masculine sock" of male bands; also, the "feminine tendency" to "cooperate" produced a more tightly unified rhythm section than those produced by aggressively individualistic men (the same claim made about the cooperative commonwealth bands). Finally, Rio asserted that women presented a more "delightful picture" than the "trite male band in its uniform tuxedo." "Girls find a pleasing picture does not detract from good musicianship or from thoroughness and preciseness which help to comprise the attributes of good musicianship." Even Viola Smith ended her polemic with the admonition to "think of all the showmanship that the presence of a member of the fair sex in a band would provide."[59]

Even the International Sweethearts of Rhythm, widely acknowledged as the finest of the all-girl bands and extremely popular with audiences, were criticized on gender grounds. Formed in Mississippi in the late 1930s to raise money and publicity for an all-black school, the band broke with the school in 1941 and began to tour professionally. Its first engagements were at Harlem's Apollo Theatre and Savoy ballroom. The Sweethearts immediately impressed listeners and were popular favorites during the war; by 1945 the *Amsterdam News* declared that "their place with the great name swing bands of the country is secure." But to *Metronome*'s respected critics, the Sweethearts fell short. "No matter where or how you heard this band, you'd know it was a *colored* all-girl orchestra," wrote Barry Ulanov. "For the Sweethearts kick . . . always with a moving beat that makes some of their thinnest offerings tolerable." Ulanov judged most of the band's material "too hard for the limited techniques of the girls," though "not uncommonly complex for a male crew." Ulanov's colleague Leonard Feather, who organized some of the earliest all-female recording sessions, agreed: "This is still the best-looking band around, and still, alas, the furthest off-pitch." Critics, especially Ulanov and Feather, always judged performances more severely than did audiences; clearly, too, both felt comfortable resorting to invidious gender distinctions in supporting their judgments.[60]

It was as vocalists, not as instrumentalists, that women were most visible in swing, a role that inspired as much controversy within jazz circles as did "girl musicians." For many musicians and enthusiasts, female big-band vocalists (and most males as well) were regarded as unfortunate concessions to commercial taste, ornaments who added nothing to the music and usually detracted from it. For the many aficionados who found the most commercially prominent swing bands suspect, preferring to believe that authentic jazz was produced in smaller New Orleans–style ensembles, the presence of heavily made-up, provocatively gowned young singers confirmed their view that swing was a betrayal of the real jazz. This animus was expressed in the critical nomenclature: vocalists were always "canaries," "warblers," "chirpies," "thrushes," "sparrows." When critic George Frazier launched an early diatribe against Goodman's Martha Tilton, charging in *Down Beat* that she "stinks," he was widely criticized for his lack of chivalry; his remark became emblematic of the figure of the arrogant dyspeptic critic. But attacks on the "girl singers" continued in the various publications devoted to swing.

An especially acerbic article, " 'The Gal Yippers Have No Place in Our Jazz Bands,' " conjured up an image of musicians and "billions" of radio listeners wincing "as if their ear-teeth were being yanked by the roots" at the "yodeling" of seductive but talentless "young lovelies." Environmental factors rather than the biological incapacity ascribed to female instrumentalists were judged responsible for the dearth of suitable vocalists. The problem was not that the swing vocalists lacked technique; rather, "trying to crossbreed the world's classic vocal background with the emotional blues shouting of the southern Negro" produced the musical equivalent of "drinking cream in your beer." Social restrictions had excluded American women from the black urban environs that had served as the "jazz classroom" for aspiring white musicians content to live on the edge. "So is it any wonder that, excluded (as of course she should have been) from this environment which is the only one which could have given the white girl the insight into what went into making good jazz music, she should be so barren of any appreciation of the finer points of playing jazz on an instrument, let alone trying to interpret it into vocal sounds?" It was sexual appeal, the appearance of "seducing the microphone," rather than musical merit that explained the ubiquity of the "female yowlers," whom the author suggested feeding "one by one" to the jitterbugs.[61]

Among musicians, "girl singers" were hardly more popular. *Swing* reported that vocalists were the "pet headache" of nine out of ten bandleaders. "I guess this kind of music just wasn't meant to be sung— anyway, by a gal," trumpeter and bandleader Berigan reportedly said after auditioning a series of unsatisfactory vocalists. Some instrumentalists were repelled less by musical considerations than by the excessive career ambition of the female vocalists, many of whom considered their big-band experience nothing more than preparation for a solo musical or film career. "It's amazing the number of musicians in bands who are fed up with the girl singer because she never does anything but try to build herself up, no matter at whose expense," wrote George Simon, who attributed the inability of female vocalists to achieve lasting success either to marriage or to widespread stupidity and indiscretion. In fact a career as big band vocalist required a substantial capital investment that could pay off only if a different kind of success was achieved, as *Down Beat* reported in an article titled "Heck, Chick Spends Check to Look Chic." Singers often went into debt purchasing an adequate supply of gowns at prices ranging from $100 to $150 apiece. And whether men or women, they were paid less than most of their instrumental colleagues and were sometimes required to double at other jobs with their bands.[62]

To be sure, some African-American vocalists—such as Ivie Anderson, featured with the Ellington orchestra from 1931 to 1942; Ella Fitzgerald, who became famous with Chick Webb's band; Billie Holiday, who sang with Count Basie before joining Artie Shaw; and Helen Humes, who replaced Holiday in the Basie orchestra—were exempt from the general disdain. Presumably their exposure to the jazz environment enabled them to overcome the built-in limitations of their sex and therefore be considered the peers of male musicians; taboos against working women were also less prevalent in the black community. A few white singers, such as Helen Forrest, June Christy, and Peggy Lee, also found critical favor.

A third category of women involved in swing was the "orchestra wife." Trade journals had always reported on the domestic affairs of musicians, and occasionally they printed special features on the wives of bandleaders. The dislocations of domestic life in the war years made this aspect of the industry more salient; in September 1942, a few months after a reader had called for "a column on chicks," *Down Beat* introduced a new column, "The Musician's Wife Says," intended to advise women on coping with the irregular hours and frequent absences entailed by their husbands' careers.[63] In the same year appeared the film *Orchestra Wives*, featuring the Glenn Miller band. One of the few films actually about the swing business, it reveals much about the role of women within the swing fraternity. The movie opens in a studio where the band is recording a populist wartime tribute to the average patriotic American. After the take, the band is informed that business dictates a cross-country tour. Bandleader Gene Morrison (Glenn Miller) and his manager remind the rebellious band members that, much as they despise touring, "money and reputation" are made on the road. "You don't get anywhere playing in one spot," he says. "It isn't the carriage trade that pays our salaries, boys," he tells the disgruntled sidemen. "It's those kids who put those nickels in the jukeboxes all over the country."

The Morrison band's uniqueness in the number of spouses that accompany musicians on the road sets up the film's main focus on a moral education in gender roles. At a dance in small-town Dixon, the band's womanizing trumpet star (George Montgomery) meets twenty-year-old Connie (Ann Rutherford), who has idolized his solos on the soda-fountain jukebox. She follows him to a dance the next night in a neighboring town, where the two impulsively wed. The naive Connie is brought abruptly into a backstage world of intrigue and infighting among the itinerant wives. Presided over by Natalie (Carole Landis), whose affected society accent belies a genius for acid-tongued treachery, the "orchestra wives" play bridge, correct each other's malapropisms, and carry on dalliances with each other's husbands. They gleefully plot a confrontation between Connie and Jaynie (Lynn Bari), the band vocalist and a former flame of Bill's, who immediately befriends Connie by lending her a gown for her wedding night—only to position herself, it turns out, to "knife" the newest wife. When Jaynie shrugs off their old fling as "nice, but temporary," Bill compliments her on looking "at things like a man." "Oh, don't tell anyone," the singer retorts. "I'm considered very feminine."

Craftily raising Connie's suspicions while the band is on a one-night excursion to Des Moines, the wives maneuver Connie into traveling to the hotel, where she discovers her husband in Jaynie's room. Although Bill protests innocence, Connie remains unconvinced. "Perhaps it's all part of being an orchestra wife," she charges during the ensuing argument. "If that's so, I don't want to be an orchestra wife." The next day she discovers she was the victim of a ruse, and apologizes to her affronted husband. "I think you're a lot of cats—dangerous cats!" she rails at the other wives before impishly revealing the affairs they have been carrying on behind each other's backs. A dish-throwing catfight ensues, drawing in jealous husbands and leading immediately to the band's breakup. Bill rebukes Connie in the strongest language he can muster: "Look, I married you because you were a happy kid—gay . . . cute . . . cheerful. But you've gone neurotic on me. You trail me around like a house detective. And now with one flick of your tongue you bust up our band. Last night you said you weren't an orchestra wife, and you hit the nail on the head. You aren't, and you never will be." A disconsolate Connie returns alone to Dixon, where her brave front is reduced to tears by Bill's trumpet-playing on the jukebox.

Some time later, the former band members are reunited in New York by mysterious telegrams offering them auditions for different bands. It turns out that Connie has orchestrated the reunion with the help of the wolfish piano player (Cesar Romero). Secret gifts of diamonds and mink coats, ostensibly from bandleader Morrison, inspire the feuding wives to make up and smooth their ruffled husbands. The band decides to reunite—minus Jaynie, whose unnervingly male sexual aggressiveness has no place in the new, domestically harmonized ensemble. To cap this virtuoso performance of orchestra-wifely guile, Connie teases her husband by showing up at the band's opening at Glen Island Casino with a much older love interest (actually her father). "But we haven't anything to talk about," she reminds Bill coyly. "You told me I was a terrible orchestra wife and walked out on me." The film closes with a shot of Bill's empty trumpet chair as he dances, reconciled, with his wife. In the end, the midwestern naif proves herself more than a match for the "dangerous cats" whose schemes nearly destroyed both the band and her marriage.

In reality, only a very few orchestra wives ever had the opportunity to travel with their husbands, but the movie reveals a number of contemporary stereotypes and anxieties. Even while touring with them, the women have no role in their spouses' strictly male professional world. They gossip and scheme as any isolated group of bored housewives presumably would. Only Jaynie evades her prescribed gender role, but only at the cost of an ambiguous sexual persona; she combines supposedly male sexual ends with quintessentially female sexual means. Jaynie is in fact stranded between genders; not an orchestra wife, she is also, unlike Billie Rogers, not "one of the guys." Her loyalties belong not with her professional colleagues but with their nonworking wives, with whom she conspires to disrupt the newfound domestic bliss of an ex-lover, even contributing her own gown to their wedding night. Jaynie clearly must be dropped from the reunited band, but who will replace her at the microphone? A man, possibly, or at least a more domestically attuned woman? And what of Connie? It's hard to dispute Bill's statement that she will never make a proper orchestra wife. Perhaps she will convince the other wives to stay home with her, thus easing a chronically unstable condition. More likely, the band's—or Bill's—touring days are over, to be replaced by the lucrative studio jobs to which many married musicians with families aspired.

Ironically, *Orchestra Wives* appeared when the main concern of American couples was not being thrust together unnaturally on the road, but being separated by the war. Some of its lessons still held, though. If feminine wiles could undo the all-important unity of purpose of a dance band, the movie suggests, they could also undermine a larger masculine undertaking—the war effort. Such fears were felt vividly enough to compel *Down Beat*'s editors—perhaps inspired by the film—to write on the morale-sapping impact of "catty" rumors that musicians posted overseas were "stepping out" on their wives.[64] "Dangerous cats," whether wives, vocalists, or musicians, were evidently much on the mind of the swing fraternity at a time when the manpower shortage threatened the integrity of traditional gender roles. If the war produced a lasting positive image of women's involvement in swing, it was not as musicians or singers but as the volunteer hostesses at the Hollywood Canteen, flouting local censure to dance with black servicemen. The actual making of music, the fraternity agreed, was best left to men. But changes set in motion by the war were already elevating the swing vocalists, male and female, at the expense of the big bands in which they had always served as unequal partners.

Long before V-E Day, musicians had looked ahead to the end of the war and speculated on the future of their profession. *Down Beat* predicted that combat-honed service bands would "stack up" favorably against the top civilian big bands, and projected that as many as 26,000 jobs in industrial music would await returning servicemen; early in 1944 it initiated a column called "When Johnny Comes Marching Home," on readjusting to civilian life.[65] But as early as 1943 the press sensed that the war would have far-reaching effects on the status of swing. In a June 1943 editorial titled "After the War—What of Music?" *Down Beat* predicted that the war's enforced global blending of cultures would radically change the place of American music in the world.

As reports detailed swing's symbolic importance to foreign listeners in the Allied and Axis countries alike, it was clear that a new market for jazz had coalesced. With local radio broadcasting severely disrupted during most of the war, listeners in England and the Continent depended on American records and publications to keep themselves abreast of musical developments in the United States. As the tide turned against the Axis in 1944, visits by Dinah Shore, Bing Crosby, and Glenn Miller stimulated British enthusiasm for American music. "I've got to get myself on an international slant really," joked Crosby after a tour that took him within a thousand yards of enemy lines and once into a German-held town in France. "Too many French people asked me: 'Connez-vous [*sic*] Sinatra?' " Frenchman Charles Delaunay reported that before France fell, jazz fans were either musicians or intellectuals. During the occupation, the music gained a huge mass following, representing to many a tie to the free world. The same was true of Belgium. Even in Germany and Italy, where it was banned for ideological reasons, jazz remained an important underground symbol of resistance to fascism. Michael Kater has documented how jazz adapted to the hostile cultural climate of the Third Reich, persisting in broadcasts, recordings, and live performances despite ferocious but ineffectual campaigns by the Nazis against the "Nigger-Jew" music. Similarly, an Italian observer wrote in 1945 that jazz had served as inspiration to partisans opposing the government; after Mussolini's overthrow, jazz enjoyed a period of great public enthusiasm, aided by low record prices and high salaries for musicians. Spread by overseas U.S. army radio stations, dances, and festivals, jazz was ubiquitous within two years after D-Day, and widely recognized as promoting American democracy and international harmony.[66]

This enthusiasm extended well beyond Europe, which had long lionized American jazz. A radio executive with the OWI who had recently returned from Sydney reported that Australians were wildly enthusiastic about the music. Native populations were touched as well. "It's amazing how these primitive people picked up the rhythm of the drum breaks," remarked a marine drummer who observed two thousand Fiji Islanders dancing to a service band's rendition of "Two O'Clock Jump." The commercial possibilities were dazzling. "The world has been introduced to Americans and American music as never before," *Down Beat* observed. "If we proceed fairly and diplomatically, we and everyone else will profit." With a "great market" and "marvelous product to sell," American musicians' interests would be best served by a free-trade policy to replace the swing protectionism that had obtained before the war. "For every band they can send, we can send ten." But the industry had some vital homework to do before it could take full advantage of this "world revolution in music." It needed to solve its union difficulties, adapt to popular tastes in the United States, and attend to economic necessities before worrying about the creation of "art."[67]

5

Swing and Its Discontents

When the press began predicting the imminent demise of swing in late 1946, longtime contributors like Duke Ellington could be excused for dismissing the rumors as yet another premature epitaph. "As far back as I can remember . . . some people have been saying 'hot music' was really through," he told a reporter. "The same thing is being said today, only now they refer to the corpse as swing. Well, it just happens that a lot of the mourners are not in the music business regularly and their answers aren't so accurate or helpful." Ellington's memory was accurate. As early as 1938, when media attention was at a peak, patrons of "hinterland ballrooms" were showing a marked preference for "sweet" bands and nonswing tunes, according to the *New York Times*. Older and more affluent patrons were observed to "prefer rhythms to which they can dance without resembling a chimpanzee suffering from delirium tremens."[1]

The future of swing was questioned again the following year. Backing away from earlier predictions, Paul Whiteman labeled the music a "fad . . . on the wane," unsuited to the "deep-seated romantic sentiment" prevalent among college students, who dismissed swing as "high-school stuff." As an experiment, a New York bandleader played a Viennese waltz before a "shagging, jitterbug crowd," and was amazed to find dancers bursting into applause. The experience led him to conclude that "swing music is slowly but surely losing its popularity and form and . . . will eventually evolve into a more danceable, melodious type of music."[2]

The approach and onset of world war deflected public attention from the issue of swing's longevity, but the winding down of hostilities brought further prophecies that swing's demise was finally at hand. After completing a lengthy wartime tour of U.S. service camps, a veteran bandleader predicted a public vogue for ballads and sweet, melodious songs. He based his projections on a long pattern of dialectically oscillating preferences for popular music: ragtime (1890–1900) had given rise to sweet music (1900–1915), which produced torrid early jazz (1917–1925), after which ensued semisymphonic sweet music (1925–1932), and finally, swing (1932–1944). The next sweep of the pendulum would be bolstered by the aftereffects of war. "Returning servicemen, high-strung from their part in battle, demand smooth music to soothe their shattered nerves," he averred; such music had been employed to rehabilitate veterans suffering from nervous breakdowns. The new music, while retaining the more defined prominent beat characteristic of swing, would feature warm, soothing timbres, vibrato, and string sections.[3]

All these predictions shared the notion that swing was a static form, while the audience was the dynamic factor that seemed always on the verge of abandoning a music that had ceased to speak to it. Ellington's confident demurral expressed this sense that swing, whatever transitory label it went by, would maintain its musical integrity and retain its true audience. His statement reflected the historical relativism that had earlier enabled the swing community to defend the music by asserting that it was a reflection of its times. But if swing itself was fluid, able to evolve away from its audience, perhaps the historical pattern would be broken. By 1947 the familiar predictions were accompanied by a host of unprecedented and ominous signs.

Attendance dropped sharply at hotels, ballrooms, nightclubs, and one-night locations. Many venues cut back from six to four or five nights a week, sometimes to weekends only, while promoters, burned by losses, suspended their operations. Venues known for top-name swing ensembles switched to smaller, lesser-known and society-style bands. Unable to find enough profitable engagements to maintain their large payrolls and high overhead, many big bands dissolved; some reorganized, but with fewer members. During the winter of 1946–47, bands led by Benny Goodman, Woody Herman, Artie Shaw, Tommy Dorsey,

Les Brown, Harry James, Jack Teagarden, and Benny Carter dissolved, provoking a blizzard of press stories. In May 1947 commercial sponsors abruptly canceled dozens of radio shows, including Goodman's, to protest the allegedly inflated prices of their performers.[4]

This time, apparently, the swing industry faced a genuine crisis. In the face of this preponderance of evidence, those who performed, managed, or wrote about swing addressed themselves to two questions: Why had the music's fortunes so suddenly and drastically declined? And could anything be done to resuscitate the business? Because swing presumably could not be revived unless its malaise were properly diagnosed, responses to the second question depended on answers to the first. For the first time, the swing community confronted the possibility that the problem lay not on the demand side, with the audience, but with the musical product itself.

If swing had fallen victim to the general postwar economic malaise that had hit the entertainment industry especially hard, its recovery depended on fluctuations of the business cycle over which it had no control. But if its failure was the result of inflated salaries and a talent glut released at the end of the war, its survival required letting the market adjust conditions in the music industry. If swing's declining audience was due to inevitable shifts in popular taste or to demographic change—the aging of its core audience of high school and college students, and the unwillingness of potential new consumers to take up an "old" fad—then prospects for saving swing were limited. But if these problems were caused by big bands betraying their audience by playing undanceable tempos or lacing their charts with the controversial modernisms of what was coming to be called bebop, swing could rescue itself only by returning to the musical conventions practiced by its most successful ensembles.

A number of explanations for swing's collapse were advanced, all stressing changes in the audience or in the media that distributed the music.[5] But big-band jazz itself had changed since Pearl Harbor. Ensembles had grown larger, more assertive. The typical prewar aggregation of sixteen had increased by ten or fifteen pieces with the inclusion of string sections. Larger frequently meant louder, and sometimes faster tempos. More subtle were the changes in swing's cultural status.

Since Goodman, swing artists had aspired, at least occasionally, to the cultural legitimacy accorded by the concert hall. But the enormous demand for wartime entertainment, in the opinion of some critics, had caused band leaders to lose touch with their dancing audience in favor of the enthusiasts who clustered rapt around the bandstand. Ironically, this increased emphasis on swing as a listener's music made swing more vulnerable to the exigencies of the market.

With the rise of bebop, the cycle of swing came full circle. Just as swing had been defended by its early proponents as merely an updated version of once-scandalous dance crazes, bop was explained as an appropriate response to the times: "the hair shirt with which [its fans] will meet an atomic world," as *Newsweek* put it, suggesting that swing's mellifluousness no longer fitted the Cold War mood.[6] If, as signs suggested, bop was to become the postwar equivalent of swing, forward-thinking bandleaders would be well advised to adapt to the new trend. Many did, but only briefly. For it soon became clear to most in the musical community that bop would never achieve the mass popularity of swing; in fact, bebop was eventually blamed by many for the postwar decline of swing. Rather than a radical departure from swing, bebop is better understood as a variation of swing that emerged at an inopportune historical moment, whose brief cultural trajectory reveals as much as swing's longer ascent and decline.

Swing's postwar predicament illuminates a larger debate about the relative power of the culture industry and the consumers of culture. Some have followed the Frankfurt school in emphasizing the power of a monolithic mass culture industry to impose its productions on a passive audience; others stress the ability of consumers to exercise choice and exert a countervailing force against the impulses of corporate culture. In the study of popular music, this issue has pitted those in the Adornian tradition of suspicion toward technology and the market (which are in this view fundamentally linked) against those who follow Walter Benjamin in stressing the utopian potential of technology. The contemporary debate over swing's decline underscores the problems inherent in bifurcating cultural production and consumption. The music industry of the late 1940s was both responding to the changing tastes of its audience and working to redefine those tastes. Rather than being seen as opposing forces, swing's producers and distributors and its audience should be understood as joined in constant dialectic exchange.[7]

Tension Music and Concertitis

The swing community anticipated the war's end with a mixture of expectancy and trepidation. "1946 will be a great year for jazz, just as the year before it, and the year before it," wrote Leonard Feather. "So much was accomplished, incredibly, during the years of war, that it's hard to conceive what may develop in a world at peace." The conflict had been good for swing. Domestically, it had generated increased demand as well as income among swing consumers; internationally, it had provided the opportunity and means to proselytize a world market. The end of midnight curfews and of gasoline, rubber, and shellac rationing would eliminate swing's worst wartime hobbles. An unprecedented influx of talent was occurring with the return of military personnel. "The number of brilliant young jazzmen arriving on the scene has reached bewildering proportions," observed Feather. "Even more staggering has been the gold rush in the recording studios," prompting an "increased output of great jazz."[8]

The music itself had evolved impressively, incorporating sophisticated formal elements from European music and bringing its practitioners' technical skills to a new peak. Bands led by Ellington, Herman, and Boyd Raeburn had pushed jazz to a new plateau, incorporating the harmonic advances of such European art composers as Bartok, Schönberg, Ravel, and Stravinsky. *Down Beat* observed proudly that the "virtual musical revolution" of jazz had raised the standards of American listeners to the "world's highest": Ellington had prepared the public's ears for Shostakovitch, Herman for Stravinsky.[9]

At the same time, and for the same reasons, the end of war posed unprecedented challenges of adjustment for the musicians who staffed the big bands and for their audience. The trade press had periodically warned that the wartime employment conditions would not last, that excesses of salary and personal behavior would eventually haunt the industry. *Down Beat* questioned whether the thousands of returning service musicians would find their old jobs waiting for them. Even the increased musical sophistication of swing contained peril. *Metronome* warned that the music had evolved so rapidly during the war that musicians would need "to study hard and earnestly to come abreast of" it. "Harmonically, jazz is not at all what it was in 1939; its colors are different; its resources are so much broader that comparison with the music of that blissful era is ridiculous."[10]

While the music industry faced the challenge of employing thousands of veterans, the return of millions of military personnel augured a cultural sea change that might dramatically alter the demand for swing. The conclusion of the previous world war had ushered in the Jazz Age, with all the accompanying cultural changes; there was every reason to expect that the end of this war would bring an equally radical shift in popular taste. Because of the wartime record ban and shellac shortage, much of the public had lost contact with swing's stylistic evolution. How would audiences preoccupied by years of war mobilization react to the forms that swing had developed since 1941? Did consumers of swing actually wish to have their cultural standards raised to the heady levels promised by its enthusiasts? Jazz had succeeded under wartime conditions, but its appeal was largely retrospective, conditioned on its ability to conjure memories of more familiar, settled times. Frank Sinatra's enormous solo success beginning in 1943 foreshadowed the possibility that the bandleaders' title "King of Swing" might be less worth contesting than it had been a few years earlier.

Moreover, as several bandleaders acknowledged, the postwar climate had created the need for different musical forms. The "national mood of the moment is one of uncertainty verging on pessimism," wrote Ray McKinley. "And swing and pessimism don't mix." Since the war, Americans have become "very neurotic . . . overwhelmed by a feeling of insecurity" and nostalgic yearnings, suggested Lennie Tristano. "They're afraid to experience . . . the kind of intense emotion, for instance, that's brought on by good jazz. There's more vitality in jazz than in any other art form today. Vitality arises from an emotion that is free. But the people, being neurotic, are afraid of being affected by a free emotion and that's why they put down jazz." The United States was suffering from "a collective hangover," agreed Eddie Howard, its "jangled nerves" no longer able to tolerate demanding music. Many swing bands "just play too damn loud," admitted Benny Goodman. Even Charlie Barnet acknowledged that changes in public taste lay behind swing's declining economic fortunes. "Tension music was okay during the war," he said. "Now we're done with it."[11] Given this new cultural mood, the critical question for the swing industry was whether the music could be modified to appeal to the new taste, or was irredeemably out of step with the times.

Related to the apparent inability of big bands to cater to the emotional needs of their audience was a perceived reluctance to play the role of entertainer. Use of visual devices, stunts, and props had been a mainstay both of swing's more respected ensembles (Calloway, Lunceford) and of the more commercial bands (Kay Kyser), although swing partisans had looked askance at the practice. But the postwar crisis led cities to blame "the musical snobbishness and the patronizing attitudes" of modern swing musicians for the public's loss of enthusiasm. Musicians should reemphasize the art of courting audiences, "rubbing elbows" with and educating those less familiar with their music, urged *Down Beat*'s editors. "The public wants more than just dance music for their money," asserted Erskine Hawkins, who urged other bandleaders to develop "new forms of musical entertainment." Noting that most band salaries had dropped sharply since the war, Hawkins credited his "Dance Carnival" production with boosting admissions and salaries for his own sidemen.[12]

The migration of swing from ballrooms and theaters to concert halls struck some postwar critics as emblematic of, and perhaps indirectly responsible for, swing's eclipse. Before and during the war, all the most successful and culturally ambitious bands had given occasional formal concerts. But from Norman Granz's "Jazz at the Philharmonic" concert tour to the midnight "One-Night Stands" presented at Manhattan's Carnegie and Town halls, the concert hall was after the war an increasingly common venue for a range of jazz performers: big bands, jump combos, bebop artists, Dixieland traditionalists. "With big band business still in a hazardous state, many name sidemen today are turning to the concert halls to keep in cakes and drapes," reported *Down Beat* in a lead story. "More jazz concerts are being planned or held here at the present time than at any other era of the biz."[13]

This development was praised by people both in and outside the swing community as one that would elevate the music and its audience. Nora Holt, a tendentious highbrow music critic for the *New York Amsterdam News*, observed that European art music had gradually become limited to a "luxury class," thereby leaving younger generations of listeners susceptible to less worthy popular fare. As a result, she claimed, the "youth of America are congenitally marked by jazz." But the new synthesis of classical and popular forms, exemplified by the new "pops" concert series and "Jazz at the Philharmonic" performances at Carnegie, promised to repair this cultural damage. "Gone are the days when jazz band performances were confined to dance halls and juke box recordings," she noted. "Today they function in every species of entertainment [because of] the concert form they have achieved." This slow ascent "to the dignity of concert halls" had produced a steady improvement in the "quality and texture" of popular music. Youthful listeners even showed signs of transferring their allegiance from "the 2 B's—bop and boogie"—to the "charm and spiritual beauty of the 3 B's era—Bach, Beethoven and Brahms." Thanks to aggressive marketing of European art music, an encouraging minority of young people were "as volatile and effervescent" when experiencing the classics as "when listening to the music of Dizzy Gillespie."[14]

Similar hopes were expressed by Stan Kenton. After placing first in the 1947 *Down Beat* poll, the bandleader stated that "swing is dead, gone, finished," fated to be replaced by bands specializing either in smoothly calibrated dance numbers or in the more challenging music of a "progressive" jazz inflected by European symphonic modernism. This functional division reflected a comparable schism in the audience that had long been present but was now creating an untenable situation. The swing audience had become hopelessly divided, Kenton argued, with a sizable group opting to stand around the bandstand and listen while another contingent attempted to dance. As a result Kenton found it impossible to please more than half of his audience. "Jazz bands don't belong in ballrooms or hotel grills," he said, "not as long as they cater primarily to dancers." He soon announced that he would retire from playing in ballrooms or at dances in favor of the concert hall.[15]

The systematic elevation of swing to concert hall status struck others as an ambiguous accomplishment, questionable in its affect on both artists and their audience. Woody Herman accused the " 'progressive jazz' clan" of "defeating its own purpose" by restricting its " 'new art' " to the concert stage and expecting "the public to absorb and understand in four hours what they spent 10 to 12 years to devise." After a Town Hall concert by Dixieland revivalist Eddie Condon, a critic admitted looking "forward to the day when it won't be necessary to sit the public down in the awesome dignity of a concert hall for the purpose of playing a brand of music which was born and bred in an atmosphere of smoke, alcohol, loud talk, sex, police raids and similar factors contributing to adult delinquency. Jazz is the product of a tough, noisy environment, and that's where it ought to stay." But even the conventions of night-clubs, presumably sanctums of jazz authenticity, were changing. Condon attracted attention by "conducting" jam sessions at his Greenwich Village club. Condon "claps his hands, makes gestures which are supposed to look like the rhythms, and sings what he wants the band to play," reported the *New York Times*. "It is unorthodox conducting, but then who ever tried to conduct a group improvisation?" In deference to piano virtuoso Art Tatum, 52nd Street's Three Deuces instituted an "hour of silence" policy, which reportedly enjoyed little success from regular patrons accustomed to conversing during sets.[16]

To be sure, complying with the letter of the concert hall didn't necessarily entail internalizing its spirit. While some bemoaned the "concertizing" of swing as a betrayal of its authenticity, others charged jazz artists with undermining their own cultural stature and commercial viability by staging overpriced, shoddy, and unprofessional concerts. "I have never seen a jazz concert where the music, the production and the presentation were all of high caliber," complained *Down Beat*'s Levin. Performances were frequently marred by inferior sound systems, poor pacing and song selection, ill-rehearsed bands, and absent or indifferent guest stars. The most talented artists were often content to appear onstage with second-rate players, and pandered to their audience with superficial musical effects. "You do not give a concert by assembling a band and a singer on the stage, and running through a few of the group's more famous records," wrote Levin. A concert "should have careful planning for contrast, change of pace, color and display of every musical facet possible." Because of musicians' own lack of seriousness, concluded another writer, the ten years of concert jazz since Goodman's Carnegie debut had failed to elevate the cultural status of jazz.[17]

The unwillingness of swing artists to take their concert hall prerogatives seriously was often matched by a lack of audience decorum. The youthful exuberance of the jitterbugs, which Goodman had predicted would be sublimated with maturity, showed no sign of abating. "Jazz concert-goers have been getting increasingly irked by the applause, foot-stomping, and general carryings-on of some of the older children lately," *Down Beat* reported, adding that performances at the Metropolitan Opera House were also being disrupted by "paid claques" hired by rival divas. A midnight concert by Lionel Hampton's orchestra attracted what was described as the "most demonstrative audience" in Carnegie's history. "What used to be called jitterbugs made spectacles of themselves dancing together in the aisles and in front of the orchestra," a reporter observed, noting that "All dancers were of the male species." Likewise, a group of "Brooklyn boppists" observed at the hall for a Dizzy Gillespie concert were "just as drunkenly loud as their 1938 forebears [and] managed to clap the wrong beats just as effusively."[18]

Whether or not postwar swing conformed to the performance conventions of European art music, many big bands had clearly lost touch with the dancers who had traditionally been crucial to commercial success. This phenomenon was attributed to the war, when civilian demand for musical entertainment was so great that promoters allowed musicians to play "listening music" for their own enjoyment without fear of losing patrons. "Everyone knows that we switched from dance music to listening music during the war, also that ballrooms were so packed that operators forgot how to promote, if they ever knew," noted Tom Archer, seasoned operator of a string of midwestern dance halls. Guy Lombardo, whose undiminished commercial success at a time when his swing rivals were suffering was widely noted in the press, argued that as a result of people's wartime escapism, "money was spent indiscriminately and many hastily-put-together aggregations flourished," with a general lowering of standards. A waiter at Hollywood's enormous Palladium ballroom complained that top orchestras, including those led by Harry James, Tex Beneke, and Benny Goodman, "do not play dance music. They are all first class musicians and work hard but not one number out of five can be danced to." As a result, customers would walk off the floor and ask for their checks. As if this weren't enough, an indignant patron charged that postwar dancers "shuffled" incompetently around the dance floor, "cluttering it up" for those who had learned the steps.[19]

Many bandleaders accepted this criticism and retooled their orchestras to take the requirements of dancers into account. "We have to play sweet so they can dance," insisted Tommy Dorsey. "If they want to just listen, they'll go to a jukebox instead of a ballroom." Bandleaders "must forget about the few screaming fans who line up against the bandstand and applaud flag-wavers," agreed Barnet. "We'll have to look over their heads and watch the bulk of the audience to see whether or not they're walking back to their chairs in disgust because they can't dance to the music." The public no longer accepts "the hot stuff . . . Everything I play has to be danceable," he said.[20]

As Kenton's comments indicate, not everyone joined this consensus. After all, music consumers might be *choosing* to simply listen rather than dance; perhaps audience expectations had changed as much as the music. For the first time since before the First World War, recreational dancing seemed to be falling out of fashion. Unlike the 1930s, when high school students on Coke dates danced regularly after school in drugstores furnished with a jukebox and small dance floor, postwar youth were more inclined to stand and listen. A 1948 *Ladies' Home Journal* survey detected virtually no interest in dancing among high school students, a finding confirmed by observing behavior at high school and college dances. "Dancing has become a minor social necessity instead of a creative sport," concluded one writer. He attributed declining dance participation to wartime legislation imposing a 30 percent tax—later reduced to 20 percent—on establishments that permitted public dancing, thereby eliminating most neighborhood dance floors. (This factor was repeatedly cited by *Down Beat* and other swing proponents for encouraging small instrumental groups at the expense of vocalist-fronted big bands that catered to dancers.) The jukeboxes that had served these local venues were now located in bars and beauty shops, where a different kind of music was demanded, for background ambience or nondistracted listening rather than for dancing.[21]

Others noted that even if teenagers had wanted to dance, their ability to attend dances (or purchase records) was sharply circumscribed by the disappearance of war jobs. As in previous periods, the music industry attempted to cater to the preferences of those demographic groups with the most disposable income, which after the war included fewer teens. Acknowledging the symbiotic relationship between dance and swing, a *Down Beat* editorial bemoaned the passing of the jitterbugs ("a precious nuisance but, brother, we certainly could use them or a reasonable facsimile of the same today") and urged booking offices, press agents, bandleaders and managers, the musicians' union, ballroom promoters and operators to throw their full support behind a "National Dance Week." In this view, the onus for swing's decline was removed from musicians or songwriters; the industry was simply responding to changing consumer demand and to economic variables over which it had no control. An informal survey of students at Notre Dame's senior prom at which the Charlie Ventura band performed found agreement on one point: "a good beat" was the critical element of a dance band. Reactions to the Ventura band were mixed; too loud and fast, some thought, although others seemed pleasantly surprised that he was not as boppish as anticipated. Opinions likewise varied on whether dancing was on the way back. "I don't know if there is a big dance band revival," said one, "but I know there should be."[22]

Smothering the Market

If, as many assumed, the music industry was a zero-sum business in which swing and sweet profited at each other's expense, the contracting market for swing should have been accompanied by increased demand for a smoother, more soothing alternative. But as jazz advocates were quick to point out, the widely reported decline of swing bands was shared by frankly commercial, dance-oriented groups as well. "Sweet music of an excessively commercial sort has shown no better dividends than good dance music and jazz well executed," noted a *Down Beat* critic. Responding to "chortling" among music executives that the swing era was over, the magazine pointed out that Lombardo, Sammy Kaye, and other sweet bands had recently suffered unsuccessful tours and low grosses. It worried that by scapegoating swing for its problems, the music industry risked further undermining its own economic health. Ignoring the commercial success of Nat King Cole and Kenton in order to promote a Wayne King revival risked undermining the entire industry. *"Don't the agency men realize that if they talk themselves and their promoters into the belief that nothing will sell but syrup that they are smothering the market that has taken them out of Broadway's back closet and made them the million dollar operation they are today?"* demanded an editorial.[23]

The microeconomic difficulties faced by both swing and sweet bands, according to a number of contemporary analysts, were rooted in wartime conditions and exacerbated by the inflation and strikes that began shortly after V-J Day.[24] The entire entertainment industry, including Hollywood, was affected, but no sector more than live music. The crux of the problem was high overhead and excess capacity. During the war leaders had increased the size of their ensembles in response to consumer preference and in the belief that the extra salaries would be deducted from their high income taxes. Salaries for sidemen also increased, to $300 and up, partly because of higher living costs. Payrolls that had doubled or tripled and could reach $5,000 a week forced bands to seek guarantees of $2,000 and more from promoters, in addition to 60 percent of gate receipts. Promoters passed on the higher expenses to customers, doubling the typical dance admission charge of one dollar.

Given the high demand for and relative shortage of entertainment during the war, the industry remained in equilibrium. But falling postwar demand precipitated a devastating cycle. Consumers discouraged by high prices stayed home or went to movies; promoters went bankrupt paying high guarantees for what turned out to be sparse audiences; agencies found it more difficult to book bands at rates the musicians would accept; payroll costs prevented bandleaders from accepting lower guarantees; higher lodging and food costs prevented musicians from accepting lower salaries. To survive, bands were confronted with a stark choice: to cut payrolls, they had to decrease their size, lower musicians' salaries, or both. Some leaders simply dissolved their bands and formed smaller groups with musicians willing to accept their lower salaries.[25]

In short, the swing industry, according to those most familiar with it, was suffering from a lack of one of its defining qualities: competitiveness. "Dancedom has always done well when there were two or three bands fighting it out for top honors," *Down Beat* recalled. "The boys aren't even bothering to put the gloves on these days." A business that had witnessed a parade of pretenders to its throne seemed resigned to increasingly unprofitable practices. A good product obviated the need for high guarantees. Bandleaders were urged to follow the examples of Kenton and Dorsey, who shared losses with promoters when they occurred, or Hal McIntyre, whose contracts forbade promoters to charge dancers more than $1.10 for admission.[26]

While swing leaders seemed less willing to compete with one another for public attention, they also faced increasing competition from outside swing's musical domain. Musical categories that had seemed fairly stable for a decade were reshaping themselves in unexpected configurations. The geographic and cultural mobility that characterized the first half of the decade had resulted in the hybridization of several regional and ethnic musical forms—blues, country, Latin, polka—that swing was obliged to acknowledge in order to remain commercially viable. The boundaries dividing these ethnic genres were unusually porous in the postwar years. The swing artists who remained commercially viable did so by incorporating these various musical forms, some of which had contributed to swing but had been submerged over the course of its development.[27]

Hampton, and to a lesser extent Basie, maintained popularity in the late 1940s by streamlining and simplifying their bands' sounds, emphasizing brassy arrangements and a pronounced backbeat. Evolving away from big bands that sought to incorporate the rhythmic and harmonic innovations of bebop, Hampton looked to the African-American blues tradition known first as "race," later as "jump," and finally around 1950 as "rhythm and blues." Jump became a stylistic sanctuary for African-Americans and many whites attracted by neither the modernism of bebop nor the white sweet bands and popular vocalists; bands led by Hampton, Lucky Millinder, Bill Doggett, and Earl Bostic provided employment for scores of musicians displaced by the collapse of swing.

Jump's most successful artist, whose swing credentials like Hampton's were impeccable, was Louis Jordan. After a stint with Chick Webb, Jordan formed his own seven-piece outfit, the Tympani Five, which performed his clever jiving vocal numbers over a shuffle-boogie vamp and driving backbeat. Several of these records sold over a million copies. Also marking the trend toward smaller groups with a vocal focus was Nat Cole, another swing veteran, who coupled unusual commercial success with critical acclaim. Cole's piano playing assimilated some formal elements of jazz modernism; like a number of white vocalists who established their fame in big bands, Cole ultimately dropped his piano playing to concentrate exclusively on singing. Hampton, Jordan, and Cole inspired a wave of imitators, who were eagerly recorded by independent labels and popularized through a network of local disk jockeys.[28]

As a musical category swing was challenged by other ethnic traditions that appeared to have little in common with it. A few critics and musicians thought the future of dance music lay in incorporating Latin elements. Latin-sounding novelty numbers had appeared occasionally in the repertoire of big bands, but Dizzy Gillespie, under the influence of Mario Bauza, another trumpet player, was the first to highlight the music systematically, hiring the Cuban percussionist Chano Pozo for his late 1940s ensemble. Soon leaders as diverse as Kenton, Barnet, Krupa, Herman, Larry Clinton, and Nat Cole were incorporating some "Latin tinge" into their ensembles, at least by hiring Afro-Cuban drummers or bongo players. Latin big bands, most notably the one led by Machito, also incorporated the musical innovations of jazz, generating considerable enthusiasm among musicians. "That Afro-Cuban rhythm is real gone!" said Charlie Parker after recording with Machito. "I like to play with those drummers—man, it's so relaxed." For a time, at least, audiences shared in this enthusiasm. "A casual glance on the floor of the Palladium ballroom here, where Machito normally hangs out, will show a partnership in mutual excitement between dancers and musicians not seen since the early big band days of the middle thirties," observed one writer.[29]

Less palatable to much of the swing community was an upsurge of interest in the music once known derisively as "hillbilly," later as "country and western." Like swing, country had vastly expanded its audience during the war, and by 1950 it had become the populist-tinged vernacular music of white middle America, appealing to both rural and urban audiences. For swing fanciers, country music represented an unfortunate debasement of popular taste. "Hillbilly Boom Can Spread like Plague," warned a lead story in *Down Beat* on the popularity of barn dances around Hollywood. "Of course, Hollywood is strictly a hick town," the reporter acknowledged before recalling nervously that both Whiteman and Goodman had built on early successes there to inaugurate national trends.[30] The swing press took surprisingly little notice of western swing sensation Bob Wills, whose Texas Playboys played a blend of country, swing, and jump with shuffle-beat rhythms that attracted a mass audience of white dancers.

As the "barn dance boom" migrated east, polka bands outdrew top-name swing bands in the Midwest, attracting not older nostalgia seekers but the youth market crucial to commercial success. "They seem to know all the bands' numbers, sing along on the vocals, scream for the hippest requests, and cheer the bands on in a fashion which takes an aging observer back to Benny Goodman's 'Sing Sing Sing' days," noted a reporter present at some Brooklyn "polka fests." Even George Avakian called polka "the real music of the man in the street," adding that on the "level of genuineness, polkas have it all over jazz now." In fact the music loosely labeled polka had emerged alongside swing in the 1930s, benefiting from the same technological developments that made swing a national phenomenon and adapting swing's instrumentation and some of its musical innovations. Several of the late 1930s' most popular hits were forms of polka music, including the Yiddish "Bei Mir Bist du Schön," which Goodman helped popularize, and "Beer Barrel Polka," a runaway hit of 1939. Like country, polka greatly expanded its audience during the war, and by 1948 it had reached a new level of mass popularity. But few in the swing community took the polka craze seriously or considered the form more than an illegitimate pretender to the cultural throne rightfully occupied by swing.[31]

However distasteful this competition from other genres seemed to purists, a different, arguably more insidious threat to swing's competitiveness came not from rival musical forms but from the large entertainment conglomerates whose ascendance had accompanied the rise of swing. The recording industry, which had sprouted numerous small independent labels in response to the wartime recording ban, showed signs by 1947 of reverting to an oligopoly of the "big four": Columbia, Decca, RCA Victor, and Capitol. *Down Beat* reported that many independent labels were folding as the recording industry followed "the inevitable course of American business at large." With retail sales of $204 million in 1947, the industry enjoyed its most profitable year to date, finally surpassing the previous peak of 1921; but there were complaints about the conservative practices and products on which that commercial success was built. That bumper year was followed, moreover, by a nearly year-long recording ban precipitated both by the Taft-Hartley Act's prohibitions against record companies' payments to the AFM welfare fund and by Petrillo's hostility to disk jockeys—yet another manifestation of the hated "canned music." Then Columbia's and Victor's attempts to dominate the market with their respective new 33⅓ and 45 RPM technologies triggered what came to be called the "Battle of Speeds."[32]

Partly because of confusion over shifting technologies, consumers turned to television, boosting sales of sets by 400 percent in 1949; record sales fell to $158 million. The music industry had been preparing since the late 1930s for the arrival of television, and even optimists braced for its impact. "Television will turn the band business into show business," predicted Lionel Hampton, who hoped to exploit the new medium by simplifying his own music. "It will kill the emphasis on music and put it on production numbers, novelties, and crooners," he said.[33]

The long-term implications for swing of Hollywood appeared even more ominous. Companies like Warner Brothers and M-G-M had long exerted an important influence on the music industry through the song publishers they controlled. The migration of musical employment to

Los Angeles during the war, as musicians sought jobs in movie orchestras and relocated network radio shows, further shifted the balance of
power from New York to Los Angeles. In the uncertain postwar atmosphere, Hollywood drew special scrutiny from swing loyalists. "The
movie industry is moving in on music and every other phase of the
entertainment business with a real vengeance," wrote Michael Levin.
"Monopoly is a very ugly word but signs of it are cropping up all over."
Movie companies already in control of song publishing were moving
into the recording field, while contractual obligations required top
musical and singing talent to remain on the West Coast. "It is highly
possible in the next few years that agencies who want to plant their
attractions in films will have to agree to tie up other artists both for
records and radio in a way which the film company deems suitable,"
Levin warned.[34]

Swing stood the most to lose from this situation. As early as 1939, a
swing bandleader had blamed a surge in "anti-swing talk" on music
publishers, who found that more melodically complex sweet tunes sold
better among the sheet-music buying public than rhythmically oriented
swing tunes.[35] By 1947, according to an analysis published in the *New
York Times Magazine*, a variety of technological factors conspired to
further weaken swing's position within music publishing. Because sweet
and novelty tunes yielded better sales of sheet music than swing (and
each sheet sale netted publishers twenty times more than each record
sale), the Hollywood publishing conglomerates had a clear financial
interest in promoting sweet at the expense of swing. Further savings
could be realized by rerecording old songs already in their catalogues.
By using movies—and later, television—to promote the music they
wished, and deploying song-pluggers to persuade bandleaders and disk
jockeys to play particular songs, the conglomerates could manipulate
both the demand and supply side of musical taste. In response to the
resulting record sales, and popularity among radio listeners and dance
hall patrons, MCA and other booking agencies dropped swing as
unprofitable, a condition exacerbated by the higher wages swing musicians customarily received relative to their sweet counterparts.[36]

In addition to the perceived decline of swing relative to sweet, a more
sweeping transformation was taking place in the swing industry, the full

impact of which would not be apparent for several years. Since the commercial development of the phonograph, recordings had been treated as secondary to published sheet music. The standard industry practice since before swing had been that songs were written and published before being sold to bands to record. Often a number of "covers" of a given popular tune were recorded within a short period, with no particular benefits accruing to the first. For example, following Chick Webb's 1934 recording of "Stompin' at the Savoy," twelve recordings were made by different bands in 1936. The radio networks' creation of BMI in the early 1940s began to change the relative financial importance of published music and recordings. By the late 1940s, as the sale of sheet music fell, these sales increasingly followed successful recordings. Working through A & R (artists and repertoire) agents at recording companies, songwriters were able to get their songs recorded, then publish them on their own. By the early 1950s, television had largely replaced radio for promoting sheet music sales. "Everybody but the music publishers, who used to be pretty good at that, nowadays picks songs," complained a veteran songwriter. "Today we don't dare publish a song until some artist perhaps liked it, or when the whim of an A & R genius decided it should be done . . . A record should be a by-product of publishing, not the spark plug of songwriting and publishing." In short, a print medium was metamorphosing into an aural medium that bypassed musical notation. Although this development was not intrinsically harmful to swing, a genre based on written arrangements, it was linked to the ascent of the popular vocalists whose star presence ensured that particular songs would be identified with them, thereby reducing the songs' usefulness to other artists.[37]

Related to the rise of A & R departments and the changing relations between sheet music and recordings was the appearance of disk jockeys, identified by *Metronome* as "a species of parasites . . . the Musical Mushroom . . . of 1947." In the same way that jukeboxes shaped the swing industry of the 1930s, disk jockeys transformed the dissemination of music after the war. Bandleaders and recording companies had lost the battle to control the broadcasting of their performances in 1940; "platter-spinners" further eroded the commercial appeal of live network radio and the economic viability of live musicians. Disk jockeys were widely suspected by musicians of engineering the sudden rise of the popular singers at the expense of instrumental bands, whether swing or sweet. Moreover, they could influence more directly the patterns of consumer taste. Although the route to a jukebox playlist had hardly been a model of free market economics, the consumer was granted an element of choice. Through "payola" by record companies and song publishers, disk jockeys were blamed for contributing to the general monopolistic distortion thought to be overtaking the entertainment market. Their significance was indicated by *Variety*'s establishment of a full-page weekly chart to gauge the popularity of songs and recordings on the basis of reports by roughly 100 major disk jockeys across the United States.[38]

Even apart from the disturbing consequences of disk jockeys, the swing community found much to criticize about postwar network radio (as they had before the war as well). One fan complained that while as recently as 1942 "one could snap on [the] radio at night and enjoy really fine dance bands from all over the country," broadcasts now featured "truly unknown mickey mouse or hershey bar bands." The reader wondered: "Are all the famous dance spots closed?" Insiders blamed the inherent conservatism of corporate radio. *Down Beat*'s editors charged that radio, "after a quarter century development into a billion dollar industry, is more immature than ever in its attitude toward jazz and swing." Sampling the national airwaves during a cross-country drive, George Simon was pleasantly surprised by the "snatches of jazz" interspersed amid the ubiquitous diet of hillbilly and western music in places like North Carolina, Alabama, and Texas. Only in big cities did he discern a fear of alienating listeners by playing jazz. "It's my pet hunch that radio is selling jazz much too short," he concluded. "In radio as in many other fields, it's the big, policymaking guys who are the reactionaries, and who, like most all other reactionaries, have little idea of what the little man really wants."[39]

Crewcut, Jarb, Swixibop

In effect, the national culture industry that had arisen alongside and been shaped by swing now seemed to be mobilizing its considerable powers against it. For a decade the fortunes of big-band jazz and the music industry had seemed inextricably linked. By the late 1940s, this was no longer true; "swing" was not synonymous with American popular music, and it was difficult for some to believe it ever had been. Mystified by this turn of events, a few raised suspicions about a conspiracy against jazz in which the press was involved. Bandleader Chubby Jackson, for example, blamed widely reported statements by industry "moguls" for sticking postwar jazz with a damaging reputation for being "unintelligible . . . mechanical noise." "They sit there in their aged hypocrisies and halt the natural progress of America's only contribution to music—Jazz!" he fumed. "What chance have we as musicians or composers to present our young selves when Mr. Publisher saves a million dollars a year by refusing us and reaching in the grab bag of yesterday's hits and plugging the oldies?" *Down Beat*'s editors periodically inveighed against their colleagues in the daily press, who at one point likened the commercial appeal of a top band to "a Communist rally in Scarsdale."[40]

Cut loose from the industrial infrastructure that had supported it, a musical form that for a decade had been heard in prestigious concert halls and been discussed as the successor to European classical music was driven to seek counsel from businessmen. Paradoxically, rather than freeing swing from the demands of the market, its "elevation" from a dancer's accompaniment to a listener's art had tied it more closely to commercial considerations. Swing found itself being discussed as a commodity, a bundle of musical attributes that could be rearranged and repackaged at will. Adding a new vocalist or strings, subtracting horns, slowing the tempo, choosing different tunes, eliminating bebop motifs—these decisions had become more central than ever to bandleaders. In desperation, even sectors that had resisted this approach solicited the guidance of the market. In what it heralded as a "super-duper special issue" devoted to the decline of the band business, *Down Beat* solicited articles from bandleaders, booking agents, ballroom operators, record executives, disk jockeys, and others. The prevailing advice was that in order to survive, swing would have to adapt to the market, not educate or elevate its listeners. "The dancing public pays its money for a product, the same as when they buy anything else on the market," wrote Frank Dailey, operator of the Meadowbrook, where Glenn Miller built his national success. "When the label remains the same and the contents change (which has been the case with many of our bands), there ceases to be a demand for it." A Chicago club operator equated hiring bands with purchasing bread. "If I save three cents a pound on bread, I'm ahead at the end of the year. The same rule applies to buying a band."[41]

Emblematic of this marketing approach was *Down Beat*'s contest to designate a successor to the word *jazz*. The concern over an appropriate moniker extended well back in the history of jazz. In the 1930s, the precise distinction between "jazz" and "swing" had received endless scrutiny. In 1945, a piece had humorously proposed "swazz" and "jing" as possibilities, the former supposedly the choice of Harvard students, the latter of Yale. By 1949 the issue was no longer a joke. The magazine offered a first prize of $1,000 for the best entry; other prizes included private performances by the Charlie Barnet band and the King Cole Trio, and dates with top vocalists of both sexes. Submissions were judged by a panel that included semanticist S. I. Hayakawa and English professors from Cornell and Carleton. After much suspenseful ballyhoo, first prize was bestowed on "crewcut," a term meant to convey the opposite of "longhair." Other prize-winning submissions included "jarb," "mesmerhythm," "id," "swixibop," "blip," "idoism," "ameratonic," "schmoosic," "improphony," "syncope," and "reetbeat." Despite these "gratifying" results, *Down Beat* concurred with its panel that none of the submissions should actually replace "jazz" in common usage. Although it "might be nice to utilize 'crewcut' once in a while as a change of pace," the point was to induce people "to *think* seriously and extensively about jazz"—and presumably to generate some publicity.[42]

The more scientific side of the swing ethos, which had earlier tested the music's prurient effect on teens, was represented in the magazine's attempt to apply the scientific method to explaining the music's decline. "When scientists are confronted with a problem, they create laboratory conditions identical with those actually existing and test their products, designs, or formulas under these conditions," stated the editors. It proposed to use an unknown and untested fifteen-piece ensemble, led by

Roy Stevens, as the "guinea pig" for its "laboratory experiment"—
gauging audience reaction to Stevens in the country's real-life ballrooms, theaters, recording studios, and radio stations. But interest in
the experiment waned before much useful data had been accumulated.[43]

Bandleaders responded to the crisis in a variety of ways. Secure in
both critical and popular success, Kenton defiantly admitted his role,
along with Woody Herman and Dizzy Gillespie, in undermining the
dance-band business. "Sure, we ruined it," he declared on the front
page of *Down Beat*'s "Everybody Dance" issue. "We ruined it because
we were bound and determined to play the kind of music we wanted
to play. What we wanted to play wasn't dance music, but, despite this,
agents and promoters insisted on handling us just as they would handle
a dance band." Some musicians, including Coleman Hawkins and Art
Tatum, gave up trying to maintain regular working bands and instead
appeared as "virtuosos" fronting "skeleton bands" that might change
with every engagement.[44] Others, following prewar expatriates like
Sidney Bechet and Hawkins, fled to what they considered the more
appreciative audiences of Europe. Ellington, Armstrong, Gillespie,
Lena Horne, and Pearl Bailey were only a few of the jazz artists who
embarked on European tours in 1948, while others expatriated themselves. "If the current clamp on progressive music continues," wrote
one, "I predict that most of the jazz greats will follow my trail." But
most accepted the dictates of the marketplace, sometimes experimenting with different styles, tempos, and arrangements, at other times
pulling "the hats, noses, and beards out of the mothballs."[45]

Swing Redux

"Bop, although the subject of much discussion and controversy, has not
as yet scratched the surface publicity-wise," stated a confidential proposal for a "Bop at the Stork Club" party to be sponsored in January
1949 by Benny Goodman and Capitol Records. "The primary reason
is that Bop has not been considered quite respectable. Therefore, the
projected party rests, in the main, upon making Bop respectable and
amusing, while keeping its musical flavor and controversial approach."
The fete was to be staged in the club's Blessed Event Room, a location

that would simultaneously bestow "stature" on bop's birth and enable "the Stork" to "cash in" on its "undoubted publicity value." Approximately 150 guests would be invited, mainly from the press: editors and writers for trade publications, newspaper columnists, members of the "intelligentsia," " 'think' editors" from magazines like *Harper's* and *Atlantic*, as well as disk jockeys and music agency personnel. Although guest artists, including bop singers, jazz musicians, and vocalists would be invited, the proposal stipulated: "None of the really extreme boppers [are] to be present." Guests were to receive "Bop hats, Bop glasses, Bop ties"; "Bopanapes" would be served along with a new drink, "Benny's Bop." Prizes would go to guests coming up with the best definitions of bop (pencils and paper to be provided by the club). The bill for this bop bash was to be footed equally by Goodman and Capitol, each paying approximately $600.[46]

Like many of his swing colleagues, by 1948 Goodman was struggling to come to terms with a music whose relationship to big-band jazz remained strangely undefined. Earlier he had dismissed the modernists as "not real musicians . . . bebop reminds me of guys who refuse to write a major chord even if it's going to sound good." "They're just writing or playing for effect," he concluded, "and a lot of it doesn't swing." As recently as August he had professed his dislike for a music he called "nervous more than exciting," based on chords that were "just pretentious tripe." He complained further of "the morals of these guys. Before you can give some of them a job in your band, you've got to screen them, like the FBI." At the same time, however, Goodman was collaborating with modernists Red Rodney and Wardell Gray and recruiting young musicians for a new bop-oriented big band. In a Westchester County appearance in July, Goodman's septet managed to appeal both to dancers expecting his familiar swing-era hits and to "the goatee–beret–horn rimmed glasses set" that was satisfied to "gather and gape" at the band. "The group doesn't come on in a manner that will scare any swing addicts, bop being predominately displayed in fine, if somewhat subdued, taste," a reviewer noted. "Benny does a job of selling the new product to his old public."[47]

By December, when he unveiled his new big band at New York's Paramount Theatre, Goodman had apparently reconsidered the merits of bop. "I still don't know what bop is," he confessed to *Newsweek*, "and I do not believe anyone really does. It's only good or bad music and call mine bop or schmop, it's good. These boys have spirit. They're out to make a name, and it's a combination of what they do and what I know." Although the band appeared in "the fast-fading uniform of the bebop fraternity"—red berets, black-rimmed glasses, and bow ties—most critics resisted the notion that Goodman had made a radical break with his past. "He has made certain concessions to bop, but he does not have a bop band," said Leonard Feather. "I don't see much difference between this and the Goodman band of 1936," agreed a colleague. But the campaign to identify himself with bop continued, with the Stork Club party, the Truman inaugural, and through much of 1949.[48]

Abrupt stylistic departures designed to recapture a disenchanted audience had long been commonplace in popular music; swing itself had been born out of such an impulse. These shifts often involved the appropriation of African-American musical forms by whites. "Bop at the Stork Club" only recapitulated at a more patently self-conscious level what had occurred nearly fifteen years earlier when John Hammond and Willard Alexander persuaded Goodman to reorganize his band around the arrangements of Fletcher Henderson. The incongruity of Goodman as a standard-bearer for bebop arises from a distorted notion of the relationship between swing and bebop. Because of the apparent contrasts between these two genres, both as music and as cultural style, historians and others have seen them as polar opposites, often attributing differences where similarities should be emphasized, and vice versa. Swing has been depicted as primarily a white phenomenon, bop as African-American; swing as widely popular functional music performed by big bands, bop as small-group art music that spurned commercial success; swing as participatory, bop as detached; swing as embodying the politics of consensus, bop as militant harbinger of the race consciousness that would bloom during the 1950s and afterward. Such characterizations are as misleading about swing as about bop.

Even at the level of cultural style, the continuities between swing and bop are more striking than any discontinuities. Like swing, bop was notorious for its distinctive argot (which its most prominent figures

Earl Hines and His Orchestra, featuring the Bluebonnets, in 1943, when many bands were enlarging dramatically.

A segregated wartime audience enjoys a Duke Ellington concert at Fort Dix, New Jersey.

Lionel Hampton with his 1950–1951 orchestra, one of the few to survive the postwar band slump.

SWING—"Jump" tunes don't satisfy post-war customers.

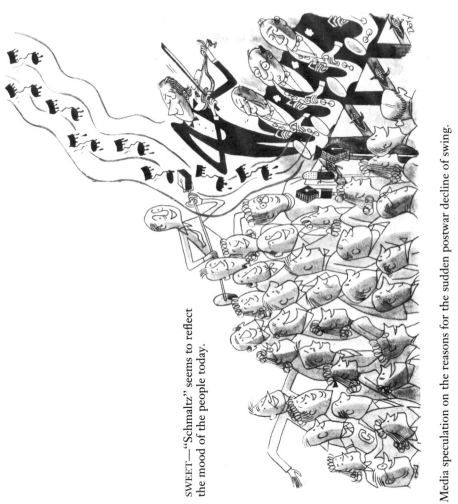

SWEET—"Schmaltz" seems to reflect the mood of the people today.

Media speculation on the reasons for the sudden postwar decline of swing.

Dizzy Gillespie greeted by fans upon his March 1948 return from a two-month tour of Europe.

Benny Goodman with Mrs. Betty Henderson at the Bop Goes to the Stork Club party in New York City in January 1949.

disowned); many of its terms had changed ("hep" had become passé and was replaced by "hip"), but obsolescence is expected of slang. And much of this nomenclature had clear roots in swing and earlier, particularly in the dialects created by swing icon Lester Young and by Cab Calloway. Likewise, the concern with illicit drug use among bop musicians and their followers had been anticipated a decade earlier (although the object of concern had shifted from marijuana—then considered a narcotic—to true narcotics like heroin). In their ambivalence toward their cultish disciples and the styles with which they were associated, in their aspirations toward both cultural legitimacy and commercial success, musicians associated with bebop resembled their swing predecessors more than they differed from them.[49]

"History is repeating itself," observed a 1949 *Down Beat* editorial noting the parallels between the "commotion" created by swing and bop: uninitiated patrons complaining that the music was undanceable "noise," leaders and publicists willing to feed the public's demand for explanations of the new music, use of broadcasting to introduce the form to a new and initially skeptical audience. "The boppists may be all excited about the commotion centering around the introduction of their product," the editors claimed, "but it is no greater than and no different from the hubbub that was under way in January, 1936, over that puzzling, unknown quantity of music—swing."[50]

This familiar historicist thinking resurfaced often in comments and writings by proponents of the new jazz. A Capitol Records publication explained the rise of bop as yet another turn in the inexorable "cycle of change" of the musical world. "One form spawns and is in turn devoured by the next. The art progresses." Confronted with predictions of bebop's demise, Gillespie directed critics to magazine and newspaper articles around 1936 and 1937. "People were saying EXACTLY the same thing about swing, which was supposed to be just a new fad then," he observed. Ellington, alert as always to historical parallels, asked: "Why be surprised that bop is ridiculed? Jazz and swing got the same treatment in their early days, too."[51]

Unlike much of the coverage by the mainstream press, which treated bebop as if it had dropped in from another planet, this line of argument implied bop's essential continuity with its musical antecedents while at the same time acknowledging its difference. That is, the new jazz belonged to an established musical tradition even as it represented a cyclical variation of that tradition. With historical hindsight, these continuities are more striking than the divergences. Just as swing's luminaries were grounded in 1920s jazz, bop's leading practitioners had apprenticed in the big bands and smaller jump bands of the war years. Although its roots were various, there is general agreement that bop was worked out beginning around 1940 in informal after-hour sessions at Harlem clubs by young musicians gainfully employed in swing outfits. Dizzy Gillespie had apprenticed with Teddy Hill and Cab Calloway, among others; drummer Kenny Clarke likewise worked with Hill. Bud Powell played with Cootie Williams, Howard McGhee with Charlie Barnet, Mary Lou Williams with Andy Kirk, and so on. Charlie Parker traveled east to New York in 1942 with the Kansas City–based orchestra led by Jay McShann. Throughout the 1940s, bop reached its largest live audiences under the aegis of big bands, beginning with Earl Hines's and continuing through those led by Billy Eckstine, Dizzy Gillespie, Woody Herman, and Charlie Ventura. Only in 1944 did bebop appear in public in a small-group format, on 52nd Street. Owing to these circumstances, distinctions among swing, jump, and bop are difficult to draw with any precision. The same musician was likely to be a swing artist by day or during a tour, a bebopper after two in the morning or on hiatus between tours in New York City.[52]

Like swing, bop was puzzling to contemporaries because it seemed to appear *ex nihilo* and fully formed, its historical roots obscured by conditions in the music industry. Just as the formative preswing years of the early 1930s had been elided by the post-Crash collapse of the entertainment business, particularly the recording industry, bebop's lengthy incubation period coincided with the distraction of world war. The 1942–1944 recording ban, moreover, ensured that the prime vehicle for disseminating the new music was unavailable for nearly two years. When bop first began attracting media attention, in 1946, it generated much the same coverage as early swing had: tongue-in-cheek accounts of moral panics followed by endless efforts to explain and define a label that postdated the music to which it had been attached.

The word first appeared as *re-bop*, later *be-bop*, *bebop*, and finally

simply *bop*. News reports accurately described the term as onomato-
poeic, referring to the scat-sung phrases through which Gillespie and
others communicated their musical ideas; some accounts also looked
back to earlier vocal improvisations by Armstrong, Calloway, and
Waller, all of which contained the sound "be-bop." When pressed for
explanations, the jazz modernists spoke of a new way of phrasing and
accenting, use of a wider harmonic range, new chords, and previously
shunned intervals like flatted fifths and ninths.[53]

Early on, the media tended to associate the music with vice. A ripple
followed the decision by a Los Angeles radio station to ban "rebop":
"hot jive music" that encouraged juvenile delinquency and "arouses
degenerative instincts and emotions." The story was picked up by *Time*,
which glossed Gillespie's explanation of bop with its own ominous definition: "hot jazz overheated, with overdone lyrics full of bawdiness,
references to narcotics, and doubletalk." It designated as "the bigwig
of be-bop" singer Harry "The Hipster" Gibson, who with guitarist
Slim Gaillard had recorded such reputed bop anthems as "Who Put
the Benzedrine in Mrs. Murphy's Ovaltine?" (which owed far more to
Fats Waller than to bebop).[54]

This misleading association of bop with novelty vocal numbers was
short-lived, but a moral taint continued to haunt the music. "Not since
the early days of the swing craze, when daily newspapers would come
out with the most fantastic definitions of the word swing, have I seen
a branch of music so methodically maligned and mauled in the magazines and other media as Bebop," fumed Leonard Feather. *Down Beat*
complained periodically of an "anti-bop feeling" in the press that
unfairly linked the music to various depravities. Newspapers had been
quick to pounce on narcotics arrests and other contretemps involving
a tiny minority of musicians as evidence that the music itself was morally culpable. "There are classical men who have some of the worst
morals in the world," charged Nat Cole. "But nowadays it's always the
bop musician who gets the rap." Cole vowed to become a sort of character witness for the music: "I figure I can help by telling the public,
'Now I'm going to play bop, and we'll see if it changes my morals.' "[55]

Part of bop's image problem was that the term itself had been a label
publicized by the media; musicians disliked it because it lacked speci-

ficity and could be applied to what they considered unrelated phenomena. Because the label was overdetermined, it was loosely applied to a bewildering range of musicians, from Muggsy Spanier and Louis Armstrong to Sammy Kaye and Perry Como, who could not be construed as having any affinities with the music. "The public is confused about bop now," commented Nat Cole. "They think everything they hear is bop—even an old-fashioned swing saxophone solo." Lionel Hampton, whose pronouncements on bop were taken at face value by a gullible media, added to the confusion. "B-bop is the chord structure, Re-bop is the rhythm," he explained. "We combine both and call it the New Movement." Hampton also recorded an album of tunes titled "Zoo-bop," "oo-bop," "re-bop," and "ee-bop," which were described as variants of bebop. If the term continued to be used indiscriminately, *Down Beat* speculated hopefully, the public would eventually forget its origins, and the music would lose its stigma.[56]

Because the term *bebop* contained novelty value, this ambiguity could work in its favor as well as against it. Swing trumpeter Lee Castle found that audiences hungry for bebop were satisfied by two-beat Dixieland arrangements played loudly, which they assumed were some "new kind of bop." "Kids would come up and ask, 'Have you got any bop?' " he told *Down Beat*. "I'd say, 'Yeah, South Rampart Street [a Dixieland standard].' So we'd play it, and the kids would come back and say, 'That's fine. Got any more bop?' " Citizens in Muscatine, Iowa, in 1949 formed the Royal Society of Be Bop, which met Hot Club style every week in an establishment called Granny's Grill; details of the club's activities make it doubtful that the music consumed was actually bebop. But hostile media coverage compensated for this positive response. Unsympathetic critics were willing to feed the public's curiosity with facetious definitions. "Be-bop is to music what Gertrude Stein is to literature and Salvatore Dali is to painting," went one of the kinder ones. "It is an abstraction followed by a weird cult of musicians and an even weirder group of stone faced listeners." Syndicated columnists like Frank Conniff took delight in baiting the music and its adherents. Robert Ruark deemed bebop "a kind of musical outrage for which some people profess a fondness. It is played by people who wear goatees and berets. Its language has been compared to that spoken by the Cro-

Magnon man, obviously the mental equal of the modern bopster."
Pianist George Shearing, a bebop popularizer, asserted that "the only
thing that can do anything bad for bop is the word itself. People consider it something they don't like."[57]

This stigma extended beyond the musicians to their devotees. In
1950, for example, the decision by the Milwaukee archdiocese to bar
from Catholic schools young beboppers—"teenagers with freakish
haircuts and gangster tendencies"—was widely reported. Press
accounts cited confessions by two "former be-bop girls" that they followed a "formulated policy of vice and misconduct." A police officer
warned that bebop cliques went beyond devotion to the music and
indulged in "drinking, marijuana smoking, shoplifting, and illicit sex
relationships." The costume depicted in these accounts was not far
removed from what jitterbugs had worn: for boys, loud jackets, pleated
pants with narrow cuffs, long hair combed straight back and parted
down the back of the head; for girls, tight-fitting long skirts, jackets,
and saddle shoes. "The term bop is being kicked around so loosely in
the columns of newspapers that it is just a matter of time until it will
be employed to designate juvenile delinquents," complained *Down
Beat.*[58]

In short, the dangerous excesses popularly associated with bebop—
juvenile delinquency, illicit drug use, sexual promiscuity, outrageous
language and dress—were similar to what had earlier been assigned to
swing's jitterbugs and ickies. Few danced to bop, to be sure, but neither
had many jitterbugs danced to swing. And the figure that came to be
known as the "hipster" emerged imperceptibly out of the same urban
environment that sustained swing. "They come with their zoot suits,
long haircuts, reefers, and 'zombie' jive to night spots that feature jazz
talent," according to a report on so-called zombies (of both races) who
congregated on 52nd Street during and after the war, befriending musicians and driving the regular patrons downtown to the relative purity
of Greenwich Village.[59]

There was a subtle difference in the media response to bop, however.
Whereas early press accounts of swing maintained a measure of respect
for its bandleaders and musicians, leveling their sarcasm at swing's exuberant followers, media coverage of bebop regularly demeaned the art-

ists themselves. Swing's most conspicuous public faces, not coincidentally, had been white: Goodman, Shaw, Dorsey, Miller. The public
image of bebop, on the other hand, was established almost totally by
Dizzy Gillespie. Just as no magazine article in the early swing years
could fail to mention Goodman, no feature on bebop in the late 1940s
was complete without a description and photograph of Gillespie. With
his trademark goatee, glasses, beret, and meerschaum pipe, later aug-
mented with a leopard-skin jacket, his balloon-cheeked embouchure,
soprano laugh, and loose, bowlegged walk, Gillespie served as a perfect
visual embodiment of the cult of bop. But unlike the media figures of
swing, whose appearance and deportment remained distant from the
outlandish spectacle of the jitterbugs, Gillespie seemed to welcome the
role, serving as the energy center of the new subcultural style.

In fact, however, the modernists were as concerned to distance themselves from such perceived excesses as their swing predecessors had
been. Even the style-setting Gillespie was quick to point out that even
such subcultural icons as his goatee and beret should not be misinter-
preted as significant statements; their rationales were comfort and con-
venience. His rumpled, unbuttoned clothes and beat-up horn were likewise accidental. Parker, who contributed nothing to bebop's sartorial
style, readily admitted his heroin addiction but warned younger musicians in the strongest terms to avoid emulating his habit. Perhaps there
was an element of coyness in Gillespie's disclaimers; he was perfectly
willing to be photographed signing autographs for teenaged girls
wearing painted-on goatees, and bowing to Mecca (a publicity stunt he
later rued).[60] In any event, subcultural style need not be thought out
consciously in order to be significant.

Still, the jazz modernists were less concerned with style statements
than with cultural acceptance. In fact bebop artists were at least as concerned with cultural legitimacy as their swing predecessors had been
and pursued it in many of the same forms. The classical concert hall
remained a potent symbol for the new generation of musicians. "Bop
is the Negroes' entree to Carnegie hall on something approaching equal
status with the New York Philharmonic, or any other recognized longhair outfit," asserted one critic. As Goodman had, many of the bop
artists emphasized their respect for and indebtedness to such European

composers as Ravel, Debussy, Prokofiev, and Schönberg. A *Down Beat* writer found the "fantastic and exciting 're-bop' style . . . in most all of Stravinsky's works, particularly *Rite of Spring*." The Russian émigré even composed a work for the Woody Herman band, *Ebony Concerto*, which premiered at Carnegie Hall in 1946 before Herman toured with it. Parker, who claimed to have developed his style independently of the swing era's most influential players in the relative isolation of Kansas City, described bop as "no love-child of jazz," even "something entirely separate and apart" from that tradition; he idolized Hindemith and professed a profound desire to study composition with Varese.[61] Such considerations underlay his controversial decision to perform with a string section, recordings of which Parker claimed were his personal favorites.

A watershed occurred in September 1947, when Carnegie Hall hosted an all-bop concert featuring Dizzy Gillespie, who led his big band and played in a quintet with Charlie Parker and Ella Fitzgerald. Although bop artists and modernist tendencies had appeared earlier in Norman Granz's "Jazz at the Philharmonic" concerts and through Woody Herman's band, the Carnegie debut was publicized and reviewed as representing the same sort of milestone as Goodman's had nearly a decade earlier. Organized by Leonard Feather, the concert attracted a sellout crowd; a front-page review in *Down Beat* described it as "an excellent concert, one of the freshest musically heard since the first Ellington 1942 set to." Soon Gillespie was playing fifty concerts annually at such distinguished venues as Boston's Symphony Hall and Philadelphia's Academy of Music, in addition to New York's Carnegie and Town halls.[62]

A romance with the symbols of high culture and learning pervaded the bop subculture, as it had swing. Whatever its utilitarian considerations, the bop dress code seemed lifted from the Parisian avant-garde. Psychoanalysts reportedly competed for the privilege of treating certain musicians, one of whom kept a Dali original locked in a strongbox in the middle of his tiny apartment. Others learned Arabic in order to study the Koran. In addition to paying homage to avant-garde European composers, the jazz modernists gave their compositions quasi-academic titles like "Epistrophy" and "Ornithology." Much was made of bop artists' ability to converse about intellectual matters; one described Gillespie as "deep," and Parker as someone who "could converse on any level about anything." Gillespie recalled lengthy discussions with Parker about philosophy, politics, "the social order," "lifestyle," Marcantonio, and Baudelaire. Even antibop drummer Panama Francis, who derided the beboppers as "rejects from the big bands," complained that the "bebop era was really born from the intellectuals."[63]

Actually performing the music required a sophisticated knowledge of music theory, particularly chord substitutions, much of which was conveyed by Gillespie in informal tutorials. Swing music had also required considerable musical training, but bop brought a new self-consciousness. "It was different from the 'swing' music that had preceded it, the technology of the whole thing . . . it was the most intelligent era of jazz," recalled drummer Kenny Clarke. Several bop artists had attended conservatories and conceived their role as that of educators, both of other musicians and of audiences unlikely to be prepared to appreciate the new jazz. "We tried to educate the people," recalled Sarah Vaughan of Eckstine's band, which included Parker, Gillespie, Art Blakey, Lucky Thompson, and Fats Navarro. "We used to play dances, and there were just a very few who understood who would be in a corner, jitterbugging forever, while the rest just stood staring at us."[64] Bebop sometimes received the benefit of the doubt from musicians who considered themselves unqualified to pass judgment on such apparently cerebral music.

Although they acquired a reputation for indifference to their audience, bop artists, who like their big-band counterparts struggled to remain commercially viable, recognized the need to prepare audiences for their music. In practical terms, this did not involve educating the audience as much as meeting it halfway. Contrary to the perception that has colored subsequent appraisals of bebop as "art for art's sake," the modernists did not deliberately flout commercial success; many avidly sought, and occasionally received, popular success of the kind that swing bandleaders took for granted. The charges often made against bop—that it was excessively loud, fast, dissonant, and unsuited to dancing—were also leveled at the postwar swing bands, and some musicians associated with bop willingly modified their music in the same ways as their swing counterparts.

General confusion about exactly what bop was made it possible for Goodman and others to graft certain musical devices onto a traditional swing sound and exploit the novelty value of bop through the extra-musical gimmicks. Others adapted the new music in a less ostentatious manner. "I don't go for the more wild type of bop, so the boys in the band and I have perfected a more relaxed, listenable form that we call relaxed bop," explained Lester Young. "After all for any new music to catch on it has to have commercial appeal and bop has now been commercialized." Musicians reminded themselves and one another that audiences expected to hear melodies they could recognize and remember. For Gillespie, the answer was not to discard bop, but to apply its harmonic and rhythmic principles to familiar standards. "We're going to have the melody going along with some countermelodies so they can understand what we're doing," he said. Tenor player Charlie Ventura achieved critical and popular success in 1948 by harmonizing the singing voices of Jackie Cain and Roy Kral with saxophones to create a "voice-instrument" sound both distinctive yet commercially salable. "Our music is composed, arranged and performed for both a listening and dancing audience, and while using original ideas and incorporating 'new sounds' into music, we do not lose the general structure of a melody, line or rhythm," he said. By embellishing rather than obscuring familiar melodies, "we do not alienate the many, who have not as yet come to completely accept the rapid changes being made in popular music and jazz these days."[65]

Even more fundamental to commercial success than melody, perhaps, was maintaining the proper rhythm. Faced with losing the patronage of customers whose main criterion was a danceable beat, some chose to moderate their tempi. Responding to Parker's published claim that bop differed from jazz in its lack of a steady tempo, Gillespie argued that such an attitude was responsible for bop's commercial difficulties. "We'll never get bop across to a wide audience until they can dance to it," he said. "They're not particular about whether you're playing a flatted fifth or a ruptured 129th as long as they can dance." With the advice of his wife, a former dancer who circulated in the audience to sample its reaction, and manager Willard Alexander, Gillespie decided to keep bop's harmonic innovations while avoiding "variations in the beat" that discouraged dancers. He praised pianist George Shearing as "the greatest thing that's happened to bop in the past year" because he played "so the average person can understand" and dance to it. Likewise, Ventura discovered that his reputation as a bop musician "scare[d] the dancers," who stood listening until they realized that the band was in fact playing music they could dance to.[66]

Although some of bop's difficulty with dancers was attributed to a decrease in their skills, some adapted to the new tempi by taking their steps in half-time. "I've seen people dancing to our band and to our RCA Victor recordings . . . all over the country . . . they think the Afro-Cuban rhythm effects are especially interesting to a dancer," Gillespie insisted. "Whether it was Young playing a dance in St. Louis or Parker at the Pershing in Chicago," recalled an observer, "the ballroom was crowded with listeners *and* dancers." Mary Lou Williams recalled dancers at Harlem's Savoy adapting to bebop, and Cecil Taylor remembered "the most creative dancers" at Parker performances "trying to create new patterns to fit that new sound that they heard."[67]

But did bop have to be marketed as dance music in order to be commercially successful? Theaters and recordings had been a major source of income for swing bands, and the increasing number of formal concerts offered bop a further source of earnings. Kenton's "progressive jazz," though not considered bebop, had demonstrated that a big band could ignore the dancing clientele and still enjoy commercial success through concert performances and recordings. Bop "should stay where it belongs . . . as a concert proposition," insisted Frank Dailey. "It's like swing on 52nd Street in the old days. People went there to listen to it, and it stayed there. The same applies to bop." Gillespie likewise observed that "very often people don't want to dance, they just want to come up to the bandstand and listen to the music . . . Is that bad?"[68]

In fact a number of marketing innovations were introduced in order to exploit bop's idiosyncrasies. In the summer of 1948, a Broadway club called the Royal Roost initiated an extremely successful bebop-only music policy that served as a model for several other establishments. Recognizing the bop clientele's financial constraints and serious appreciation for the music, management opened a fenced-off section where for ninety cents one could sit and listen until closing without paying a minimum or buying drinks. A milk bar installed for underage patrons was reported to account for 20 percent of the club's business. The bebop policy began as a Tuesday-night experiment, but within weeks it was in place seven nights a week. Promoter Monte Kay and disk jockey Symphony Sid popularized the club through flamboyant publicity and persistent radio plugs; Gillespie led the audience in "community sings." Nicknames followed: the Roost was dubbed the "Metropolitan Bopera House" or "the House That Bop Built." Shows attracted mainly but not exclusively bop musicians and cultists. "In the few months it has been featuring bop," reported *Down Beat*, "the Roost has advanced from a haunt of the students and followers of this type of music to a key spot on the itinerary of visiting trades persons, orchestral and radio personalities and 'hip' tourists." Each attraction seemed to outdraw the preceding one. The Roost formula was imitated at Bop City, the Clique, and Birdland, a club named after Parker that opened in 1949.[69]

Although bop artists had a reputation for eschewing showmanship, Gillespie appeared to heed the voices urging musicians to devote more attention to the visual entertainment value of their art. He criticized colleagues who adopted a bored or superior air toward their audience for undermining bop's public appeal. "You won't see my band operating that way," he said. "My boys work hard, and I work them hard. We have something to sell, and we've gotta use good showmanship to do it. The first thing they learn in this respect is to play up to their audiences." Gillespie's clowning, bumping, and grinding irritated some critics, especially when it took place on a concert stage. "Showmanship is one thing," groused Michael Levin after Gillespie's epochal Carnegie show. "Acting like a bawdy house doorman is another." At another Carnegie concert, Gillespie introduced the creator of "those mad bop ties the band is wearing" and announced that free ties would be given away at the end of the concert. Even Parker looked askance at Gillespie's antics. "The leopard coats and the wild hats are just another part of the managers' routines to make him box office," he said.[70] Such comments are further evidence that for many of the modernists, style was inspired less by cultural politics than by commercial motives.

Another sign of growing popular acceptance of bop was its appearance on bills with popular nonjazz groups. Gillespie's big band, for example, appeared at Bop City in a triple bill with vocalist Dinah Washington and the Ravens in what was described as "the most diversified show to have hit the main stem in many a moon." Later that year he appeared with a doo-wop group, the Orioles, at Harlem's Apollo Theatre.[71]

Bop's continuity with swing was further underscored by the ease with which it was incorporated into the system that had disseminated swing so effectively. After earlier versions of his big band failed commercially, Gillespie achieved national success as a bandleader in 1947 and 1948 through the promotional techniques devised in the late 1920s for Ellington by Irving Mills and institutionalized during swing's heyday. Billy Shaw, a seasoned manager with experience at MCA and William Morris, negotiated Gillespie a contract with RCA Victor (as Mills had for Ellington), helped organize the 1947 Carnegie bebop inaugural, and planned a concert tour through the United States and Europe. A steady stream of press releases and article reprints gave Gillespie a high media profile. "At the end of the year, Dizzy and Billy and the men who play Dizzy's music could breathe more easily, could smile expectantly, could look forward to more folding money," commented *Metronome* in naming Gillespie's ensemble Band of the Year for 1947. "Maybe Dizzy wasn't a threat to Sammy Kaye yet, or Stan Kenton, but he was moving ahead, he was beginning to crowd the bop men, he was proving that a colored band with a difficult music could make enough sense to enough people to pay off."[72]

Gillespie's success continued through 1948. On his return from an enormously successful European tour, his ship was welcomed by hundreds of milling fans. "A turnout at the North River pier equalled only by those greeting returning soldiers testified to the wild enthusiasm that characterizes his followers," reported the *New York Amsterdam News*. A gala party in a Broadway club that drew "virtually every important figure in the amusement and writing field" was followed by a sold-out concert at Town Hall. Belying the notion that bop appealed only to New Yorkers, the band's success continued on the West Coast, where four years earlier a foray by Gillespie and Parker had encountered hostility. His engagement at the Cricket Club was held over for a third week after a "near riot" ensued when patrons were turned away. A concert in the Pasadena Civic Auditorium attracted a standing-room-only crowd. In the Bay area, Gillespie attracted large crowds comprising musicians and bop fanciers as well as dancers and "a lot of customers who were there purely to see what it was the band does that causes so much excitement." One maintained that "you can't get away from the fact that [bebop] is the thing now. Everywhere you go you hear a little bop even on the radio, and any musician who misses hearing this band doesn't deserve to be a musician." Reminiscent of Goodman's triumphant 1935 West Coast tour, audiences at San Francisco's Trianon had memorized the band's arrangements and sang along with them.[73]

Partly because of its tradition of live music in local bars, Chicago had the reputation of being an even bigger bop-playing center than New York. In strip joints and other dives, wrote one observer dryly, "the dissonances and ear-bending chords of bop pass without the customers screaming." Two North Side clubs specialized in bop, while the South Side's Savoy and New Congo Club, among others, regularly presented the music. "Bop attracts a younger crowd," said one manager. "They haven't much money to spend, but you make it up by having a crowded room." Chicago's "highbrow" disk jockey, Dave Garroway, introduced listeners to bebop in a regular midnight broadcast over WMAQ.[74]

For Gillespie, the broadcasts and films that had developed a national audience for swing were achieving the same result for bebop. Initially hostile to the new music, disk jockeys were suddenly promoting it. In addition to Symphony Sid's nightly bop broadcast over WMCA, such disk jockeys as WWRL's Dan Burley, WMGM's and WHN's Leonard Feather, WHOM's Roy Carroll and Willie Bryant, WOV's Fred Robbins and Bill Williams, WAAT's Bill Cook and WLIB's Woody Woodard all gave the new music air time.[75] Even the columnists who had taken such pleasure in skewering the modernists conceded that bop was replenishing popular music and might usefully be assimilated into the cultural mainstream.

By 1948 bop appeared "to be more or less accepted by the popular music lovers." The *New York Amsterdam News* reported that "the radical departure from conventional jazz is growing like wildfire," with the bebop contingent establishing itself in "the choice spots once occupied by the 'swing' addicts." Lester Young confirmed that "the majority" of his audience was "on a bop kick. Even the older dance band conscious people have been affected with the urge to bop." A 1949 poll of *Down Beat* readers for its "All-Time Jazz Hall of Fame" showed bop artists to be as well respected as traditional or swing players: the top three trumpet selections were Armstrong, Gillespie, and Miles Davis; Johnny Hodges, Parker, and Carter drew the most votes on alto saxophone. Even with 1949's general downturn in the band business, Gillespie held his own against such diverse rivals as Lombardo, Kaye, Dorsey, and Goodman, while in Detroit Parker reportedly outdrew Ellington, Herman, and Armstrong.[76]

Support for bop was particularly widespread among young African-Americans in northern cities, according to Ira Gitler: "whenever I went into a black neighborhood in the years 1945–1949, whether it was at a record store in Harlem, a shoeshine stand in St. Louis, a rib joint in Chicago, or someone's apartment in Brooklyn, I heard bebop coming out of loudspeakers, juke boxes, and an assortment of phonographs from consoles to portables." But bop found support even outside metropolitan centers. Booked to play a small establishment in Pennsylvania mining country, a bandleader was encouraged by the manager to "bop all over the place": " 'Howard McGhee was here last week playing bop, and it was sensational.' " During the show, three youths walked in wearing goatees and horn-rimmed glasses. Regional appreciation for bop varied, according to musicians who toured. Audiences in the Southwest disliked it, according to Parker; African-Americans in the Midwest liked it, while southerners preferred the blues.[77] By 1949 the tide of public opinion had apparently turned in favor of the new music.

Despite efforts to make bop more melodious, danceable, visually engaging, and marketable, an uneasiness clouded bop's popularity; many in the music business feared a short half-life to its appeal. Partisans could quarrel over periodic reports in *Variety* and others that bop's end was near, but a persistent sense held that it would not long outlast the decade. The proprietor of a record distribution business reported that sales around the country showed that the public overwhelmingly preferred music with a strong beat—Dinah Washington, the Ravens, spirituals, and hillbilly music—and that sales of bebop records were negligible. By late 1949 these fears were expressed by bandleaders who had recently embraced bop. Informed that some students at the University of Minnesota were conducting a mock funeral for bebop in December 1949, Charlie Ventura expressed his relief that the genre was "really dead." "To me, the word be-bop means 'mud' or 'blah,' " he said. "It scares most persons and makes us orchestra players look like a lot of weird characters." Buddy Rich, after pressure from his booking agency and a "verbal spanking" from Goodman, who thought Rich had lost control of his sidemen, fired his entire band for its modernist propensities. "It's not that I dislike bop," he insisted, but these musicians seemed unable to play anything else.[78]

In 1950 Gene Krupa reorganized his own band to play "good sensible dance" arrangements of familiar standards. The leader had concluded that although there was "a definite place for bop in the jazz picture . . . the timing was bad" for promoting it as popular music. "I guess we're all a little guilty of trying to force bop" onto the public, he admitted. "We played our share of it in this band, but it received good reception only in scattered spots—a few college kids were with it and some of the jazz disciples around New York, Chicago and Hollywood caught on. But on the whole, it was a lost cause." Announcing a turn toward more commercial music, Nat Cole suggested that bop had fallen into "the wrong hands. It would have been all right if they'd let Dizzy and Charlie Parker alone," he said. "But the musicians ruined bop themselves." Cole noted Parker's decision to surround himself with strings. "Pure bop goes only so far," he concluded.[79]

Even bop's most visible artist was forced to reexamine his musical objectives in light of disappointing audience response. "We can't play small places that hold 100 or 200 persons," Gillespie said after consultations with Willard Alexander. "We're playing big auditoriums that hold a couple of thousand, and you can't rely on the extremists to support you there." Despite his best efforts to make the band more rhythmically accessible, he recalled later, the audience would "just stand around the bandstand and gawk, so the dance-hall operators stopped sending for us. There weren't that many concert dates available, and I found myself watching what I had left dwindle." Finally his wife, who had been gauging audience response, delivered an ultimatum: " 'Look, you've had it. Do you want all them raggedy-assed niggers, or do you want me? Either way . . .' So that's when the band broke up. I broke it up in 1950, in Chicago at a place on the North Side, the Silhouette Club. Everybody was sorry about that, man; cats were crying, not making any money. So was I." The surge of publicity that had assisted bop's ascendance was partly responsible for its sudden demise. "We were so excited and having so much fun," Gillespie reflected, "we forgot to emphasize in the publicity the most important thing, the music, and we were helping to make bebop seem like just another fad, which it wasn't."[80]

Within three years bebop achieved and lost both media notoriety and a notable amount of public acclaim. Its trajectory was closely linked to the desperate efforts of many in the swing industry to stave off the sharp decline in public support for the jazz-oriented big bands that had begun shortly after the war. But to the majority of its artists, as Gillespie's comment suggests, bebop was only tangentially related to the media fad that defined its public image. That the musical conventions of bop permanently altered the idioms of jazz is clear decades after the fact, but was also noted by contemporaries. Marshall Stearns observed in 1950 that although bop's "musical revolution" had largely passed, "the clichés of Bop, watered down almost past recognition, are beginning to appear in the arrangements of dance bands all over the country . . . jazz will never be the same." Before long, he predicted, even Guy Lombardo would adopt "the more simple melodic twists of yesterday's Bop."[81] Another cycle of swing had passed.

6

Cracks in the Coalition

W hat if swing had never been "king?" If its mass popularity had been a myth, an exaggeration if not a colossal delusion, the vexing mystery of its sudden decline would be moot. So argued Tex Beneke, a saxophonist in the Glenn Miller organization who took over as leader after Miller's mysterious 1944 disappearance over the English Channel. Swing was still "within a degree of being as popular as it ever was," Beneke insisted; both its mass appeal and heralded demise had been mostly media events. Popular taste had always favored sweet, which for a time had masqueraded under the swing label in order to exploit the latter's "romantic" image and novelty. True, a minority of youthful enthusiasts and jitterbugs—"Susie Q. and her pals at Polytechnic High School"—had supported the genuine swing outfits and still worshipped the bands led by Ellington, Herman, Kenton, and Raeburn. But a majority had always and still preferred the more commercial product, the music that represented most of the recorded output of the Miller, Goodman, and Dorsey bands.[1]

Beneke's "steady-state" theory of the business was a version of Ellington's notion that swing was simply a transient label for a kind of music that had existed before 1935 and would continue long after its fad appeal was gone. But this revisionist view was promptly challenged by Ray McKinley, a former colleague who argued that big-band jazz had indeed shaped national tastes and musical styles in a way far out of proportion to its representation in repertoires or among the hundreds of dance bands crisscrossing the continent. "From 1936 to 1940 the pace was set by Goodman, TD and Shaw, and with these three kingpins sweet came off a poor second," he wrote. McKinley allowed that "swing took a nose dive during the early war years," with the resurgence in sentimental sweet music. But as Allied war fortunes improved, swing "came back upon the national scene and held its own here at home during the last two and a half years of the war and for about six months thereafter."[2]

The Beneke-McKinley exchange, conducted in the familiar language of polemic and hyperbole, was an argument in which both sides were partially correct; swing did exert a cultural influence disproportionate to its actual representation in the music industry. But the controversy again highlighted the tenuous consensus that had enabled swing to encompass and balance cultural oppositions. Swing's very definition was the result of an unstable consensus that hadn't much mattered to musicians during the boom years but was inclined to disintegrate under the stress of postwar conditions. Reviving swing presupposed some agreement on what swing was, but agreement was harder to achieve in an industry facing both internal and external challenges. Swing's success, argued Michael Levin, had been possible in the 1930s only because large numbers of the general public accepted the musical preferences of jazz musicians and their youthful cognoscenti. This alliance had collapsed during the war. "Thus you now have a very strong cleavage among the musicians themselves, a cleavage among the kids . . . and a general public thoroughly confused by the jazz they hear around them."[3]

In addition to the cleavages discussed earlier—the competition posed to the big bands by musical forms like jump, country, Latin, and polka; and the dissonance between bandleaders concerned with musical innovation and cultural authority, and patrons interested in dancing—there were significant divisions among the swing community's musicians and critics. As a result of these various schisms, the Americanist swing ideology of the late 1930s and war years began to lose its focus. It did not fade entirely; the ideology was carried forward in the "Jazz at the Philharmonic" concert series, for instance. But it became caught up in a complex current of conflicting political impulses that robbed it of whatever clarity it had once possessed.

Big-band jazz had always struck its proponents as the musical expres-

sion of the New Deal, and the fragmentation of the swing community
reflected changes in the larger political culture of the United States.
The Roosevelt coalition of workers, urban ethnics, African-Americans,
farmers, and intellectuals that had undergirded the politics of the previous half-generation faced formidable dilemmas after the war. By 1948
the Democratic Party was confronting challenges from two former con-
stituencies: on the right, from the southern Dixiecrats, and on the left,
from Henry Wallace and the Progressive Party. Harry Truman
adopted a strategy that enabled him to capture a long-shot victory in
the 1948 election, but at the cost of exacerbating the strains already
afflicting his party. After that year the coalition he had inherited was
no longer tenable. For this reason 1948 can be pointed to as the end
of the 1930s, and it marked the end of swing as well.

That Modern Malice

Although several prominent bandleaders overcame their initial suspicion to ally themselves with bebop, some leading members of the swing
community resisted the new idiom. "Of all the cruelties in the world,
be-bop is the most phenomenal," observed Fletcher Henderson in
1948. "Of course, I don't know what be-bop is," continued the man
responsible for pioneering swing's musical conventions. "But it isn't
music to me. I heard Dizzy's band in Los Angeles, and I must say he
has a great band. Whatever be-bop is, Dizzy is one of the few who can
play it, and he doesn't give it to you all night long."[4] Henderson's
remarkable comment, with its hyperbole and self-contradictions, was
typical of the response of an important minority of the swing community as it struggled to come to terms with its strange musical
progeny. Even at its popular peak in 1948, bop endured persistent criticism from musicians who, unlike Goodman, Young, Herman, and
others, were unable or unwilling to embrace the new music.

The highly publicized disputes between partisans of bebop, or
modern jazz more generally, and Dixieland or traditional jazz—a faction sometimes called "moldy figs"—have been adduced to prove
bebop's significance as a radical rupture of the jazz tradition. Some
historians have attributed to the popular music industry, particularly

the trade press, a reflexive, subtly racist animosity toward bebop, a musical form depicted as the protest music of alienated African-Americans motivated by a newfound race consciousness. But this representation, though not wholly false, blurs the categories and distorts the dynamics of change in the postwar jazz community. The polarization and infighting of the postwar years is best understood not simply as a response to bebop, but as part of a longer struggle between critics and musicians, extending back to the mid-1930s, over the authority to define jazz. Moreover, exchanges among musicians and critics over the validity of bebop were taking place in a larger context of widespread concern over the demise of swing—the economic viability of the jazz-oriented dance bands and of live music in general. At the heart of antibop sentiment among both musicians and critics was the fear that bop was hastening and exacerbating the decline of all jazz.

No criticism attracted more attention or carried more weight than that of Louis Armstrong, universally admired within the jazz community and not known for belittling fellow musicians. On some occasions Armstrong derided bop as music he'd heard in 1918, at other times as meaningless and unmelodic. But his most consistent ground for criticism was the damage he sensed bebop posing to the already tenuous commercial viability of jazz. "All them young cats playing them weird chords," he groused. "And what happens? No one's working." His antipathy encapsulated a number of insecurities facing jazz musicians in the postswing era:

> These young cats now they want to make money first and the hell with the music. And then they want to carve everyone else because they're full of malice, and all they want to do is show you up, and any old way will do as long as it's different from the way you played it before. So you get all them weird chords which don't mean nothing, and first people get curious about it just because it's new, but soon they get tired of it because it's really no good and you got no melody to remember and no beat to dance to. So they're all poor again and nobody is working, and that's what that modern malice done for you.

Armstrong was gently chided by *Down Beat* and the *New York Amsterdam News* for his remarks, which they labeled "sour grapes" and argued would further alienate the public. Armstrong's criticisms involved the same sort of self-contradictions that characterized Henderson's riposte. "Them bebop boys are great technicians," he told *Time* for a cover story. "Mistakes—that's all bebop is. Man, you've gotta be a technician to know when you make 'em. Them cats play too much music—a whole lot of notes, weird notes." If the boppers were making mistakes, in what sense was their technique "great"? Or were these "mistakes" only in the ears of the hearer? Ironically, his group, the All-Stars, broke attendance records at Bop City during a September 1949 engagement.[5]

Prominent musicians willing to be quoted generally distanced themselves from Armstrong's views, professing their inability to comment on bop or a belief that it would eventually yield benefits to jazz. Stan Kenton praised bop for "educating the people's ears" to more challenging musical forms, while Woody Herman pointed out that Armstrong's own style had resulted from an openness to " 'progressive' music and 'new' ideas." Only the Henderson brothers, Fletcher and Horace, expressed unequivocal agreement. "No truer—and more courageous words—were ever spoken," opined Fletcher. "He's as right as Truth itself." In fact few musicians judged the music as harshly as Armstrong or Henderson, at least for attribution. Most expressed a weary acceptance of inevitable stylistic change. "Time marches on," noted Ellington saxophonist Ben Webster, in a remark typical of many older musicians; "you must move, too." Others defended bebop more aggressively. After an especially intemperate attack by Tommy Dorsey, colleagues attributed his remarks to professional jealousy and desire for publicity. "Well, swing was paying him off," observed Nat Cole during a radio symposium on Dorsey's comments. "After bop starts to pay off, which I am sure it is going to do, he'll be one of the ones hollering up there."[6]

Occasionally this dispute between jazz traditionalists and modernists took the familiar form of controlled competition. Bebop was paired not with swing, however, but with the older music of New Orleans. In 1947 a Treasury Department radio program called "Bands for Bonds" hosted the first live comparison of the two styles. A New Orleans band comprising Wild Bill Davison, Edmond Hall, Danny Barker, Pops Foster,

Baby Dodds, and others and organized by Rudi Blesh competed in Mutual Broadcasting's New York studio with a bop aggregation assembled by Ulanov featuring Gillespie, Parker, Tristano, Ray Brown, and Max Roach. A more public showdown took place in 1949 at the Waldorf Astoria, when some three thousand high school students invited by the *Herald Tribune* heard ensembles led by Sidney Bechet and Charlie Parker. "According to the thundering ovation which followed," the *New York Amsterdam News* reported, "classic jazz won a complete and undisputed victory."[7] For the most part, however, there was too little common ground between the two factions to be resolved through the familiar rituals of band battles.

Contrary to the received wisdom, the music press's animosity to jazz modernism was no more pronounced than that of swing musicians. In fact the white-dominated trade press was quite favorable to the new music. Under the direction of Barry Ulanov and Leonard Feather, *Metronome* was militantly probop; *Down Beat* continued its traditional policy of editorial eclecticism, but one of its most prolific concert and record reviewers during the late 1940s, Michael Levin, was clearly sympathetic to bebop. Although polemical disputes flared periodically, they were no more contentious than earlier contests over critical standards and the debate over swing versus traditional jazz. *Down Beat*'s penchant for bitter polemics was never better represented than in a 1949 issue whose front page included articles suggesting that Ellington dissolve his band, calling into question the "Armstrong myth," and berating critics for giving up the righteous war against bebop. Such polemical exchanges, however, were the exception, at least in a periodical that a decade earlier had resounded with violent clashes.[8]

Some observed that a sense of disillusionment and ennui had overtaken their ranks. Reflecting on the recent critical firestorm in which he had been embroiled, Michael Levin cast a backward glance on jazz criticism. The pioneer critics of the mid-1930s—Hammond, Stearns, Frazier, Winthrop Sargeant, Paul Eduard Miller—might have been juvenile and musically ignorant, but they were sincere and "helped give [jazz] a small niche in the U.S. intellectual cubbyholes of culture." Their successors—Dave Dexter, Simon, Feather, Ulanov, Bill Gottlieb, Blesh, Levin himself—possessed a more sophisticated knowledge of music, but at times let their preoccupation with the music industry overshadow a "sheer love of the music itself." For Levin, this group continued to exert an unhealthy stranglehold on the business of criticism. "Almost all the men now criticizing jazz are hangovers from the days of the '30s in jazz and before," he wrote. "Unlike Coleman Hawkins, they don't seem to have adapted too well to the changes." With a dearth of "new champions of fresh and enthusiastic vision to battle its cause," bop in particular had been disadvantaged by the stagnant world of criticism. Only Leonard Feather had made "a conscientious effort to stay up with the changes in jazz"; his colleague, Barry Ulanov, prone to what Levin called "shifting bouts of mysticism and icy dogmatism," seemed to acknowledge his own disillusionment with the apparently ineluctable process of commercial co-optation.[9]

In fact the earliest observations on the controversy over the new music, at a time when the term *bebop* was relatively fluid and undefined, explicitly linked Gillespie and Parker to "modernists" like Benny Carter, Charlie Shavers, Johnny Hodges, Teddy Wilson, Don Byas, Trummy Young, and Ben Webster, some of whom had risen to prominence even before swing. Of this old guard, Coleman Hawkins, who regularly recorded and performed with younger bop players, was most closely linked to the new music. One reader rebuked *Down Beat* for catering "all out of proportion to the re-boppian school of thought . . . Not everyone defines jazz as Dizzy Gillespie's goatee, or Coleman Hawkins' latest rhapsody." *Metronome*'s George Simon, who dissented from his magazine's prevailing probop stance, criticized the "hysterical" tempos of what he called the "frantic era of swing," singling out those "adolescent Hawkins and Lester Young and Gillespie imitators." The fiercely antibop *Record Changer* even grouped Gillespie with Calloway and Whiteman, complaining: "Every single year there's a new crop of phoneys—black and white—trying to pervert or suppress or emasculate jazz."[10] In short, the critical community initially perceived bebop not as a break with swing, but as a tendency within or extension of swing.

Moreover, criticism of bop tended to be musically informed rather than reflexive. The music was sometimes charged with being too frantic, lacking the relaxed quality of ease associated with swing, an observation few could quarrel with. But nearly all those who criticized bop, whether musicians or critics, made exceptions for Gillespie and Parker; their stature as innovative musicians was nearly unquestioned. (The charms of Thelonious Monk were largely lost on contemporary critics, however.) What irked many critics were the lesser bebop musicians who, in their view, adopted the trappings of the subculture and made the music into a cliché. This criticism was shared by the artists themselves, who resented the trivialization of their art, and resembled the disdain with which the swing musicians had viewed "ickies." The first extended analysis of Gillespie's style to appear in *Down Beat*, after detailing the reach of his influence in contemporary music of early 1946, noted the unfortunate tendency of his "devotees" to copy his appearance and behavior:

> Musicians wear goatee beards because Dizzy wears a goatee beard; musicians wear the ridiculous little hats that have been seen around lately because Dizzy wears one; musicians have started to laugh in a loud, broken way because that's the way Dizzy laughs; musicians now stand with a figure "S" posture, copying Dizzy who appears too apathetic to stand erect—and so on down the list. Surely this *copycatism* accomplishes nothing for the Dizzy fan, but, just as surely, it does Dizzy much harm.

The easily caricatured bop look was the frequent target of cartoons in *Down Beat*, which had always allowed its artists a leeway that resulted in occasional bad taste. "What's be-bop?" exclaimed one representative strung-out and bereted character. "Why, man, the inevitable! It's a classic protest against the chaos, the desolation, the abject melancholia of our times." In 1949 Ulanov noted elegiacally: "Early in bop's history, the mimicry reached a point where every graceless step taken by Bird or Dizzy or anybody else in the inner circle became a model of perfection. It was not enough to play like them, to look and talk and walk like them; if some new means of self-torture could be discovered locked in the past of one of these heroic figures or twisting its way into their present, then it was fundamental to bop survival to inculcate the same rotten habit."[11]

Inferior imitation of the musical idiom was also offensive to both musicians and critics. The opinion that "there's nothing worse than bad bebop" was widely held. Michael Levin bemoaned "the truly distressing playing" of "lesser bop satellites" during a Royal Roost appearance by Miles Davis and Max Roach. "In no other section of jazz is there such a tremendous gulf between the really good practitioners of the art and the young 'uns starting in," he commented. Pianist Lennie Tristano blasted the "little monkey-men of music" who "steal note for note the phrases" of master musicians like Gillespie and "contribute nothing" original. "Their endless repetition of these phrases makes living in their midst like fighting one's way through a nightmare in which bebop pours out of the walls, the heavens, and the coffeepot," he wrote. A "light-fingered mob" of "larcenous lads" had desecrated bop, according to Ulanov, vulgarizing its rhythmic complexities and characteristic vibratoless tone. Young musicians with relatively little training attempted to perform what all agreed was the most technically and theoretically demanding genre of jazz yet to appear, a tendency Gillespie cautioned against. "They have to learn all the rudiments, just as the rest of us did," he said. "When I was growing up, all I wanted to play was swing, but I had to learn the other stuff, too."[12]

Critics were also unanimous in condemning the narcotics use that seemed an unfortunate by-product of the new music. Continuing a crusade that reached back to the mid-1930s, Down Beat blasted in increasingly harsh terms what it alleged were a tiny minority of miscreants for hurting their own careers as well as the profession: "[t]he threat to music today is not a red scare . . . it's a head scare . . . Unless music and marijuana are branded as irreconcilable as gasoline and alcohol, the hophead cats will start thinking THEY'RE Santa Claus come Christmas, with a leisurely stroll out some third story window the result." Steadfastly defending musicians against the media image of drug addicts, Down Beat cited the Ventura band as comprising upstanding family men, self-proclaimed Coca-Cola "addicts." Before long the editors realized that the real threat was no longer marijuana but heroin, and threatened to publicize the names of those arrested. Excepting Gillespie, Kenton, Herman, and Ventura, George Simon castigated musicians whose "morals, and . . . personal habits, have resulted in a degeneracy that has affected innocent members of their movement and which has also, directly and indirectly, brought about the destruction, even the death, of promising musicians"; his colleague Ulanov argued that musicians were better understood as unbalanced and undisciplined than as "dope fiends."[13]

In short, the main opposition to bop as a genre came from those critical circles that had earlier opposed swing; those who, like George Avakian, believed the word *jazz* had since the mid-1930s been "kicked around too freely." They despised bop's modernism because they linked it to a larger decline of authentic jazz into commercialism. The most militant of the moldy figs, such as Rudi Blesh, labeled swing "completely anti-jazz, anti-New Orleans, opposed to the real musical values which jazz represents," defining the latter so strictly as to exclude Ellington and virtually everyone else. This critique was not limited to moldy figs, however. African-American poet and journalist Frank Marshall Davis recalled that he had initially "resented bop, not so much because of the radical sound but because some of its practitioners admitted they were trying to curve jazz into a form acceptable to traditional white standards" (precisely the charge sometimes leveled at swing). "They wanted to make it 'respectable' for use on the concert stage."[14]

Bop was in fact supported if not championed by the mainstream jazz press, who reserved their critical barbs for those who aspired to play bop but lacked sufficient skill. Furious exchanges did erupt, pitting outspoken partisans of bebop like Leonard Feather and *Metronome* against traditionalists Rudi Blesh and *Record Changer*; exceptional bitterness arose from *Esquire*'s sudden purge of non-Dixieland advocates from its annual critics poll. But the "progressive jazz" of Stan Kenton generated more attention and controversy in the trade press than bop did during most of the late 1940s.[15]

Jazz Is America's Own

A corollary of the widely misunderstood schism between bop and its forerunners was the politicization of genres. Jazz had long carried a range of political meanings, but never before had it been possible to position rival factions on a political spectrum. The terms of the debate were set by Feather in 1945: "Just as the fascists tend to divide group against group and distinguish between Negroes, Jews, Italians and 'real Americans,' so do the moldy figs try to categorize New Orleans, Chicago, swing music and 'the real jazz.' Just as the fascists have tried to foist their views on the public through the vermin press . . . so have the Figs yapped their heads off in the *Jazz Record*, *Jazz Session* and *Record Changer*." This political schema was picked up the next year in a well-publicized interview with drummer Dave Tough, who averred that while Dixieland was once "revolutionary stuff," it had become "just a Straight-Republican-Ticket kind of music." Former musical compatriot Wild Bill Davison responded in kind, calling Tough "the Dizzy Gillespie of the cymbals . . . one of those modern liberals who are the first to holler 'fascist' any time they can't run things their own way." Lionel Hampton also entered the fray, claiming that whenever "I see any injustice or any unfair action against my own race or any other minority groups 'Hey Ba Ba Rebop' stimulates the desire to destroy such prejudice and discrimination." He offered this illustration: "The poll tax must go!! *Hey Ba Ba Rebop*."[16] The thrust of these disparate remarks seemed clear: bebop represented a progressive force of the left pitted against the reactionary, backward impulses of the New Orleans revival.

The reality was more complex. Tough was an archetypal swing drummer who had developed his style in the 1920s listening to New Orleans players before working in the Goodman, Dorsey, Shaw, and Herman bands. His initial reaction to bebop was more bewildered than favorable. "These cats snatched up their horns and blew crazy stuff," he said. "One would stop all of a sudden and another would start for no reason at all." His comments reflected the bitterness of an internecine dispute among the mainly white performers associated with Eddie Condon, some of whom were more tolerant of stylistic innovation (swing *or* bop) than others. "We're not exactly playing re-bop music," he admitted, although his group's repertoire did include bebop tunes. Tough dismissed Dixieland enthusiasts as "snobs who affect a 'pose' " in order to relive their lost youth. "They like to think it's still prohibition and they're wild young cats up from Princeton for a hot time," he said. "All they need is a volume of F. Scott Fitzgerald sticking out of their pockets." Hampton's comprehension of and support for bebop was equally tenuous, although he attempted to capitalize on the music's publicity. (Hampton was first attracted to the G.O.P. by a young California congressman, Richard Nixon.) When Leonard Feather attacked the left as "reactionary" for ignoring modern jazz in favor of workers' songs, folk music, and traditional jazz, he was soundly rebuked by the *Daily Worker*. And when columnist Frank Conniff launched a Red-baiting attack on Artie Shaw's support for the Paris Peace Congress, he mocked the musician's highbrow pretensions rather than his modernism. "Jazz, a true people's music nourished by the immense vitality of a young and virile land, is no longer good enough for Artie Shaw," he charged.[17]

Clearly, the categories of left and right are inadequate to characterize the politics of postwar jazz. Bebop's politics resist assimilation to any clear-cut political model. Contemporaries noted the belief that modern jazz expressed protest against a society and musical industry dominated by often-hostile whites. Some musicians' comments further support the view that race was central to the genesis and meaning of bebop. Billie Holiday accused "ofays" of "copping" swing, then bop. "Benny Goodman had been named the 'King of Swing,' so they had some cats who was playin' swing music," is how Howard McGhee put it. "We figured, what the hell, we can't do no more than what's been done with it, we gotta do somethin' else."[18]

Without dismissing the element of cultural nationalism, bop's most pronounced fault line was generational rather than racial; its rapid tempi and difficult key signatures were color-blind, excluding older musicians of both races. To describe the bop artists as "a new community of avant-garde outsiders in rebellion against racism and the failures of a rationalized, exclusive world" is to romanticize them beyond their own recognition and that of their contemporaries. Moreover, it was bebop's ability to bring whites and African-Americans together that appeared most threatening to those groups that opposed it on New York's 52nd Street and Los Angeles' Central Avenue. "What these red-neck [Los Angeles] cops didn't realize was that the bebop and jazz that the black musicians were playing was bringing the races closer together," recalled Roy Porter.[19] Bop's racial politics were neither wholly separatist or integrationist.

Both the modernist and more traditionalist strains of postwar jazz are best understood as participating in politics at two different levels. As Eric Lott has argued, bop's politics were most pronounced at the level of "style," as the play of subversive signifiers, visual and musical. Gillespie later phrased it: "We just played our music and let it go at that. The music proclaimed our identity; it made every statement we truly wanted to make."[20] In this sense, bebop inherited the tradition of cultural politics descended from swing's hepsters and jitterbugs. In contrast, the more explicit and traditional politics of postwar jazz—a direct outgrowth of the previous decade's ideology of racial equality and democracy—were expressed most clearly by more traditional jazz artists. African-American musicians were indeed energized by their war-time experiences, but it was those musicians affiliated with swing, not with bop, who were most active promoting racial equality. At the same time, the other face of the swing ideology—glorifying the American way of life and American exceptionalism—also came into sharper focus during the late 1940s as jazz was promoted as a weapon in the Cold War. That the same musicians sometimes participated in both levels simultaneously makes any strict demarcation between or among these political and musical realms impossible.

These political meanings were of course played against a broader historical backdrop. The relaxation of racial barriers that had taken place during the swing era faced new challenges in the uncertain climate after 1945, as African-Americans pondered how to solidify and advance gains made during the war. In 1946 the Daughters of the American Revolution again voted to ban an African-American, pianist Hazel Scott, from Constitution Hall, a decision that further outraged African-Americans when President Truman refused to denounce the action. An "anti-Negro" faction at Indiana University nearly succeeded in blocking the reappointment of Marshall Stearns, who resigned anyway to go to Cornell. In New York City a black bassist was brutally beaten by police after a dispute with a cab driver, inspiring a petition of protest signed by 2,300 people. After fatal violence occurred at dances in its city auditorium, Atlanta barred African-American dances, a decision that bandleader Lucky Millinder successfully lobbied to overturn. Millinder was later forced to make changes in his band. "Tour before the last we had seven white boys in the band and no trouble anywhere," he said, "but recently there's been talk of trouble and turmoil and the Klan marching again, so I don't have a mixed band now." Bandleader Andy Kirk observed that because of changes in civil rights law, his band was no longer booked by locations that feared he might attract a large black audience, which they would have to admit. An engagement by the Billy Eckstine band at Boston's Rio Casino was canceled after a near riot there when an intoxicated white woman shouted some racial insults at the bandleader. A series of raids, ostensibly for underage drinking, closed Philadelphia's Downbeat Club, which was known for attracting interracial audiences of bop enthusiasts. And Café Society, that symbol of the Popular Front and racial mixing, was forced out of business, largely as the result of a campaign waged against Barney Josephson and his brother by the news media because of their alleged Communist sympathies.[21]

The same years presented other, more promising signs of improving race relations in popular music. In 1947 NBC established "Nat King Cole Trio Time," an all-black radio show sponsored by Kraft and expected to open the way for additional commercially sponsored programs featuring African-Americans. A Philadelphia radio station banned the song "Shine" in 1948 on the ground that "the number is considered uncomplimentary by a segment of our listening audience." The following summer, after a crusade pushed by National Records, *Billboard* magazine replaced the category of "race" records with the term "rhythm and blues," leading other trade magazines to do likewise. In 1950 Hampton's became the first black band to play midtown Manhattan's Palladium in the ballroom's ten-year history. "It was democracy in action, colored and white fellows dancing with white and colored girls, and not one unpleasant incident," according to one report.[22]

The decline of Harlem as an entertainment Mecca for whites symbolized the uncertain legacy of earlier civil rights advances. Since the 1935 riot, Harlem had faced periodic campaigns to discourage white patronage, but swing's peak years saw significant traffic uptown. This patronage fell off during the war, partly because of the increased range of entertainment presented on 52nd Street. Woody Herman's 1946 appearance in Harlem was the first in four years by a big-name white band, but it did not establish a precedent. Proprietors complained of "vicious propaganda" designed to convinced potential patrons "that above 110th Street is cannibal country," and called on city government to encourage a return to prewar conditions, when Harlem's nightspots were well attended by white tourists and theatergoers. "Our people are good and our night clubs are good," insisted one club owner. But some interpreted the loss of tourist trade as a positive sign; if integration was working downtown, what need was there to travel to Harlem? Though sorry to see "the passing of a Harlem where every little block on Seventh Avenue had a fine little jump band," Michael Levin thought it worth the price if it led to an improvement of the surrounding neighborhood and a decrease in segregation. But these desired results were not forthcoming.[23]

Increasingly, African-Americans in the music industry looked to race solidarity and entrepreneurial self-sufficiency. Nat Cole and Louis Jordan demonstrated that it was possibile for artists to use black promoters, a practice formerly unheard of. "Reports are around that it is as hard to find a Negro promoter using name Negro attractions in the South as it is to find Negro social callers in Bilbo's living room in Jackson, Mississippi," complained the *New York Amsterdam News.* Lionel and Gladys Hampton founded the Hamp Tone Record Company in 1946 hoping to attract black businessmen to an operation intended to build the careers of black musicians and vocalists. Journalist Dan Burley and composer J. C. Johnson spearheaded a campaign to encourage black bandleaders to plug songs written by fellow African-Americans unable to compete because of discrimination on Tin Pan Alley. "Save for a scattered few, the ranks of outstanding colored songsmiths have been depleted to the point of almost complete dissolution because . . . Tin Pan Alley is practically closed to them," wrote Burley. He complained of "cute little white girl songwriters or doddering old-time white composers, with half-baked compositions . . . running in and out of some Negro band leader's dressing room . . . gaining auditions for as much as an hour while the colored writers . . . have to cool their heels in the corridors hoping against hope to get a few words with the great maestro." Burley's proposal that bandleaders hold white songwriters to the same quota system used to limit employment for African-Americans was enthusiastically supported by his readers. The columnist also initiated a crusade to promote the hiring of black disk jockeys. While Whiteman, Dorsey, Herman, and others had radio shows, black luminaries like Armstrong, Hines, and Ellington were passed over. As a result, Burley wrote, "we find radio in the same class with Hollywood as one of the major hurdles to overcome before the educational message for tolerance, brotherhood can be broadcast to a nation that surely needs it."[24]

Despite these efforts at promoting racial solidarity (none of which specifically involved bebop), the integrationist impulse in jazz remained strong. Its most conspicuous postwar vehicle was the concert series "Jazz at the Philharmonic," or JATP, organized by Norman Granz. Born and raised in Los Angeles, Granz, a former film cutter, early in the war organized an integrated jam session in a Hollywood club to prove that customers of different races could mix. In 1944 he organized a benefit concert for twenty-one Mexicans convicted of crimes in the aftermath of the Los Angeles "zoot-suit" riots; later benefits supported Fair Employment Practices Commission and antilynching legislation. He followed this in 1945 with an eighteen-concert series at Los Angeles' Philharmonic Hall, whose manager initially stipulated that Granz not use the word *jazz* in advertising and that no more than half of the performers be African-American, and forbade him to publicize the concerts over the radio. Early in 1947 Granz inaugurated his most ambitious campaign: a nationwide tour featuring Coleman Hawkins, Roy Eldridge, Buck Clayton, Trummy Young, Flip Phillips, and Buddy Rich, and a drive to encourage bandleaders to adopt an antidiscrimination clause in their contracts.[25]

In a letter to thirty top swing bandleaders, Granz urged them to follow the example of Actors' Equity (and himself) by adopting a contractual clause guaranteeing that they would not be forced to play in segregated establishments. In the event of discrimination in ticket sales or seating policies, the artist retained the right to cancel the concert and retain one-half of the contract price. The clause, which Granz had used for two years, would be "like an FEPC among bandleaders," he suggested. In the South, where Jim Crow was statutory, the campaign would aim at guaranteeing equal facilities for both races and at defeating the laws. Granz received enthusiastic pledges of support from

Artie Shaw, Tommy Dorsey, Charlie Barnet, Nat Cole, Count Basie, Buddy Rich, and Coleman Hawkins. The strategy had already been adopted in 1945 by Paul Robeson, Hazel Scott, and Count Basie, and in 1947 by Lionel Hampton, who had succeeded in integrating previously whites-only establishments in New York, Chicago, and Los Angeles.[26]

The concert clause was only one aspect of a larger crusade that sought to use jazz as a means of furthering racial equality. All JATP literature carried the following announcement, which perfectly encapsulated the swing ideology that had taken shape well before the war:

> Jazz is America's own. It is the music which grew out of a young and vigorous melting-pot nation. It is a product of all America, deriving much of its inspiration and creation from the Negro people.
>
> Jazz holds up no superficial bars. It is played and listened to by all peoples—in harmony, together. Pigmentation differences have no place in jazz. As in genuine democracy, only performance counts. Jazz is truly the music of democratic America. It is an ideal medium for bringing about a better understanding among all peoples.

Granz hoped to form a nationwide network of JATP fan clubs to spread jazz's message of democracy and racial equality throughout the country. The main target was American youth. Using a mailing list of some 10,000 names compiled from record sales, Granz planned to distribute to club members a publication featuring "stories about jazz and racial equality." Members would also get reduced prices on records and concert tickets. "Whenever I come to a town where there's a club," Granz promised, "I'll stop in and talk to the members, stressing the democratic nature of jazz." For Granz, the quality of the music he presented was secondary to its ideological value. "I would rather sell mediocre jazz to 9000 people and sell my pitch on race relations along with it than operate in a vacuum . . . I never get in a public argument about jazz," he said.[27] A typical JATP year would include a seven-month tour involving 150 concerts across North America, Europe, and Asia.

Alongside Granz's campaign were international efforts that capitalized on swing's war-expanded horizons. The same music that could help highlight and strengthen the democratic ideals of the country of its origin could also promote those ideals in a hostile world, particularly the bloc that had suddenly and disturbingly fallen under Soviet domination. "The 'teenagers' in Russia are no different than our own 'teenagers,'" insisted Benny Goodman in a plea for State Department broadcasts to the Soviet Union, "and they will respond to the same music." As consulting director of Popular Music for Voice of America, an unsalaried position he assumed in April 1947, Goodman selected two recordings—roughly seven minutes—for broadcast each day. The selections, he claimed, were "representative of music which has been accepted by the American public" and included swing (the broadcast opened with Goodman's theme, "Let's Dance") as well as sweet, musical comedy, hillbilly, and western ballads. "Our portion of the 'Voice of America' programs indirectly stresses democracy, showing that artists of every race, color and creed have succeeded in the popular music world in this country," said Goodman. "I suppose it could be called propaganda, but it is the right kind of propaganda. In a world filled with so many doubts, music is one common bond." Goodman was allegedly the most popular American musician among Soviets, and his willingness to serve was linked by some to his desire to play a concert tour there. "I feel that we have much to sell the Russians and I would like to have the opportunity to continue presenting our case," he wrote in protest against plans to abolish the broadcasts. Goodman was soon embroiled in a different controversy: a group of jazz critics, including Barry Ulanov and George Simon, accused the bandleader of short-changing jazz in his effort to include a representative variety of American popular music. Goodman had described the program as "no current hit parade" and included some records that were twenty years old. After heated exchanges in *Metronome* and a meeting among the disgruntled critics, Voice of America agreed to increase the time allotted to popular music from forty-nine to ninety minutes a week. Editors from *Down Beat* and *Metronome* were invited to help Goodman select a more up-to-date jazz program.[28]

Goodman was not the only swing figure to tout jazz as a vehicle for world peace. Bandleader Cootie Williams, who had played with Ellington and Goodman, proposed that the United States "try music as a common language rather than the devious double talk of diplomatic wordage." Williams was less concerned with the bipolar rivalry than with promoting increased international understanding more generally. "Music is the product of an honest mind and therefore free access to music of different people would aid in gaining mutual understanding of peoples," he said. "It is the language of peace, why not make full use of it in attempting to gain that end?" Williams' thoughts were echoed almost word for word by fellow trumpeter Carlo Bonlaender, from Frankfurt, Germany. Calling jazz "the most democratic thing in the world," he stressed that it "unites people of various races and nationalities and teaches them to work together and understand each other, to respect and appreciate one another's ideas." In Germany, jazz was wildly popular in both zones. Though branded a "Marshall Plan export sent from America to deaden the minds of the masses" by the Eastern bloc, West German broadcasts found a large audience in the Communist East Zone, including its press chief, Gerhart Eisler.[29]

A considerable distance separated the politics of Voice of America broadcasts and antibias contracts from the politics of goatees, needle-injected drugs, and oblique horn phrases. The dual politics of postwar jazz—music as a vehicle for promoting civil rights and democratic values, and music as oppositional style—would be continually transformed in the years that followed. By 1955 Gillespie was leading goodwill tours for the State Department, at the same time that the cultural style he helped create, embodied by the figure of the hipster, was gathering momentum through the writings of Jack Kerouac, Norman Mailer, and others. In fact this image from the later 1950s has shaped subsequent understanding of the artists originally associated with bop. But the stylistic politics of modern jazz represented only one strain of a postwar politics that often carried a more overt message and dated back to the mid-1930s; both strains had their origins in swing.

Epilogue: Shall We Dance?

Within a few years, the bilious cleavages of the late 1940s struck even ardent partisans as misguided. Summing up the previous decade's internecine conflict, Leonard Feather noted in 1953 that despite the waste of "a tremendous amount of breath, paper, and choler," the divisions had been healed.

> You find bop, or modern changes or whatever you want to call it, in the style of at least half the *Down Beat* poll winners. This doesn't mean that Dixieland or swing music is dead; on the contrary, Dixie has passed from the status of specialized, esoteric jazz into a new acceptance as popular music. Dixieland is as simple for today's musician to play as it is for today's fan to understand. Similarly you can hear swing music, such as the bands of the '30s provided, on any major TV show today; it's being played by house musicians who may have played that way as pioneers 15 years ago, who today do it as part of a job, to make an anonymous living.

Even erstwhile traditionalists Rudi Blesh and George Avakian had made peace with the modernists, supervising their recording sessions and praising them in print. "Yes, the dust has settled and the contestants have gone about their business," Feather concluded. "*Hot vs. Cool* is just a gag, in which both sides are shadow boxing. Shall we dance?"[30] The contentious realm of jazz had apparently found harmony in the decade retrospectively associated with social and political consensus. That outcome could not have surprised anyone who had followed the life cycle of swing. It also reflected a new reality. Now that swing's moment as mass culture had irrevocably passed, the stakes were lower; it no longer made sense for the vestiges of the swing community to expend energy demonizing one another for excessive commercialism or cultism.

This new mood of tolerance did not indicate that those with a vested interest in swing were prepared to give up its claim on the public, however. The very question "Was swing ever king?" understandably failed to engage the attention of more than a handful in the swing industry, who recalled that at the very least the music had provided thousands of musicians and their media associates with livelihoods and a certain amount of public acclaim. There seemed no reason why that appeal couldn't be perpetuated, given ingenuity and a willingness to conform to the demands of the audience.

Following the precipitous decline of bebop, various sectors of the industry tried persistently during the 1950s to revive the triumphs of the previous decades. For a time it appeared that Dixieland might inherit the swing following; the revival of New Orleans jazz attracted the attention of disk jockeys, recording companies, and music publishers. But a mass audience was not forthcoming. Recording companies attempted to rouse the public by cultivating and promoting new orchestras while simultaneously reissuing classic recordings on long-playing formats. Columbia's release of the 1938 Goodman Carnegie concert received wide press coverage that suggested a resurgence of swing, now perceived nostalgically. RCA Victor and Capitol, on the other hand, sought to capture the future by assembling studio bands and aggressively promoting them as America's "Number One Band." This approach was sharply different from the route by which bands achieved mass popularity in the boom years, but it achieved some success in the early 1950s with a band led by Ralph Flanagan, which grossed $600,000 in 1951, not much less than perennial commercial leaders Sammy Kaye ($900,000) and Guy Lombardo ($850,000). The experiment inspired a wave of veteran swing artists—including Sy Oliver, Buddy Rich, Lee Castle, Shorty Rogers, and Neil Hefti—to form dance bands in late 1951 and 1952. In 1952, after two years of preparation and recording, veteran arrangers Eddie Sauter and Bill Finegan unveiled an "experimental" big band, which RCA Victor attempted to promote through a tie-in with its new line of "living sound" high-fidelity sets.[31]

Broadcasters also tried to rebuild public enthusiasm for swing. In 1953 *Billboard* announced that a big band "revival is not limited to a few stations and deejays, but is widespread and on stations all over the country." Industry expectations were boosted by the recollection that swing's ascent had followed a period in the early 1930s dominated by vocalists; perhaps history would repeat itself. The networks' most ambitious campaign came three years later, when NBC announced the debut of "Bandstand," a short-lived program designed to showcase big bands on weekdays from ten until noon.[32] But the remote broadcasts that had played such a crucial role in the popularization of swing were being phased out.

While these media were perceived as crucial to the viability of the music industry and of particular artists, some believed that commercial success depended on attracting live audiences. Ballroom operators formed a trade association in the late 1940s that in 1951 succeeded in repealing the despised wartime cabaret tax. The National Ballroom Operators' Association also joined forces with the AFM to generate enthusiasm for dance bands by sponsoring a nationwide contest to identify and promote the country's best band. The winner, chosen after a round of regional competitions, was awarded a television appearance and a six-week sponsored tour. Such efforts yielded few lasting benefits. In 1949 bandleader Andy Kirk noticed that familiar ballrooms were being converted to supermarkets, bowling alleys, and roller-skating rinks, a pattern that continued through the 1950s. At the same time, theaters that had provided a major source of income for the top national bands ceased hiring them as stage attractions. Hotels likewise declined to feature name bands, opting instead for star attractions backed by house bands.[33]

Just as swing's demise had been regularly predicted during the peak years, the 1950s witnessed recurrent rumors of a revival. But performers who had options in other sectors of the entertainment industry took them. The more famous bandleaders parlayed their fame into book and movie contracts or found work as disk jockeys. Others migrated to Hollywood or television networks, where they functioned behind the scenes as arrangers or musical directors. A few retired, able to live off the savings they had amassed during their stardom. Some continued to maintain bands and tour: Ellington, Basie, Kenton, Harry James, Les Brown. Other swing veterans continued to form bands during and after the 1960s, sometimes scaling them down to more economical size. In 1965 Basie veteran Thad Jones and drummer Mel Lewis formed the most critically acclaimed big band of the following decade, playing Monday night at New York's Village Vanguard when not touring. The following year Buddy Rich, who had worked with Harry James and the Dorseys during the 1950s, formed his own big band, which won international acclaim through the mid-1970s. Trumpeter Maynard Ferguson formed a number of bands during the late 1960s and 1970s that tapped a new audience drawn to jazz-rock fusion. And in 1973 pianist Toshiko Akiyoshi, who took up jazz while living in Japan, formed a big band with Lew Tabackin that by the 1980s was widely considered the leading jazz-oriented big band. Yet none of these ensembles, which built to varying degrees on the musical idiom of swing, sought to connect with the dancers swing had reached. Their audiences were listeners, primarily jazz fans who gathered at jazz festivals and in concert halls, nightclubs, and college auditoriums.

Whatever success and visibility these bands attained had little in common with the response generated by swing. The coalition of African-American and white musicians—often from middle-class backgrounds—patrician writers and critics, and a diverse audience that comprised jitterbugs and ickies, blacks and whites drawn from both urban and rural areas, did not survive the war. Much of its energy was absorbed from the mid-1950s on by rock and roll, which constructed a different demographic coalition. Although it appealed to middle-class whites, of course, rock and roll's impetus came from the southern working class that had migrated during the war. It too represented an ethnic hybrid, of African-American blues and white country music. At first, not surprisingly, prominent swing figures greeted the new music with disdain. Sinatra told a congressional committee that rock and roll was "the most brutal, ugly, desperate, vicious form of expression it has been my misfortune to hear . . . the martial music of every sideburned delinquent on the face of the earth."[34] But by the 1970s most leaders of big bands were incorporating elements of rock and roll in order to remain commercially viable.

In the increasingly circumscribed jazz world, the late 1950s and 1960s saw the emergence of an ideology of race consciousness much more explicit than had accompanied bebop. Many African-American musicians were rediscovering musical roots like blues and gospel, and experimenting with harmonic structures native to India and other Eastern cultures. Titles like "Tanganyika Strut," "Better Git Hit in Your Soul," and *We Insist!: Freedom Now Suite* expressed this combination of cultural roots and political militance. By the 1960s a small but highly vocal cadre of musicians were formulating a clear ideological role for their music. "We are only an extension of that entire civil rights, Black Muslim, black-nationalist movement that is taking place in America," said Archie Shepp, its most visible spokesman. This music, sometimes called "free jazz" or "the new thing," was linked to opposition to the Vietnam War, to support for Cuba, and to "the liberation of all people." Accompanying this global focus was an attack on the supposedly reactionary, white-dominated music industry: the critics, recording companies, and unions that had long irked musicians. Club owners were reviled as "cockroach capitalists" who in Shepp's view operated "crude stables where black men are run until they bleed, or else hacked up outright for Lepage's glue." In this climate, where jazz could be enlisted as marching music in a race/class struggle, it was tempting to seek a usable past in bebop by projecting the concerns of 1960s radicals on musical innovators like Gillespie and Parker, thereby defining swing as the historical enemy of authentic black music.[35]

Swing continues to reassert itself, reaching new audiences but always cloaked in nostalgia. Its latest standard-bearer is Harry Connick, Jr., whose stage presence and pianistic and vocal talents suggest to some both Sinatra and Nat Cole. Born the year before Woodstock, Connick has transgenerational appeal, something that could not be said of swing performers like Sinatra at comparable stages in their careers. But his meteoric rise was aided by a classic swing industry tie-in, his performance on the 1989 soundtrack to the hit movie *When Harry Met Sally . . .* Among musicians, swing has new practitioners like saxophonist Scott Hamilton, a protégé of Bud Freeman. Fan clubs like the Glenn Miller Birthplace Society continue to draw new members, as do swing dance clubs and lessons, which attract both couples who grew up with swing and people in their twenties eager to learn the lindy hop and jitterbug. Public television has discovered swing as a potent fundraising vehicle, staging "extravaganzas" like "Big Band Ballroom Bash," which featured professional dancers acting out scenes from the 1930s and 1940s to the music of a reconstituted Artie Shaw band (one skit showed a ballroom brawl between Second World War–era soldiers and sailors).

A half-century later, swing has been absorbed by the culture, both musically and ideologically. Just as bebop's innovations were quickly incorporated by subsequent musicians, swing's idioms have worked their way into television studio orchestras, movie soundtracks, New Year's Eve celebrations, and FM easy-listening stations. Its Americanist ideology has likewise been absorbed by American society, contributing to the cultural politics of later musical genres whose versions of racial syncretism strike the ears as worlds apart from the lush, seamless orchestrations of the big bands. Swing's sociological lesson—the possibility of tolerance, mutual respect, even affection, between African-Americans and whites—has long since become an established virtue in American society—an ideal still honored as much in the breach as in the observance.[36] By demonstrating that whites could indulge their long-standing fascination for African-American culture without the protective coloration of blackface, swing inaugurated a new chapter in race relations, one in which culture and race could be imagined as separate and distinct. But the dubious equating of skin color and culture has been continually reasserted (and attacked) in the decades since the ballrooms were converted to bowling alleys. This is a debate located close to the American bone, and it shows no sign of abating.

Notes

Introduction: Understanding Swing

1. Ralph Ellison, "What America Would Be Like without Blacks," *Time* 95 (April 6, 1970), p. 55.
2. Gama Gilbert, "Higher Soars the Swing Fever," *New York Times Magazine*, Aug. 14, 1938, p. 6.
3. For this argument about the blues artist Leadbelly, see Benjamin Filene, " 'Our Singing Country': John and Alan Lomax, Leadbelly, and the Construction of an American Past," *American Quarterly* 43 (Dec. 1991), p. 616.
4. Benny Goodman as told to Ted Shane, "Now Take the Jitterbug," *Collier's* 103 (Feb. 25, 1939), p. 60. "Swing, Swing, Oh Beautiful Swing!" *Metronome* 52 (Feb. 1936), pp. 19, 33; "Swing Still Up in the Air," *Metronome* 52 (March 1936), p. 16; Scotty Lawrence, "Swing Is Here to Stay," *Metronome* 53 (Aug. 1937), p. 13. " 'Round and Around," *Literary Digest* 121 (April 4, 1936), p. 26. Benny Goodman and Irving Kolodin, *The Kingdom of Swing* (New York: Stackpole Sons, 1939), pp. 174–175.
5. "Swing, Swing, Oh Beautiful Swing!" pp. 19, 33; *Metronome* 53 (Aug. 1937); W. F. Ludwig, "Why the Public Likes Swing," *Metronome* 52 (Oct. 1936), p. 18.
6. Virgil Thomson, "Swing Music," *Modern Music* 13 (May–June 1936), pp. 12–17; "Swing Again," *Modern Music* 15 (March–April 1938), pp. 160–166. The most recent attempt to define swing is that of Gunther Schuller in *The Swing Era: The Development of Jazz, 1930–1945* (New York: Oxford University Press, 1989), pp. 223–225.
7. *Down Beat*, Feb. 1939, p. 2. Gama Gilbert, "Swing," *New York Times Magazine*, Nov. 19, 1939, p. 14. "No Swing at Carnegie," *Metronome* 55 (Jan. 1939), p. 38. "Jazz versus Swing," *Metronome* 60 (April 1944), p. 23. Russ Morgan, "Why I Hate Swing," *Swing* 1 (Oct. 1938), p. 14.
8. John O'Hara, "Take It!" *New Republic* 101 (Dec. 27, 1939), p. 287. "Jazz

versus Swing," pp. 22–23. See also "Louis on Jazz and Swing," *Metronome* 61 (June 1945), pp. 26–27.

9. For an account of this tour, see Goodman and Kolodin, *The Kingdom of Swing*, pp. 197–200; Arthur Rollini, *Thirty Years with the Big Bands* (Urbana: University of Illinois Press, 1987), pp. 34–70.

10. "Whoa-ho-ho-ho-ho-ho!" *Time* 27 (Jan. 20, 1936), p. 30; Arnold Shaw, *52nd Street: The Street of Jazz* (New York: Da Capo, 1977), pp. 68–74. See also *Literary Digest* 121 (April 4, 1936), p. 26; Frank Norris, "The Music Goes 'Round and Around," *New Republic* 85 (Jan. 29, 1936), pp. 334–335.

11. William S. Dutton, "We've Got Rhythm," *American Magazine* 119 (March 1935), pp. 52, 53, 126–128.

12. For a thorough investigation of the formalist and historicist approaches to jazz criticism, see John Gennari, "Jazz Criticism: Its Development and Ideologies," *Black American Literature Forum* 25 (Fall 1991), pp. 449–523. The approach I advocate has been taken by Gary Tomlinson, whose study of Monteverdi devotes as much attention to the composer's intentions and the cultural context of Renaissance Italy as to relations between and among individual compositions. But as a music historian, Tomlinson's primary texts are works of music, his stated objective being to describe their meanings. See his *Monteverdi and the End of the Renaissance* (Berkeley: University of California Press, 1987), pp. ix–xi. Scott DeVeaux has made a similar argument regarding jazz in "Constructing the Jazz Tradition: Jazz Historiography," *Black American Literature Forum* 25 (Fall 1991), pp. 525–560. For a full discussion of problems raised by the historical interpretation, see David W. Stowe, "Historians, Homologies, and Music as Cultural Text," paper presented at the annual meeting of the American Studies Association, Boston, November 1993.

13. See Frank Tirro, "The Silent Theme Tradition in Jazz," *Musical Quarterly* 53 (July 1967), pp. 313–334.

14. Erika Doss, "The Art of Cultural Politics: From Regionalism and Abstract Expressionism," in Lary May, ed., *Recasting America: Culture and Politics in the Age of Cold War* (Chicago: University of Chicago Press, 1989), pp. 195–220; Serge Guilbaut, *How New York Stole the Idea of Modern Art: Abstract Expressionism, Freedom, and the Cold War* (Chicago: University of Chicago Press, 1983). Karal Ann Marling, *Wall-to-Wall America: A Cultural History of Post Office Murals in the Great Depression* (Minneapolis: University of Minnesota Press, 1982).

15. Rumors that James hired only musicians who could play baseball were exaggerated, although he did put a skilled pitcher on the payroll for one day, long enough to play in an important rematch. Drew Page, *Drew's*

Blues: A Sideman's Life with the Big Bands (Baton Rouge: Louisiana State University Press, 1980), pp. 117–118. Krupa quoted in George T. Simon, *The Big Bands* (New York: Schirmer Books, 1981), p. 21. See also Ira Gitler, *Swing to Bop: An Oral History of the Transition in Jazz in the 1940s* (New York: Oxford University Press, 1985), pp. 239–240.

16. Irving Kolodin, "Number One Swing Man," *Harper's* 179 (Sept. 1939), p. 433. In a special fiftieth-birthday issue on Louis Armstrong, *Down Beat's* editors compared him to Babe Ruth. *Down Beat*, July 14, 1950, p. 10.

17. Jules Tygiel, *Baseball's Great Experiment: Jackie Robinson and His Legacy* (New York: Oxford University Press, 1983). On Communist Party pressure to integrate baseball, see pp. 36–37. "Simon Sez," *Metronome* 63 (May 1947), p. 50. Nelson George, *The Death of Rhythm & Blues* (New York: Pantheon, 1988), pp. 57–58.

18. On the New Deal as cultural movement, see Alan Lawson, "The Cultural Legacy of the New Deal," in Harvard Sitkoff, ed., *Fifty Years Later: The New Deal Evaluated* (New York: Knopf, 1985), pp. 155–181.

    Roosevelt's commitment to racial equality, to be sure, has been debated by historians. "The New Deal, in spite of a small number of token gestures, had little to offer blacks in particular, and as such left the segregationist social organization of the South unchallenged," writes Ira Katznelson in a statement that encapsulates recent thinking. See "Was the Great Society a Lost Opportunity?" in Steve Fraser and Gary Gerstle, eds., *The Rise and Fall of the New Deal Order, 1930–1980* (Princeton: Princeton University Press, 1989), pp. 185–211. See also Richard Polenberg, *One Nation Divisible: Class, Race, and Ethnicity in the United States since 1938* (New York: Penguin, 1980), pp. 31–34; idem, *War and Society: The United States, 1941–1945* (New York: J. B. Lippincott, 1972), pp. 107–112. For earlier, more generous assessments, see William E. Leuchtenberg, *Franklin Roosevelt and the New Deal* (New York: Harper & Row, 1963), pp. 184–187; Arthur M. Schlesinger, Jr., *The Age of Roosevelt*, vol. 3, *The Politics of Upheaval* (Boston: Houghton Mifflin, 1960), pp. 425–438.

19. For a brilliant interpretation of blackface minstrelsy in antebellum America, see Eric Lott, *Love and Theft: Blackface Minstrelsy and the American Working Class* (New York: Oxford University Press, 1993).

20. Warren I. Susman, *Culture as History: The Transformation of American Society in the Twentieth Century* (New York: Pantheon, 1984), p. 197; Lawson, "The Cultural Legacy of the New Deal," pp. 155–181; William Stott, *Documentary Expression in Thirties America* (New York: Oxford University Press, 1973).

21. Lawrence W. Levine, "American Culture and the Great Depression," in

The Unpredictable Past: Explorations in American Cultural History (New York: Oxford University Press, 1993), pp. 206–230. Susman, *Culture as History*, pp. 193–209; William Graebner, *The Age of Doubt: American Thought and Culture in the 1940s* (Boston: Twayne Publishers, 1991).

22. Michael Harrington, *Fragments of the Century* (New York: Saturday Review Press, 1973), p. 64.

1. The Tempo of the Time

1. Gama Gilbert, "Swing It! And Even in a Temple of Music," *New York Times Magazine*, Jan. 16, 1938, p. 7.

2. Account of concert drawn from *Down Beat*, Feb. 1938, pp. 1, 5–7; George T. Simon, "Benny and Cats Make Carnegie Debut Real Howling Success," *Metronome* 54 (Feb. 1938), pp. 1, 18, 44; *New York Times*, Jan. 17, 1938, p. 11; Irving Kolodin, liner notes to *Benny Goodman's Carnegie Hall Concert*, Columbia 814–816.

3. *Down Beat*, June 1937, pp. 1–2. "Basie's Brilliant Band Conquers Chick's," *Metronome* 54 (Feb. 1938), pp. 1, 20.

4. Maurice Zolotow, "Harlem's Great White Father," *Saturday Evening Post* 214 (Sept. 27, 1941), p. 64. Otis Ferguson, "Breakfast Dance, in Harlem," in Dorothy Chamberlain and Robert Wilson, eds., *The Otis Ferguson Reader* (Highland, Ill.: December Press, 1982), p. 59.

5. "Basie's Brilliant Band Conquers Chick's," pp. 1, 20. No consensus has emerged regarding the winner of the contest. Critic Helen Oakley Dance, who was doing publicity work for Webb at the time, claims she set up the battle, knowing Basie would win, in order to shake up Webb. She felt the drummer was allowing Ella Fitzgerald to dominate his band to an unhealthy extent. Dance quoted in Burt Korall, *Drummin' Men: The Heartbeat of Jazz* (New York: Schirmer Books, 1990), pp. 36–37.

6. For an account of this process, see Lawrence Levine, *Highbrow/Lowbrow: The Emergence of a Cultural Hierarchy in America* (Cambridge, Mass.: Harvard University Press, 1988).

7. Quoted in Philip K. Eberly, *Music in the Air: America's Changing Tastes in Popular Music, 1920–1980* (New York: Hastings House, 1982), pp. 102–104. For a sample of the argument over 1920s jazz, see John R. McMahon's classic "Unspeakable Jazz Must Go!" *Ladies' Home Journal* 38 (Nov. 1921), pp. 38, 115. See also Kathy J. Ogren, *The Jazz Revolution: Twenties America and the Meaning of Jazz* (New York: Oxford University

Press, 1989), pp. 139–161; Lawrence Levine, "Jazz and American Culture," in *The Unpredictable Past: Explorations in American Cultural History* (New York: Oxford University Press, 1993), pp. 172–188.

8. *New York Times*, Oct. 26, 1938, p. 20; Nov. 2, 1938, p. 25; Jan. 18, 1938, p. 22; Jan. 23, 1938, sec. 11, p. 8; May 31, 1938, p. 18. "But there was not a mite of harm in them," the *Times* continued. "They were of all races, all colors, all walks—or rather all swings and shags—of life."

9. *New York Times*, Feb. 26, 1939, p. E9. Larry Clinton, "Swing Grows Up," *Good Housekeeping* 107 (Oct. 1938), p. 13. *New York Times*, Jan. 23, 1938, sec. 11, p. 8.

10. One bandleader worked out a theory of two-year cycles: the "golden financial era" of 1926–1928 produced 6/8 marches; "weirdly balanced songs" dominated the next two years; imported Cuban rhumbas held sway through 1932, followed by a two-year boom in cowboy songs and hillbilly music. Finally, ballads dominated in the two years before swing, 1934–1936. *Down Beat*, Dec. 1937, p. 2.

11. *New York Times*, July 27, 1938, p. 19. "How Long Will Swing Last?" *Metronome* 54 (March 1938), p. 9. Charles E. Green, "1937 Models in Dance, Club, and Ballroom," *Metronome* 53 (Jan. 1937), p. 16.

12. *Down Beat*, March 1938, p. 10; *New York Times*, Sept. 24, 1939, sec. 4, p. 9.

13. Gama Gilbert, "Higher Soars the Swing Fever," *New York Times Magazine*, Aug. 14, 1938, p. 6. Clinton, "Swing Grows Up," p. 13. *Down Beat*, Dec. 15, 1940, p. 14.

14. Gilbert, "Swing It!" p. 21; Gilbert, "Higher Soars the Swing Fever," p. 19. For a discussion of 1920s jazz as an engine for cultural relativism see Ogren, *Jazz Revolution*, pp. 161–165. Neil Leonard has also demonstrated how jazz shed its morally suspect reputation and achieved a measure of cultural legitimacy during the 1930s; *Jazz and the White Americans: The Acceptance of a New Art Form* (Chicago: University of Chicago Press, 1962). Morroe Berger's survey of press reviews from the 1920s and 1930s also supports this view; see his "Jazz: A Model of Cultural Diffusion," in Charles Nanry, ed., *American Music: From Storyville to Woodstock* (New Brunswick, N.J.: Transaction Books), pp. 12–27.

15. "A Sage Looks at Swing," *Time* 35 (May 20, 1940), p. 41.

16. Quoted in *New York Times*, Aug. 14, 1938, sec. 9, p. 10. *New York Times*, Oct. 30, 1938, sec. 9, p. 7.

17. *New York Amsterdam News*, Oct. 29, 1938, p. 20. "Sixty Years," *Metronome* 59 (Oct. 1943), p. 11.

18. *Bridgeport Telegram*, Nov. 2, 1942, in Benny Goodman Papers, MSS 53,

Yale Music Library (hereafter YML). Benny Goodman and Irving Kolodin, *The Kingdom of Swing* (New York: Stackpole Sons, 1939), pp. 242–243.

19. Goodman and Kolodin, *Kingdom of Swing*, p. 182. Gilbert, "Higher Soars the Swing Fever," p. 19.

20. AP Newsbrief, May 19, 1937, in Goodman Papers, YML. "Swing Secrets Taught in High School," *Metronome* 55 (March 1939), p. 12. *New York Times*, Dec. 15, 1938, p. 8.

21. H. I. Phillips, "The Once Over," May 27, 1937, in Goodman Papers, YML. Will Roland, "Educators: Fight Jazz Prejudices," *Metronome* 61 (April 1945), p. 23. For a description of the diffusion of cultural relativism through U.S. academic culture, see Edward A. Purcell, Jr., *The Crisis of Democratic Theory: Scientific Naturalism and the Problem of Value* (Lexington: University Press of Kentucky, 1973), especially pp. 66–73. Ruth Benedict's best-selling *Patterns of Culture*, a manifesto of cultural relativism, was published in 1934.

22. Benny Goodman as told to Ted Shane, "Now Take the Jitterbug!" *Collier's* 103 (Feb. 25, 1939), pp. 11–12; Gilbert, "Higher Soars the Swing Fever," p. 6. An irate reader pointed out that Goodman's account of this "first" encounter was concocted: the band did not play in Kansas City until three years after the event was alleged to have occurred; *Down Beat*, April 1939, p. 10.

23. Frank Norris, "The Killer-Diller: The Life and Four-Four Time of Benny Goodman," *Saturday Evening Post* 210 (May 7, 1938), p. 22. J. F. Considine, "Boston Swings to Swing," *Metronome* 54 (Dec. 1938), p. 32; "Ickies' Antics Submerge Goodman-Basie Battle," *Metronome* 54 (July 1938), p. 39. Paul E. Wittenmyer, "Jitterbugs Wreck Chicago Stadium," *Metronome* 54 (Oct. 1938), p. 16. Jack Hirshberg, "6,000 Jitterbugs Riot at Lunceford Date," *Metronome* 56 (April 1940), p. 10. *Down Beat*, May 1, 1941, p. 7.

24. *Down Beat*, Dec. 1938, p. 44; Feb. 1939, p. 23; April 1, 1943, p. 19.

25. "Jazz Enters the Laboratory for Psychological Study," *Science News Letter* 36 (July 1, 1939), pp. 12–13. *Down Beat*, March 1939, p. 14; April 1939, p. 27.

26. *Down Beat*, Oct. 1937, p. 6. Gilbert, "Higher Soars the Swing Fever," p. 6.

27. *Down Beat*, Dec. 1937, p. 2.

28. "Swing Is Art and Is Becoming Great Art," *Science News Letter* 38 (Dec. 14, 1940), p. 377. *Down Beat*, May 1939, p. 9; Oct. 1938, p. 12. *New York Times*, Sept. 8, 1938, p. 25.

29. Marshall Stearns and Jean Stearns, *Jazz Dance: The Story of American Vernacular Dance* (New York: Macmillan, 1968), pp. 315–334.

30. Quoted in Stanley Dance, *The World of Swing* (New York: Scribner's, 1974), p. 124. Dicky Wells as told to Stanley Dance, *The Night People: Reminiscences of a Jazzman* (Boston: Crescendo Books, 1971), pp. 34–36. Goodman and Shane, "Now Take the Jitterbug!" p. 60. Stearns and Stearns, *Jazz Dance*, pp. 322–323. The *New York Times* quote appears in ibid., p. 331.

31. David M. Faulkner and Farnsworth Elliot, "Swing's for Listeners—Not for Dancers!" *Metronome* 55 (Oct. 1939), p. 19. *Down Beat*, July 1937, p. 8.

32. Goodman and Shane, "Now Take the Jitterbug!" p. 60. "Jimmy Dorsey on Swing," *Metronome* 56 (March 1940), p. 18, reprinted from *Chicago Daily News*. *Down Beat*, Jan. 15, 1940, p. 7; Dec. 15, 1941, p. 4. Frankie Masters, "Now Take Swing," *Swing* 1 (March 1939), p. 16. For an argument that jazz increasingly embraced "traditional values" during the 1930s, see Leonard, *Jazz and the White Americans*, pp. 119–132.

33. On the Jitterbug Society, see *Down Beat*, Sept. 23, 1946, pp. 17–18. An exotic argot particular to jazz would surface again ten years later during the bebop sensation, at which time it would again be presented as a novelty. But such language predated even the swing era; many of its distinctive forms apparently originated with Armstrong in the 1920s. See Albert Murray, *Stomping the Blues* (New York: Da Capo, 1976), p. 238.

34. Cab Calloway and Bryant Rollins, *Of Minnie the Moocher and Me* (New York: Crowell, 1976), p. 252. *New York Amsterdam News*, May 20, 1944; *New York Times*, July 12, 1942, p. 27.

35. "The Jive Language," *Metronome* 55 (June 1939), p. 20. Otis Ferguson, "Man . . . You're Jiving Me Crazy," reprinted in Chamberlain and Wilson, *Otis Ferguson Reader*, p. 48.

36. *Down Beat*, July 1936, p. 1; March 15, 1944, p. 1.

37. *Down Beat*, June 1, 1940, pp. 2, 11; Sept. 15, 1941, p. 10; Jan. 15, 1943, pp. 1, 10; "They Are Innocent until Proved Guilty!" *Metronome* 59 (Feb. 1943), p. 34; "No Rye for FBI; They'll Take Tea," *Metronome* 61 (Aug. 1945), p. 7.

38. *Down Beat*, Dec. 1937, p. 2. Goodman and Shane, "Now Take the Jitterbug!" p. 12. *Down Beat*, Dec. 1, 1939, p. 10.

39. *Downbeat*, Dec. 1935–Jan. 1936, pp. 1, 9; Helen Oakley, "Chicago Letter," *Jazz Hot*, April 1936, p. 11. *Boston Herald*, May 26, 1937, in Goodman Papers, YML. Henry Anton Steig, "Alligators' Idol," *New Yorker* 13 (April 17, 1937), p. 31.

40. Faulkner and Elliot, "Swing's for Listeners," p. 19. See also Alice C. Browning, *Lionel Hampton's Swing Book* (Chicago: Negro Story Press, 1946), p. 79. Gilbert Seldes, "No More Swing?" *Scribner's* 100 (Nov. 1936), p. 71. Leon James quoted in Stearns and Stearns, *Jazz Dance*, p. 323.

41. Irving Kolodin, "The Dance Band Business: A Study in Black and White," *Harper's* 183 (June 1941), pp. 76–77; John Desmond, "Making Catnip for the Hepcats," *New York Times Magazine*, June 20, 1943, p. 17. Woody Herman and Stuart Troup, *The Woodchopper's Ball: The Autobiography of Woody Herman* (New York: E. P. Dutton, 1990), p. 36. Norris, "The Killer-Diller," p. 22; Steig, "Alligators' Idol," p. 31.

Reliable demographic data on the swing audiences are difficult to come by. A poll of Chicago nightclub patrons conducted by Music Corporation of America (MCA) in 1937 found that the enthusiasm for swing was most pronounced up to age twenty-three. Patrons aged twenty-three to twenty-nine preferred "sweeter" music, while the musical preferences of those over twenty-nine were unclear. For a demographic analysis of the audience at Boston's Cocoanut Grove on the evening when fire destroyed the ballroom in November 1942, see Lewis Erenberg, "From New York to Middletown: Repeal and the Legitimization of Nightlife in the Great Depression," *American Quarterly* 38 (Winter 1986), p. 774. Erenberg found that the audience consisted mainly of members of the upper-middle class, students, defense workers, and servicemen.

42. Erenberg, "From New York to Middletown," pp. 761–778.

43. Ralph Cooper with Steve Dougherty, *Amateur Night at the Apollo* (New York: Harper Collins, 1990), pp. 50–51. *Down Beat*, Oct. 1936, p. 15. Langston Hughes, "When the Negro Was in Vogue," in *The Langston Hughes Reader* (New York: George Braziller, 1958), p. 370. Malcolm X as told to Alex Haley, *The Autobiography of Malcolm X* (New York: Ballantine Books, 1965), pp. 74, 49. Chip Deffaa, *Swing Legacy* (Metuchen, N.J.: Institute for Jazz Studies, 1989), p. 191.

44. *Down Beat*, April 1937, p. 16. "White Bands Big in Harlem," *Metronome* 56 (Jan. 1940), p. 10. Bud Freeman as told to Robert Wolf, *Crazeology: The Autobiography of a Chicago Jazzman* (Urbana: University of Illinois Press, 1989), p. 42.

45. "Making a Ballroom a Social and Financial Success," *Metronome* 52 (Jan. 1936), p. 44. Cooper, *Amateur Night*, pp. 49–50. "Making a Ballroom a Success," p. 23; *Down Beat*, Dec. 1936, p. 25.

46. *Down Beat*, May 1939, p. 2. Malcolm X, *Autobiography*, p. 82; Bill Coleman, *Trumpet Story* (Boston: Northeastern University Press, 1991), p. 56.

47. Erenberg, "From New York to Middletown," pp. 770–772. Devoting so

much attention to the urban ballrooms and dance halls runs the risk of ignoring the large variety of other venues in which big bands performed. Swing was performed and danced to in a variety of places, including auditoriums, stadiums, armories, skating rinks, warehouses, barns, roadhouses, and open fields. But the streamlined *art moderne* style was associated with the swing bands and exerted a powerful influence on the design of ballrooms across the country.

48. A sideman recalled Ellington preparing for an important engagement at New York's Roxy Theater: "In his dressing room there were sketches of the stage set. Duke scanned these for days while we were playing the Apollo Theatre uptown, and then we were told to go to the tailor for fittings on the new uniforms . . . cinnamon-brown slacks, chocolate-brown jackets, billiard-green shirts, pastel-yellow ties . . . However, at the dress rehearsal at the Roxy, Duke took one look at our color scheme and immediately dashed to the phone and awakened some shirt manufacturer with an order for several dozen shirts of a different color. Then, he explained that the original shirts muddied our features under the lights. But we used them for one-nighters later"; Rex Stewart, *Jazz Masters of the 30s* (New York: Da Capo, 1972), p. 84.

49. Glen Gray quoted in Jack O'Brien, "New York," May 16, 1948, in Goodman Papers, YML. On territory bands, see David W. Stowe, "Jazz in the West: Cultural Frontier and Region during the Swing Era," *Western Historical Quarterly* 23 (Feb. 1992), pp. 53–73.

50. *Down Beat*, April 1, 1940, p. 7.

51. "Jitterbugs in Jersey," *Time* 34 (March 6, 1939), p. 39; "New King: Glenn Miller," *Time* 34 (Nov. 27, 1939), p. 56. Deffaa, *Swing Legacy*, p. 25. Miller responded: "I don't want to be the king of swing or anything else. I'd rather have a reputation as one of the best all-round bands."

52. On the ballot-stuffing controversy, see *Down Beat*, Jan. 1, 1940, p. 1. *Chicago Defender*, Dec. 7, 1940, p. 13.

53. Marcela Breton, ed., *Hot and Cool: Jazz Short Stories* (New York: Plume, 1990), pp. 12–28. "Common Meter" originally appeared in 1930 in the *Baltimore Afro-American*, demonstrating that the conventions of swing were well established among African-Americans years before swing became a national fad.

2. Between Conjure and Kapital

1. *Down Beat*, April 1939, pp. 4, 9. The title of this chapter comes from Bernard Wolfe's *The Late Risers* (New York: Random House, 1954).

2. *Down Beat*, May 1939, p. 10.
3. *Down Beat*, November 1935, pp. 1, 6. Hammond remained dissatisfied with Ellington to the end, complaining in his 1977 memoir about Ellington's "inability to get people up on a floor to dance," his opposition to efforts to create integrated bands, and his loss of contact with his origins. "None of this is to suggest that Duke was not proud of his own people," Hammond added. "In his way he fought the battle for equal rights as effectively as any other Negro leader." John Hammond with Irving Townsend, *John Hammond on Record: An Autobiography* (New York: Ridge Press, 1977), pp. 133–139.
4. A 1936 interview revealed that Ellington had refused to study formal composition because he felt that academic training would stifle an intangible element in his music, "something essentially Negro." "He is a black man fully conscious of the extraordinary talents of his race AND PROUD BECAUSE HE IS A BLACK MAN," the article began, probably responding to Hammond's charges. "He thinks and acts in Negroid ways. He is not a black edition of a white man, and he is not trying to imitate a white man as is the case with many negroes who prostitute their own fine talents trying to copy or emulate those of the white"; *Down Beat*, July 1936, p. 6. In 1939, decrying the controversy and faddism that had come to surround "swing," Ellington asserted that his "aim has always been the development of an authentic Negro music, of which swing is only one element . . . Our music is always intended to be definitely and purely racial"; *Down Beat*, Feb. 1939, pp. 2, 16–17. Even Ellington's language appeared to reveal his racial consciousness. A 1936 profile in *The Crisis* proudly pointed out that despite the significant popular and critical recognition accorded Ellington, he had not forsaken his cultural roots. "He still persists in speaking in the Negro idiom. Instead of the routine request for a *presto* or an *allegro con spirito*, Ellington will tell his men to '*sock it.*' When a symphonic conductor would call for a solemn *andante* the *hot* jazz command would be, '*Come on boys—let's go to church*' "; Chester Rosenberg, "Duke Ellington," *The Crisis* 43 (Feb. 1936), p. 60.
5. For discussions of the cultural significance of jazz in the 1920s, see Kathy Ogren, *The Jazz Revolution: Twenties America and the Meaning of Jazz* (New York: Oxford University Press, 1989); Lawrence Levine, "Jazz in American Culture," in *The Unpredictable Past: Explorations in American Cultural History* (New York: Oxford University Press, 1993), pp. 172–188; Berendt Ostendorf, "Social Mobility and Cultural Stigma: The Case of Chicago Jazz," in *Black Literature in White America* (Totowa, N.J.: Barnes and

Noble, 1982), pp. 95–117; Neil Leonard, *Jazz and the White Americans: The Acceptance of a New Art Form* (Chicago: University of Chicago Press, 1962).

6. Dorothy Chamberlain and Robert Wilson, eds., *The Otis Ferguson Reader* (Highland, Ill.: December Press, 1982), p. 98 (originally published in the *H.R.S. Rag*, Sept. 1938). Details on Hammond's biography drawn from Hammond, *On Record*; E. J. Kahn, Jr., "Young Man with a Viola," *New Yorker* 15 (July 29, 1939), pp. 19–24; Irving Kolodin, "Number One Swing Man," *Harper's* 179 (Sept. 1939), pp. 431–440.

7. Kolodin, "Number One Swing Man," pp. 433, 432, 438.

8. Ibid., p. 431. Kahn, "Young Man," p. 19. *New York Journal-American*, Jan. 2, 1939. Hammond, *On Record*, p. 177.

9. Chamberlain and Wilson, *Otis Ferguson Reader*, p. 99. *Down Beat*, July 15, 1940, p. 6.

10. Chamberlain and Wilson, *Otis Ferguson Reader*, p. 100. *Down Beat*, July 15, 1940, p. 6.

11. Kolodin, "Number One Swing Man," p. 438. Chamberlain and Wilson, *Otis Ferguson Reader*, p. 101. Ferguson's ambivalence toward Hammond might be expected, given his temperament and strong personal prejudices. Alfred Kazin remembers Ferguson, not unfondly, as "one of the real roughs of the Thirties . . . who laughed at all revolutionary intellectuals as impossible utopians and fantasists . . . a desperate man, a sorehead, a fatalist"; Alfred Kazin, *Starting Out in the Thirties* (Boston: Little, Brown, 1965), pp. 30–31. See also Malcolm Cowley's foreword to Chamberlain and Wilson, *Otis Ferguson Reader* (p. xiii), which notes that Ferguson's pieces were "read with admiration by jazz musicians . . . who had never before opened a journal of opinion and would never open one again, after Otis died."

12. *Down Beat*, April 1939, p. 9. Such charges were later made against Leonard Feather, another prominent critic-producer.

13. Chamberlain and Wilson, *Otis Ferguson Reader*, p. 101.

14. *Down Beat*, June 1937, p. 6. Guy Sykes, "Reviewing the Reviewers," *Metronome* 53 (Oct. 1937), p. 18. Chamberlain and Wilson, *Otis Ferguson Reader*, p. 99. Kahn, "Young Man," p. 24. K. R. McIntire, "Memorandum to Mr. Kramer," June 11, 1941, File 100-25561, Federal Bureau of Investigation, U.S. Department of Justice, Washington D.C. (hereafter FBI).

15. Kahn, "Young Man," p. 22. Chamberlain and Wilson, *Otis Ferguson Reader*, p. 102. Henry Johnson, "The Negro and the Jazz Band," *New*

Masses 20 (Nov. 17, 1936), p. 15. *New York Times*, Dec. 18, 1938, sec. 9, p. 9.

16. "Internal Security (C)," July 8, 1942, New York, N.Y., File 100-12265, FBI.

17. P. E. Foxworth to Director, Oct. 3, 1941, File 100-25561; John Edgar Hoover to Special Agent in Charge, May 27, 1942; Foxworth to Director, June 9 and June 22, 1942. "Internal Security (C)," July 8, 1942, New York; "Security Matter—C," April 3, 1951, New York; "Communist Infiltration of the National Association for the Advancement of Colored People (NAACP), Internal Security—C," June 6, 1958, NY 100-7629 Sub C, New York; all FBI.

18. Hammond, *On Record*, pp. 155–156, 187–190, 238–241.

19. Kolodin, "Number One Swing Man," p. 434.

20. Kahn, "Young Man," p. 20. Johnson, "The Negro and the Jazz Band," p. 15. "Internal Security (C)," July 8, 1942, p. 3, FBI. Hammond, *On Record*, p. 200.

21. "Internal Security–C: Custodial Detention," Feb. 15, 1943, p. 2, New York, FBI.

22. See S. Frederick Starr, *Red and Hot: The Fate of Jazz in the Soviet Union, 1917–1980* (New York: Oxford University Press, 1983).

23. For a close study of the cultural politics of communism in Harlem, see Mark Naison, *Communists in Harlem during the Depression* (New York: Grove Press, 1983), esp. pp. 193–219, 287–314.

24. Ibid., pp. 211–213; quotation from p. 213. *Down Beat*, April 15, 1944, p. 2. Norman Macleod, "Me and Louis Armstrong," *The Crisis* 43 (June 1936), p. 168.

25. Dizzy Gillespie with Al Fraser, *To Be, or Not . . . to Bop* (Garden City, N.Y.: Doubleday, 1979), p. 80. Roy Porter with David Keller, *There and Back: The Roy Porter Story* (Baton Rouge: Louisiana State University Press, 1991), p. 50. Despite the presence of mixed couples at Camp Unity, Sidney Bechet forbade sidemen from fraternizing with white women, thinking it would cost him the engagement. See Bill Coleman's account in *Trumpet Story* (Boston: Northeastern University Press, 1991), p. 129.

26. J. Edgar Hoover to Special Agent in Charge, New York, July 15, 1943, File 100-48754, FBI; Special Agent in Charge to Director, April 3, 1947, File 100-48754-90, FBI. The FBI's 2,100-page file on Josephson contains numerous press clippings on Café Society; see esp. File 100-48754-10 and -11. For Billie Holiday's recollections, see Holiday with William Dufty, *Lady Sings the Blues* (New York: Penguin, 1984), pp. 83–91.

27. *Daily Worker*, Nov. 24, 1938, p. 7.
28. *Daily Worker*, Dec. 2, 1938, p. 9.
29. *Daily Worker*, Dec. 29, 1938, p. 7.
30. Naison, *Communists in Harlem*, p. 303.
31. "Security Information—Confidential," FBI memo to State Department File 100-434443, April 21, 1953, p. 1, FBI. Edward Kennedy Ellington, *Music Is My Mistress* (Garden City, N.Y.: Doubleday, 1973), p. 175. FBI to State, April 21, 1953, pp. 1–2.
32. *New York Amsterdam News*, Nov. 4, 1944, p. 2-A. FBI to State, April 21, 1953, pp. 2–4.
33. FBI to State, April 21, 1953, pp. 4–5.
34. *Down Beat*, March 1938, p. 10. "Prof. Goodman Gives Lecture," *Metronome* 55 (Jan. 1939), p. 13. Liner notes to *Count Basie Super Chief*, Columbia G31224.
35. Bob White, letter, *New Republic* 102 (Feb. 12, 1940), p. 215. Rex Stewart, *Boy Meets Horn* (Ann Arbor: University of Michigan Press, 1991), p. 202.
36. As historian Maurice Isserman has noted, "nobody was born a Communist ... American Communists [were] real human beings who held and discarded illusions, learned some lessons from their mistakes and failed to learn others, integrated events as either substantiation or refutation of passionately held beliefs—in short ... a group of people involved in, shaping, and shaped by an historical process." See his excellent review article, "Three Generations: Historians View American Communism," *Labor History* 26 (Fall 1985), pp. 517–545; quotation from p. 540. For a persuasive call for a more nuanced understanding of "fellow travelers," see Dave Roediger's foreward to Jessie Lloyd O'Connor, Harvey O'Connor, and Susan M. Bowler, *Harvey and Jessie: A Couple of Radicals* (Philadelphia: Temple University Press, 1988), pp. vii–xiii. Irving Howe offers a succinct interpretation of the Popular Front in *Socialism and America* (New York: Harcourt Brace Jovanovich, 1985), pp. 87–104.
37. *Down Beat*, Jan. 1, 1941, p. 10; Jan. 1, 1942, p. 5.
38. Gary Gerstle, *Working-Class Americanism: The Politics of Labor in a Textile City, 1914–1960* (Cambridge: Cambridge University Press, 1989). For a concise discussion of the discourse of Americanism among workers, employers, and religious and political leaders in Woonsocket, Rhode Island, see pp. 5–15. See also Lawrence Levine, "The Historian and the Icon," in *The Unpredictable Past: Explorations in American Cultural History* (New York: Oxford University Press, 1993), pp. 283–285.
39. Robert Crandall, "What's Wrong with Down Beat?" *Music and Rhythm* 1

(Dec. 1940), p. 84. An editorial page from 1937 serves as a useful metonymy for the magazine's editorial policy: a flagrantly racist cartoon depicting "native" Africans playing a drum, listening to a record player, and speaking in a debased dialect; three letters from readers angrily attacking an earlier letter that had complained about the excessive space awarded black jazz in *Down Beat*; and an ambivalent editorial on the subject of racially mixed bands; *Down Beat*, Dec. 1937, p. 12. For a helpful contemporary survey of swing journalism by a participant, see Dave Dexter, Jr., "The Fourth Estate," in *Jazz Cavalcade* (New York: Da Capo, 1977), pp. 114–126.

40. *Down Beat*, Oct. 1936, p. 4; April 1939, p. 10.
41. *Down Beat*, Oct. 1936, p. 4; May 1936, p. 2; Oct. 1937, p. 3.
42. *Down Beat*, Dec. 1937, p. 12; Oct. 15, 1939, pp. 1, 10.
43. *Down Beat*, Dec. 1938, p. 10; Aug. 1, 1940, p. 10; Oct. 1, 1939, p. 10.
44. *Down Beat*, Aug. 1, 1940, p. 10; June 15, 1941, pp. 1, 10; Aug. 15, 1941, p. 10.
45. *Down Beat*, Oct. 1936, p. 4; May 1937, p. 3; Jan. 15, 1941, p. 2.
46. *Down Beat*, Oct. 1936, p. 5; Nov. 1936, p. 10.
47. *Down Beat*, April 1, 1940, p. 7. Another writer criticized Billie Holiday for wasting her talents with Artie Shaw, whose band played "white man's jazz and that's no backing for Billie's singing, which even during its more commercial moments, has a definite 'race' flavor"; *Down Beat*, Aug. 1938, p. 5.
48. *Down Beat*, Jan. 1938, p. 18; June 1938, p. 5. To be sure, both assumptions continue to exert a powerful grip on contemporary views concerning ethnicity, particularly in the realm of literature. See Henry Louis Gates, Jr., " 'Authenticity,' or the Lesson of Little Tree," *New York Times Book Review*, Nov. 24, 1991, pp. 1, 26–30.
49. *Down Beat*, Nov. 1936, p. 17. Regardless of its credence within the jazz community, La Rocca's claim was accepted by a "March of Time" newsreel on the origin of swing, provoking a guest column by Five Pennies trumpeter Red Nichols, who countered that *Time*'s editors were "mixed up" and that the newsreel was a "serious blow" to the music industry. *Down Beat*, May 1937, p. 7. *Time* responded, in effect, that experts disagree. For a representative dispute over the first integrated band, see *Down Beat*, July 15, 1943, p. 4.
50. Hammond quoted in Ronald G. Welburn, "American Jazz Criticism 1914–1940" (Ph.D. diss., New York University, 1983), p. 208. Disdain for jazz among African-American intellectuals of course extended back to the

1920s. See Nathan Irwin Huggins, *Harlem Renaissance* (London: Oxford University Press, 1971), pp. 9–11, 197–198.

51. Marshall W. Stearns, "Fondation de la Fédération Internationale Des Hot Clubs," *Jazz Hot*, Sept.–Oct. 1935, p. 1.

52. *Down Beat*, Dec. 1936, p. 22. Arnold Shaw, *52nd Street: The Street of Jazz* (New York: Da Capo, 1977), p. 245. *Down Beat*, Nov. 1938, pp. 2, 19. As a result of the scandal, Stearns was demoted from secretary general to adviser.

53. Paul Bacon, "Jazz Fan," in Frank Driggs and Harris Lewine, *Black Beauty, White Heat: A Pictorial History of Classic Jazz, 1920–1950* (New York: W. Morrow, 1982), p. 10. Charles Miller, "Swing Nostalgia," *New Republic* 116 (May 12, 1947), p. 35.

54. For an influential formulation of this argument, see Christopher Lasch, *The New Radicalism in America, 1889–1963: The Intellectual as a Social Type* (New York: W. W. Norton, 1986).

55. Frank Norris, "Music Goes 'Round and Around," *New Republic* 85 (Jan. 29, 1936), p. 334.

56. Gunther Schuller calls Frazier's lyrics "probably the most sophisticated and cryptic blues lyrics ever contrived (including even Joni Mitchell's). It is not clear whether Jimmy Rushing really understood what he was singing, but it certainly sounds convincing." See *The Swing Era: The Development of Jazz, 1930–1945* (New York: Oxford University Press, 1989), pp. 254–257.

57. Andy Kirk, *Twenty Years on Wheels* (Ann Arbor: University of Michigan Press, 1989), p. 117. *New York Amsterdam News*, May 16, 1942, p. 17. *Down Beat*, June 15, 1942, p. 17; Nov. 1937, p. 11; March 1939, p. 1; May 1939, p. 2. Philip K. Eberly, *Music in the Air: America's Changing Tastes in Popular Music, 1920–1980* (New York: Hastings House, 1982), pp. 119–120, 138, 144–145. For observations on the relationship between parodies of scholarship, cultural capital, and hip, see Andrew Ross, *No Respect: Intellectuals and Popular Culture* (New York: Routledge, 1989), pp. 80–82.

58. Bob White, letter, *New Republic* 102 (Feb. 12, 1940), p. 215. *Down Beat*, Aug. 1939, p. 10; March 15, 1944, p. 10; Nov. 18, 1946, p. 10.

59. In "American Jazz Criticism, 1914–1940," Welburn offers a brief but helpful study of the struggles of writers in the 1920s and 1930s to develop a language and method for jazz criticism. Unfortunately, he does little to contextualize the activities of this small community of writers and journalists within the larger cultural and social struggles taking place during

the swing era. Welburn does offer a useful sense of the internecine battles among competing writers and the publications that proliferated during this period.

60. James Lincoln Collier, *The Reception of Jazz in America: A New View* (New York: Institute for Studies in American Music, 1988), pp. 29–41.

61. Ibid., pp. 52–66. George Frazier, "Swing Critics," *Jazz Hot*, July 1936, p. 3.

62. *Down Beat*, Nov. 1, 1940, p. 6. Bob White, "Critics' Opinions Come 'A Dime a Dozen'!" *Music and Rhythm* 1 (April 1941), p. 55. *Down Beat*, Feb. 15, 1941, p. 8.

63. Carter quoted in "Do Critics Really Know What It's All About?" *Metronome* 53 (May 1937), p. 17. *Down Beat*, April 1939, pp. 4, 9; May 1939, p. 14.

64. *Down Beat*, Aug. 1938, p. 4. "Do Critics Really Know What It's All About?" p. 17.

65. "Do Critics Really Know What It's All About?" p. 17.

66. *Down Beat*, March 1939, p. 3; Feb. 15, 1941, p. 8. He was promptly reminded that his readers included people "who have had more education than you, whose reading is broader, and whose intellects are probably better, who could tear your pretentious little manifesto to shreds if they cared to take the time." White, "Critics' Opinions Come 'A Dime a Dozen'!" pp. 54–55.

67. *Down Beat*, Sept. 1939, p. 9; July 15, 1940, p. 6.

68. *Down Beat*, Jan. 15, 1940, p. 8; Aug. 1, 1940, p. 9.

69. Welburn, "American Jazz Criticism, 1914–1940," pp. 250–251.

70. Carl Cons, "What MUSIC and RHYTHM Stands For," *Music and Rhythm* 2 (May 1942), p. 49. John Hammond, "Why Has Benny Goodman Changed?" *Music and Rhythm* 2 (June 1942), pp. 13, 33.

71. Warren Susman, *Culture as History: The Transformation of American Society in the Twentieth Century* (New York: Pantheon, 1984), pp. 170–174.

72. Francis Newton [Eric Hobsbawm], *The Jazz Scene* (New York: Da Capo, 1975), p. 243.

3. The Incorporation of Swing

1. *New York Times*, Oct. 27, 1938, p. 1.

2. *Down Beat*, April 1938, p. 1; May 1938, p. 1; Chip Deffaa, *Swing Legacy* (Metuchen, N.J.: Institute for Jazz Studies, 1989), pp. 87–88. "Mowing Down Mendelssohn," *Newsweek* 14 (Sept. 18, 1939), p. 39. See also Gun-

ther Schuller, *The Swing Era: The Development of Jazz, 1930–1945* (New York: Oxford University Press, 1989), p. 297. This practice of adapting the classics extended back at least to the 1920s.

3. *New York Times*, Nov. 6, 1938, sec. 9, p. 12.
4. Ibid; *New York Times*, Oct. 30, 1938, sec. 9, pp. 7, 12.
5. *New York Times*, Oct. 30, 1938, sec. 9, p. 12.
6. "Takes a Stand on Swing," *Metronome* 55 (Jan. 1939), p. 39. *Down Beat*, April 1939, p. 23.
7. *New York Amsterdam News*, Dec. 28, 1940, p. 16. *Down Beat*, June 1937, p. 14.
8. Deffaa, *Swing Legacy*, pp. 87–88; Arnold Shaw, *52nd Street: The Street of Jazz* (New York: Da Capo, 1977), p. 98.
9. Thomas J. Hennessey, "From Jazz to Swing: Black Musicians and Their Music, 1917–1935" (Ph.D. diss., Northwestern University, 1973), p. 440.
10. Doron K. Antrim, ed., *Secrets of Dance Band Success* (New York: Famous Stars, 1936), p. 23.
11. Ibid., p. 22. *Down Beat*, March 1935, p. 1; Dec. 1936, p. 1.
12. Hennessey, "From Jazz to Swing," p. 491.
13. Artie Shaw with Bob Maxwell, "Music Is a Business," *Saturday Evening Post* 214 (Dec. 2, 1939), pp. 14–15, 66–68. For a more detailed indictment of the industry, see Shaw's *The Trouble with Cinderella: An Outline of Identity* (New York: Farrar, Straus and Young, 1952), pp. 256–261, 380–381, 385–387.
14. *Down Beat*, Dec. 15, 1939, pp. 1, 28. Quote from Rex Stewart, *Jazz Masters of the 30s* (New York: Da Capo, 1972), p. 23. Hennessey, "From Jazz to Swing," pp. 300–306; Brian Priestley, *Jazz on Record: A History* (New York: Billboard Books, 1991), pp. 40–42; Duke Ellington, *Music Is My Mistress* (Garden City, N.Y.: Doubleday, 1973), p. 77. For an account of a sideman who played with both Henderson and Ellington, see Rex Stewart, *Boy Meets Horn*, ed. Claire P. Gordon (Ann Arbor: University of Michigan Press, 1991), p. 119. On Mills and Ellington, see Barney Bigard, *With Louis and the Duke* (New York: Oxford University Press, 1986), pp. 48, 58–59.
15. Bigard, *With Louis and the Duke*, p. 52. "The Booking of Bands," *Metronome* 61 (Oct. 1945), pp. 18–22.
16. George T. Simon, *The Big Bands* (New York: Schirmer Books, 1981), p. 47; Woody Herman and Stuart Troup, *The Woodchopper's Ball: The Autobiography of Woody Herman* (New York: E. P. Dutton, 1990), pp. 28–29.
17. Maurice Zolotow, "Harlem's Great White Father," *Saturday Evening Post* 214 (Sept. 27, 1941), p. 37.

18. Leo Walker, *The Wonderful Era of the Great Dance Bands* (New York: Da Capo, 1990), p. 236. *Down Beat*, April 1936, p. 1. *Variety* survey reported in *Down Beat*, Jan. 1938, p. 6. *Down Beat*, Dec. 15, 1939, pp. 1, 28. Irving Kolodin, "The Dance Band Business: A Study in Black and White," *Harper's* 183 (June 1941), p. 72.

19. Simon, *The Big Bands*, p. 48. William S. Dutton, "We've Got Rhythm," *American Magazine* 119 (March 1935), p. 127. Lyric quoted in Kolodin, "Dance Band Business," p. 72.

20. *Down Beat*, Dec. 15, 1939, pp. 1, 28; Simon, *The Big Bands*, pp. 46–49; *Down Beat*, July 1938, p. 20.

21. For a detailed and well-illustrated account of such publicity stunts, see Walker, *The Wonderful Era*, pp. 249–269. For a first-person account by a press agent, see "How the P.A. Works on a Tour of One Nighters," *Metronome* 52 (May 1936), pp. 13, 26. See also Cab Calloway and Bryant Rollins, *Of Minnie the Moocher and Me* (New York: Crowell, 1976), p. 248.

22. Walker, *The Wonderful Era*, p. 236.

23. Reported in *Down Beat*, Jan. 1938, p. 6. Accurate data on industry earnings are difficult to obtain, especially since the boundaries between swing and other forms of popular music were indeterminate.

24. *Down Beat*, March 1935, p. 6. On the significance of radio in fostering musical exchanges between urban centers and the western "territories," see David W. Stowe, "Jazz in the West: Cultural Frontier and Region during the Swing Era," *Western Historical Quarterly* 23 (Feb. 1992), pp. 68–71.

25. Walker, *The Wonderful Era*, p. 217. Crosby's was one of the bands to rise suddenly that year. See Jack Mosher, "A Swing Band Is Born," *Collier's* 103 (May 20, 1939), p. 17.

26. Kolodin, "Dance Band Business," p. 76; "New King," *Time* 34 (Nov. 27, 1939), p. 56. Shaw, *Trouble with Cinderella*, pp. 128–129. Philip K. Eberly, *In the Air: America's Changing Tastes in Popular Music, 1920–1980* (New York: Hastings House, 1982), pp. 272–274.

27. Simon, *The Big Bands*, pp. 56–57; Walker, *The Wonderful Era*, pp. 169–170. Kolodin, "Dance Band Business," p. 79. *Down Beat*, July 1937, p. 8; April 1939, p. 10. For the impact of tobacco companies on radio broadcasting, see Eberly, *In the Air*, pp. 114–124.

28. *Down Beat*, Feb. 1, 1945, p. 10. George Simon, "Simon Sez," *Metronome* 61 (May 1945), p. 34.

29. Russell Sanjek, *American Popular Music and Its Business: The First Four Hundred Years*, vol. 3, *From 1900 to 1984* (New York: Oxford University Press, 1988), pp. 165–168, 176.

30. "ASCAP and BMI Explain Music War," *Metronome* 56 (Nov. 1940), p. 11; Minna Lederman, "Music and Monopoly," *The Nation* 151 (Dec. 29, 1940), pp. 655–656.

31. *Down Beat*, Nov. 1, 1940, p. 1. Sanjek, *American Popular Music*, p. 181. "More Light and Less Heat Can End This War," *Metronome* 56 (Nov. 1940), p. 11. *Down Beat*, Oct. 1, 1940, p. 10.

32. Simon, *The Big Bands*, pp. 61, 63; Deffaa, *Swing Legacy*, pp. 92–93. Sanjek, *American Popular Music*, p. 262.

33. Evan Eisenberg, *The Recording Angel: Explorations in Phonography* (New York: McGraw-Hill, 1987), pp. 31–32. Lawrence W. Levine, "The Folklore of Industrial Society: Popular Culture and Its Audience," *American Historical Review* 97 (Dec. 1992), pp. 1377–79, 1393–95. Eisenberg, *The Recording Angel*, pp. 73–74, 142–150, 158.

34. Estimates of record sales and industry earnings, which are imprecise for this period and vary by source, come from Sanjek, *American Popular Music*; and Walker, *The Wonderful Era*. Roland Gelatt, *The Fabulous Phonograph: From Tin Foil to High Fidelity* (Philadelphia: J. B. Lippincott, 1955), estimates sales slightly lower: 6 million in 1932, 33 million in 1938.

35. *Down Beat*, Aug. 1939, p. 4.

36. "Phonograph Boom," *Time* 34 (Sept. 4, 1939), p. 36; Barry Ulanov, "The Jukes Take Over Swing," *American Mercury* 51 (Oct. 1940), p. 176. Sanjek, *American Popular Music*, p. 145.

37. Sanjek, *American Popular Music*, p. 143.

38. Ulanov, "The Jukes," pp. 172–177.

39. Sanjek, *American Popular Music*, p. 170.

40. Ibid., pp. 143–144. Joseph Horowitz writes that the 1940 decision "eventually undermined both studio orchestras and the distinctive 'big bands'— appreciated by . . . composers if not by the music appreciators—radio had helped create"; Joseph Horowitz, *Understanding Toscanini: How He Became a American Culture-God and Helped Create a New Audience for Music* (New York: Alfred A. Knopf, 1987), p. 411.

41. Bernard B. Smith, "What's Petrillo Up To? The Fight against Canned Music, and a Possible Solution," *Harper's* 186 (Dec. 1942), pp. 90–95. John Hammond, "Petrillo Needs a Press Agent," *Music and Rhythm* 3 (Aug. 1942), pp. 8, 19, 31, 35; "Petriller-Diller!" *Metronome* 59 (Aug. 1943), p. 4; *Down Beat*, May 15, 1944, p. 10.

42. Simon, *The Big Bands*, p. 54. *Down Beat*, July 1, 1942, p. 10; Aug. 1, 1942, p. 10. *New York Amsterdam News*, July 18, 1942, p. 15. Sanjek, *American Popular Music*, p. 218.

43. Robert D. Leiter, *The Musicians and Petrillo* (New York: Octagon Books,

1974), p. 103. Kolodin, "Dance Band Business," p. 75; Andy Kirk, *Twenty Years on Wheels* (Ann Arbor: University of Michigan Press, 1989), pp. 63–64. Dizzy Gillespie and Al Fraser, *To Be, or Not . . . to Bop* (Garden City, N.Y.: Doubleday, 1979), pp. 139–140, 149. Leiter, *Musicians and Petrillo*, p. 103.

44. Hennessey, "From Jazz to Swing," pp. 287–289; 457–461. Hennessey overestimates the extent to which this professional ethic was universalized, as a reading of virtually any of the memoirs of swing-era musicians will confirm, but the general impulse is correct, perhaps more for black than for white bands. Irving Kolodin wrote in 1941 that "one would be hard pressed to form even a single complete hot band of college graduates," although a college background was more common among purveyors of more commercially oriented "sweet" swing. "The real sturdy stuff of jazz is produced by the men who have been gutter-rats in their time, out on their own at seventeen, clubbing round in night spots, honky-tonks, and gin-mills before they were old enough to vote." Again, this "sturdy stuff" was not the mainstay of swing orchestras. Kolodin, "Dance Band Business," p. 81–82.

45. Deffaa, *Swing Legacy*, p. 123. Arthur Rollini, *Thirty Years with the Big Bands* (Urbana: University of Illinois Press, 1987), p. 53. Deffaa, *Swing Legacy*, p. 161. On fines in the Calloway band, see Danny Barker, *A Life in Jazz* (New York: Oxford University Press, 1986), pp. 172–177. Joe Bookman's "One-Night Tour," *Collier's* 108 (Nov. 1, 1941), pp. 22–23, provides an evocative account of a week in the life of a struggling band, as do many musicians' memoirs.

46. "Wanted: Side-Men!" *Metronome* 55 (Sept. 1939), p. 26; "Don't Start a Band Now!" *Metronome* 55 (Oct. 1939), p. 20; *Down Beat*, May 15, 1941, p. 5.

47. Lewis A. Erenberg, "Things to Come: Swing Bands, Bebop, and the Rise of a Postwar Jazz Scene," in Lary May, ed., *Recasting America: Culture and Politics in the Age of Cold War* (Chicago: University of Chicago, 1989), pp. 235–236.

48. George T. Simon, *Glenn Miller and His Orchestra* (New York: T. Y. Crowell, 1974), p. 161.

49. For Miller's rise, see Simon, *Glenn Miller*, pp. 160–192; *Down Beat*, Feb. 1, 1940, p. 8; Sept. 15, 1940, p. 18; "New King," *Time* 34 (Nov. 27, 1939), p. 56; Kolodin, "Dance Band Business," pp. 78–79.

50. *Down Beat*, Feb. 1, 1940, p. 8.

51. Kolodin, "Dance Band Business," p. 78. Deffaa, *Swing Legacy*, pp. 118–125.

52. *Down Beat*, July 1938, p. 20.
53. *Down Beat*, Dec. 1, 1940, pp. 2, 23; Dec. 15, 1940, p. 5; *New York Amsterdam News*, Nov. 23, 1940, p. 16; Dec. 21, 1940, p. 20.
54. Hennessey, "From Jazz to Swing," pp. 442–445; Scott Knowles DeVeaux, "Jazz in Transition: Coleman Hawkins and Howard McGhee, 1935–1945" (Ph.D. diss., University of California at Berkeley, 1985), pp. 143–162.
55. *Down Beat*, Dec. 15, 1940, p. 1.
56. Elliott Grenard, "Being Ignored by Big-Money Radio Is Main Factor in Keeping Earnings Down," *PM*, Aug. 24, 1941; Kolodin, "Dance Band Business," pp. 79–80; *Down Beat*, Dec. 1, 1940, pp. 2, 23; DeVeaux, "Jazz in Transition," pp. 152–153. Fears that black bands would be unable to survive were belied by the unprecedented wartime success of ensembles led by Basie, Hampton, and others able to retain their personnel despite the war mobilization. See Count Basie as told to Albert Murray, *Good Morning Blues: The Autobiography of Count Basie* (New York: Random House, 1985), pp. 254–256; *New York Amsterdam News*, Jan. 17, 1942, p. 16.
57. Gerald Early, *Tuxedo Junction: Essays on American Culture* (New York: Ecco, 1989), pp. 280–281. Early is responding to the simplistic account offered by Amiri Baraka (LeRoi Jones) in *Blues People* (New York: Morrow Quill, 1963). Writes Gunther Schuller: "The question of what *is* black and what *is* white in jazz, and what influences affected which musicians and when, are enormously complex ones, generally defying detailed precise answers—that is, beyond the uncontestable reality that jazz originated with black Americans and that all its major developments and innovations have derived from them. It is when one probes beneath that general truth that one may encounter vexing and virtually unanswerable questions of artistic pedigree and authorship." Schuller, *The Swing Era*, p. 729.
58. Hennessey, "From Jazz to Swing," pp. 224–226, 385; Deffaa, *Swing Legacy*, p. 252. Rex Stewart recalled the "amazed, angry, morose, and bewildered" reaction of the Fletcher Henderson band, riding high in 1927 and regarded as the "world's greatest dance orchestra," as they were definitively "cut" on their home turf, Roseland, by a "Johnny-come-lately white band from out in the sticks." "The facts were that we simply could not compete with Jean Goldkette's Victor Recording Orchestra. Their arrangements were too imaginative and their rhythm too strong, what with Steve Brown slapping hell out of that bass fiddle and Frankie Trumbauer's inspiring leadership as he stood in front wailing on his C-melody saxophone"; Stewart, *Jazz Masters of the 30s*, pp. 11–12.

59. Kirk, *Twenty Years on Wheels*, pp. 83, 57. DeVeaux, "Jazz in Transition," p. 149.

60. Roy Porter with David Keller, *There and Back: The Roy Porter Story* (Baton Rouge: Louisiana State University Press, 1991), pp. 29–30.

61. Stewart, *Boy Meets Horn*, pp. 113–114. See also Stewart, "The Business of Recording," in *Jazz Masters of the 1930s*, pp. 28–36.

62. Ironically, the tune, adapted from an unsuccessful stage show that Kirk heard in Kansas City, was originally titled "A Slave Song"; Kirk, *Twenty Years on Wheels*, pp. 84–87.

63. Barker, *A Life in Jazz*, pp. 157–162; Priestley, *Jazz on Record*, p. 22. Basie, *Good Morning Blues*, pp. 167–168; Priestley, *Jazz on Record*, p. 65. Ironically, a similar crisis occurred when Basie left Columbia for RCA Victor. See John Hammond with Irving Townsend, *John Hammond on Record: An Autobiography* (New York: Ridge Press, 1977), pp. 275–276.

64. Lionel Hampton with James Haskins, *Hamp: An Autobiography* (New York: Warner Books, 1989), p. 75. See also interview with Art Blakey in Robert D. Rusch, *Jazztalk: The Cadence Interview* (Secaucus, N.J.: Lyle Stuart, 1984), p. 118. *Down Beat*, Aug. 1937, p. 2. Ira Gitler, *Swing to Bop: An Oral History of the Transition in Jazz in the 1940s* (New York: Oxford University Press, 1985), pp. 14–15. Whitney Balliett, *American Musicians: Fifty-six Portraits in Jazz* (New York: Oxford University Press, 1986), pp. 88–89.

65. Nat Shapiro and Nat Hentoff, eds., *Hear Me Talkin' to Ya: The Story of Jazz as Told by the Men Who Made It* (New York: Rinehart, 1955), 326–327. Balliett, *American Musicians*, p. 89. Gitler, *Swing to Bop*, pp. 13, 14; Garvin Bushell with Mark Tucker, *Jazz from the Beginning* (Ann Arbor: University of Michigan Press, 1988), p. 93. Kirk, *Twenty Years on Wheels*, p. 98.

Oral histories and memoirs of swing-era musicians provide a nearly inexhaustible supply of such war stories, particularly from Ellington and Calloway alumni, who have been more thoroughly recorded than others. In particular see Gitler, *Swing to Bop*, pp. 9–31; Shapiro and Hentoff, *Hear Me Talkin'*, pp. 313–332; Bushell, *Jazz from the Beginning*, pp. 90–96; Hampton, *Hamp*, pp. 62–65; Kirk, *Twenty Years on Wheels*, pp. 87–114; Dicky Wells as told to Stanley Dance, *The Night People: Reminiscences of a Jazzman* (Boston: Crescendo Books, 1971), pp. 41–54; Barker, *A Life in Jazz*, pp. 163–169. Earl Hines, who first toured the South in 1931, and Art Blakey, who toured with the Henderson band in the late 1930s, both considered themselves precursors to the Freedom Riders of the early 1960s. See Rusch, *Jazztalk*, p. 118; Balliett, *American Musicians*, pp. 88–89.

66. Billie Holiday with William Dufty, *Lady Sings the Blues* (New York: Penguin, 1984), p. 81. *New York Amsterdam News*, Oct. 29, 1949, p. 1; Holiday, *Lady Sings*, p. 61. *Down Beat*, Sept. 1, 1940, p. 1.
67. *Down Beat*, Dec. 15, 1943, p. 3. Sanjek, *American Popular Music*, p. 140. "John Hammond Says," *Music and Rhythm* 2 (May 1942), p. 22.
68. "Benny Goodman was no civil rights activist," recalled Lionel Hampton. "He didn't talk much about racism. His whole concentration was on music, but it galled him that something as petty as race prejudice could mess up the music he wanted to hear and play"; Hampton, *Hamp*, p. 65.
69. Holiday, *Lady Sings*, pp. 70–71; *Down Beat*, Oct. 1, 1941, p. 2; Dec. 15, 1941, p. 1. For a sobering account of racism on the part of both patrons and musicians, see Roy Eldridge, "Jim Crow Is Killing Jazz," *Negro Digest*, Oct. 1950, pp. 44–49; quotation from p. 46.
70. *Down Beat*, June 1938, p. 5; Oct. 15, 1939, pp. 1, 10. Tellingly, none of these musicians allowed their names to be printed.
71. Simon, *Glenn Miller*, pp. 182–184. Stewart, *Boy Meets Horn*, p. 137. Jefferson quoted in Dempsey J. Travis, *An Autobiography of Black Jazz* (Chicago: Urban Research Institute, 1983), p. 403. Bill Coleman, *Trumpet Story* (Boston: Northeastern University Press, 1991), p. 96.
72. Salary figure from Stewart, *Boy Meets Horn*, p. 25; "Cootie and the King," *Metronome* 56 (Nov. 1940), p. 22. Another account states that Williams left Ellington, who was paying $150 a week, for Goodman's offer of $200. "The Press Agent's Mind at Work," *Metronome* 61 (March 1945), p. 24. While unofficial salary figures are available, the ranges for both white and black bands are so broad, and changed so readily in response to the market, that direct comparisons are difficult. For example, sidemen in the Woody Herman band were paid fifty dollars a week at Roseland in 1936, while Fletcher Henderson's top players received double that salary in the early 1930s. Herman, *Woodchopper's Ball*, p. 23; Stewart, *Boy Meets Horn*, p. 131. But according to the unanimous testimony of musicians and writers, among comparable bands in comparable situations, whites were routinely better paid.
73. *New York Amsterdam News*, Nov. 23, 1940, p. 14; *Down Beat*, Dec. 1, 1943, p. 11.
74. Cornel West quoted in Andrew Ross, ed., *Universal Abandon? The Politics of Postmodernism* (Minneapolis: University of Minnesota Press, 1989), p. 278.
75. *New York Amsterdam News*, Oct. 29, 1938, p. 20. Shaw, *52nd Street*, p. 127. For a perceptive contemporary discussion of black influences on white

popular music, see William Grant Still, "The Men behind American Music," *The Crisis* 51 (Jan. 1944), pp. 12–15.

76. *Down Beat*, Dec. 15, 1943, p. 3; Feb. 15, 1944, p. 1. Bigard never mentions the incident in his memoir. Gitler, *Swing to Bop*, pp. 308–309. *Down Beat*, Dec. 1, 1944, p. 6, reported that the studio had requested that Kessel be removed from the band.

77. See Milton Mezzrow and Raymond Wolfe, *Really the Blues* (New York: Random House, 1946); and Andrew Ross's discussion in *No Respect: Intellectuals and Popular Culture* (New York: Routledge, 1989), pp. 79–81.

78. Dorothy Baker, *Young Man with a Horn* (New York: Readers Club, 1943), p. 131. Hampton, *Hamp*, p. 85. Melvin Patrick Ely, *The Adventures of Amos'n'Andy* (New York: Free Press, 1991), pp. 60–63.

79. Hampton, *Hamp*, pp. 28–29. Ironically, Hampton appears to have been a great favorite of Hollywood whites. "They consider him one of the finest examples of young Negro manhood; compliment his business acumen, his deportment at all times, and his passionate concern for the advancement of his people"; *New York Amsterdam News*, Nov. 23, 1940, p. 17. For a book-length study of jazz in California with some attention to social conditions, see Ted Gioia, *West Coast Jazz: Modern Jazz in California* (New York: Oxford University Press, 1992).

80. Just as the failure of the television version of "Amos'n'Andy" was due not only to changes in the self-conception and cultural authority of African-Americans between 1931 and 1951 but also to the fact that seeing characters presented difficulties not apparent in a purely aural medium; Ely, *Adventures of Amos'n'Andy*, pp. 203–244.

81. For a brilliant analysis of the ideological work performed by blackface and Vitaphone in *The Jazz Singer*, see Michael Rogin, "Blackface, White Noise: The Jewish Jazz Singer Finds His Voice," *Critical Inquiry* 18 (Spring 1992), pp. 417–453.

82. Leiter, *Musicians and Petrillo*, pp. 56–57; Hampton, *Hamp*, p. 49.

83. Ely, *Adventures of Amos'n'Andy*, pp. 167–168. Frank Norris, "The Music Goes 'Round and Around," *New Republic* 85 (Jan. 29, 1936), p. 335.

84. Simon, *Glenn Miller*, p. 252.

85. *Down Beat*, Dec. 1938, p. 4. Simon, *The Big Bands*, p. 66.

86. *Down Beat*, Dec. 1938, p. 4; April 15, 1941, p. 13; Sept. 15, 1941, p. 10; Aug. 1, 1943, p. 10; Sept. 1, 1944, p. 10; Oct. 15, 1943, p. 6. Barry Ulanov, "The Film, Phony and Otherwise," *Metronome* 59 (July 1943), p. 15. For Hammond's disillusionment with the film directed by William Dieterle and released as "Syncopation," see "John Hammond Says," *Music and Rhythm* 2 (July 1942), p. 30.

87. *Down Beat*, Oct. 15, 1943, p. 6. Simon, *The Big Bands*, p. 66.
88. Dalton Trumbo, "Blackface, Hollywood Style," *The Crisis* 52 (Dec. 1945), p. 366. *New York Amsterdam News*, March 27, 1943, p. 16; Oct. 7, 1944, p. 8-B. Barry Ulanov, "Cabin in Sky Just Gets By," *Metronome* 59 (March 1943), p. 13. *New York Amsterdam News*, July 22, 1944, p. 8-B. For hopeful reports on the status of blacks in films, see *New York Amsterdam News*, Jan. 9, 1943, p. 15; April 10, 1943, p. 17; June 12, 1943, p. 17. Thomas Cripps provides a useful analysis of race in wartime movies in "Racial Ambiguities in American Propaganda Movies," in K. R. M. Short, ed., *Film and Radio Propaganda in World War II* (Knoxville: University of Tennessee Press, 1983), pp. 125–145.
89. *Down Beat*, July 29, 1946, p. 10.
90. *Down Beat*, Aug. 15, 1943, p. 7. *Metronome*'s review was somewhat more generous, placing *Stormy Weather* "way ahead of the other scrawny attempts to picture the band business and the allied arts and crafts"; Barry Ulanov, "The Films," *Metronome* 59 (July 1943), p. 15.
91. "New Orleans," *Ebony* 2 (Feb. 1947), pp. 26–27. Bigard, *With Louis and the Duke*, pp. 92–95; Holiday, *Lady Sings*, pp. 119–122. See also Charles Emge's lukewarm review in *Down Beat*, May 21, 1947, p. 11.
92. Holiday, *Lady Sings*, pp. 93–94. Ellington, *Music Is My Mistress*, pp. 239–241; *Down Beat*, June 15, 1942, p. 6; Frank Brady, *Citizen Welles: A Biography of Orson Welles* (New York: Scribner's, 1989), pp. 333–334; Charles Higham, *Orson Welles: The Rise and Fall of an American Genius* (New York: St. Martin's, 1985), pp. 181, 189, 205, 207; Bigard, *With Louis and the Duke*, pp. 85–86.

4. The Conscription of Swing

1. *Down Beat*, Dec. 15, 1944, p. 10.
2. Philip Gleason, "World War II and the Development of American Studies," *American Quarterly* 36 (1984), pp. 343–358. Gleason's "Americans All: World War II and the Shaping of American Identity," *Review of Politics* 43 (Oct. 1981), pp. 483–518, highlights the ambiguities of and tension between cultural pluralism and assimilation, between ethnicity and the ideology of Americanism, during this period. Koussevitzky quoted in *New York Times*, Jan. 17, 1943, sec. 8, p. 7.
3. *New York Times*, June 19, 1941, p. 23. *Down Beat* Jan. 1, 1943, p. 1; *New York Daily Worker*, Sept. 24, 1942.
4. Quoted in Sherna Berger Gluck, *Rosie the Riveter Revisited: Women, the War, and Social Change* (Boston: Twayne Publishers, 1987), p. 10.

5. For the argument that war forced the participation of women in the workplace and that public attitudes eventually changed as a result, see William H. Chafe, *The American Woman: Her Changing Social, Economic, and Political Role* (New York: Oxford University Press, 1972); Gluck, *Rosie the Riveter Revisited,* pp. 259–270. This argument has been challenged by Leila J. Rupp, *Mobilizing Women for War: German and American Propaganda, 1939–1945* (Princeton: Princeton University Press, 1978), pp. 137–166; 176–177. See also Karen Anderson, *Wartime Women: Sex Roles, Family Relations, and the Status of Women during World War II* (Westport, Conn.: Greenwood Press, 1981), esp. pp. 1–11; Maureen Honey, *Creating Rosie the Riveter: Class, Gender, and Propaganda during World War II* (Amherst: University of Massachusetts Press, 1984). For additional interpretations, see D'Ann Campbell, *Women at War with America: Private Lives in a Patriotic Era* (Cambridge, Mass.: Harvard University Press, 1984); Susan Hartman, *The Home Front and Beyond: American Women in the 1940s* (Boston: Twayne Publishers, 1982).

6. *Down Beat,* Jan. 1, 1942, p. 1, 22; Feb. 15, 1942, p. 2; March 15, 1942, p. 1; May 1, 1942, pp. 1, 21; May 15, 1942, pp. 1, 21; Oct. 15, 1942, p. 1; May 1, 1944, p. 1; March 15, 1945, p. 1. John Hammond, Dave Dexter, and Elliott Grennard, "Music Faces Its Crisis," *Music and Rhythm* 3 (Aug. 1942), p. 12.

7. Pvt. Frank S. Hoerger, "Musicians for Morale!" *Metronome* 60 (Jan. 1944), p. 44. *Down Beat,* Jan. 15, 1944, pp. 1, 19; May 1, 1945, p. 7.

8. *Down Beat,* Jan. 1, 1942, pp. 1, 22; Jan. 15, 1942, p. 2; July 1, 1942, p. 7; Dec. 15, 1943, p. 6.

9. *Down Beat,* Feb. 15, 1943, p. 1. "Classico, Psycho, Educator Rebuke Raving Rodzinski," *Metronome* 60 (March 1944), p. 8.

10. *Down Beat,* July 1, 1943, p. 10. "Classico, Psycho, Educator Rebuke Raving Rodzinski." For a discussion of wartime strains on the family, see Richard Polenberg, *War and Society: The United States, 1941–1945* (Philadelphia: J. B. Lippincott, 1972), pp. 145–150.

11. *New York Post,* Oct. 14, 1942.

12. *Down Beat,* March 15, 1943, p. 12; Jan. 1, 1942, p. 10; April 1, 1943, p. 21. Mike Daniels, "Musician of the Year," *Metronome* 60 (Jan. 1944), pp. 18–20; *Down Beat,* Dec. 1, 1943, p. 15; Dec. 15, 1943, pp. 1, 29. Shaw suffered an exhaustion-induced breakdown following the tour. See Artie Shaw, *The Trouble with Cinderella* (New York: Farrar, Straus and Young, 1952), pp. 372–374.

13. *Down Beat,* Jan. 15, 1942, pp. 1, 20; Dec. 15, 1942, p. 1; Nov. 15, 1943, p. 15; March 1, 1943, p. 4.

14. Woody Herman and Stuart Troup, *The Woodchopper's Ball: The Autobiography of Woody Herman* (New York: E. P. Dutton, 1990), pp. 29–30. *New York Amsterdam News*, Nov. 14, 1942, p. 16. Buck Clayton assisted by Nancy Miller Elliott, *Buck Clayton's Jazz World* (New York: Oxford University Press, 1987), pp. 114–116. Dizzy Gillespie and Al Fraser, *To Be, or Not . . . to Bop* (Garden City, N.Y.: Doubleday, 1979), p. 120.

15. *Down Beat*, Dec. 15, 1943, p. 1; April 1, 1943, p. 10; Sept. 1, 1943, p. 10; April 15, 1943, p. 10. As Robert Westbrook has shown, such private obligations—to buddies, family, American womanhood, the American Way of Life—were crucial to mobilizing support for the war in lieu of unselfish obligation to the state, which the United States was unable to command. Robert B. Westbrook, " 'I Want a Girl, Just Like the Girl That Married Harry James': American Women and the Problem of Political Obligation in World War II," *American Quarterly* 42 (Dec. 1990), pp. 587–614.

16. *Down Beat*, April 15, 1945, p. 10; Jan. 1, 1944, p. 7. "Letters from the Editor," *Metronome* 59 (Dec. 1943), p. 4; "Gripers are Snipers!" *Metronome* 61 (Feb. 1945), p. 5. *Down Beat*, Feb. 15, 1945, p. 13.

17. "War Producing Specialized Songs, Says U.S.O. Music Head," *Metronome* 59 (May 1943), p. 25. Sanjek concurs: "Unlike the home front, where motorized vehicles languished because of gasoline rationing and rubber shortages, and the buses on which name bands had been traveling were confiscated for the war effort, everything used by the armed forces was mechanized, and the march rhythm sought by the OWI [Office of War Information] was out of place"; Russell Sanjek, *American Popular Music and Its Business*, vol. 3, *From 1900 to 1984* (New York: Oxford University Press, 1988), p. 251.

18. *Down Beat*, Feb. 1, 1943, p. 17. *New York Times*, Jan. 13, 1943, p. 17; "War Producing Specialized Songs," *Metronome* 59 (May 1943), p. 25.

19. *New York Times*, Jan. 13, 1943, p. 17. *Down Beat*, May 1, 1942, p. 10.

20. *Down Beat*, March 15, 1945, p. 10. Hammond, Dexter, and Grennard, "Music Faces Its Crisis," p. 46. OWI head quoted in Sanjek, *American Popular Music*, p. 251. *Down Beat*, Dec. 15, 1942, p. 34; Feb. 15, 1942, p. 11; Jan. 1, 1942, p. 2.

21. *Down Beat*, Feb. 15, 1944, p. 13; July 15, 1945, p. 11.

22. Philip K. Eberly, *Music in the Air: America's Changing Tastes in Popular Music, 1920–1980* (New York: Hastings House, 1982), p. 74. *Down Beat*, Nov. 15, 1944, p. 5; Dec. 15, 1943, p. 29.

23. Barry Ulanov, "V Discs: A great army service waxes sweet and hot for the boys in khaki," *Metronome* 60 (May 1944), p. 20; *Down Beat*, Oct. 15, 1944, p. 13; Feb. 1, 1944, p. 16; July 15, 1945, p. 11. Early in the war, nearly the

entire recording industry had formed Records for Our Fighting Men, Inc., to collect old records and send new recordings to U.S. forces; *Down Beat*, June 15, 1942, p. 1.

24. *Down Beat*, March 15, 1944, p. 3; Oct. 1, 1945, p. 2. *Philadelphia Inquirer*, Jan. 15, 1946. *Down Beat*, Dec. 15, 1944, pp. 1, 15.

25. Ray McKinley, " 'Ooh, What You Said, Tex!' " *Metronome* 60 (March 1947), pp. 39–40. *Down Beat*, Nov. 1, 1944, p. 10.

26. "Miller Over There," *Metronome* 60 (Sept. 1944), p. 26; "Miller a Killer!" *Metronome* 60 (Nov. 1944), p. 15. That *Metronome* printed the critical notice apparently sent Miller into a cold fury. George T. Simon, *Glenn Miller and His Orchestra* (New York: T. Y. Crowell, 1974), pp. 382–387.

27. Neil A. Wynn, *The Afro-American and the Second World War* (London: Paul Elek, 1976), pp. 88–89. Gunther Schuller contends that swing split into three factions during the war: rhythm and blues, modern jazz, and vocalist-dominated commercial dance music. Gunther Schuller, *The Swing Era: The Development of Jazz, 1930–1945* (New York: Oxford University Press, 1989), pp. 390–391.

28. *Down Beat*, Oct. 15, 1943, p. 10; Oct. 15, 1944, p. 2.

29. Band member quoted in Alice C. Browning, *Lionel Hampton's Swing Book* (Chicago: Negro Story Press, 1946), pp. 81–82. Bud Freeman as told to Robert Wolf, *Crazeology: The Autobiography of a Chicago Jazzman* (Urbana: University of Illinois Press, 1989), pp. 60–61.

30. See Studs Terkel, *"The Good War": An Oral History of World War Two* (New York: Pantheon, 1984); and the essays collected in "A Round Table: The Living and Reliving of World War II," *Journal of American History* 77 (Sept. 1990), pp. 553–593, particularly John Hope Franklin's "Their War and Mine" and David Brion Davis' "World War II and Memory." For a good overview of wartime race relations, see Polenberg, *War and Society*, pp. 99–130, and John M. Blum, *V Was for Victory* (New York: Harcourt Brace Jovanovich, 1975), pp. 182–220. For race relations in the wartime entertainment industry, see Wynn, *The Afro-American and the Second World War*, pp. 79–98; and Alan Pomerance, *Repeal of the Blues* (Secaucus, N.J.: Citadel Press, 1988), pp. 165–183.

31. *New York Amsterdam News*, March 10, 1945, p. 7-B.

32. *New York Amsterdam News*, May 22, 1943, p. 14; "Nazis Okay, Negroes Not, Lena Leaves Army Camp," *Metronome* 61 (Feb. 1945), p. 11; "Union Nixes USO Show," *Metronome* 60 (Jan. 1944), p. 10.

33. *Down Beat*, Nov. 1, 1942, p. 2; Jan. 1981, pp. 17–19, which includes

excerpts from Young's military transcript. For different views on whether these experiences permanently scarred Young musically or personally see Clayton, *Buck Clayton's Jazz World*, p. 119; Whitney Balliett, *American Musicians: Fifty-six Portraits in Jazz* (New York: Oxford University Press, 1986), p. 238; Harry "Sweets" Edison quoted in Fred Hall, *More Dialogues in Swing* (Ventura: Pathfinder Publishing of California, 1991), p. 29. Young's mistreatment at the hands of the military was thinly fictionalized in the film *'Round Midnight* (1986).

34. *New York Amsterdam News*, Sept. 26, 1942, p. 17.
35. Clayton, *Buck Clayton's Jazz World*, pp. 117–128.
36. John Hammond with Irving Townsend, *John Hammond on Record* (New York: Ridge Press, 1977), pp. 249–261; quotations from pp. 247, 269.
37. For an insightful discussion of these factors, see Scott DeVeaux, "Jazz in Transition: Coleman Hawkins and Howard McGhee, 1935–1945" (Ph.D. diss., University of California at Berkeley, 1985), pp. 217–243.
38. *Down Beat*, July 15, 1942, pp. 1, 8; Aug. 1, 1942, p. 23; Sept. 15, 1942, p. 15; Feb. 1, 1943, p. 2.
39. *New York Amsterdam News*, Sept. 11, 1943, p. 12-A; Aug. 12, 1944, p. 11-A. The anthem's talismanic quality was first demonstrated in the early hours of the war. Bandleader Jimmy Dorsey was broadcasting a radio program when news of the Japanese attack on Pearl Harbor broke. During the one-hour program, Dorsey was interrupted by news bulletins forty-two times; one tune alone was interrupted six times. Finally Dorsey departed from the arranged repertoire and led his band in "The Star-Spangled Banner"; this time he was not interrupted; *Down Beat*, Jan. 1, 1942, p. 1.
40. Barry Ulanov, "California Melodies," *Metronome* 60 (July 1944), p. 17.
41. *Down Beat*, March 1, 1943, p. 6; April 15, 1943, p. 1; Jan. 15, 1944, p. 15; "Hollywood Canteen," *Metronome* 59 (Dec. 1943), p. 12.
42. *New York Amsterdam News*, Jan. 9, 1943. *Down Beat*, March 1, 1943, p. 6; Oct. 1, 1943, p. 10; "An Ugly Story," *Metronome* 59 (Nov. 1943), p. 4. *Down Beat*, March 1, 1945, p. 6; Sept. 1, 1945, p. 6; Dec. 1, 1945, p. 6.
43. Chester B. Himes, "Zoot Riots Are Race Riots," *The Crisis* 50 (July 1943), pp. 200–201, 222. *Down Beat*, Aug. 1, 1944, p. 1; on scapegoating, see Irving Kolodin, "The Dance Band Business: A Study in Black and White," *Harper's* 179 (Sept. 1939), p. 80. *Down Beat*, Oct. 1, 1943, 10.
44. *Down Beat*, May 15, 1943, p. 1; Nov. 15, 1943, p. 2. Arnold Shaw, *52nd Street: The Street of Jazz* (New York: Da Capo, 1977); Sammy Price and Caroline Richmond, eds., *What Do They Want? A Jazz Autobiography*

(Urbana: University of Illinois Press, 1990), p. 55; *Down Beat*, June 15, 1944, p. 1; Nov. 15, 1945, p. 1.

45. *New York Amsterdam News*, July 15, 1944, p. 12-A; July 22, 1944, p. 11-A; July 22, 1944, p. 1-A.

46. *Down Beat*, June 15, 1944, p. 1; Nov. 15, 1945, p. 1; *New York Amsterdam News*, Nov. 10, 1945, p. 1; July 29, 1944, p. 1-A. Gillespie, *To Be . . .*, pp. 210–211.

47. *New York Amsterdam News*, Nov. 13, 1943, p. 8-B; Nov. 20, 1943, p. 8-B; May 12, 1945, p. 8-B.

48. *Down Beat*, Sept. 15, 1945, p. 10; Dec. 1, 1945, p. 10. *New York Amsterdam News*, July 1, 1944, pp. 1-A, 5-A; July 15, 1944, p. 10-A.

49. "John Hammond Says," *Music and Rhythm* 2 (March 1942), p. 22. *Down Beat*, Oct. 15, 1944, p. 1; Oct. 1, 1944, p. 12. "Why?" *Metronome* 59 (March 1943), p. 34; "Editorial," *Metronome* 59 (July 1943), p. 5. Andy Kirk, *Twenty Years on Wheels* (Ann Arbor: University of Michigan Press, 1989), pp. 107–109. *New York Amsterdam News*, June 30, 1945, p. 1; May 12, 1945, p. 8-B. *Down Beat*, Nov. 15, 1945, p. 1.

50. For other arguments on the connection between swing, the war, and a new black politics, see Lewis Erenberg, "Things to Come: Swing Bands, Bebop, and the Rise of a Postwar Jazz Scene," in Lary May, ed., *Recasting America: Culture and Politics in the Age of Cold War* (Chicago: University of Chicago Press, 1989). pp. 235–238; Eric Lott, "Double V, Double-Time: Bebop's Politics of Style," *Callaloo* 11 (Summer 1988), pp. 597–599. Both arguments exaggerate the political content of bop, as will be shown in the next chapter.

51. *New York Amsterdam News*, Jan. 24, 1942, p. 17. John Desmond, "Making Catnip for the Hepcats," *New York Times Magazine*, June 20, 1943, p. 16. *Down Beat*, Sept. 15, 1943, p. 10. Describing how bands circumvented Office of Price Administration wage-stabilization guidelines by reclassifying sidemen, *Metronome* called on sidemen to "pay more attention to conscience" and the bandleader "to use his head as well as his heart" by not bidding up musicians' salaries to outrageous levels; "Musicians: Have a Head as Well as a Heart!" *Metronome* 59 (Jan. 1943), p. 42.

52. See Linda Dahl, *Stormy Weather: The Music and Lives of a Century of Jazz-women* (New York: Limelight Editions, 1989), esp. pp. 35–93. *Down Beat*, Feb. 1, 1942, p. 8.

53. Dahl, *Stormy Weather*, p. 39. See also Ellen Koskoff, ed., *Women and Music in Cross-Cultural Perspective* (Westport, Conn.: Greenwood Press, 1987), particularly Koskoff's "An Introduction to Women, Music, and Culture," pp. 1–23.

54. "Male Throb Dept," *Metronome* 59 (Aug. 1943), p. 24. The editors complied with the request. See also *Down Beat*, Feb. 1, 1942, p. 10.

55. "Rita Rio and Her All-Girl Orchestra," *Swing* 1 (Oct. 1938), p. 17. *Down Beat*, March 15, 1943, p. 12. Maurice Zolotow, "Phil Spitalny and His All-Girl Orchestra," *Swing* 1 (Aug. 1938), p. 19.

56. *New York Amsterdam News*, Sept. 14, 1943, p. 13-A. *Down Beat*, March 15, 1943, p. 12.

57. *Down Beat*, Feb. 1938, p. 4.

58. *Down Beat*, March 15, 1943, p. 12; Feb. 1, 1942, p. 8.

59. *Down Beat*, Feb. 1938, p. 4; Feb. 1, 1942, p. 8. Polemical exchanges of opinions on the ability of women to play swing long predated the destabilizing impact of wartime conscription. In 1936 *Metronome* provided space for Gypsie Cooper, first alto saxophonist with the Spitalny orchestra, to argue that women could in fact "swing," whatever that word was taken to mean. "It seems strange for me, a woman—and a lady, I hope—to inject my voice into this man's magazine," began her typically apologetic piece. "But the editor is responsible—blame him." Citing a trend toward women's "seeking independence rather than romance" and a list of names of female contributors to music, Cooper acknowledged that the double standard that made audiences more inclined to judge harshly minor squeaks or note cracks made by women undermined the self-confidence requisite for swing. She counseled prospective women swing musicians to "analyze yourself," prepare to face a sexual double standard, and avoid romance "at least until you have made the grade." Ironically, Cooper's piece appeared next to an article titled "A Good Musician Is Not Born but Made"; Gypsie Cooper, "Can Women Swing?" *Metronome* 52 (Sept. 1936), p. 30.

60. *New York Amsterdam News*, Jan. 31, 1942, p. 16, for history of the Sweethearts. *New York Amsterdam News*, March 1, 1945, p. 5-B. "Sweethearts of Rhythm: Not Slick but Kicks," *Metronome* 59 (Feb. 1943), p. 19; "Sweethearts of Rhythm: Without Anna-mation," *Metronome* 60 (March 1944), p. 33. On the Feather recording sessions of women (of which he was quite proud), see *New York Amsterdam News*, March 31, 1945, p. 9-B; Leonard Feather, *The Jazz Years: Earwitness to an Era* (New York: Da Capo, 1987), pp. 127–143, 159–164.

61. *Down Beat*, Oct. 15, 1939, p. 18. On environmental factors, see Michael J. Budds, "African-American Women in Blues and Jazz," in Karin Pendle, ed., *Women & Music* (Bloomington: Indiana University Press, 1991), pp. 282–297.

62. Dahl, *Stormy Weather*, 124. *Down Beat*, Feb. 1, 1942, p. 6; Oct. 15, 1939, p. 18. "Simon Sez," *Metronome* 59 (May 1943), p. 6. *Down Beat*, Dec. 15,

1944, p. 4. George T. Simon, *The Big Bands* (New York: Schirmer Books, 1981), pp. 33–39; Leo Walker, *The Wonderful Era of the Great Dance Bands* (New York: Da Capo, 1990), pp. 285–294.

63. *Down Beat*, Sept. 15, 1942, p. 23.
64. *Down Beat*, June 1, 1943, p. 10.
65. *Down Beat*, Nov. 15, 1944, p. 2; Aug. 1, 1944, p. 10; March 15, 1944, p. 1.
66. *Down Beat*, July 1, 1940, p. 7; Oct. 1, 1944, p. 2; Nov. 1, 1944, p. 1; Aug. 26, 1946, p. 4. Michael H. Kater, *Different Drummers: Jazz in the Culture of Nazi Germany* (New York: Oxford University Press, 1992). *Down Beat*, Nov. 1, 1945, p. 10; Jan. 14, 1946, p. 12.
67. *Down Beat*, May 1, 1945, p. 11; Oct. 1, 1944, p. 1; Aug. 1, 1944, p. 11; July 15, 1944, p. 1.

5. Swing and Its Discontents

1. Steve Roper, United Press column, May 1947, Benny Goodman Papers, MSS 53, YML. "How Long Will Swing Last?" *Metronome* 54 (March 1938), p. 9; *New York Times*, Aug. 7, 1938, sec. 9, p. 8. When *Newsweek* asked various bandleaders and music critics their prognosis for swing in 1938, Paul Whiteman, Tommy Dorsey, Hal Kemp, and Shep Fields were among those who felt swing was increasing in popularity, while Kay Kyser and Al Donahue cited evidence that public interest was waning. "Swing Is On the Way, but Up or Down? Embattled Experts Can't Agree," *Newsweek* 12 (July 25, 1938), p. 26.
2. *New York Times*, Sept. 14, 1939, p. 19; May 2, 1939, p. 22.
3. *Down Beat*, June 15, 1944, p. 4.
4. Associated Press column, May 22, 1947, Goodman Papers, YML.
5. The wartime recording ban, followed by another strike during 1948, had frustrated the record-buying audience, which was further discouraged by the struggle between Columbia and RCA Victor over recording technology. The increasingly Hollywood-dominated music industry apparently preferred to promote nonswing music. Many musicians blamed the wartime entertainment tax imposed on dancing. Disc jockeys, the latest purveyors of "canned music," were accused of depriving musicians of work and royalties while fueling public adulation for singers like Frank Sinatra, Dinah Shore, Perry Como, Dick Haymes, and Mel Torme. Some felt that the songs available to big bands were inferior to their 1930s repertoire. Others believed a pervasive kind of cultural change was responsible for

swing's hardship. Americans seemed anxious and neurotic in the postwar years, not the proper frame of mind associated with swing, and many were turning inward, focusing on careers and families. Television represented a beguiling alternative to the public culture of dance and concert halls.

6. "B. G. and Bebop," *Newsweek* 32 (Dec. 27, 1948), p. 66.

7. The literature on mass and popular culture, technology, and the market is vast. For its roots, see Theodor Adorno, "On the Fetish-Character in Music and the Regression of Listening," in Andrew Arato and Eike Gebhardt, eds., *The Essential Frankfurt School Reader* (New York: Urizen Books, 1978), pp. 270–299; Walter Benjamin, "The Work of Art in the Age of Mechanical Reproduction," in Hannah Arendt, ed., *Illuminations*, trans. Harry Zohn (New York: Schocken Books, 1968), pp. 219–253. For influential recent formulations, see Fredric Jameson, "Reification and Utopia in Mass Culture," *Social Text* 1 (1979), pp. 13–48; Stuart Hall, "Notes on Deconstructing 'the Popular,'" in Raphael Samuel, ed., *People's History and Socialist Theory* (London: Routledge & Kegan Paul), 1981, pp. 227–239.

 The best discussion of these issues involving music is Richard Middleton, *Studying Popular Music* (Milton Keynes and Philadelphia: Open University Press, 1990), chaps. 2 and 3. See also Georgina Born, "Modern Music Culture: On Shock, Pop and Synthesis," *New Formations* 2 (Summer 1987), pp. 51–78; George Lipsitz, "Against the Wind: Dialogic Aspects of Rock and Roll," in *Time Passages: Collective Memory and American Popular Music* (Minneapolis: University of Minnesota Press, 1990), pp. 99–132. Virtually all the work informed by these issues has focused on rock music, for example, Simon Frith's *Sound Effects: Youth, Leisure, and the Politics of Rock'n'Roll* (New York: Pantheon, 1981). While there are no unreconstructed Adornians writing about popular music, his influence is perceptible. For an excellent sympathetic critique of Adorno's position, see Bernard Gendron, "Theodor Adorno Meets the Cadillacs," in Tania Modleski, ed., *Studies in Entertainment: Critical Approaches to Mass Culture* (Bloomington: University of Indiana Press, 1986), pp. 18–36.

 Ironically, Adorno's final word on jazz could be taken as a fairly apt summary of my own study. "Certainly, jazz has the potential of a musical breakout from this culture on the part of those who were either refused admittance to it or annoyed by its mendacity," he writes in *Introduction to the Sociology of Music*. "Time and again, however, jazz became a captive of the culture industry and thus of musical and social conformism; famed devices of its phases, such as 'swing,' 'bebop,' 'cool jazz,' are both advertising slogans and marks of that process of absorption"; *Introduction to the Sociology of Music*, trans. E. B. Ashton (New York: Seabury Press, 1976), pp. 33–34.

8. Paul Eduard Miller, ed., *Esquire's 1946 Jazz Book* (New York: A. S. Barnes, 1946), pp. 163, 151.

9. "The Beginning," *Metronome* 61 (Sept. 1945), p. 6; *Down Beat*, Aug. 26, 1946, p. 10.

10. "The Beginning," *Metronome* 61 (Sept. 1945), p. 6.

11. Ray McKinley, " 'Ooh, What You Said, Tex!' " *Metronome* 63 (March 1947), pp. 40–41. *Down Beat*, Oct. 6, 1950, p. 1. Alice Mosby, "Hollywood," July 21, 1947, Goodman Papers, YML; "The Swing from Swing," *Time* 48 (Sept. 9, 1946), p. 94. For an ambitious demonstration of how this mood of anxiety permeated all sectors of U.S. popular culture, see William Graebner, *The Age of Doubt: American Thought and Culture in the 1940s* (Boston: Twayne Publishers, 1991).

12. *Down Beat*, July 29, 1949, p. 10. *New York Amsterdam News*, June 26, 1948, p. 25.

13. *Down Beat*, April 9, 1947, p. 1. On this development see Scott DeVeaux, "The Emergence of the Jazz Concert, 1935–1945," *American Music* 7 (Spring 1989), pp. 6–29.

14. *New York Amsterdam News*, May 11, 1946, p. 8; May 10, 1947, p. 8; Aug. 13, 1949, p. 13.

15. *Down Beat*, Jan. 14, 1948, pp. 1, 18; Dec. 15, 1948, p. 1.

16. *Down Beat*, May 5, 1948, p. 1. Charles Miller, "Jazz without Beers," *New Republic* 115 (Aug. 12, 1946), p. 174. *New York Times*, Aug. 24, 1947, sec. 2, p. 5; *Down Beat*, July 1, 1944, p. 5.

17. *Down Beat*, Nov. 19, 1947, p. 11; Jan. 14, 1948, p. 5.

18. *New York Times*, Feb. 1, 1948, sec. 2, p. 7; *Down Beat*, April 9, 1947, p. 17; May 5, 1948, p. 2; Jan. 14, 1949, p. 3.

19. *Down Beat*, May 19, 1950, p. 13; Feb. 24, 1950, p. 10; Dec. 14, 1951, p. 10.

20. Bob Thomas, "Hollywood," July 25, 1947, Goodman Papers, YML; *Down Beat*, Aug. 12, 1946, p. 12.

21. Jeffrey Fleece, "Kids, Taxes, and Popular Songs," *Saturday Review of Literature* 32 (July 30, 1949), pp. 43–44. The price of a jukebox selection also doubled, to ten cents, after the war.

22. *Down Beat*, Oct. 6, 1948, p. 10; June 30, 1950, p. 16. For an early report of the decline of popular dancing, see *Down Beat*, Aug. 1, 1945, p. 3.

23. *Down Beat*, Nov. 18, 1946, p. 4; Jan. 29, 1947, p. 10; italics in original.

24. See George Lipsitz, *Class and Culture in Cold War America: "A Rainbow at Midnight"* (New York: Praeger, 1981), pp. 37–101.

25. *Down Beat*, Aug. 12, 1946, pp. 1, 12; Dec. 11, 1946, pp. 1, 4–5.

26. *Down Beat*, May 7, 1947, p. 8; Nov. 18, 1946, pp. 4–5.

27. For a useful map of popular music's postwar terrain, see Lipsitz, *Class and Culture*, pp. 195–225.

28. Russell Sanjek, *American Popular Music and Its Business*, vol. 3, *From 1900 to 1984* (New York: Oxford University Press, 1988), pp. 240–241; Nelson George, *The Death of Rhythm & Blues* (New York: Pantheon, 1988), pp. 19–57.

29. Marshall W. Stearns, "Rebop, Bebop, and Bop," *Harper's* 200 (April 1950), pp. 94–95; anonymous manuscript, n.d., in Bebop file, Institute for Jazz Studies, Newark, N.J. (hereafter IJS). *Down Beat*, Feb. 11, 1948, p. 5.

30. Sanjek, *American Popular Music*, pp. 240–246. *Down Beat*, May 6, 1949, p. 1.

31. Avakian quoted in *Down Beat*, July 15, 1949, p. 3. On the rise of polka, see Victor Greene, *A Passion for Polka: Old-Time Ethnic Music in America* (Berkeley: University of California Press, 1992).

32. *Down Beat*, May 7, 1947, p. 1. Sanjek, *American Popular Music*, pp. 229–235; Roland Gelatt, *The Fabulous Phonograph: From Tin Foil to High Fidelity* (Philadelphia: J. B. Lippincott, 1955), p. 295.

33. *Down Beat*, June 3, 1949, p. 2. For a detailed chronicle of early relations between the music industry and television, see Sanjek, *American Popular Music*, pp. 291–330.

34. *Down Beat*, March 12, 1947, p. 4.

35. "But let's have no more about swing's slipping," commented Vincent Lopez at that time. "That's just rot—and a way for college professors to get publicity"; *Down Beat*, August 1939, p. 12.

36. Murray Schumach, " 'Revolution' in Tin Pan Alley," *New York Times Magazine*, Oct. 19, 1947, pp. 20, 69–71.

37. Sanjek, *American Popular Music*, pp. 291–330, esp. 293–294, 318–319, 324; quotation from pp. 329–330.

38. "Phenomenon of the Year," *Metronome* 64 (Jan. 1948), p. 28; *Down Beat*, April 21, 1950, p. 1; Sanjek, *American Popular Music*, pp. 223, 286.

39. *Down Beat*, Feb. 12, 1947, p. 10; Feb. 25, 1946, p. 10. George Simon, "There's Jazz in Them Thar Hills!" *Metronome* 64 (June 1948), p. 42.

40. *Down Beat*, March 10, 1948, p. 1; Dec. 1, 1948, p. 10.

41. *Down Beat*, May 19, 1950, p. 3.

42. *Down Beat*, July 15, 1949, p. 10; Nov. 4, 1949, pp.1, 10.

43. *Down Beat*, Dec. 30, 1949, p. 1; Jan. 13, 1950, p. 1.

44. This trend began late in the war. *New York Amsterdam News*, April 21, 1945, p. 16-A.

45. *Down Beat*, May 19, 1950, p. 1; July 14, 1948, p. 1; December 29, 1948, p. 10.
46. Memo, Hal Davis to Goodman, "Bop Goes to the Stork," Goodman Papers, YML.
47. George Simon, "B. G. Explains," *Metronome* 62 (Oct. 1946), p. 49; "Benny Blows Bop," *Metronome* 64 (Aug. 1948), p. 24. *Down Beat*, July 14, 1948, p. 6.
48. "B. G. and Bebop," *Newsweek* 32 (Dec. 27, 1948), pp. 66–67.
49. For an excellent review of the literature on the place of swing and bop within the jazz tradition, see Scott DeVeaux, "Jazz in Transition: Coleman Hawkins and Howard McGhee, 1935–1945" (Ph.D. diss., University of California at Berkeley, 1985), pp. 1–48. DeVeaux concludes that musicology-oriented scholars—André Hodeir, Ross Russell, Martin Williams—understand the transition from swing to bop as evolution, whereas scholars with a sociological perspective—Amiri Baraka, Eric Hobsbawm, Frank Tirro (recent interpretations by Eric Lott and Lewis Erenberg could be adduced)—see the transition as revolution. See also DeVeaux, "Constructing the Jazz Tradition," pp. 525–560.
50. *Down Beat*, Jan. 14, 1949, p. 10.
51. Capitol Records pamphlet in Bebop file, IJS; Dizzy Gillespie, "Bop Is Here To Stay," n.d., Bebop file, IJS; "Who Killed Bop?" *Ebony* 5 (April 1950), p. 74.
52. DeVeaux, "Jazz in Transition," pp. 228–233.
53. See, for example, the responses of McGhee, Gillespie, and Parker to the question "What is be-bop?" *Down Beat*, Sept. 10, 1947, p. 6. See also *New York Times*, Dec. 5, 1948, sec. 2, p. 13.
54. *Down Beat*, April 8, 1946, p. 10; "Be-bop Be-bopped," *Time* 47 (March 25, 1946), p. 52.
55. Leonard Feather, "Inside Bebop," Jan. 1949, Bebop file, IJS. *Down Beat*, April 22, 1949, p. 1.
56. *Down Beat*, Dec. 15, 1950, p. 10; April 22, 1949, p. 1. Leonard Feather, *Inside Jazz* (New York: Da Capo, 1977), p. 42. *Down Beat*, Dec. 12, 1950, p. 10. Gillespie claims that Ellington later told him, "Birks, you should've never let them put a label, like bebop, on your music." Dizzy Gillespie and Al Fraser, *To Be, or Not . . . to Bop* (Garden City, N.Y.: Doubleday, 1979), p. 344. For an article touting Hampton as spokesman of the "new movement" in jazz, see *The Afro-American*, July 3, 1948, p. 6.
57. *Down Beat*, April 22, 1949, p. 1. J. Harvey Burham to George Hoefer, April 12, 1949; George Hoefer, untitled manuscript; Robert C. Ruark, "Bop? It's an Escape," n.d.; all in Bebop file, IJS. *Down Beat*, May 3, 1950, p. 3.

58. *Down Beat*, Dec. 16, 1949, p. 10; April 22, 1949, p. 1; Dec. 15, 1950, p. 10.
59. *Down Beat*, Feb. 25, 1946, p. 3.
60. Boyer, "Bop," p. 28; Gillespie and Fraser, *To Be* . . . , pp. 278–281. "Bebop," *Life* 25 (Oct. 11, 1948), pp. 138–142.
61. *Down Beat*, May 6, 1949, p. 2; Sept. 1, 1945, p. 3; Woody Herman and Stuart Troup, *The Woodchopper's Ball: The Autobiography of Woody Herman* (New York: E. P. Dutton, 1990), pp. 64–67. *Down Beat*, Sept. 9, 1949, p. 1.
62. *Down Beat*, Oct. 22, 1947, pp. 1, 3; Gillespie and Fraser, *To Be* . . . , p. 312. See also preconcert announcements, *Down Beat*, Sept. 24, 1947, p. 5; *New York Amsterdam News*, Sept. 27, 1947, p. 21. Boyer, "Bop," p. 30.
63. Boyer, "Bop," p. 31. Bob Redcross quoted in Gillespie and Fraser, *To Be* . . . , p. 197; ibid., p. 287; Ira Gitler, *Swing to Bop: An Oral History of the Transition in Jazz in the 1940s* (New York: Oxford University Press, 1985), pp. 172–173. Chip Deffaa, *Swing Legacy* (Metuchen, N.J.: Institute for Jazz Studies, 1989), p. 186. Andrew Ross attributes the affinity among hipsters, intellectuals, and bop musicians to their common structural relation to cultural capital, as refracted through postwar patterns of consumption and leisure; Andrew Ross, *No Respect: Intellectuals and Popular Culture* (New York: Routledge, 1989), pp. 79–83.
64. Clarke quoted in Gillespie and Fraser, *To Be* . . . , p. 100; ibid., p. 192.
65. *New York Amsterdam News*, Oct. 2, 1948, p. 24. *Down Beat*, March 11, 1949, p. 3. *New York Amsterdam News*, Feb. 12, 1949, p. 24. Vocalized bop had been pioneered in 1945 with Dave Lambert and Buddy Stewart in Gene Krupa's band. See Feather, *Inside Jazz*, pp. 39–40.
66. *Down Beat*, Oct. 7, 1949 p. 1; Sept. 23, 1949, p. 3.
67. Gillespie, "Bop Is Here to Stay," n.d., Bebop file, IJS. Gitler, *Swing to Bop*, p. 5. Williams quoted in Nat Shapiro and Nat Hentoff, eds., *Hear Me Talkin' to Ya: The Story of Jazz as Told by the Men Who Made It* (New York: Rinehart, 1955), p. 351. Taylor quoted in A. B. Spellman, *Four Lives in the Bebop Business* (London: MacGibbon and Kee, 1967), p. 63.
68. *Down Beat*, Jan. 27, 1950, p. 1. Gillespie, "Bop Is Here to Stay," n.d., Bebop file, IJS.
69. *Down Beat*, Aug. 25, 1948, p. 3; June 3, 1949, p. 19; *New York Amsterdam News*, Oct. 2, 1948, p. 23; *Chicago Tribune*, April 3, p. 1949.
70. *Down Beat*, Nov. 17, 1948, p. 1; Sept. 24, 1947, p. 5; Jan. 14, 1949, p. 3; Sept. 9, 1949, p. 1.
71. *New York Amsterdam News*, July 16, 1949, p. 29; Dec. 24, 1949, p. 17.
72. "Band of the Year," *Metronome* 64 (Jan. 1948), p. 18.
73. *New York Amsterdam News*, March 27, 1948, p. 23; Aug. 7, 1948, p. 25. *Down Beat*, Aug. 25, 1948, p. 16. Only a year earlier critic Dave Dexter

had reported a total loss of interest in bebop in southern California; *The Capitol*, March 1947, Bebop file, IJS.

74. Gitler, *Swing to Bop*, pp. 4–5; Harry Henderson and Sam Shaw, "And Now We Go Bebop!" *Collier's* 121 (March 20, 1948), pp. 16–17.

75. *New York Amsterdam News*, June 12, 1948, p. 25; Oct. 30, 1948, p. 29.

76. *New York Amsterdam News*, Oct. 30, 1948, p. 29; June 4, 1949, p. 25; Oct. 2, 1948, p. 24. *Down Beat*, March 11, 1949, p. 11. Barry Ulanov, "Variety Lays an Egg," *Metronome* 65 (July 1949), p. 34. A cartoon depicted a mink-clad dowager telling a record salesman, "I'd really prefer something a little on the be-bop kick . . ."; *Down Beat*, May 19, 1948, p. 14.

77. Gitler, *Swing to Bop*, pp. 4–5. *Down Beat*, April 22, 1949, p. 1. Feather, *Inside Jazz*, p. 31.

78. Ulanov, "Variety Lays an Egg," p. 34; *New York Amsterdam News*, May 21, 1949, p. 24. *Down Beat*, Dec. 16, 1949, p. 12.

79. *Down Beat*, Jan. 14, 1949, p. 1; Aug. 25, 1950, p. 3; Oct. 6, 1950, pp. 1, 19.

80. *Down Beat*, Oct. 7, 1949, p. 1. Gillespie and Fraser, *To Be . . .* , pp. 343, 356–357.

81. Stearns, "Rebop, Bebop, and Bop," pp. 94–95.

6. Cracks in the Coalition

1. Tex Beneke, "Swing Was Never King!" *Metronome* 63 (Feb. 1947), 20–21, p. 37.

2. Ray McKinley, " 'Ooh, What You Said, Tex!' " *Metronome* 63 (March 1947), 19, pp. 39–41.

3. *Down Beat*, Oct. 7, 1949, p. 19.

4. *Down Beat*, Sept. 8, 1948, p. 1. Henderson also praised Parker and Coleman Hawkins, a member of his big band two decades earlier, who was able to play bop "when he wants to," but in the end always reverted to "playing Hawkins again."

5. *Time* interview quoted in *Amsterdam News*, Nov. 15, 1947, p. 23; *Down Beat*, April 7, 1948, p. 2. *New York Amsterdam News*, Nov. 15, 1947, p. 23; "Pops Cops Bop's Tops," *Metronome* 65 (Oct. 1949), p. 8.

6. "Armstrong Blast at Bebop Creates West Coast Furore," *Capitol News*, n.d., Bebop file, IJS. *Down Beat*, Feb. 25, 1949, p. 12; Sept. 23, 1949, pp. 1, 12–13. For a sample of contemporary responses, see *Down Beat*, Jan. 28, 1949, p. 2 (Hodges, Hibbler, Carney, and Webster); March 30, 1948, p. 15 (Louis Jordan); Jan. 14, 1949, p. 11 (Hampton); *Amsterdam News*, March

8, 1947, p. 19 (Lucky Millinder); Nov. 29, 1947, p. 23 ("Stuff" Smith); March 19, 1949, p. 25 (Eddie Wilcox); April 29, 1950, p. 27 (anonymous musician).

7. Barry Ulanov, "Moldy Figs vs. Moderns," *Metronome* 63 (Nov. 1947), pp. 15, 23. *New York Amsterdam News,* March 12, 1949, p. 24.

8. *Down Beat,* June 17, 1949, p. 1. For responses, see *Down Beat,* July 1, 1949, p. 1; July 15, 1949, pp. 1, 12; July 29, 1949, p. 12. Ironically, one of the issue's most controversial claims was a profession of nostalgia for the bare-knuckled era of jazz criticism. "A curious cult of 'broadmindedness' has taken over jazz criticism," charged D. Leon Wolff, an occasional contributor to *Down Beat.* "Gone are the shrill cries of yesterday, the intramural onslaughts that ripped the sham from certain jazz and jazzmen. Now the tune is: 'If you can't boost, don't knock.' " *Down Beat* provided space to the editor of *Record Changer,* formerly an antibop "haven of reactionaries," to defend his journal against the charge of aesthetic relativism. "The moth-eaten old doctrine of dog-eat-dog in jazz criticism, the shrill and often meaningless cries that the other fellow's kind of jazz is a dirty fraud, is back to haunt us," wrote Orrin Keepnews. The point of this "nastiness school of criticism," he argued, was to fill space and boost circulation rather than encourage understanding or appreciation; its essence was contained in the claim: "No controversy means no standards." *Down Beat,* July 15, 1949, p. 12.

9. *Down Beat,* July 29, 1949, p. 19. For Ulanov, see "Are We Cantankerous?" *Metronome* 65 (April 1949), p. 15.

10. *Down Beat,* Feb. 11, 1946, p. 14; Nov. 4, 1946, pp. 10, 14; April 22, 1946, p. 10. "Simon Says," *Metronome* 61 (Aug. 1945), p. 34. *Record Changer* quoted in Leonard Feather, *The Jazz Years: Earwitness to an Era* (New York: Da Capo, 1987), p. 87.

11. *Down Beat,* Feb. 11, 1946, p. 14; April 21, 1948, p. 3. Barry Ulanov, "Skip Bop and Jump," *Metronome* 65 (Dec. 1949), p. 37.

12. *New York Amsterdam News,* Dec. 10, 1949, p. 30. *Down Beat,* June 16, 1948, p. 18. Lennie Tristano, "What's Wrong with the Beboppers," *Metronome* 63 (June 1947), p. 16. Ulanov, "Skip Bop and Jump," p. 37. *Down Beat,* Nov. 17, 1948, p.1.

13. *Down Beat,* Dec. 17, 1947, p. 10; April 8, 1949, p. 10; July 1, 1949, p. 10; Nov. 17, 1950, p. 10. George Simon, "The Good Old vs. the Bad New Days," *Metronome* 65 (Jan. 1949), p. 50; Barry Ulanov, "Musicians Are Not Dope Fiends," *Metronome* 63 (Aug. 1947), pp. 12–13. For a number of musicians' reflections on drug use in the bop community, see Ira Gitler,

Swing to Bop: An Oral History of the Transition in Jazz in the 1940s (New York: Oxford University Press, 1985), pp. 274–290.

14. *Down Beat*, June 15, 1945, p. 10. Rudi Blesh, *Shining Trumpets: A History of Jazz* (New York: Alfred A. Knopf, 1946), p. 290. Blesh comes off as an incongruous hybrid of Leroi Jones and Theodor Adorno. Frank Marshall Davis, *Livin' the Blues: Memoirs of a Black Journalist and Poet*, ed. John Edgar Tidwell (Madison: University of Wisconsin Press, 1992), p. 288. On the anticommercial leanings of the white traditionalists, see Burton Peretti, *The Creation of Jazz: Music, Race, and Culture in Urban America* (Urbana: University of Illinois Press, 1992), pp. 174–176.

15. Leonard Feather, the prime combatant in these critical wars, gives an excellent retrospective account, particularly of the *Esquire* jazz poll flap. He admits being guilty of "mean-spirited, clumsily written words . . . If the writers in both camps had moderated their tone and concentrated on trying to advance the cause of the musicians they believed in, without denouncing those they opposed, much of the ill feeling could have been avoided"; Feather, *The Jazz Years*, pp. 76–94; quotation from p. 89. For the perspective of a victim of Feather's virulence who actually sued *Metronome*, see Art Hodes and Chadwick Hansen, *Hot Man: The Life of Art Hodes* (Urbana: University of Illinois Press, 1992), pp. 59–63.

    Thus Eric Lott's argument that "much of the forties music press . . . figured as law and order trying to stem the furious tide" is exaggerated. See his "Double V, Double-Time: Bebop's Politics of Style," *Callalo* 11 (Summer 1988), p. 603. The mainstream critics most hostile to bop had ceased to write for trade publications. Hammond, for example, dismissed bop as "a collection of nauseating clichés, repeated ad infinitum." See "B. G. and Bebop," *Newsweek* 32 (Dec. 27, 1948), p. 67. Irving Kolodin charged bop with "intellectual poverty" and excessive concern with "method," mainly because its most noteworthy compositions were built on old chord changes. See "A Feather in the Cap of Bop," *Saturday Review of Literature* 32 (July 30, 1949), p. 45.

16. Leonard Feather, "On Musical Fascism," *Metronome* 61 (Sept. 1945), p. 16. *Down Beat*, Sept. 23, 1946, p. 4; March 26, 1947, p. 11; Dec. 16, 1946, p. 8.

17. Burt Korall, *Drummin' Men: The Heartbeat of Jazz* (New York: Schirmer Books, 1990), pp. 206–247. Tough was also widely known and respected for his literary acumen. Tough quoted in Lott, "Double V, Double-Time," p. 600, who later cites Tough's comments on Dixieland as evidence for bebop's leftist politics. *Down Beat*, Sept. 23, 1946, p. 4. *Daily*

Worker, June 20, 1947, p. 11. Frank Conniff, "Artie Shaw Makes Music with Reds," April 1949, Goodman Papers, YML.

18. McGhee quoted in Gitler, *Swing to Bop,* p. 324; Billie Holiday with William Dufty, *Lady Sings the Blues* (New York: Penguin, 1984), p. 97. For contemporary views of modern jazz, see Richard O. Boyer, "Bop," *New Yorker* 24 (July 3, 1948), p. 30; *Down Beat,* Feb. 11, 1948, p. 16; Sidney Finkelstein, *Jazz: A People's Music* (New York: International Publishers, 1988), pp. 146–150; Marshall Stearns, "Rebop, Bebop, and Bop," *Harper's* 200 (April 1950), p. 96.

19. Lewis Erenberg, "Shape of Things to Come: Swing Bands, Bebop, and the Rise of a Postwar Jazz Scene," in Lary May, ed., *Recasting America: Culture and Politics in the Age of Cold War* (Chicago: University of Chicago Press, 1989), p. 238. Roy Porter with David Keller, *There and Back: The Roy Porter Story* (Baton Rouge: Louisiana State University Press, 1991), p. 67. For the claim that "interracial teamwork among the bop-conscious was too much for 'white reactionaries,' " see "Who Killed Bop?" *Ebony* 5 (April 1950), 74.

20. Dizzy Gillespie and Al Fraser, *To Be, or Not . . . to Bop* (Garden City, N.Y.: Doubleday, 1979), p. 291.

21. *Down Beat,* July 15, 1946, p. 14; July 29, 1946, 1. *New York Amsterdam News,* Jan. 19, 1946, p. 19. *Down Beat,* March 24, 1948, p. 23. Andy Kirk, *Twenty Years on Wheels* (Ann Arbor: University of Michigan Press, 1989), p. 113. *Down Beat,* Jan. 15, 1947, p. 4; Jan. 14, 1949, p. 20.

22. *New York Amsterdam News,* Feb. 1, 1947, p. 21; Jan. 31, 1948, p. 13. *Down Beat,* June 2, 1948, p. 14. *New York Amsterdam News,* July 9, 1949, p. 27; Nov. 18, 1950, p. 26.

23. *New York Amsterdam News,* March 9, 1946, p. 19; Oct. 26, 1946, p. 24. *Down Beat,* Aug. 26, 1946, p. 9.

24. *New York Amsterdam News,* Jan. 26, 1946, p. 21; April 20, 1946, p. 20; July 20, 1946, p. 17; April 6, 1946, p. 18; April 20, 1946, p. 20; Sept. 13, 1947, p. 21.

25. On Granz see *PM,* Feb. 13, 1947, p. 17; *New York Amsterdam News,* Feb. 15, 1947, p. 21; "Granz and the Jazz Philharmonic," *The Crisis* 54 (May 1947), pp. 143–144. On restrictions at Philharmonic Hall, see *Down Beat,* June 15, 1945, p. 1; Dec. 1, 1945, p. 16.

26. *New York Amsterdam News,* March 9, 1946, p. 19; May 12, 1945, p. 8-B; June 30, 1945, p. 1; Oct. 25, 1947, p. 23.

27. "Granz and the Jazz Philharmonic," *The Crisis* 54 (May 1947), p. 144. *PM,* Feb. 13, 1947, p. 17.

28. *New York Times,* May 3, 1947, p. 16; May 4, 1947, sec. 10, p. 9; " 'Beat Me, Ivan,' " *Newsweek* 30 (Aug. 4, 1947), p. 66; *New York Times,* May 3, 1947, p. 16. "Point and Counterpoint," *Metronome* 63 (June 1947), p. 6; "Benny Goodman Complains . . ." *Metronome* 63 (Aug. 1947), pp. 16–17.

29. *New York Amsterdam News,* June 28, 1947, p. 25. Richard Manser, "U.S. Conquest: Hot 'Yahtz,' " *New York Times Magazine,* Aug. 20, 1950, p. 26.

30. *Down Beat,* May 6, 1953, p. 21.

31. Milt Gabler, "Hot Renaissance of Dixieland Jazz," *New York Times Magazine,* Sept. 24, 1950, pp. 26–27, 38. Leo Walker, *The Wonderful Era of the Great Dance Bands* (New York: Da Capo, 1990), pp. 113–118; Philip K. Eberly, *Music in the Air: America's Changing Tastes in Popular Music, 1920–1980* (New York: Hastings House, 1982), p. 182.

32. *Billboard* quoted in Eberly, *Music in the Air,* pp. 181–182; ibid., p. 175.

33. Walker, *The Wonderful Era,* pp. 115, 128, 131. Kirk, *Twenty Years on Wheels,* p. 116. Walker, *The Wonderful Era,* p. 122.

34. Sinatra quoted in George Lipsitz, "Against the Wind: Dialogic Aspects of Rock and Roll," in *Time Passages: Collective Memory and American Popular Culture* (Minneapolis: University of Minnesota Press, 1990), p. 123; for a persuasive account of the social and cultural roots of rock and roll, see pp. 116–130.

35. Shepp quoted in "Point of Contact: A Discussion," *Down Beat Music '66,* pp. 29, 20; Frank Kofsky, *Black Nationalism and the Revolution in Music* (New York: Pathfinder Press, 1970), pp. 145–153. For an influential contemporary interpretation of bebop as protest, see LeRoi Jones [Amiri Baraka], *Blues People: Negro Music in White America* (New York: Morrow Quill, 1963), pp. 199–202.

36. The distance traveled, since the decline of swing, in our culture's sensitivity to racist stereotypes was brought home to me forcefully as I attempted to obtain illustrations for this book. Several sources held the copyright on cartoons that, in addition to conveying valuable information about the current social roles of swing music and its purveyors, portrayed African-Americans with exaggerated physical characteristics that reflected current racial biases. All these sources refused permission to reproduce the cartoons.

Index

Adams, Wilhelmina, 166
Adorno, Theodor, 183, 279n7
AFM (American Federation of Musicians), 77, 98, 133, 196, 242; opposition to "canned music," 114–117; recording ban, 115–117, 136, 145, 153, 161, 206; discrimination in, 127, 157, 166–167
Akiyoshi, Toshiko, 242
Alexander, Willard, 56, 105, 204, 214, 219
"Alexander's Ragtime Band," 146
American Expeditionary Service, 152, 153
American Federation of Musicians. *See* AFM
Americanism, 73–74, 143
American Society of Composers, Arrangers, and Publishers. *See* ASCAP
Ammons, Albert, 61, 66
"Amos 'n' Andy," 131, 133
Anderson, Marian, 61, 75
Apollo Theatre, 43, 135, 155, 172, 216
Arcadia ballroom, 43, 44
Archer, Tom, 189
Arlen, Harold, 111
Armstrong, Louis, 3, 12, 18, 36, 66, 82, 105, 135, 137, 202, 208, 218, 226; criticisms of bebop, 224–225
Arnold, Thurmond, 111

Artists and repertoire (A & R) agents, 198
ASCAP (American Society of Composers, Arrangers, and Publishers), 98, 103, 110–112, 152
Audiences: at Carnegie Hall, 17–19, 21–22; classical and swing, 28, 46; conventions of, 35–36, 40–42; and race, 42–44, 124, 125–127, 236–237; competition for, 47–48; Popular Front, 65–68; and phonographs, 112; and Glenn Miller, 120–121; and musicians, 160; international, 178–179; postwar, 180–184, 186–189, 200–202; for bebop, 212–220; in Harlem, 234–235; composition of, 254n41
Avakian, George, 83, 89, 195, 230, 240

Bach, Johann Sebastian, 27, 28, 30, 94–96
Bach Society of New Jersey, 94, 97, 98
Bailey, Buster, 82
Bailey, Mildred, 109, 128, 153
Bailey, Pearl, 202
Baker, Dorothy, 131
Ball of Fire, 134, 137
Ballrooms, 25, 34, 42–45, 46, 103–104, 107, 126, 161–162, 180, 181, 186–187, 189–191, 202, 242. *See also specific ballrooms*
Band battles. *See* Cutting contests

Bandleaders, 45–46, 101–102, 236–237. *See also individual names*
Barker, Danny, 125, 225
Barnet, Charlie, 38, 43, 79, 90, 117, 119, 135, 137, 186, 190, 194, 201, 206
Baseball, 12–13, 92, 129
Basie, Count, 8, 23, 41, 47, 48, 84, 162, 174, 193, 242; at Savoy ballroom, 18–21, 46, 48, 49; and classics, 27, 97; and John Hammond, 52, 56, 61, 63, 125, 159; and music industry, 109, 125; and race, 126–127, 129, 130
Bauza, Mario, 194
Bebop, 9, 36, 39, 40, 43, 60, 153, 159, 162, 186, 187, 191, 194, 197, 202–220, 236, 240; politics of, 11–12, 14, 230–233, 239, 243–244; as subculture, 14, 209–212; relation to swing, 183, 204–205; origins, 206–207; press criticism, 207–220, 223–230; and high culture, 211–212; commercial success, 214–218; decline of, 218–220
Bechet, Sidney, 61, 205, 226
"Beer Barrel Polka," 195
"Begin the Beguine," 152
Beiderbecke, Bix, 18, 90, 123
"Bei Mir Bist Du Schön," 195
Bellson, Louis, 135
Beneke, Tex, 190, 221–222
Benjamin, Walter, 183
Benton, Thomas Hart, 11
Berigan, Bunny, 113, 170, 174
Berkeley, Busby, 39
Berlin, Irving, 85, 111, 135, 146
Bernie, Ben, 8
Berry, Connie, 168
Bigard, Barney, 103, 130, 138
Big Broadcast of 1937, The, 77, 118
"Big John's Special," 23
Billboard, 234
"Black and Tan Fantasy," 51–52
Blackface, 5, 14, 126, 131–132, 138
Blakey, Art, 212, 268n65
Blesh, Rudi, 226, 230, 240

Blue Devils, 101
"Blue Reverie," 18
BMI (Broadcast Music, Inc.), 110–111, 152, 198
Bonlaender, Carlo, 239
Booking agencies, 83, 98–99, 101–107
Bop City, 225
Bostic, Earl, 194
Boston, 41, 43, 234
Boswell, Connie, 95
Bridges, Harry, 62, 77
Broadcast Music, Inc. *See* BMI
Broonzy, Bill, 61
"Brother, Can You Spare a Dime?" 151
Broun, Heywood Hale, 91
Browder, Earl, 53, 65
Brown, Ray, 226
Brown, Les, 182
Brunswick records, 56, 82
Budge, Don, 26
Burley, Dan, 37, 81, 129–130, 165, 217, 235–236
Byas, Don, 84, 227

Café Society, 66–67, 168, 234
Cain, Jackie, 213
Calloway, Cab, 36–37, 39, 48, 67, 85, 186; and music industry, 102, 106, 107, 160; and race, 121, 122, 126, 157; and bebop, 205, 206, 207, 227
Camp Unity, 66
Capitol records, 116, 202–203
Carnegie Hall, 17–19, 21–23, 24, 27, 34, 46, 49, 56, 61, 65, 67, 70, 71, 79, 186–187, 189, 210, 211, 215, 241
Carter, Benny, 27, 46, 80, 87, 88, 103, 162, 182, 218, 227
Casa Loma, 46, 100, 105, 109, 119
Castle, Lee, 208, 241
CBS, 7, 96, 99, 102, 108, 109, 111, 120, 139
"Chant of the Weed," 36
Chicago, 7, 41, 58, 74, 104, 115, 214, 217, 218, 219, 220, 231, 237

Chicago Defender, 47, 84
Christian, Charlie, 76, 129
Christy, June, 174
Clarke, Kenny, 206, 212
Class relations, 42, 46, 51–53, 66, 69, 72, 73–74, 83–86, 231–232, 244, 254n41
Classical music. *See* European art music
Clayton, Buck, 18, 20, 149, 158, 236
Clinton, Larry, 24, 95, 109, 113, 194
Cold War, 11, 233
Cole, Nat King, 192, 194, 207, 225, 234, 235, 237, 244
Coleman, Bill, 128
Columbia records, 55, 113
Commodore Record Shop, 82, 91
Communist Party, 13, 50, 64–72, 77, 100, 234, 259n36
Como, Perry, 155, 208
Concert halls, 186–190, 210–211
Condon, Eddie, 90, 188, 231
Connick, Harry, Jr., 244
Conniff, Frank, 208, 232
Cons, Carl, 88
Consolidated Radio Artists, 105, 121
Coon-Sanders Nighthawks, 123
Cooperative bands, 100–101
Coquettes Orchestra, 171
Cotton Club, 22, 36, 51, 102
Coughlin, Father Charles, 31, 112
Country music, 155, 195, 199, 238
Crawford, Jimmy, 34
Cremin, Arthur, 32
"Creole Love Call," 51
Crisis, The, 80
Criticism, jazz, 50, 52–54, 80–93, 226–230, 285n8; and the Ivy League, 83–85, 201
Crooners, 23, 25
Crosby, Bing, 23, 37, 155, 178
Crosby, Bob, 4, 47, 91, 108, 153, 162
Cugat, Xavier, 104, 162
Culture industry, 183–184
Cutting contests, 20, 46–48, 169, 225–226

Dailey, Frank, 200–201, 214
Daily Worker, 55, 65, 67–68, 70–71, 232
Dance halls. *See* Ballrooms
Dancing, 31, 33–35, 40–44, 189–191, 213–214. *See also* Audiences; Jitterbugs
Daughters of the American Revolution, 75, 233
Davis, Benjamin, Jr., 70, 166
Davis, Frank Marshall, 230
Davis, Meyer, 8
Davis, Miles, 218, 229
Davison, Wild Bill, 225, 231
Decca records, 7, 113, 114, 116, 125, 127, 196
Delaunay, Charles, 178
Democratic Party, 14, 223
Depression, 16, 24–25, 26, 72, 103, 104, 110, 112, 134
Dexter, Dave, Jr., 226
Dickerson, Reed, 78–79
Disk jockeys, 198–199, 236
Dixieland. *See* Traditional jazz
Dodds, Baby, 226
Doggett, Bill, 194
"Don't Mean a Thing If It Ain't Got That Swing," 5
Dorsey, Jimmy, 27, 35, 105, 108, 135, 162
Dorsey, Tommy, 8, 27, 32, 90, 94–95, 117, 118, 221; and music industry, 103, 104, 108, 109, 113, 119, 237; and Hollywood, 135, 136, 162; and postwar decline, 181, 193; and bebop, 225
Down Beat, 25, 52, 54, 71, 86, 160; and swing ideology, 74–80, 166; and AFM, 111, 116; and Hollywood, 136; and postwar decline of swing, 184, 186, 190, 191–192, 193, 195, 199, 200–202; and bebop, 205, 207–208, 211, 218, 226, 228, 229, 240
Downes, Olin, 6, 96
"Drop Me Off in Harlem," 52

Drugs, 36, 38–39, 205, 209, 229–230, 239
Duke Is Tops, The, 135

Early, Gerald, 123
Eberle, Ray, 169
Eckstine, Billy, 159, 206, 212, 234
Eisler, Gerhart, 239
Eldridge, Roy, 67, 128, 137, 170, 236
Ellington, Duke, 3, 5, 6, 8, 21, 26, 27, 29, 32, 61, 78, 83, 97, 184, 202, 218, 221, 236, 242; and critics, 50–52, 79, 88, 226, 230, 256nn3,4; and Popular Front, 69–71, 72; and music industry, 102–103, 105; and race, 121, 122, 124, 125, 126, 128, 129; and Hollywood, 133, 139; and Second World War, 157, 162, 166; on decline of swing, 180–181; on bebop, 205
Ellington, Mercer, 158
Ellison, Ralph, 1
Ely, Melvin, 131
"Epistrophy," 211
Erenberg, Lewis, 45
Esquire, 153, 230
European art music, 27–28, 32, 40, 184, 187, 189, 200; "swinging the classics," 94–98; and bebop, 210–211
Evans, Gil, 158
Evans, Herschel, 20

Fair Employment Practices Commission, 157, 236
Farley, Mike, 7
Fascism, 24, 53, 73, 142, 143, 157, 178–179, 166
FBI (Federal Bureau of Investigation), 50–51, 60, 62, 64, 69–70
Federal Communications Commission, 95, 96, 97
Feather, Leonard, 83, 172, 184, 204, 207, 211, 217, 226, 227, 230, 231, 232, 240, 286n15
Ferguson, Maynard, 242
Ferguson, Otis, 37, 58, 88–89

Fields, Shep, 153
52nd Street, 6, 23, 39, 108, 206, 209, 214, 232, 234; racial incidents, 163–165
Film. *See* Hollywood
Finegan, Bill, 241
First World War, 142, 150
Fisher, Rudolph, 48
Fitzgerald, Ella, 21, 103, 159, 174, 211
Flanagan, Ralph, 241
Forrest, Helen, 174
Foster, Pops, 225
Foster, Stephen, 95
Francis, Panama, 212
Frankfurt School, 183, 279n7
Frazier, George, 83, 84, 87, 88, 173, 226
Freedman, Marvin, 79
Free jazz, 243–244
"From Spirituals to Swing," 56, 64, 65, 68

Gabler, Milt, 82
Gaillard, Slim, 207
Gale, Moe, 103–104, 160
Garber, Jan, 159
Gender relations in swing, 23, 53, 143, 167–178. *See also* Women in jazz
General Amusement Corporation, 99
George, Nelson, 13
Germany, 53, 178–179, 239
Gershwin, George, 22, 29, 110, 111
Gibson, Harry "The Hipster," 207
Gillespie, Dizzy, 66, 117, 149, 165, 187, 189, 194, 202, 239; and bebop, 206, 207, 210–220, 223, 226, 227, 228, 229, 233; commercial success, 215–217
Gitler, Ira, 218
Glaser, Joe, 103, 105, 121, 138
Gleason, Ralph, 91
Glen Island Casino, 119, 176
"God Bless America," 146
Golden Gate Quartet, 67
Goldkette, Jean, 123, 267n58
Goodman, Benny, 3, 4, 5, 8, 43, 45, 47, 84, 195, 221, 231; at Carnegie

Hall, 6, 17–19, 23, 24, 27–28, 34, 46, 49, 61, 79, 95, 183, 189, 241; and Communist Party, 18, 71; and education, 28–29, 40–41, 210–211; and jitterbugs, 30–31, 35, 37, 40, 42; and Hammond, 55, 91–92, 107; and Popular Front, 71–72, 73; and race, 75–76, 77–78, 80, 127, 129, 130, 131; as bandleader, 101, 104, 105, 118; on film, 135; in Second World War, 143, 147, 150, 153; postwar, 181–182, 185–186, 189–190; and bebop, 202–204, 218, 223; and Voice of America, 238
Gottlieb, Bill, 226
Grand Terrace, 124
Granz, Norman, 186, 211, 236–238
Gray, Glen, 46, 100–101
Gray, Wardell, 203
Green, Freddy, 19
Greenwich Village, 66, 209

Hackett, Bobby, 47, 170
Hall, Edmond, 225
Hall Johnson Singers, 61
Hamilton, Scott, 244
Hammond, John, 4, 35, 38, 54–60, 116; and Ellington, 50–52; and race, 60–61; and Popular Front, 62–64, 66, 68, 77; as critic, 76, 83, 88, 91–92, 226; and Hot Clubs, 81, 82; as producer, 83, 90, 125; and Goodman, 91–92, 107, 127, 204; in Second World War, 159
Hampton, Lionel, 19, 21, 28, 38, 67, 78, 105, 135, 153, 189; and race, 127, 131, 132, 137, 157; postwar success, 193, 194, 235; and television, 196; and bebop, 231, 232
Harlem, 19, 33, 48, 103, 138, 147, 163; and Communist Party, 65, 69; and whites, 42–43, 85, 128, 234–235; and bebop, 206, 218
"Harlem Air Shaft," 52
"Harlem Speaks," 52
Hart, Lorenz, 110

Harvard, 83, 84, 85, 201
"Harvard Blues," 84
Hawkins, Coleman, 27, 103, 202, 227, 236, 237, 239
Hawkins, Erskine, 103, 160, 163, 186
Hayakawa, S. I., 201
Haymes, Dick, 155, 169
Hefti, Neil, 241
Heidt, Horace, 104, 109, 162
Henderson, Fletcher, 6, 46, 102, 121, 124–125, 149, 204, 223, 225, 267n58
Henderson, Horace, 157, 225
Herman, Woody, 42, 91, 103, 105, 108, 109, 135, 138, 148–149, 150, 170, 181, 184, 188, 194, 202, 206, 211, 218, 221, 223, 225, 229, 231, 234, 236
Hill, Teddy, 206
Himes, Chester, 162
Hindemith, Paul, 211
Hines, Earl, 43, 47, 124, 157, 161, 170, 206, 236
Historical relativism, 26–27, 30, 95–96, 147, 181, 205
Hodges, Johnny, 218, 227
Holiday, Billie, 6, 21, 52, 66, 126–127, 138–139, 174, 232
Hollywood, 39, 69, 70, 96–97, 99, 225, 244; and race, 130–132, 137–140; and jazz, 132–136, 195, 196–197; and Second World War, 161–162
Holt, Nora, 187
Hoover, J. Edgar, 50, 62, 67
Horne, Lena, 138, 153, 157, 202
Hot Clubs, 81–83
Hot Record Society, 91
Howard, Eddie, 185
Hughes, Langston, 43, 51, 166
Humes, Helen, 184
Hutton, Ina Ray, 169

Ideology: swing, 1, 11, 13, 52–54, 73–74, 125, 143–144, 167, 222, 237; Popular Front, 64–66; Americanism, 73–74; cultural pluralism, 76–77; bebop, 230–233; race, 243–245

"I'm Coming, Virginia," 18
Ink Spots, 103, 158, 159
International Sweethearts of Rhythm, 172
"It's the Same Old South," 71–72

Jackson, Chubby, 200
James, Harry, 12, 18, 56, 79, 109, 135, 162, 182, 190, 242
Jammin' the Blues, 131
"Jazz at the Philharmonic," 186, 211, 236–237
Jazz Hot, 81
Jazz Singer, The, 132–133
Jefferson, Viola, 128
Jitterbugs, 19, 30–36, 42, 57, 147, 165, 180, 189. *See also* Dancing; Swing subculture
Johnson, J. C., 235
Johnson, Pete, 61, 68
Jolson, Al, 5, 132
Jones, Joe, 28
Jones, Thad, 123, 242
Jordan, Louis, 159, 194, 235
Josephson, Barney, 66–67, 234
Josephson, Leon, 67
Jukeboxes, 114–115, 120, 145, 147, 190–191, 198, 218
"Jump for Joy," 69, 139
Jump music, 9, 155, 193–194, 234
Juvenile delinquency, 146–157, 209

Kansas City, 20, 211
Kapp, Jack, 125
Kater, Michael, 178–179
Kay, Monte, 215
Kaye, Sammy, 104, 123, 135–136, 150, 192, 208, 216, 218
Kemp, Hal, 29, 109
Kenton, Stan, 187, 190, 192, 193, 194, 202, 216, 221, 225, 229, 230, 242
Kern, Jerome, 110
Kerouac, Jack, 239

Kessel, Barney, 131
King, Wayne, 3, 8, 29, 104, 192
Kolodin, Irving, 63
Koussevitzky, Serge, 142–143
Kral, Roy, 213
Krupa, Gene, 4, 12, 18, 19, 21, 28, 36, 38, 39, 55, 119, 127–128, 135, 136, 137, 194, 219
Kyser, Kay, 85, 107, 109, 123, 134, 149, 150, 162, 186

Ladnier, Tommy, 61
LaGuardia, Fiorello, 166
La Rocca, Nick, 80
Las Vegas Nights, 136
Latin jazz, 194–195
Lee, Canada, 166
Lee, Peggy, 174
"Let's Dance," 7, 95
Levin, Michael, 154, 166–167, 188, 197, 215, 222, 226–227, 229, 235
Levine, Lawrence, 15, 112
Lewis, Meade "Lux," 61, 66
Lewis, Mel, 242
Life magazine, 82
Lindy Hop, 33, 43. *See also* Jitterbugs
"Little Brown Jug," 120
"Loch Lomond," 19, 95, 109
Lombardo, Guy, 8, 104, 123, 150, 192, 218, 220, 241
Long, Huey, 31, 112
Lopez, Vincent, 33
Los Angeles, 7, 31, 44, 196–197, 207, 232, 236, 237; wartime racial tension, 147, 161–163, 165. *See also* Hollywood
Lott, Eric, 233, 286n15
Lunceford, Jimmy, 8, 31, 46, 48, 67, 111, 121, 136, 158, 186

Machito, 194–195
Macleod, Norman, 66
Mailer, Norman, 239
"Make Believe Ballroom," 109, 115, 140
Malcolm X, 43

Mannone, Wingy, 4
Marcantonio, Vito, 62, 66, 212
MCA (Music Corporation of America), 56, 99, 104–106, 107, 121, 197, 216
McCall, Bruce, 67–68
McGhee, Howard, 206, 218, 232
McIntyre, Hal, 193
McKinley, Ray, 154, 185, 221–222
McShann, Jay, 58, 206
Meadowbrook Club, 119, 140, 201
Meet the People, 71
Mercer, Johnny, 111
Metronome, 38, 52, 54, 59, 80, 83, 111, 116, 129, 169; and Second World War, 148, 150, 154–155, 161; and bebop, 226, 227, 230, 238
Mezzrow, Mezz, 59, 131
Miley, Bubber, 51
Miller, Glenn, 4, 8, 43, 45, 47, 79, 90, 101, 103, 105, 108, 113, 128, 135, 221, 244; rise of, 119–123; in Second World War, 148, 150–151, 152, 153, 154–155
Miller, Paul Eduard, 78, 226
Millinder, Lucky, 103, 122, 194, 233–234
Mills, Irving, 102–103, 121, 216
Mills Brothers, 125
"Minnie the Moocher," 36
Mitchell's Christian Singers, 61
"Moldy figs," 223
Mole, Miff, 123
Monk, Thelonious, 228
Monroe, Al, 48
"Moonlight Serenade," 120
Moten, Benny, 6, 122
Movies. *See* Hollywood
Music Corporation of America. *See* MCA
Music and Rhythm, 91–92, 127
"Music Goes 'Round and Around," 7
Musicians; professionalization, 117–118; road tours, 125–126; salaries, 192; expatriation of, 202
Music industry, 93, 98–140, 221–223; music publishers, 98, 99, 102, 110,

132, 151, 168–198, 200; booking agencies, 102–107; radio, 107–112; recording, 112–117; pressures of, 117–119; race relations, 121–130, 235; cross-country tours, 125–126; film industry, 130–140; in Second World War, 145, 155–156, 159–160, 175, 179; postwar slump, 180–202, 242–244; rise of bebop, 202–218; decline of bebop, 218–220
Mutual Broadcast System, 111, 226

NAACP (National Association for the Advancement of Colored People), 80
Nanton, Tricky Sam, 51
National Association of Broadcasters, 116
National Ballroom Operators' Association, 242
Navarro, Fats, 212
Nazi-Soviet pact, 68
NBC, 7, 28, 99, 109, 111, 234, 241
Negro Freedom Rally, 166
Negro Labor Victory Committee, 166
Nelson, Ozzie, 119
Newark, 82
New Deal, 11, 13–16, 69, 222–223
New Masses, 56, 59, 64
New Orleans, 138–139
New Orleans jazz. *See* Traditional jazz
New Orleans revival, 231–232, 241
New York Amsterdam News, 80–81, 187
New York City, 7, 28–29, 33, 54–55, 71, 78, 82, 83, 91, 104, 107, 118, 126, 197, 216, 219, 233; in film, 134, 135; in Second World War, 153, 159, 163–166. *See also* 52nd Street; Harlem
New York Philharmonic, 17, 27, 147, 210
Nightclubs, 45, 188, 214–215; cabaret tax, 145, 190
Nixon, Richard, 232
Noble, Ray, 19
Norris, Frank, 83
Norvo, Red, 4, 21, 150, 153

Oakley, Helen, 81, 88
Office of Defense Transportation, 160
Office of War Information, 137, 151, 179
Oliver, Sy, 130–158, 241
"One O'Clock Jump," 23, 113, 130
Onyx Club, 7, 41, 155
Orchestra Wives, 75–77
Original Dixieland Jazz Band, 18, 80
"Ornithology," 211
Ory, Kid, 138

Page, Oran "Lips," 127
Page, Walter, 18
Painting, 11
Palladium: Los Angeles, 189–190; New York, 234
Palomar ballroom, 7, 44, 118
Panassie, Hugues, 81, 87, 89
Paramount Pictures, 77–78
Paramount Theatre, 43, 169, 203
Parker, Charlie, 194, 211, 216, 218, 219, 226–228
Petrillo, James, 115–116, 196
Philadelphia, 43–44, 236
Philharmonic Hall (Los Angeles), 236
Phillips, Flip, 236
Polka music, 195–196
Pollack, Ben, 119
Polls, 47–48, 52, 218
Popular Front, 53–54, 62, 65–69, 72, 77, 234
Porter, Cole, 110
Porter, Roy, 124, 232
Powell, Adam Clayton, Jr., 166
Powell, Mel, 169
Pozo, Chano, 194
Primus, Pearl, 166
Progressive jazz, 187, 188, 230. *See also* Kenton, Stan

Race, 13, 23, 47, 51–52, 245; and John Hammond, 60–61; and jazz criticism, 77–80, 85; in swing industry, 121–130;
in Hollywood, 130–133, 137–140; in Second World War, 143–144, 156–167; in Los Angeles, 161–162; in New York City, 163–166; in bebop, 204, 210, 218, 226, 230, 232–233; postwar climate, 233–237, 239; in free jazz, 243–244
Race riots, 147, 162–163, 234
Radio, 8, 12, 52, 84; and "swinging the classics," 94, 95–98; and rise of swing, 99, 102–105, 107–112; and ASCAP, 110–112; and recordings, 112–117; and AFM, 115–116; and Glenn Miller, 119–121; and African-Americans, 123–124, 140, 234, 236; in Second World War, 148, 151–153, 161, 178–179, 197; and postwar retrenchment, 182, 197, 199, 241; and disk jockeys, 198–199, 200, 217; and bebop, 205, 207, 215, 217, 218; and Voice of America, 238, 239
Raeburn, Boyd, 221
Ravens, The, 216, 219
RCA Victor, 102, 113, 115, 117, 120, 127, 153, 214, 216, 241
Recordings, 75, 82, 93, 172, 175; and John Hammond, 59–60, 63, 64, 90, 91; royalties, 98, 114; jazz, 112–118; and AFM, 114–117, 136, 161; recording ban, 115–117, 136, 161, 206; and African-Americans, 124–125, 127, 244; and Second World War, 145, 153, 154; postwar innovations, 196, 199, 241
Redman, Don, 6, 36, 46, 58
"Reefer Man," 36
Reisman, Leo, 122
Relativism. *See* Historical relativism
Rhapsody in Blue, 22, 28, 153
Rhythm and blues. *See* Jump music
Rich, Buddy, 219, 236, 237, 242
Riley, Mike, 7
Rio, Rita, 169, 171
Rite of Spring, 211

Roach, Max, 226, 229
Robeson, Paul, 61, 237
Robinson, Jackie, 12, 13
Rock and roll, 243
Rockwell-O'Keefe, 105, 121
Rodgers, Richard, 110
Rodney, Red, 203
Rodzinski, Artur, 147
Rogers, Billie, 170, 171
Rogers, Shorty, 241
Rogin, Michael, 133
Roosevelt, Eleanor, 67, 97
Roosevelt, Franklin D., 11, 13, 15, 26, 31, 41, 70, 110, 112, 116, 143, 144, 155, 157, 223, 249n18; Executive Order 8802, 157
Roseland ballroom, 43, 124–125
Royal Roost, 214, 219
Rushing, Jimmy, 71, 84

Sanjek, Russell, 91
Sargeant, Winthrop, 226
Sarnoff, David, 63
Sauter, Eddie, 241
Savitt, Jan, 105
Savoy ballroom, 19–23, 28, 33, 42–44, 46–48, 58, 103, 120, 163, 172, 214
Scheherazade, 27
Schribman brothers, 103
Scott, Hazel, 233, 237
Scott, Raymond, 95, 129
Second World War, 8–9, 15–16, 65, 141–179, 189; cultural after-effects, 15, 185–186; and swing ideology, 143–145; and music industry, 145–156, 160, 184–185, 189; and musicians, 148–150; and V Discs, 153; and popularity of jazz, 153–155, 178–179; and race relations, 156–167; and Los Angeles, 161–163; and New York City, 163–166; and women, 167–169, 177–178; postwar music industry, 192–193

"Sensation Rag," 18
Shavers, Charlie, 227
Shaw, Artie, 8, 27, 34, 45, 47, 79, 174, 221, 231, 232; and music industry, 101–102, 103, 105, 108, 109, 113; and race, 127, 137; and Second World War, 148, 149–150, 152, 244; and postwar decline, 181
Shaw, Billy, 216
Shearing, George, 209, 214
Sheet music, 197–198. See also Music industry
Shepp, Archie, 243–244
"Shine," 18, 234
Shore, Dinah, 178
Simon, George, 13, 83, 88, 110, 116, 199, 226, 227, 229–230, 238
Sinatra, Frank, 147, 155, 167, 169, 178, 185, 243, 244
Singleton, Zutty, 138
Slang, 37–38, 204–205
"Slumming on Park Avenue," 85
Smith, Gerald L. K., 31
Smith, Tab, 84
Smith, Viola, 171, 172
"So Lovely," 29
Song Is Born, A, 135, 137
"Song of the Jitterbug," 36
"Song of the Vipers," 36
"South Rampart Street," 208
Soviet Union, 65, 238
Spanier, Muggsy, 149, 208
Spencer, Onah, 80
Spitalny, Phil, 169–170
Spotlight Bands, 152
Stacy, Jess, 55, 76, 77
"Star Dust," 66
"Star-Spangled Banner, The," 160–161
Stearns, Marshall, 4, 51, 81, 83, 88, 220, 226, 233
Stevens, Roy, 201–202
Stewart, Rex, 72
"St. Louis Blues," 141
"Stompin' at the Savoy," 23, 198

Stork Club, 206
Stormy Weather, 138, 153
Stravinsky, Igor, 30, 184, 211
Strike Up the Band, 39–40
Sullivan, Ed, 164
Sullivan, Maxine, 67, 95, 97, 109
"Sunrise Serenade," 120
Sun Valley Serenade, 120, 135
Susman, Warren, 15
"Sweet" music, 24, 55, 122, 124, 135, 143, 154, 191, 194, 197, 221, 238
Swinging the classics, 27, 94–98, 111
Swing It, Professor, 134
Swing subculture, 30–39, 52–54, 66–67, 80–93, 156, 163–165, 187, 189, 195; and women, 144–145, 168–174; and bebop, 204–205, 209; fragmentation of, 221–223, 240
Symphonic jazz, 17
Symphony Sid, 215, 217

Tabackin, Lew, 243
Taft-Hartley Act, 196
Tatum, Art, 66, 188
Taylor, Cecil, 214
Teagarden, Jack, 79, 124, 182
Television, 196
Templeton, Alec, 95
Territory bands, 46, 100
"Texas Tea Party," 36
Theaters, 42, 108, 133, 134. *See also specific theaters*
Thompson, Lucky, 212
Thomson, Virgil, 4, 42
Three Deuces, 188
Tibbett, Lawrence, 151
Tilton, Martha, 19, 173
Tin Pan Alley, 10, 25, 135, 151, 235
Toscanini, Arturo, 18, 28, 57, 169
Totalitarianism, 23–24, 31
Tough, Dave, 28, 128, 231–232
Traditional jazz, 5, 10, 173, 231–232, 234, 240, 241, 251n14

Trianon ballroom, 162, 217
Tristano, Lennie, 185, 226, 229
Truman, Harry S, 204, 223, 233
Trumbauer, Frank, 123, 148
Turner, Joe, 61, 66

Ulanov, Barry, 114, 136, 172, 226, 227, 228, 229–230, 238
"Until the Real Thing Comes Along," 125
USO (United Service Organization), 148, 149–150, 157, 159

V Discs, 153–154
Vallee, Rudy, 8, 29, 109, 162
Varese, Edgar, 211
Vaughan, Sarah, 212
Ventura, Charlie, 191, 206, 213, 214, 219, 229
Venuti, Joe, 79, 128
Village Vanguard, 242
Vitaphone, 114, 133
Vocalists, 54, 155, 173–174, 177, 178, 194, 198, 241. *See also* Crooners
Voice of America, 238

Wallace, Henry, 223
Waller, Fats, 3, 36, 67, 70, 121, 133, 138, 148, 153, 157, 207
Waring, Fred, 8, 109, 115
Washington, Dinah, 216, 218
Webb, Chick, 3, 20, 21, 103
Webster, Ben, 129, 225, 227
Welles, Orson, 62, 139
Wells, Dicky, 34
West, Cornel, 130
When Harry Met Sally . . ., 244
White, Josh, 166
White, Walter, 80, 137, 160
White, William Allen, 26
Whiteman, Paul, 4, 6, 17, 22, 39, 96, 105, 109, 115, 120, 122, 123, 128, 133, 148, 153, 180, 195, 227, 236
White Rose Inn, 164

"Who Put the Benzedrine in Mrs. Murphy's Ovaltine?" 207
Wilkins, Roy, 80
William Morris, 99, 105, 121, 216
Williams, Cootie, 129, 159, 206, 238–239
Williams, Mary Lou, 66, 170, 206, 214
Williams, Mayo "Ink," 125
Willkie, Wendell, 137
Wills, Bob, 195
Wilson, Teddy, 19, 66, 75–76, 227

Winchell, Walter, 106, 164
Women in jazz, 167–178; all-female bands, 169–172; vocalists, 173–174; in Second World War, 177–178

Yale, 36, 55, 81, 83, 84, 201
Young, Lester, 18, 20, 129, 131, 158, 218, 223, 227
Young, Trummy, 129, 227, 236
Young Man With a Horn, 131
"Your Hit Parade," 109